SEVENTY LESSONS
IN TEACHING AND
PREACHING CHRIST

GEORGE GOODMAN

Marshall Pickering

Pickering and Inglis
Marshall Pickering
3 Beggarwood Lane, Basingstoke, Hants RG23 7LP, UK

Copyright © 1939 by George Goodman

First published in 1939 by Pickering and Inglis Ltd.
Reprinted in 1942, 1944, 1946, 1948, 1954, 1957, 1961,
1965
Re-issued in this format in 1986 by
Pickering and Inglis Ltd.
Part of the Marshall Pickering Holdings Group
A subsidiary of the Zondervan Corporation

British Library Cataloguing in Publication Data
Goodman, George
   Seventy lessons in teaching and preaching
   Christ.
   1. Bible. N.T.—Homiletical use
   2. Preaching
   I. Title
   251   BV4211.2

   ISBN 0-7208-0696-8

Printed in Great Britain by
The Guernsey Press Co. Ltd., Guernsey, Channel Islands.

Introduction

IN the previous three volumes, *70 Best Bible Stories, 70 Familiar Bible Stories* and *70 Less-Known Bible Stories,* I dealt with the histories of incidents in the lives of the outstanding characters in the Bible. The principal events in the Life of the Lord were considered, but His teaching only as it was incidental to His parables and miracles, death and resurrection.

I have for a long time been looking forward to supplementing those volumes with a fourth, which should have as its theme: *The Lord Jesus Himself in all the beauty and dignity of His person, offices, work and teaching.*

The Apostles and those who followed in their train " preached Christ." Paul confessed, " We preach Christ, even Him crucified "; and the first disciples, we read went everywhere " teaching and preaching Christ."

I fear a great deal of the preaching today could hardly be so described. In the second article I seek to show how even when Christ is named He is often not preached in the sense that the Apostles preached Christ. They proclaimed Him to men, and pressed upon their hearers the necessity of receiving Him and closing with His offers of mercy and life. For them He was a living present person who, having died, had risen, and now invited sinners to come to Him for salvation.

These studies display the pre-eminence of Christ in all its remarkable outstanding characteristics.

I trust the bringing together and setting out in a simple manner these glories of Christ will enable many to preach Him to others and to rejoice in Him for themselves as the all-sufficient Saviour and Lord.

Men need Christ today as ever. Morality, ethics, social philosophical teaching and religion make their various appeals, but what the heart of man needs is a personal Saviour and guide, and nothing will ever meet that need but the faithful and loving preaching of Christ.

GEORGE GOODMAN

The Two Desires

Thou, Lord, hast wrought within my heart
   Two prevalent desires:
The first that Thou be glorified—
   To this my soul aspires;
The other that I may be saved
   Who am so full of sin.
But how these two can e'er agree,
   I find no light within.

Thy glory and Thy righteousness
   Demand the sinner's death;
I would not have Thine honour dimmed,
   Nor seek a false relief
That does not render praise to Thee
   Who art Supreme above,
Or tarnishes in least degree
   Thy wisdom and Thy love.

Lo, in the Gospel of Thy grace,
   The Cross of Calvary,
I see these two desires fulfilled,
   And praise the Mystery.
There in the Mediator's death
   Thy glory is revealed,
Thy righteousness is satisfied,
   And my poor soul is healed.

Then blessèd be Thy matchless grace,
   Thy wisdom and Thy power,
That reconciled these diverse ends
   In Calvary's awful hour.
There Mercy met with Truth, there Peace
   And Righteousness embraced;
There Thy great Name was glorified
   And I, the sinner, graced.

G. G.

Contents

Seventy Lessons in Teaching and Preaching Christ

THE PRE-EMINENCE OF CHRIST

"That in all Things He Might Have the Pre-eminence"

THAT the Name of Jesus is the widest known, the best loved, indeed the outstanding name in the world, not even the bitterest opponent can deny. Its praises are sung without ceasing day and night. From every quarter of the globe ascend songs of gladness from the lips of those whose lives have been lightened with the knowledge of that Name.

It is in very fact the "*Name that is above every name.*" The press never stops printing books and tracts of which He is the theme; poets sing His praise in sacred poetry and in solemn hymns; artists find inspiration in the incidents of His life and death for their greatest masterpieces; daily tens of thousands of teachers and preachers go forth, often asking no reward, to proclaim His name and speak of His dying love. Martyrs triumphed in the flames or endured patiently in dungeons, and unnumbered hosts have suffered the loss of all things for love of His Name, desiring only the privilege of spending and being spent for His sake. There is no sphere of human life or activity in which His Name is not the one of greatest influence and power for righteousness and goodness.

Even science must confess Him as the One Who taught it to love truth and hate hypocrisy and superstition, to judge righteous judgment, for on these does all true science depend.

9

It is a tremendous claim that *in ALL things* He must have the pre-eminence, but the wonderful truth is that it must be accorded to Him. Nothing noble, beautiful or worthy in the world exists that must not ascribe to Him the first place in influence and power.

He is *the Outstanding Figure in History*; *the Greatest Person in the World of Men*; He is, to use His own words, which express better than any others this exalted claim, "*the Light of the World*."

Where is any rival ? Who will come forward to dispute the fact that even now in this sin-troubled world that rejects Christ's claim, He is the First, the Pre-eminent One ?

But His pre-eminence is something far greater than all this. True, His place of influence in the world is assured as the first and the highest, but there are glories far beyond this in which He stands out pre-eminent and alone.

I. THE DIGNITY OF HIS PERSON

As John Bunyan wrote: "This One hath not His fellow," for though He is spoken of as "God's fellow" (Zech. 13. 7) and also is not ashamed to call His people brethren, yet none can claim as He to be *both God and Man*.

This was the outstanding wonder of all God's purposes, His greatest work, the great Mystery of Godliness, that He who was Himself God should be manifested in flesh, should be found in fashion as a man.

There have been great men in the world who have won fame and renown and whose names are honoured and beloved; but all must give way to Him Who is more than Man, the Lord, the Heir of all things, the Creator and Upholder of the universe.

II. HIS SINLESS LIFE AND PERFECT CHARACTER

He must be accorded pre-eminence in this also, that in a world of sinners He alone was without sin. The holiest of the sons of men have been the first to acknowledge their sinfulness and how far short they fall of the glory of God, for " there is no man that sinneth not," and " in many things we offend all " except One, and He stands out pre-eminent in holiness and sinless purity.

Though meek and lowly in heart, He never confessed to sin nor apologized for failure. He only could face His fellow-men and say: "Which of you convinceth Me of sin ?"

His character was perfect in all virtue. We do not think of Him as we do of other men, as being distinguished for some particular quality. He had all in perfect balance.

If a circular disc be painted with the colours of the rainbow in equal proportions, when it is spun round it will appear white, for the rainbow is but a pure white light split by a prism into its component hues. So in Christ all the virtues are in such perfect proportion that as seen in Him none stands out above others ; all are merged in perfect white—the beauty of holiness.

III. THE NOBILITY OF HIS DEATH

Many men have died noble deaths, have laid down their lives gloriously, and their memory is precious to us; but which of them will we place in comparison with the solemn scene on Calvary ?

There was in that death something with which no other could compare. It was a Substitutionary Sacrifice for Sin, such as only a Sinless Victim could offer. Unlike other men who came into the world to live, the Lord Jesus came to die, to put away sin by the sacrifice of Himself. His life was incidental to His death. That dark scene was ever before Him, and when the hour was come He voluntarily laid down His life, no man taking it from Him, except in so far as they fulfilled the determinate counsel and foreknowledge of God.

It was not the love of it, though that was great, or the patient endurance of the physical torture, or the example of suffering wrongfully, or the tenderness of the seven utterances on the Cross, that gave it its pre-eminence. It was the sacrificial character that did so. " Christ died for our sins." None other could have done this. His death, the Just for the unjust to bring us to God, gives Him in this also the unchallengeable pre-eminence.

Mahomet is sometimes quoted as a rival to Christ in his influence on men. Let us contrast the death of each.

Mahomet died in a warlike camp, while he was making preparation for an unprovoked attack on a tribe which had done him no wrong, but upon which he had resolved to force his religion at the point of the sword. Ere his bloodthirsty purpose could be carried out he died in the arms of one of his many wives, with the noise of battle preparation in his ears.

Now let us turn our eyes to Calvary and hear the gracious words, " Father, forgive them, they know not what they do," as thus the Son of God prayed for those who slew Him.

IV.—THE GLORY OF HIS RESURRECTION

In this He has the pre-eminence, as the first who has risen triumphant over death and the grave. There are seven cases recorded in the Bible of those who were called back from death; but only for a season—they died again, death would not yield up its claim.

But the Lord Jesus is the First Begotten from the dead, for it was not possible that He should be holden of death. He dieth no more, death hath no more dominion over Him.

Now is Christ risen and become the Firstfruits of them that sleep.

V. THE PURITY OF HIS TEACHING

There have been moralists and teachers in the world, but never one whose doctrine was perfect. Amidst much that was good there was much of falsehood, a great deal that was mere theory, often false sentiment and untrustworthy exaggeration. Each can be heard only in part; to none can a whole obedience be rendered.

But the Lord Jesus stands out pre-eminent in this, that no word He ever spoke can be challenged as untrue, or false in sentiment, or weak in expression, or unreliable as a guide in life. Authority is stamped on every word.

Grace and truth in perfect balance are found in all He said and did. Search those words such as never man spake and you will find nothing light or careless; nothing sentimental or foolish; nothing uncertain or hesitating; nothing proud or puffed up; in bold denunciation of evil nothing cruel or unfair; in gracious words to the sinful, no excuse for or palliation of sin.

The beauty of the words is unequalled in all literature; the convicting power of them is absent from other writings. What comfort for the weary; what hope for the sinful; what wise counsel for the direction of life; what solemn warning to the rebel; what promises for the seeker; what assurance for the believer; what prospects for the future! Search the myriad books of the world and see if any can hold a candle to this pre-eminent of all teachers.

VI.—THE WONDER OF HIS SALVATION

It was said of Him at His birth, "He shall save His people from their sins." What a unique and outstanding claim! Did any man ever propose to save another from his sins? It cannot be done. In this, then, He must have the pre-eminence.

Yet the claim is true. Thousands of millions since the angel spoke those words to Mary have testified of Him that He has saved them from their sins. Well might the prophet of old ask, "Where is any other that can save you?"

Mothers would willingly die if by so doing they could recall a prodigal son to the path of purity. Fathers would gladly pay their last penny if salvation could thereby be purchased for a wayward child.

Only One has ever been able to say to the believer, "Thy faith hath saved thee; go in peace."

How hopeless would this sin-stricken world be if there were no Saviour for sinners! But there is One, and only One. It is He Who has in this, as in all else, the pre-eminence.

He Himself put forward this extraordinary claim in unmistakable terms, "I am the Door; by Me if any man enter in he shall be saved." "I am the Way, the Truth, and the Life; no man cometh to the Father but by Me."

What other could bid his fellow-men, "Come unto Me, all ye that labour and are heavy laden, and I will give you rest"? On the lips of any other that would be outrageous nonsense.

And such a word as this, who else dare utter it ?—"I am the Resurrection and the Life; he that believeth on Me, though he were dead, yet shall he live; and he that liveth and believeth on Me shall never die."

Yet One stood among us Who uttered these words in all sincerity and gentleness. We must ascribe to Him the pre-eminence.

VII.—HIS GLORY AS HEAD OF THE CHURCH.

When He walked this earth in humiliation, a man of sorrows and acquainted with grief, He said, "I will build My Church." He foretold its course, a stormy, persecuted one, hated of all men, yet overcoming and spreading to all parts of the earth, until an innumerable company that no man can number should be gathered out of every tribe and kindred and nation, forming an invisible spiritual organism of which He Himself would be the unseen yet living Head; in which the Holy Spirit Whom He would send from the Father should abide as in a temple, sanctifying and guiding it in its course in the world.

This He has brought about, so that something unknown before in the history of the world has appeared. A company of redeemed and saved people, unlimited by nationality or language, having a common life, confessing His Name, and walking in love and good works—yet persecuted and downtrodden, but triumphing over all in His Name.

In this as in all else He has the pre-eminence.

It is of this Pre-eminent One these papers treat.

WHAT IS MEANT BY PREACHING CHRIST?

THERE is a great deal of preaching, excellent in its way, that cannot be said to be preaching Christ. It is *about* Him, but it fails in this, that it does not *preach* Him.

The difference is well illustrated by the recent remark of an Indian preacher who saw and lamented the lack of the faithful preaching of Christ. He said, "*If we knew that Christ were actually come into our village we should stop talking about Him and bid the hearers go at once to see and hear Him for themselves.*"

This is what preaching Christ really means. It is not only teaching about Him but the presentation of Him before the hearers as One actually present and ready to receive and bless them.

The result of such preaching will be that the hearers will not only know about Him, which is excellent, but will come to know Him, which is far, far better.

We preach Christ, then,

(i) *When we represent Him as a Living Person as distinct from an historical character* of whom we read in the Bible. Other religions reverence the memory, treasure the relics, and study the teaching of their long-since-dead founders. Buddha's tooth has a wonderful temple shrine, Mahomet's bones rest in a greatly revered coffin at Medina; and their followers proclaim their past virtues and repeat their sayings, and cover their shrines with holy carpets; but Christianity is something far removed from such things. Jesus lives! We have a glorified and glorious Saviour. Our preaching must obviously be something quite different.

As an illustration of preaching Christ as a Living Saviour let me tell of a child longing to know how to be saved. On the table in her own home she saw a sermon by Mr. Moody. It was lying face downwards so that the last page was uppermost. The child's eyes fell on the closing words of the sermon. They were these: "*If anyone wants to come to Jesus, He's here now—tell Him so.*" It brought

light, salvation and joy to the child as she told her Lord
she came to Him.

Mr. Moody knew how to preach Christ !

(ii) We preach Christ when we remind the hearers that *He
is present in the gathering*.   The hymn expresses it simply:

> " Jesus Christ is passing by,
> Sinner, lift to Him thine eye."

His promises are undeniable.   " Go and preach . . . and
lo, I am with you alway."   He is present to work with us
and confirm the word with signs following.

Faith does not wait to feel or even realize this fact.
Faith believes it and acts as recognizing it to be true.

He who preaches Christ calls the attention of the
people to the fact that they are in the presence of the
Lord.

Faith has been aptly described as *"making allowance for
a thing."*   If the preacher really believes his Lord present,
he will make allowance for it and act accordingly.

To present a Living Present Saviour with conviction is
truly preaching Christ.

(iii) We preach Christ *when we represent ourselves as
His ambassadors bringing a message from Him*.

A preacher to children used often to begin his address
to the little ones thus: " Children, I am not Mr. ——
merely, *I am the servant of the Lord Jesus, Who has sent me
to tell you something*.   You must listen to me as His
ambassador."   Needless to say, it arrested attention and
no doubt added great weight to the message of salvation
he brought.

It of course entails a solemn responsibility to be faithful
to so solemn a commission.   To talk lightly or unimpres-
sively after such an announcement would be like taking
the Name of the Lord in vain.   " We pray you in Christ's
stead," " as though God did beseech you by us."   What
a grand and dignified business, but how solemn the responsibility it carries with it !

(iv) We preach Christ *when we press His claim upon
the hearers*.   We might give an excellent address on Christ
as the Lamb of God.   As a Scripture study it might be

most interesting and useful, but we must go further. We must cry, " Behold the Lamb of God !"

Dr. John Kerr, an eminent Scots divine, says very truly, " *To point to Christ as He walks and say, ' Behold the Lamb of God,' is an appeal which reaches men without argument.*"

To refer to Mr. Moody again, I once heard him preach on " Herod." It was a meeting for men only, and the matter of sin was brought home to the conscience in a masterly manner. Then Christ was preached as the Saviour present and ready to save. His final appeal was, " *Now, men, what are you going to do ?*" The response was immediate and remarkable.

(v) We preach Christ *when we tell of the finished work of Christ and testify that His Blood cleanseth from all sin.* Not as a doctrine or a theory merely, but as a blessed fact of which the hearer may then and there avail himself —that the Lord, on the ground of the great Sacrifice for sins, still says to the sinner who is willing to hear and believe, " Thy sins be forgiven thee."

It is one thing to repeat regularly " I believe in the forgiveness of sins " and another to rejoice in the assurance that my sins, even mine, are actually and truly remitted. It is this that we insist upon when we preach Christ.

(vi) Very similar is the preaching of Christ, *as a Present Deliverer from the power of sin*—that He still says to the Satan-bound, "Thou art loosed "; to the sin-paralysed, " Arise and walk."

We insist, the Good Physician is present to heal, and as many as touch Him are made whole. Our urgent appeal is,

> " O touch the hem of His garment
> And thou too shalt be free."

An evangelist once sat in a meeting listening to a great preacher, an eloquent orator, who swayed the audience with the magic of his words. It was all about Christ too, a complimentary testimony to Him; but the audience rose and left having enjoyed the usual weekly thrill, but with no sign that anything more had to be done. The evangelist's heart sank with heaviness as he watched them go and muttered to himself, " Oh that after that eloquent eulogy to my Lord I might for five minutes *preach Christ to them as present to save*, and call on them to yield to Him now !"

(vii) We preach Christ *when we warn sinners that to reject Him is to perish*.   God has committed all judgment to Him, He has appointed the day in which He will judge the world by that Man Whom He hath ordained.   The day draws near, the time is short, the call is urgent.

" That One now offers to be your Lord and Saviour; He will then be your Judge !"

Such, then, should be our preaching of Christ, so that those who hear us confess, whether they obey the word or not, that they have been brought face to face with their Lord, they have had to do with Christ, He has been presented to them in very truth.

SECTION I

Our Lord Jesus Christ:
His Personal Glory

The NAME above every Name

We sing the Name o'er every name,
  Of Jesus Christ the Lord,
Who being in the form of God,
  Is equally adored.

Who made Himself of no repute,
  The servant's form He bore,
And found in fashion as a man,
  Our likeness, too, He wore.

Who fashioned thus has bowed Himself,
  Obedient unto death,
O cruel reproach, a cross of shame,
  That body compasseth !

Now God hath high exalted Him,
  At His right hand in grace,
And given Him the mighty Name,
  In Heaven the highest place.

All knees shall bow, all tongues confess
  That Jesus Christ is Lord,
And things in heaven and things on earth,
  Glory to God accord.

                                        G. G.

LESSON 1

"Before the World Was"

I. **Text.** " Whose goings forth have been from of old, from everlasting " (Micah 5. 2).

II. **Main Lesson.** That Christ was no created being, limited by time, but was from eternity very God of very God—the Eternal Son.

III. **Scripture to Study:** Proverbs 8. 22-36. Christ, under the figure of *Wisdom personified*, speaks.

v. 22. *One with the Father* (*cf.* John 10. 30 and 38; 14. 9-12). " Jehovah possessed Me in the beginning of His way, before His works of old."

v. 23. *He was " In the Beginning "* (*cf.* John 1. 1 and 1 John 1. 1). " I was set up from everlasting, from the beginning, or ever the earth was."

vv. 24-27. *Before Creation.* " When there were no depths." . . . " No fountains abounding with water." " Before the mountains were settled." . . . " While as yet He had not made the earth." . . .

vv. 28-29. *At Creation* (see Lesson 2). " When He prepared the heavens I was there " . . . "the depth " . . . "the clouds (R.V. skies) " . . . "the fountains of the deep " . . . "when He gave the sea his decree " . . . "when He appointed the foundations of the earth."

v. 30. *God's "Fellow" and "Delight"* (*cf.* Zech. 13. 7; John 3. 16). " I was by Him as One brought up with Him, and I was daily His delight, rejoicing always before Him."

v. 31. *His Delight in Man.* " . . . My delights were with the sons of men."

vv. 32-35. *His Call to Men to Hear and to Find Life in Him* (*cf.* John 1. 4 and 14. 6). " Hearken unto Me, O ye children." " Blessed is the man that heareth Me . . . Whoso findeth *Me* findeth life."

v. 36. *Danger of Rejecting Him.* " He that sinneth against Me wrongeth his own soul, all they that hate Me love death."

21

IV. **Before the World was.**   The foregoing has introduced us to the fact that the Lord Jesus Christ was with the Father in the beginning (that is, there was no beginning when He was not).   In other words, He is "the Eternal Son."

This leads to an equally wonderful truth that *All the Great Work of Our Salvation* was purposed and planned in the councils of eternity before the world was.

Sin did not take God by surprise.   He foresaw, when giving man a free will, that he would use it in rebellion, and so before his creation appointed his Redeemer and planned his Salvation.

Seven things are said to have been *before the world was.*

1. THE GLORY OF THE SON WITH THE FATHER.   In His prayer (John 17. 5) the Lord Jesus speaks of the glory " I had with Thee before the world was."

2. THE LOVE OF THE FATHER TO THE SON.   In the same prayer the Lord says: " Thou lovedst Me before the foundation of the world."

3. THE PURPOSE TO SAVE SINFUL MAN IN GRACE.   We read in 2 Timothy 1. 9 that God "saved us . . . according to His own purpose and grace, which was given us in Christ Jesus before the world began."

4. THE WISDOM THAT CONCEIVED THE PLAN was ordained before the world (1 Cor. 2. 7).

No wonder that the Apostle Paul apostrophizes in Romans 11. 33: " O the depth of the riches both of the wisdom and knowledge of God ! How unsearchable are His judgments, and His ways past finding out !"

5. THE PROMISE OF ETERNAL LIFE was made and given by God, Who cannot lie, " before the world began " (Titus 1. 2).

6. THE LAMB WAS SLAIN in the purpose of God " before the foundation of the world " (1 Pet. 1. 20); so that in Revelation 13. 8 He is spoken of as " the Lamb slain from the foundation of the world."

7. THE CHOICE OF THE ELECT was made in the wondrous foreknowledge of God " before the foundation of the world " (Eph. 1. 4).

What a dignity and majesty these seven facts give to

our salvation! It was no afterthought of God, as if sin had disarranged His plans and a remedy had to be found, but the purpose of the Eternal Wisdom and Perfect Love that knows the end from the beginning.

V. Other Lessons from the Subject.

1. THE "WISDOM" AND THE "WORD." On reading the passage above set out, Proverbs 8. 22-36, one will at once notice its similarity to that in John 1. 1-5. There Christ is the Word, in the beginning with God, and Himself God, acting in creation and giving Life to and becoming Light to the sons of men.

Wisdom may be unrevealed, but the Word is spoken or revealed.

I may be wise and no one perceive it, but when I speak that wisdom is known and perceived.

It is so with Christ. In the Old Testament, He is the Wisdom of God (not yet manifested); in the New Testament, He is the Word of God, for in these last days God hath spoken unto us by His Son. The Word was made flesh. The Wisdom of God was manifested in the Word of God.

2. OUR SAVIOUR IS OUR GOD AND OUR CREATOR. This is not sufficiently emphasized in the preaching of the Gospel.

Dr. Watts strikes this awe-inspiring note in the beautiful verse on the death of Christ.

> " Well might the Sun in darkness hide
> And shut his glories in,
> When Christ *THE MIGHTY MAKER* died
> For man the creature's sin."

3. THE FOREKNOWLEDGE OF GOD. Our finite minds have in the wisdom of God been limited to the past and present. The future is forbidden us. Men try to lift the veil, often by unlawful means, but nothing save that which God has been pleased to tell us can be known of what is coming.

But God is not restricted in this manner. Past, present and future all lie before His infinite understanding: as David says, " Thine understanding is infinite "; and thank God " His love is perfect."

What comfort this brings !

> " I cannot read His future plans,
> But this I know:
> I have the shining of His Face,
> And all the riches of His grace,
> While here below."

4. THE DEATH OF CHRIST DETERMINED FROM ETERNITY.
This is asserted in the Scriptures—

(i) *By the Lord Himself.* In John 10. 17 He says, "I have authority to lay (my life) down, and I have authority to take it again. This commandment have I received of My Father "—that commandment being the decree of the Eternal God.

(ii) *By Peter on the Day of Pentecost* (Acts 2. 23). " (Christ) being delivered by the determinate counsel and foreknowledge of God, ye have taken, and by wicked hands have crucified and slain."

(iii) *Again in Acts* 4. 28. " To do whatsoever Thy hand and Thy counsel determined before to be done."

So the Lamb was slain from the foundation of the world.

VI. Application.

(i) The One of Whom these things are true demands our adoration and worship. Let us follow the example of the once-doubting but believing Thomas and fall at His feet saying, " My Lord and my God."

(ii) How shall we escape if we neglect *so great a Salvation?* —decreed from eternity; effected by the Lord our Creator; and presented to us in the Gospel.

OUTLINE

Christ was from Eternity—

(i) The LORD of Glory (John 17. 5.　See IV. 1).

(ii) The LOVED of the Father (John 17. 14.　See IV. 2).

(iii) The LIGHT of the World (2 Tim. 1. 9 and 1 Cor. 2. 7. See IV. 3-4).

(iv) The LIFE giver (Titus 1. 2.　See IV. 5).

(v) The LAMB slain (1 Peter 1. 20, Rev. 13. 8.　See IV. 6).

Creator and Upholder of All Things

I. Text. "Unto the Son He saith . . . Thou, Lord, in the beginning hast laid the foundation of the earth; and the Heavens are the works of Thine hands " (Heb. 1. 10).

II. Main Lesson. To show the majesty and glory of the Lord Jesus as Creator and Upholder of all things. That our faith in Him as our Lord and Saviour may be strengthened.

III. Scripture for Study: Isaiah 40. 25-31. In the light of our text we are justified in applying this glorious passage to the Lord Jesus, the Holy One of God.

v. 25. *He Challenges Comparison.* "To whom then will ye liken Me, or shall I be equal? saith the Holy One."

v. 26. *He bids us Look at the Skies.* "Lift up your eyes on high and behold Who hath created these things that bringeth out their host by number."

v. 26. *His Infinite Knowledge.* "He calleth them all by name."

v. 26. *The Greatness of His Might.* "By the greatness of His might, for that He is strong in power."

v. 26. *He Upholds them all.* "Not one faileth."

v. 27. *He Rebukes Mistrust.* "Why sayest thou, O Jacob, . . . My way is hid from the Lord?"

v. 28. *He cannot Fail in Power.* "Hast thou not known? The Everlasting God, Jehovah, the Creator of the ends of the earth, fainteth not, neither is weary."

v. 28. *Nor in Wisdom.* "There is no searching of His understanding."

v. 29. *His Power is available for all who wait upon Him.* "He giveth power to the faint. . . . Even the youths shall faint and be weary, and the young men shall utterly fall. But they that wait upon the Lord shall renew their strength; they shall mount up with wings as eagles; they shall run and not be weary; and they shall walk, and not faint."

By this infinite and beneficent Creator strength is given to them that wait on Him to do all His will.

IV. Eight Passages that Speak of Christ as the Creator and Upholder of all Things.

(i) Hebrews 1. 10 (see our text above).

(ii) John 1. 1-3: " In the Beginning was the Word, and the Word was with God, and the Word was God. . . . *All things were made by Him*; and without Him was not any thing made that was made," v. 14, " And the Word was made flesh, and dwelt among us."

(iii) Hebrews 1. 2, 3: " His Son, . . . *by Whom also He made the worlds*, Who being the brightness of His glory, and the express image of His person, and *upholding all things* by the Word of His power, . . ."

(iv) Colossians 1. 15-17: " Who is the Image of the Invisible God, the Firstborn (see Psa. 89. 27) of all creation, *for by Him were all things created*, in Heaven, in earth, visible and invisible . . . *all things were created by Him* and for Him, and He is before all things and *by Him all things consist* " (maintain their being and place).

(v) Ephesians 3. 9: " *Who created all things* by Jesus Christ."

(vi) 1 Corinthians 8. 6: " To us there is . . . one Lord Jesus Christ *by Whom are all things* and we by Him."

(vii) Revelation 3. 14: " The Amen, the Faithful and True Witness, *the Beginning* (author) *of the Creation of God*."

(viii) Revelation 14. 1 and 7: " Lo, a Lamb stood on the Mount Sion. . . . Worship Him that made Heaven and Earth and the Sea and the Fountains of Waters."

To these must be added the remarkable passage in which Christ Himself claimed to be One with God in the creation and upholding of all things: John 5. 17, " My Father worketh hitherto, and *I work*. Therefore the Jews sought to kill Him, because He not only had broken the Sabbath, but said also that God was His Father, making Himself *equal with God*."

The rest of God after His creation was not the rest of inactivity but of satisfaction and delight in all He had made. He still works in upholding and maintaining all things, and this work the Lord Jesus claimed to share.

The Jews did not misunderstand Him—He made Himself equal with God.

V. Other Lessons from the Subject.

1. THE IMMENSITY OF CREATION. Some years ago one of the stars blazed up as if on fire and after some time disappeared. It is so distant that the astronomers tell us that the conflagration took place in Queen Elizabeth's reign, the light of it only now reaching us. In *Eos*, a book recently published by the American Astronomer J. H. Jeans, D.Sc., LL.D., F.R.S., we read: It has been " found that the most remote objects visible in the biggest telescope on earth are so distant that light travelling 186,000 miles a second takes 140 million years to come from them to us " (p. 14).

" Who hath created these things that bringeth out their host by number ?" What number ? To quote again from *Eos*: " The sun, which is a million times as big as the earth and 300,000 times as massive, proves to be something less than a grain of sand on the seashore. It forms one of a family whose number must certainly be counted in thousands of millions; Dr. Seares has estimated it at thirty thousand million " (p. 19).

Well might David exclaim: "When I behold the Heavens the work of Thy fingers, the moon and the stars, which Thou hast ordained; What is man that Thou art mindful of him or the son of man that Thou visitest him ?" (Psa. 8. 3-4).

2. THE BEAUTY OF CREATION. " He hath made everything beautiful in his time " (Eccl. 3. 11), and this is because He Himself is beautiful, altogether lovely. Creation is but His thoughts put into being.

True holiness is pure beauty. So we read of " the beauty of holiness," and the " beauty of the Lord our God " (Psa. 29. 2, 27. 4).

The two things to which God likens Himself are light and love (1 John 1. 5, 4. 16)—the most beautiful things in the physical and moral realms.

3. THE PURPOSE OF CREATION. This is stated as follows in Scripture:

(i) *For His Pleasure*. " For Thy pleasure they are and were created " (Rev. 4. 11); " The Lord taketh pleasure in them that fear Him; in their prosperity " (Psa. 35. 27); " in their prayers " (Prov. 15. 2). His delights are with the sons of men.

(ii) *To Display His Glory.* The Heavens declare the glory of God. God loves to display Himself to the sons of men. Display in man is offensive because man has nothing in himself worthy of display, but with God infinite wisdom and perfect love are revealed in all He does and says for the happiness of His creatures. He delights, then, to make known Himself to us (John 17. 3).

(iii) *To have Objects for His Love.* Therefore, " It became Him for Whom are all things and by Whom are all things *in bringing many sons to glory* to make the Captain of their Salvation perfect through sufferings."

(iv) *That Christ might have Companions through all Eternity.* Redeemed and sanctified by His precious Blood and conformed to His image, so that He might be the First-born among many brethren.

God's original purpose made men in His own image, in His likeness; that image marred by sin is restored in Christ.

4. THE UPHOLDING OF ALL THINGS. It is often stated that the world is governed by law. This is only relatively so. It is governed by a Person—the eternal and ever-blessed Son of God. His regular methods we call " laws," but all down to the smallest detail is directed and upheld by His infinite wisdom, mighty power and perfect love. Even the hairs of your head are all numbered !

When this is realized, how great should be our peace !

VI. Application.

(i) If by faith we lay hold of the fact that the worlds were framed by the Word of God (Heb. 11. 3), it will be easy to trust the One Whose power is so great.

(ii) Let us then delight ourselves in the wonders of creation that we may discover in them more of the greatness, goodness and grace of Him Who made them.

OUTLINES

Seven Questions as to Creation

BY WHOM ? The Triune God (Gen. 1. 1).
THROUGH WHOM ? The Lord Jesus Christ (Heb. 1. 2).
FOR WHOM ? Him Who is " Heir of all things " (Col. 1. 15-17).

How ? " He spake and it was done " (Psa. 33. 9).
When ? " In the beginning " (Gen. 1. 1).
In what Time ? " Six days " (Exod. 20. 11).
Why ? " For His pleasure " (Rev. 4. 11).

The Testimony of Creation

Declares the Glory of God (Psa. 19. 1) and
Shows His Handiwork (Psa. 19. 1).
His wondrous works declare Him Perfect in Knowledge
(Job 37. 16) and
Show His Terror and Greatness (Psa. 66. 3).
His Works are Manifold (many and varied) (Psa. 104. 24).
His Tender Mercies are over them all (Psa. 145. 9).
They Praise Him (Psa. 145. 10).
He is holy in them all (Psa. 145. 17).
All beautiful in their season (Eccles. 3. 11).
His Eternal Power and Godhead revealed to all in them,
leaving all without excuse (Rom. 1. 20).

Three Worlds in 2 Peter 3. 6-13

(i) The World that then was (6) perished in the flood
in the days of Noah.
(ii) The Heavens and the earth which are now (7)
reserved unto fire against the day of judgment.
(iii) New Heavens and a New Earth (13) wherein dwelleth
righteousness (Isa. 65. 17, 66. 22).

The Old and the New Creations

The Old Creation.	*The New Creation.*
Subject to Vanity (Rom. 8. 20);	Created in righteousness and true holiness (Eph. 5. 24);
Groaning and travailing (22);	Entered by Faith in Christ (2 Cor. 5. 17);
Waiting for the manifestation (19);	Wherein dwelleth righteousness (2 Pet. 3. 13);
To be delivered from corruption (21).	Eternal (2 Cor. 5. 1)

The Old Creation (seen and temporal) is a Parable of
the New Creation (unseen and eternal). The Invisible is
understood by the Visible (Rom. 1. 20).

His Coming Anticipated in the Old Testament

I. Text. "We have found Him, of whom Moses in the law, and the prophets, did write, Jesus of Nazareth" (John 1. 45).

II. Main Lesson. The coming of Christ was foretold in many Old Testament Scriptures.

The Lord said of them, "These are they which testify of Me," and asserted that Moses wrote of Him.

He frequently applied the Old Testament Scriptures to Himself.

III. Scriptures to Study (being some of those to which the Lord referred as speaking of Him).

In the Synagogue at Nazareth (Luke 4. 18-21; Isa. 61. 1, 2): "The Spirit of the Lord is upon Me, because He hath anointed Me to preach the Gospel to the poor; He hath sent Me to heal the broken-hearted, to preach deliverance to the captives and recovering of sight to the blind, to set at liberty them that are bruised, to preach the acceptable year of the Lord. . . . This day is this Scripture fulfilled in your ears."

The Stone which the Builders Rejected (Matt. 21. 42; Luke 20. 17; Psa. 118. 26): "Did ye never read in the Scriptures, The stone which the builders rejected, the same is become the Head of the Corner: This is the Lord's doing, and it is marvellous in our eyes?"

Christ—whose Son is He? (Matt. 22. 42-45; Psa. 110. 1): "What think ye of Christ? Whose Son is He? They say unto Him, The Son of David. He saith unto them, How then doth David in spirit call Him Lord, saying, The Lord said unto my Lord, Sit Thou on My right hand, till I make Thine enemies Thy footstool? If David then call Him Lord, how is He his Son?"

His Last Words to Jerusalem (Matt. 23. 39; Psa. 118. 26): "Ye shall not see Me henceforth—till ye shall say, Blessed is He that cometh in the Name of the Lord."

The Betrayal by Judas (John 13. 18; Psa. 41. 9): "I speak not of you all: I know whom I have chosen: but that the scripture may be fulfilled, He that eateth bread with Me hath lifted up his heel against Me."

The Shepherd Smitten (Matt. 26. 31; Zech. 13. 7): "All ye shall be offended because of Me this night: for it is written, I will smite the Shepherd, and the sheep of the flock shall be scattered abroad."

The 53rd of Isaiah applied to Himself (Luke 22. 37; Isa. 53. 12): "I say unto you, that this that is written must yet be accomplished in Me, And He was reckoned among the transgressors: for the things concerning Me have an end " (hath fulfilment, R.V.).

His Cry on the Cross (Matt. 27. 46; Psa. 22. 1): "My God, My God, why hast Thou forsaken Me ?"

His Dying Word (Luke 23. 46; Psa. 31. 5): "Into Thy hands I commend My Spirit."

His Confession before the High Priest (Mark 14. 62; Daniel 7. 13): "The High Priest asked Him, Art Thou the Christ, the Son of the Blessed ?   And Jesus said, I am: and ye shall see the Son of Man sitting on the right hand of power and coming in the clouds of Heaven."

(For a full list of prophecies of our Lord's first advent, see my *Miracle of Prophecy*, 6d.)

IV. Some Old Testament Titles of Christ.

The Seed of the Woman (Gen. 3. 15) who should bruise (crush) the serpent's head.

Shiloh (Gen. 49. 10) of whom, dying, Jacob prophesied: "unto Him shall the gathering of the people be" and—

The Shepherd, the Stone of Israel (Gen. 49. 24).

The Star out of Jacob (Num. 24. 17).

The Sceptre out of Israel, foretold by Balaam.

The Stone (Psa. 118. 26) rejected of the builders.

A *Prophet* (Deut. 18. 15; Acts 3. 27, 7. 37), of whom Moses spoke, "from the midst of thee, of thy brethren, like unto me."

The Child Born, the Son Given (Isa. 9. 6): "The government shall be upon His shoulders, and His Name shall be called Wonderful, Counsellor, The Mighty God, The Everlasting Father, The Prince of Peace."

The Root of Jesse (Isa. 11. 10): "An ensign of the people to whom the Gentiles will seek, whose rest shall be glorious."

Emmanuel, "God with us" (Isa. 7. 14; Matt. 1. 28).

His King and His Anointed (1 Sam. 2. 10): Hannah's song, "He shall give strength unto His King and exalt the horn of His Anointed."

The Shepherd—God's Fellow (Zech. 13. 7): "Awake, O sword, against my shepherd, and against the man who is my fellow."

The Lord Our Righteousness (Jer. 23. 6): "Jehovah Tzidkenu."

The Mighty One of Jacob (Isa. 60. 16).

The Branch (Zech. 6. 12): "The man whose Name is."

The Ruler in Israel (Mic. 5. 2): "Whose goings forth have been from of old, from everlasting."

My Redeemer (Job 19. 25; Isa. 59. 20).

Sun of Righteousness (Mal. 4. 2).

The King Priest (Zech. 6. 13): After the order of Melchisedek (Psa. 110. 4).

V. Other Lessons.

1. HIM OF WHOM MOSES DID WRITE.

Our Lord said, "Had ye believed Moses ye would have believed Me: for he wrote of Me."

Moses wrote the five books of the Pentateuch. From each we can find types of Christ:

> Genesis: The Ark.
> Exodus: The Passover Lamb.
> Leviticus: The Scapegoat.
> Numbers: The Serpent lifted up.
> Deuteronomy: The City of Refuge.

These, of course, can be added to.

2. THE TESTIMONY OF THE OLD TESTAMENT SCRIPTURES TO CHRIST.

Our Lord constantly appealed to the Old Testament in support of His claim:

" Search the Scriptures for . . . they are they which testify of Me " (John 5. 39).

He applied the types of the Old Testament to Himself.

The Manna : " I am that Bread of Life. Your fathers did eat manna in the wilderness and are dead. This is the bread which cometh down from Heaven, that a man may eat thereof and never die " (John 6. 48-50).

The Brazen Serpent : " As Moses lifted up the serpent in the wilderness so must the Son of Man be lifted up " (John 3. 14).

Jonah (Matt. 12. 40): " As Jonas was three days and three nights in the whale's belly; so shall the Son of Man be three days and three nights in the heart of the earth."

(These may be searched out and added to.)

3. THE OLD TESTAMENT USED IN PREACHING THE GOSPEL.

It must be remembered that when the Gospel was first preached there was no New Testament. Peter and the other first preachers quoted from the Old Testament to confirm their testimony.

See as examples Acts 2. 25-34, 3. 22-25, 4. 11, 25, etc.

Let those who seek to disparage the value of the Old Testament consider this.

4. GOD'S WAY OF SALVATION has always been the same

down the ages. It is by grace through faith on the ground of the Blood.

The 11th of Hebrews shows that the Old Testament saints knew and rejoiced in it.

Abel was accounted righteous on the ground of a more excellent sacrifice (4).

Noah was heir to the righteousness which is by faith (7).

David describes " the blessedness of the man to whom God imputeth righteousness without works " (Rom. 4. 6; Psa. 32. 1) and so on.

They looked forward; we look back to the finished work of Christ upon the Cross.

5. THE WONDER OF THE OLD TESTAMENT TYPES.

That the Gospel should have been anticipated 1,500 years before Christ came in the types is a wonder of inspiration.

The whole plan of Salvation and Life was enacted in the historical parable of the miraculous history of the Exodus and the entry into the Promised Land.

This again can be worked out in great detail from the Passover to Solomon in all his glory.

VI. Application.

Let us search the Old Testament Scriptures, for Christ is hidden therein.

Let us rejoice in the confirmation of our faith—from those sacred oracles and their testimony to Him.

ACROSTIC

ALL SCRIPTURE is given to:

SANCTIFY.   " Sanctify them through Thy truth " (John 17. 17).

CORRECT.   " Profitable for correction " (2. Tim. 3. 16).

REJOICE.   " Rejoicing the heart " (Psa. 19. 8).

INSTRUCT.   " Profitable for instruction in righteousness " (2 Tim. 3. 16).

PURIFY.   " Purified your souls in obeying the truth " (1 Pet. 1. 22).

TEACH.   " Teach me Thy statutes " (Psa. 119. 12).

UNITE.   " Unite my heart to fear Thy Name " (Psa. 86. 11).

REPROVE.   " By them is Thy servant warned " (Psa. 19. 11).

and be EATEN.   " Thy words were found and I did eat them " (Jer. 15. 16).

"Sanctified and Sent"

I. Text. "Say ye of Him, Whom the Father hath sanctified, and sent into the world; Thou blasphemest because I said, I am the Son of God?" (John 10. 36).

II. Main Lesson. To show how Christ came forth from the Father—to do His will in life and death, and to give effect to the eternal decrees and everlasting covenant.

III. Scriptures to Study. It is in the Psalms and from the lips of the Lord Himself that we learn the secrets of eternity and of His sanctification by the Father for the work of Redemption, and His commission and appointment. We shall accordingly consider two great Messianic Psalms, written some 1,000 years before His manifestation in flesh.

Psalm 2—

This Psalm looks right on to the final apostasy and rebellion of the nations, when they attempt to cast off the authority and rule of Christ.

vv. 1-3. *The Nations Rebel Against Christ.* " Why do the nations rage and the people imagine a vain thing? The kings of the earth set themselves, and the rulers take counsel together, against the Lord, and against *His Anointed* (Christ), saying, Let us break their bands asunder, and cast away their cords from us."

vv. 4-5: *The Lord views them with Derision and Wrath.*

He that sitteth in the Heavens shall laugh; the Lord shall have them in derision. Then shall He speak unto them in His wrath and vex them in His sore displeasure.

v. 6: *God sets HIS KING upon His Holy Hill in Zion.* This was fulfilled in the resurrection of Christ (see Acts 2. 25, 4. 28; and Heb. 12. 23).

" Yet have I set My King upon My Holy Hill in Zion."

v. 7: *Christ Declares THE DECREE.* He has been declared to be the Son of God, both—

(a) By eternal begetting, and

(b) In Resurrection (Acts 13. 33; Heb. 1. 5; and Rom. 1. 4).

"I will declare the decree: the Lord (Jehovah) hath said unto Me (Christ), Thou art *MY SON*; this day have I begotten Thee" (*cf.* Matt. 3. 17, and 17. 5).

v. 8: *God Promises to Give Christ a Holy Seed.* "Ask of Me, and I shall give Thee the nations for Thine inheritance (*cf.* Eph. 1. 11, R.V.), and the uttermost parts of the earth for Thy possession."

v. 9: *And Universal Dominion.* "Thou shalt break them with a rod of iron, and Thou shalt dash them in pieces like a potter's vessel" (that is those who rebel).

vv. 10-11: *The Nations are Bidden to Submit to Christ.* "Be wise, O ye kings, be instructed, ye judges of the earth. Serve the Lord with fear, and rejoice with trembling."

v. 12: *And to be Reconciled* (*cf.* 2 Cor. 5. 20). "Kiss *THE SON* lest He be angry."

v. 12: *And Fear lest Wrath come on Them.* "And ye perish from the way, when His wrath is kindled but a little" (R.V.—"His wrath will soon be kindled").

v. 12: *Those who put their Faith in Christ are blessed.* "Blessed are all they that put their trust (R.V.M., take refuge) in Him."

Psalm 110—

v. 1: *Christ is Seated at God's Right Hand* (see Matt. 22. 44; Acts 2. 34; 1 Cor. 15. 25; Heb. 1. 13). "Jehovah said unto My Lord (Christ), Sit Thou at My right hand."

v. 1: *His Enemies will be Made to Submit to Him.* "Until I make Thine enemies Thy footstool."

v. 2: *He is to be KING in ZION.* "The Lord shall send the rod of Thy strength out of Zion: rule Thou in the midst of Thine enemies."

v. 3: *There Shall be A WILLING PEOPLE.* "Thy people shall be willing in the day of Thy power, in the beauties of holiness . . . Thou hast the dew of Thy youth."

v. 4: *The WORD of the OATH makes Christ a Continuing Priest* (*cf.* Heb. 7. 21). "Jehovah has sworn and will not repent; Thou art A PRIEST FOR EVER after the order (manner or style) of Melchisedek."

vv. 5-7: *He Shall have Universal Sway.* "The Lord (Christ) at Thy right hand shall strike through kings in the day of His wrath . . . therefore shall He lift up the head."

These two Psalms reveal to us something of the meaning of Christ's being sanctified and sent by the Father. In His—

(a) Being declared to be the Son.

(b) Being seated as King in Zion at the right hand of the Father.

(c) Being predestined by the divine decree to universal dominion.

(d) Being given a Godly seed—an inheritance in His saints—a willing and obedient people.

(e) Being appointed Judge to execute judgment (cf. John 5. 22).

IV. **Other Great Scriptures** referring to the Royal Commission.

Hebrews 1. 6: "When He bringeth His first begotten into the world He saith, Let all the angels of God worship Him."

Psalm 40. 7: "Lo, I come: in the volume of the book it is written of Me, I delight to do Thy will, O My God: Thy law is within my heart."

Psalm 45. 6 (quoted Hebrews 1. 8): "Thy throne, O God (the Son), is for ever and ever; the sceptre of Thy kingdom is a right sceptre."

V. **Our Lord's Own References to It.**

John 3. 16: "For God so loved the world, that He gave His only begotten Son."

Mark 12. 6: "Having one Son, His Well Beloved, He sent Him."

John 8. 42: "I proceeded forth and came from God; neither came I of myself, but He sent Me."

John 6. 38: "For I came down from Heaven, not to do Mine own will, but the will of Him that sent Me."

John 7. 29-30: "I am not come of Myself, but He that sent Me is true, Whom ye know not. But I know Him, and He hath sent Me."

John 8. 23: "Ye are from beneath; I am from above: ye are of this world; I am not of this world."

VI. Other Lessons from the Study.

1. FREE GRACE IN THE GIFT.   It is sometimes said or implied that God had to send His Son, that He had no other way, but was under obligation to do so.   This is never so represented in Scripture.

It was of the great love of His heart that He chose this way to save man, the giving of His best.   " He so loved that He gave."

His grace was free to act as it would, and the way He acted revealed His grace, and that He was rich in mercy.

2. THE SANCTIFICATION OF THE SON by the Father means that He set Him apart for the great work of redemption. To this the Son responded by setting Himself apart and devoting Himself to God for the work to which He was appointed.   So Jesus said, " For their sakes I sanctify Myself."

This, too, was voluntary.   He became obedient to the commandment received from the Father, and voluntarily laid down His life, thus drawing out the love of the Father's heart (see John 10. 17-18; and Phil. 2. 8).

3. A STRANGER IN THE EARTH.   " He was in the world, and the world was made by Him, and the world knew Him not " (John 1. 10).   He came unto His own (possessions), and His own (people) received Him not."

Well might Jeremiah ask, " O Hope of Israel, the Saviour thereof in the day of trouble, why shouldst Thou be as a stranger in the land, and as a wayfaring man that turneth aside to tarry for a night ?" (14. 8.)

4 THE DECREE IRREVERSIBLE.   When Christ declared the decree he announced the immutable counsel of God. Nothing can reverse or defeat the purposes of God.

The One Whom men cast out and slew shall reign— God has decreed it.

The Crowning Day is coming when He who wore the Crown of Thorns will have upon His head the many diadems.

VII. Application.

No better application could be made than that of Psalm 2. 12.

" Kiss (be reconciled to) the Son lest He be angry, and ye perish from the way."

OUTLINES

The teaching of the above can readily be cast into the alliterative form thus:

THE ONE SON, THE WELL BELOVED.

1. SANCTIFIED by the Father.
2. SENT into the world.
3. STRANGER on the earth.
4. SEATED at the right hand of God.
5. SWAYING A SCEPTRE of righteousness; King of kings and Lord of lords.

SANCTIFIED

1. By God the Father (Jude 1).
2. By the Holy Ghost (Rom. 15. 16).
3. In Christ Jesus (1 Cor. 1. 2).
4. By the Word of God (John 17. 17, 1 Tim. 4. 5).
5. By Faith (Acts 26. 18).
6. Through the Offering of the Body of Christ (Heb. 10. 10).
7. Meet for the Master's use (2 Tim. 2. 21).

Threefold Sanctification of the Son

(i) By the Father (John 10. 36).
(ii) By His own act (John 17. 19).
(iii) By His obedience (Heb. 7. 26).

The Great Mystery of Godliness

" GOD WAS MANIFEST IN THE FLESH."

I. Text. " And without controversy great is the mystery of godliness: God was manifest in the flesh " (1 Tim. 3. 16).

II. Main Lesson. That Jesus of Nazareth was God manifested in flesh. This is the foundation truth (confessed by Peter, Matt. 16. 16) upon which the whole of Christianity rests.

The greatest mystery and the most wonderful fact, before which we can only stand in awe and worship.

III. Scripture to Study : 1 Timothy 3. 16.

" *Without Controversy.* " It is a matter beyond the reason of man. Controversy is futile and out of place.

" *Great is the Mystery.* " A mystery in Scripture is one of God's secrets, which could not be discovered by science, nor guessed, nor known until God is pleased to reveal or uncover it. It is then an open secret for all who are enlightened by the Spirit.

" *Of Godliness.* " The object of our faith, reverence and godly contemplation.

" *God.* " (θεός). We do well to hold fast to the A.V. rendering here. The alternative readings, " He who " (ὅς) as in the R.V., or " which " (ὅ), are not so suitable to the meaning of the context. (For a full discussion of the evidence see Burgon's *Revision Revised*, p. 424 *et seq.*)

" *Was manifested in flesh* "—that is, " was found in fashion as a man " in a body prepared Him of God, " in the likeness of sinful flesh," but without sin.

" *Justified in the Spirit.* " The Spirit He manifested when He walked on earth justified the claim He made to be the Son of God.

" *Seen of angels.* " They welcomed His birth; they ministered to Him in His temptation and in the Garden of Gethsemane; they desired to look into these great events.

40

"*Preached unto the Gentiles.*" For He came not only to confirm the promises made unto the fathers, but "that the Gentiles might glorify God for His mercy " (Rom. 15. 8).

"*Believed on in the world.*" For though many refuse the testimony, some believed and still do so.

"*Received up into glory.*" "Was taken up into and reigns in glory."

We may notice in this verse the three striking contrasts:

Flesh	Spirit.
Angels	Gentiles.
World	Glory.

IV. Our Lord's Testimony to His Deity.

(*a*) *He asserts it plainly :*

John 10. 30. " I and My Father are One " ($\check{\epsilon}\nu$=neuter; not one Person but one in essence).

John 14. 9. " He that hath seen Me hath seen the Father also."

John 8. 58. " Before Abraham was, I AM."

John 6. 42. " I came down from Heaven." 16. 27. " I came out from God."

John 5. 23. " All men should honour the Son even as they honour the Father."

(*b*) *Every page of the Gospel* has on it words or works recorded that no mere man could have said or done. Open the Gospel at any page and see.

(*c*) *He behaved as if He were God.*

He forgives sins (Matt. 9. 2; Mark 2. 7; Luke 7. 48).

He accepts worship (Matt.{ 2. 11, 8. 2, 9. 18, 14. 32-33, 28. 9; John 9. 35).

He answers prayer (John 14. 13-14).

He raises the dead.

(This subject is so great that it cannot be set out fully here. The reader is referred to my pamphlet *The Deity of Christ*, 1d.).

V. Other Lessons.

1. The Body of Our Lord.

(*a*) This was *specially prepared* for Him. " A body hast Thou prepared Me " (Heb. 10. 5).

It is spoken of as *the Tabernacle* in which He dwelt (taber-nacled) amongst us (John 1. 14), and is described in Hebrews 8. 2 and 9. 11 as:

" The true Tabernacle which the Lord pitched, and not man."

" A greater and more perfect Tabernacle, not made with hands—that is to say, not of this creation."

Of it we read—

(b) It was " *in the likeness of sinful flesh*," but not sinful. What sinless flesh was like we do not know.   Some think man was " covered with light as with a garment " (Psa. 104. 2), being made in God's image.

(c) It was *without sin.*   " In Him was no sin."   That holy thing " conceived of the Holy Ghost " (Luke 2. 35) had no law of sin and death in its members as we have.   He inherited no taint of Adam's transgression (John 14. 30).

(d) *After His resurrection* it was a glorified body (the body of His glory, Phil. 3. 21, R.V.).   It was a spiritual body (1 Cor. 15. 44), not a spirit only without flesh and bones (Luke 24. 39).

2. THE REASONS FOR IT:

(a) We read in Hebrews 2. 17, " *It behoved Him to be made like unto His brethren.*"   So that it could be said, " He that sanctifieth and they who are sanctified are all of one."   He can therefore call them His brethren.

(b) *He became man* that as man He might die for us men (Heb. 2. 9: " That He by the grace of God should taste death for every man ").

(c) *That He might be perfected through sufferings* (Heb. 2. 10), and so be fitted by this experience to become *Captain* (Heb. 2. 10), *High Priest*, merciful and faithful (Heb. 2. 17), *Saviour* and *Intercessor* (Heb. 7. 25-26), *Sympathizer* (Heb. 4. 15), and *Forerunner* (Heb. 6. 20) of His people.

3. HE RETAINS HIS BODY IN HEAVEN with the marks of His passion in it (John 20. 27).   He is seen in Heaven, " A Lamb as it had been slain " (Rev. 5. 6).   There is a Man upon the throne.

4. THE GREATEST WONDER OF ALL THE MIGHTY WORKS OF GOD was this, that He Who was Himself God should be also man.

" *That the Mighty God should be a child born and the Everlasting Father a Son given unto us may well entitle Him unto the name of Wonderful* " (J. Owen).

The Incarnation of the Son of God is to be admired as the most adorable effect of Divine Wisdom.

VI. Application.

Let us adore the Wisdom and Grace of God in this Great Mystery of Godliness.

Let us confess and rejoice in Christ as " our Lord and our God."

The Mystery of Godliness.

What ?   Did the Lord come down from Heaven to earth ?
And did He condescend to human birth ?
In swaddling clothes within the manger laid,
Who spread the Heavens the wide prospect made.

O mystery of Godliness and Power !
Omniscient, He yet knew not the hour;
Omnipotent, yet was through weakness slain;
Immortal, yet within a tomb has lain.

All present, yet the weeping sisters cried:
" Hadst Thou been here, our brother had not died."
And while with Nicodemus speaking here
Yet in the bosom of the Father was He there.

Lord, grant us peace, a humble, contrite heart,
To receive with meekness what Thou dost impart.
To worship where we cannot understand,
And bless Thee for the grace wherein we stand.

                                        G. G.

The Self-Emptying

I. **Text.** " Who made Himself of no reputation " (R.V., emptied Himself), Phil. 2. 7.

II. **Main Lesson.** The marvellous grace of the Lord Jesus, Who in Eternity was rich, for our sakes becoming poor that we through His poverty might be rich. His humbling of Himself to be found in fashion as a man necessitated the emptying of Himself in the manner described below.

III. **Scripture to Study :** Philippians 2. 3-13.

1. EXHORTATION TO LOWLINESS OF MIND:

v. 3. " Let nothing be done through strife or vainglory; but in lowliness of mind let each esteem other better than themselves."

2. TO UNSELFISHNESS:

v. 4. " Look not every man on his own things (interests), but every man also on the things of others."

3. TO CHRISTLIKENESS:

v. 5. " Let this mind be in you, which was also in Christ Jesus."

4. THE GLORIOUS AND GRACIOUS EXAMPLE OF CHRIST:

v. 6. " *Who, being in the form of God.*" Since God has no outward or visible form this can only mean " of the essential being of God "—that is, Himself God.

v. 6. " *Thought it not robbery to be equal with God.*" He was not blaspheming when He made Himself " equal with God " (John 5. 18), and being a man " made (represented) Himself God " (John 10. 33) and claimed equal honour (John 5. 23), and said that He and the Father are One.

v. 7. " *But made Himself of no reputation,*" or, as in the R.V., " emptied Himself."

The verb is κενόω. It is found in Romans 4. 14 and 1 Corinthians 9. 15, " made void "; 1 Corinthians 1. 17, " made of none effect "; 2 Corinthians 9. 3, " be in vain ";

and here " made of no reputation." κενός is always rendered " empty " or " vain " (as in vv. 3 and 16).

v. 8. " *And took upon Him the form of a servant.*" He acted willingly in becoming the servant of God, so that He was equal with and servant to Him.

v. 8. " *And was made in the likeness of men.*" " Was made " by birth into the world, so that He was seen " in the likeness of sinful flesh " (Rom. 8. 3).

v. 8. " *And being found in fashion as a man, He humbled Himself* ": not only humbled to become man, but when man yet further humbled Himself.

v. 8. " *And became obedient unto death.*" The stoop down to death was an act of sublime obedience and humbling.

v. 8. " *Even the death of the Cross.*" The shame of it ! A felon's death on a Roman gibbet. So far He went in obedience.

5. The Exaltation following the Humiliation :

v. 9. " *Wherefore God hath highly exalted Him.*" As the Lord Himself taught us, " he that humbleth himself shall be exalted."

Highly exalted means to the right hand of the Majesty on high.

v. 9. " *And given Him a Name which is above every name.*" No name has the dignity and love that the name Jesus inspires. Its very mention startles the ears and warms the heart.

v. 10. " *That at the Name of Jesus every knee should bow, of things in Heaven, and things in earth, and things under the earth.*" Heaven, Earth, and Hell shall ultimately submit to and confess that Name.

v. 11. " *And that every tongue should confess that Jesus Christ is Lord, to the glory of God the Father.*" For He must reign, King of kings and Lord of lords.

6. Appeal to Follow the Great Example :

v. 12. " *Wherefore, my beloved, . . . work out your own salvation with fear and trembling.*" Let obedience mark us as it did Him.

7. THE POWER TO DO SO:

v. 13. "*For it is God which worketh in you both to will and to do of His good pleasure.*" We do not work for our salvation, but work out in obedience what He works in us—giving both the will and the power.

IV. In What Sense did Christ Empty Himself?

1. NOT IN LAYING ASIDE HIS GODHEAD OR DEITY. He did not cease to be God, nor become half God and half man, but wholly God and wholly man in a mysterious hypostatical union impossible of definition.

The Fourth Œcumenical Council held at Chalcedon A.D. 451, used the following terms: *atreptōs*, "*without any change*" in the Person of the Son of God, which the Divine Nature is not subject unto; *adiairetōs*, with a distinction of natures, but "*without any division*" of them by separate subsistences; *asugchutōs*, "*without mixture*" or confusion; *achōristōs*, "*without separation*" or distance (quoted from John Owen, Vol. I., p. 226, who adds), and *ousiōdōs*, "*substantially*," because it was of two substances or essences in the same person: "as the fulness of the Godhead dwelt in Him bodily."

2. NOT IN CEASING TO POSSESS ANY OF THE ATTRIBUTES OF DEITY. He was still omnipotent, omniscient, and omnipresent (John 3. 13 and 1. 18). For it is written, "I am, Jehovah; I change not."

But it was—

3. THE LAYING ASIDE OF ALL OUTWARD MANIFESTATION OF GLORY—the "regalia of royalty."

It would not have served His purpose to have walked among men in the shining dignity such as He displayed on the Mount of Transfiguration.

4. THE BEING FOR A SEASON MADE LOWER THAN THE ANGELS (Heb. 2. 9), although He had by inheritance obtained a more excellent name than they.

5. BECOMING A DEPENDENT BEING. Man is a dependent being, and as man He could say, "I can of mine own self do nothing" (John 5. 30); "The Son can do nothing of Himself" (John 5. 19, 8. 28, 12. 49, 14. 10).

His works were not His, but the Father's. His words were given Him to speak. His ear was opened morning by morning to hear as the instructed. Never throughout Eternity had He been dependent, but now He lived by faith (reliance) upon the Father (John 6. 57).

6. Becoming an Obedient One. Never before had He to obey, but now His whole pathway on earth was one of obedience. Obedience that was perfect and went even to the shameful death of the Cross.

7. Having Nothing (Dan. 9. 26, r.v.). He became poor —so poor as to be bereft of all. Nowhere to lay His head; until hanged upon the Cross He laid it down in death. Never was man poorer than He, when stripped of all. He died alone and forsaken.

8. In Never Availing Himself of the Inherent Powers of His Deity, except at the Father's command.

He would not command stones to become bread without the Word of God by which He lived. He would not die without a commandment from the Father (John 10. 18). He must have authority to lay down His life and take it again.

V. Other Lessons from the Passage :

1. The Lord walked the Path of Faith. Dependence and obedience are the essence of faith. They form the " obedience of faith."

He was the " Beginner and Perfecter of Faith " (Heb. 12. 2, r.v.). He would not ask His saints to walk in a path He had not Himself trod. So He became our Perfect Example of a Man of Faith.

2. An Obedient Man. For the first time God looked down from Heaven upon a perfectly obedient man. His obedience was:

(a) *From the Heart.* He delighted to do the Father's will.

(b) *Subject to the Law.* Born under the Law, He kept it and made it honourable.

(c) *Without a failure or lapse* in thought, word, or deed, He earned the title " a perfect man " (James 3. 2) by " not offending in word."

(d) *Approved of God*, the Judge of all. Speaking from Heaven He said, " This is My Beloved Son, in Whom I am well pleased."

3. A POOR MAN.   He became so poor that we find Him—
Borrowing a coin when He would draw a lesson from it (Luke 20. 24).

Bidding Peter *find a coin in a fish's mouth* with which to pay the tribute (Matt. 17. 27).

Allowing the women from Galilee *to minister to His need* (Luke 8. 3; Mark 15. 41).

Having *nowhere to lay His head* (Luke 9. 58).

Suffering hunger (Matt. 21. 18; Luke 4. 2), and asking water to quench His thirst (John 4. 7) when weary from His journey.

4. YIELDING HIMSELF TO WICKED MAN, to be mocked, scorned, beaten and crucified.

> " How didst Thou humble Thyself to be taken,
>   Led by Thy creatures and nailed to the Cross,
>   Hated of men, and of God, too, forsaken,
>   Shunning not darkness, the curse and the loss !"

VI. Application.

The appeals in the passage should serve—

(a) No strife or vainglory, but lowliness of mind.

(b) Let this mind be in you which was also in Christ Jesus.

(c) Work out in obedience your salvation with fear and trembling, as He works in you, to will and to do of His good pleasure.

"EMPTIED."

May we be as He, emptied of all
{
ENVY and ENMITY.
MALICE and MURMURING.
PRIDE and PREJUDICE.
TOUCHINESS and TEMPER.
ILL-FEELING and IMPLACABILITY.
EVIL and ESTEEM (of self).
DISOBEDIENCE and DECEIT.

His Moral Glory

I. **Text.** "We beheld His glory, the glory as of the Only-Begotten of the Father, full of grace and truth" (John 1. 14).

II. **Main Lesson.** Glory is manifested character. The character of our Lord Jesus displayed in His walk on earth was holy, harmless, undefiled and separate from sinners; He dwelt among us, "full of grace and truth." All the moral qualities of God were seen in Him in perfect balance, so that He could say, "He that hath seen Me hath seen the Father also."

III. **Scriptures to Study.** Seven Glimpses of His Moral Glory.

(i) Matthew 11. 29: *His Meekness and Lowliness.* "Learn of Me, for I am meek and lowly in heart."

(ii) Isaiah 50. 4-6: *His Attention and Submission.* "The Lord God hath given Me the tongue of the learned, that I should know how to speak a word in season to him that is weary: He wakeneth morning by morning, He wakeneth mine ear to hear as the learned. The Lord God hath opened mine ear, and I was not rebellious, neither turned away back. I gave my back to the smiters, and my cheeks to them that plucked off the hair: I hid not my face from shame and spitting."

(iii) Isaiah 53. 7: *His Patience under Shame.* "He was oppressed, and He was afflicted, yet He opened not His mouth: He is brought as a Lamb to the slaughter, and as a sheep before her shearers is dumb, so He openeth not His mouth."

(iv) Acts 10. 38: *His Going About Doing Good.* "God anointed Jesus of Nazareth with the Holy Ghost and with power: Who went about doing good, and healing all that were oppressed of the Devil."

(v) Hebrews 7. 26: *His Purity and Sinlessness.* "Such an High Priest became us, Who is holy, harmless (guileless R.V.), undefiled, separate from sinners."

49

(vi) 1 Peter 2. 21-23: *His Example of Suffering Wrong-fully.* " Christ also suffered for us, leaving us an example, that we should follow His steps: Who did no sin, neither was guile found in His mouth: Who, when He was reviled, reviled not again; when He suffered, He threatened not; but committed Himself to Him that judgeth righteously."

(vii) John 13. 4-17: *His Example of Lowly Service to Others.* " He riseth from supper, and laid aside His gar-ments; and took a towel, and girded Himself. After that He poured water into a bason and began to wash the disciples' feet, and to wipe them with the towel wherewith He was girded. . . . So after He had washed their feet, and had taken His garments, and was set down again, He said unto them, Know ye what I have done to you ? Ye call Me Master and Lord: and ye say well; for so I am. If I then, have washed your feet; ye also ought to wash one another's feet. For I have given you an example that ye should do as I have done to you."

IV. **Other Lessons** from the Study.

1. THE CHARACTER OF GOD. All through the Old Testa-ment God is depicted as Just and Gracious—Righteous and Good.

" A Just God and a Saviour."

Tender-hearted, yet holy in all His ways; slow to anger and of great mercy; yet terrible in righteousness and awful in holiness. The two figures chosen bear this out: " God is Light " and " God is Love."

In Creation these are evident. God said, " Let there be Light "—His first recorded utterance. Then He looked on all He had made, and, behold, it was very good, and He blessed man.

These are the two outstanding qualities that were seen in Jesus when He dwelt among us. He was " full of grace and truth."

2. GRACE AND TRUTH IN THE LORD'S WORDS AND WAYS. The Lord Jesus never showed Grace at the expense of Truth. He never dealt in Righteousness without showing Mercy.

Illustrations of Grace and Truth.

(a) *The Man at the Pool of Bethesda* (John 5. 8 and 14):
Grace said, " Rise, take up thy bed, and walk."
Truth said, " Go, and sin no more, lest a worse thing
come unto thee."

(b) *The Woman Taken in Adultery* (John 8. 11):
Grace said, " Neither do I condemn thee."
Truth said, " Go, and sin no more."

(c) *The Syro-Phœnician Woman* (Matt. 15. 26 and 28):
Truth said, " It is not meet to take the children's bread,
and to cast it to dogs."
Grace said, " O woman, great is thy faith: be it unto thee
as thou wilt."

(d) *The Nobleman of Capernaum* (John 4. 48 and 50):
Truth said, " Except ye see signs and wonders, ye will
not believe."
Grace said, " Go thy way; thy son liveth."

(e) *The Guilty City—Jerusalem* (Matt. 23. 37-39):
Truth pronounced its doom.
Grace wept over it, and foretold a day when it would
welcome Him, saying, " Blessed is He that cometh in the
Name of the Lord."

(f) *In the Gospel Message* (John 3. 36):
Grace says, " He that believeth on the Son hath everlasting life."
Truth says, " He that believeth (obeyeth) not the Son
shall not see life; but the wrath of God abideth on him."

3. THE SINLESSNESS OF CHRIST. This is attested:

(a) *By His own Challenge and Confession*—
John 8. 46: " Which of you convinceth (convicteth) Me
of sin ?"
John 14. 30: " The prince of this world cometh, and hath
nothing in Me."
John 8. 29: " I do always those things that please Him
(the Father)."

(b) *By the Testimony of His Enemies and Others*—
Pilate (three times): " I find no fault in this Man "
(John 18. 38, 19. 4 and 6).
Herod : " Nor yet Herod " (Luke 23. 15).

Pilate's Wife : " Have thou nothing to do with that just Man " (Matt. 27. 19).

Judas : " I have betrayed the innocent blood " (Matt. 27. 4).

The Thief on the Cross : " This Man hath done nothing amiss " (Luke 23. 41).

The Centurion : " Truly this Man was the Son of God " (Mark 15. 39).

" Certainly this was a righteous Man " (Luke 23. 47).

(c) *By the Father, speaking from Heaven* (twice): " This is My Beloved Son, in Whom I am well pleased " (Matt. 4. 17, 17. 5).

4. THE WISDOM THAT IS FROM ABOVE.   James, the Lord's brother, writing of the Wisdom that is from above, may well have had in mind the holy life lived in the home of Nazareth, of which he had been a witness, when he wrote: " *The Wisdom that is from above (cf.* 1 Cor. 1. 24) *is first pure, then peaceable, gentle, and easy to be intreated, full of mercy and good fruits, without partiality, and without hypocrisy* " (James 3. 17).

V. Application.

Let us *Look on Him* as He walked, and seek to walk as He walked.

Learn of Him Who is meek and lowly in heart, and so become—

Like Him, having the same mind that was in Him.

Some of the Moral Beauty.

The Meekness and Gentleness of Christ (2 Cor. 10. 1).
The Love of Christ (Rom. 8. 35).
The Obedience of Christ (2 Cor. 10. 5).
The Tender Mercies of Christ (Phil. 1. 8, R.V.).
The Grace of Christ (2 Cor. 8. 9).
The Sufferings of Christ (1 Peter 1. 11 and 5. 1).
The Excellency of the Knowledge of Christ (Phil. 3. 8.)

SECTION II

Our Lord Jesus Christ: His Ministry on Earth

In Him they Marked no Pride

" The Pride of life is not of the Father, but is of the world "
(1 John 2. 16).

The Emperor passed with regal state
And glittering train the palace gate;
His mettled palfrey pawed the air
As if his glory he would share.
But as he met the cheering crowd
    I marked that he was PROUD.

The Hall was gay with light and song,
And merry the assembled throng.
The maiden trod the stately dance—
What could her loveliness enhance ?
But as her suitors round her bowed
    I marked that she was PROUD.

The Orator had ceased to speak,
His flashing eye and mantled cheek
Betokened he had spoken well
And held his audience in a spell.
But as he heard their plaudits loud
    I marked that he was PROUD.

A convict sat within his cell,
His sentence many years must tell;
He mused upon the former times
And lived again his daring crimes.
And as he thought he laughed aloud,
    For he, I marked, was PROUD.

The Son of God from Heaven stooped down,
Men plaited Him, with thorns, a crown;
Holy and harmless, undefiled,
And meek and lowly as a child.
With wicked hands His face they smote,
And gambled for His seamless coat.
Then lifted up on high He died,
Jesus the Lord they crucified—
    But though they all His claim deride,
    In Him they marked no PRIDE.   G. G.

The Wonder of His Words

I. Text. "Never man spake like this man" (John 7.
46). "The words that I speak unto you, they are spirit
and they are life" (John 6. 63).

II. Main Lesson. The words spoken by the Lord Jesus
were God's words. He received them from God. Therefore they were: *Gracious* (Luke 4. 22) and *With Authority*
(Matt. 7. 29), and such as never man spake.

He claimed that they were not spoken from Himself,
but both what He should say (the matter) and what He
should speak (the words) were given Him of His Father.

They were therefore spirit and life to those who heard
them believing.

III. Scriptures to Study.

Isaiah 50. 4: *The Lord of the Opened Ear.* "The Lord
God hath given Me the tongue of the learned, that I should
know how to speak a word in season to him that is weary:
He wakeneth morning by morning; He wakeneth Mine
ear to hear as the learned" (or instructed one—scholar).

John 8. 38: *Speaking what He saw.* "I speak that
which I have seen with My Father: . . . why do ye not
understand My words? Even because ye cannot hear
My Word."

John 12. 47, 48: *The Responsibility of Hearing.* "If
any man hear My words, and believe not, I judge him not:
for I came not to judge the world, but to save the world.
He that rejecteth Me, and receiveth not My words, hath
one that judgeth him: the word that I have spoken, the
same shall judge him in the last day."

vv. 49-50. *As the Father said unto Me, so I Speak.* "For
I have not spoken of Myself; but the Father which sent
Me, He gave Me a commandment, what I should say, and
what I should speak. And I know that His commandment
is life everlasting: whatsoever I speak therefore, even as
the Father saith unto Me, so I speak."

Matthew 7. 24-27. *The Parable of the Two Builders.*

"Whosoever heareth these sayings of mine, and doeth them, I will liken him unto a wise man, who built his house upon a rock: and the rain descended, and the floods came, and the winds blew, and beat upon that house: and it fell not: for it was founded on a rock. And everyone that heareth these sayings of mine, and doeth them not, shall be likened unto a foolish man which built his house upon the sand: and the rain descended . . . and it fell, and great was the fall thereof."

IV. Nine Things the Lord said about His Words:

1. THEY ARE SPIRIT AND LIFE (John 6. 63). They were the mediums He used to feed us upon His Body and Blood, to minister to us the Heavenly Manna, the Bread from Heaven.

2. THEY ARE LIKE SEED (Mark 4. 14). The Parable of the Sower tells us that the Son of man sows the Word. Seed has inherent life. So the Word of God brings life to the hearer. God has chosen the preaching of the Gospel as the means of saving men.

3. THEY HAVE A CLEANSING POWER (John 15. 3). "Now ye are clean through the Word which I have spoken unto you."

4. THEY ARE THE MEANS OF OUR SANCTIFICATION (John 17. 17). "Sanctify them through Thy truth: Thy Word is truth."

5. THEY BRING US INTO LIBERTY (John 8. 31-32). "If ye continue in My Words. . . . Ye shall know the truth, and the truth shall make you free."

6. THEY BRING US ETERNAL LIFE (John 5. 24). "He that heareth My Words, and believeth on Him that sent Me, hath everlasting life."

7. THOSE WHO KEEP THEM NEVER SEE DEATH (John 8. 51). "Verily, Verily, I say unto you, If a man keep My sayings, he shall never see death."

8. THEY WILL NEVER PASS AWAY (Matt. 24. 35). "Heaven and earth shall pass away, but My words shall not pass away."

9. THEY WILL JUDGE THE SINNER AT LAST (John 12. 48). "The Word that I have spoken the same shall judge him in the last day."

V. Other Lessons as to His Words.

1. THEIR BREVITY. All the recorded words of Christ could be printed in a 16-page pamphlet. His longest speech takes but fifteen minutes to read aloud.

Those words have wrought wonders in the world and revolutionized the lives of millions and brought new life, peace and rest to living and dying. Yet Rudolf Stier wrote eight volumes of 400 pages each on *The Words of the Lord Jesus* and thousands of volumes have been written by others on them. So few, yet so mighty are they.

2. THEIR BEAUTY. Judged as ordinary literature, these words are the most beautiful in the world. In this the Lord Jesus is pre-eminent also. None of the world's great writers can compare with Him. Who has ever written things to compare with " The Prodigal Son," "The Lost Sheep," "The Good Samaritan"?

One may search the world's libraries and have to say, " Never man spake like this man."

3. THEIR PURITY AND EXCELLENT MORALITY. The world has had many codes of morals. Philosophers and moralists have striven to reform men, but where is purity of such moral height as in the Sermon on the Mount? It stands out pre-eminent for simplicity, nobility and power.

4. THEIR SYMPATHY. Whoever spake so tenderly to the heart of sinful man as did Our Lord Jesus? Where can the gracious appeal of Matthew 11. 28 be matched: " Come unto Me, all ye that labour and are heavy laden, and I will give you rest "?

Sinners drew near to hear Him, for He said He had not come to condemn but to save, not to call the righteous but sinners.

5. THEIR WONDER. The strangest fact about the words of the Lord Jesus is that they centred round Himself. Yet none ever accused Him of egotism or pride.

He Himself was Salvation. Those who would find rest must come to Him.

The thirsty must come to Him and drink. Those who would have life must eat of Him.

He was the Great I AM. Would men be saved, " I am
the Door."   Would they come to the Father, " I am the
Way," Would they walk in light, " I am the Light." Would
they rise again, " I am the Resurrection and the Life."

He was Himself God. " I and the Father are One."
" He that hath seen Me hath seen the Father " (see
Lesson V).

6. THEIR PROPHETIC VALUE.   He spake of things to come.
Whole chapters are devoted to the future when He would
come again for His own and later in power and great
glory to take to Him His power and reign, and to execute
judgment.

In all these He Himself is the Judge before Whom all
nations would be gathered, and each soul give an account
of himself.

Several parables speak of the future, as " The Ten
Virgins, " The Wicked Husbandmen," " The Sheep and
the Goats."

7. THEIR DIGNITY.   In these words of our Lord is no
confusion, no uncertainty, no hesitation, no mistake ever
acknowledged, no " perhaps " or " I think " or " possibly,"
or other evidence of fallibility.   Above all, no coarseness
or vulgarity, no sentimentality, emotionalism, no sob-stuff,
no mock heroics, no trifling or lightness.   There is no
" dead fly " in the ointment.

Application.

The Same is a Perfect Man, since He offended not in
word (James 3. 2).

Let us rely wholly on His words.

Let us make them known to others.

Let us study them closely to learn of Him.

OUTLINE

The {
Wisdom and Wonder
Order and Originality
Riches and Righteousness
Dignity and Divinity
Sympathy and Strength
} of the Words of Christ

His Walk on Earth

I. Text. "He that saith he abideth in Him ought himself also to walk even as He walked" (1 John 2. 6).

II. Main Lesson. The Lord walked on earth upon the same principles as He would have us do. In this He was our perfect example.

His manner of life was simple, sincere and godly. We may learn of Him and walk after the same method, practising the same things and relying upon the same resources. As He is so are we in this world.

III. Scriptures to Study.

Luke 14. 25: *Great Multitudes follow Christ.* "And there went great multitudes with Him: and He turned and said unto them":

v. 26. *Conditions of Discipleship.* "If any man come to Me, and hate not his father, and mother, and wife, and children, and brethren, and sisters, yea, and his own life also, he cannot be My disciple."

v. 27. *Crossbearing.* "And whosoever doth not bear his cross, and come after Me, cannot be My disciple."

vv. 28-30. *Counting the Cost—A Builder.* "For which of you, intending to build a tower, sitteth not down first, and counteth the cost, whether he hath sufficient to finish it? Lest haply, after he hath laid the foundation, and is not able to finish it, all that behold it begin to mock him, saying, This man began to build, and was not able to finish."

v. 31. *Going to War—A King.* "Or what king, going to make war against another king, sitteth not down first, and consulteth whether he be able with ten thousand to meet him that cometh against him with twenty thousand? Or else, while the other is a great way off he sendeth an ambassage, and desireth conditions of peace."

v. 33. *The True Disciple.* "So likewise, whosoever he be of you that forsaketh not all that he hath, he cannot be My disciple."

IV. **How did the Lord Jesus walk?** What were the principles upon which He acted?

1. HIS AIM IN LIFE. He tells us Himself: "I do always those things that please the Father." The will of God was the end and aim of His whole life: from boyhood when He said, "Wist ye not that I must be about My Father's business?" to the last agony in the Garden when He cried, "Not My will but Thine be done." In this we may walk as He walked. "Ye know how ye ought to walk and to please God."

2. HIS PRINCIPLE OF LIFE. He lived and walked by faith, as He would have us do. "As I live by the Father, so He that eateth Me shall live by Me."

Walking in the path of dependence and obedience, He could of Himself do nothing. His words and works were from the Father; as He was instructed so He acted. He was the Beginner and Finisher of faith.

3. HIS POWER IN LIFE was the Holy Spirit, as it should be ours.

He was conceived of the Holy Ghost; anointed by the Spirit; led by the Spirit to be tempted; came up in the power of the Spirit to His ministry; by the Spirit cast out demons; and by the Eternal Spirit offered Himself without spot to God, and in the energy of that same Spirit was raised from the dead.

That Spirit is given to all believers, that they too may live by, walk in, and be led by the Holy Spirit.

4. HIS AUTHORITY AND GUIDE IN LIFE was always the Holy Scriptures. He ever appealed to them and quoted them: "What saith the Scriptures?" "How readest thou?" "What is written in the Law?"

When tempted He overcame the Devil with a thrice repeated "It is written."

In this we may "walk as He walked."

5. HIS PRACTICE OF PRAYER. He Himself tells us men ought always to pray and not to faint. "And being found in fashion as a man," He prayed.

Seven times in Luke we read of Him praying. He spoke three parables on prayer: "The Pharisee and the Publican," "The Friend at Midnight," and "The Importunate Widow and Unjust Judge." He agonized in prayer in the Garden. He died praying.

Let us then pray without ceasing, for we may walk as He walked.

6. His Joy in Life.   Although as to His circumstances He was the Man of Sorrows and acquainted with grief, yet He had a joy always before His eyes.

In this He was as the Apostle—" cast down, yet alway rejoicing."

But we never find Him rejoicing in anything but the Will of God.

" I delight to do Thy will " was His true confession. When He rejoiced in spirit over the truth being revealed to babes, it was because " it seemed good in Thy sight."

His joy was in saving sinners; in bringing many sons to glory.

So may we " rejoice in the Lord " though all is dark around, with the joy of faith that sees the unseen and looks beyond the present and temporal to the eternal.

7. His Sorrows in Life were because of the dishonour sin had brought into the world. " Rivers of water run down Mine eyes because they keep not Thy law."

He wept three times:

Once over the guilty city of Jerusalem.

Once at the grave of Lazarus.

Once in the garden of Gethsemane.

His griefs were not personal but for the miseries of sinners and the judgment on the guilty.

8. His Occupation in Life.   It is summed up in the words, " Who went about doing good."   Let it be ours. " As we have opportunity, let us do good unto all men." " To do good and communicate forget not."   Not to those who please us only, but to good or bad, friend or enemy alike, as God sends His rain upon the just and unjust.

V. Other Lessons from the Study.

1. True Discipleship is to put oneself under the teaching and discipline of Christ.   This will demand wholehearted yielding of ourselves and all we have to be at His disposal.

If anything is held back or something kept dark, the lessons
He would teach us will be spoiled.

But if all is yielded then we may learn of Him to walk
as He walked.

2. HOLINESS IS IN WALKING AS HE WALKED.   A holy life
is a Christ-like life.   As we look upon Him as He walked
so we become like Him.   As we behold His glory in the
Gospel mirror we are changed into the same image, from
glory to glory.

It is to have the mind of Christ within and the walk
of Christ without.

To be like Christ is the only way to be holy.

3. SUCH A WALK IS DESCRIBED as " Walking in Christ,"
" Walking in the Spirit," " Walking in the Truth,"
" Walking in the Light " and " Walking in Love," for so
the Lord walked, and we should walk as He walked.

VI. Application.

Study His holy walk more.

Seek to follow His footsteps.

Sanctify Him as Lord in the heart that He may teach
us how to walk.

How to Walk

In $\begin{cases} \text{Wisdom (Col. 4. 5).} \\ \text{Ancient paths (Jer. 6. 16).} \\ \text{Light (1 John 1. 7).} \\ \text{Kindness and Love (Eph. 5. 2).} \end{cases}$

In $\begin{cases} \text{LIGHT (1 John 1. 7).} \\ \text{LIBERTY (Psa. 119. 45).} \\ \text{LOVE (Eph. 5. 2).} \\ \text{LAW OF GOD (Neh. 10. 29).} \end{cases}$

LESSON 10

His Wondrous Works

I. Text. "The works that I do in My Father's name, they bear witness of Me" (John 10. 25).

II. Main Lesson. The miracles and signs that Jesus did attested His claim to be the Son of God with power. Not alone, for others have wrought miracles, but in conjunction with the other evidences.

The nature of His miracles was such as to reveal both His grace and power. They were never magical displays, nor done for show, but *beneficent works* and *parables in action* teaching profound lessons.

III. Scriptures to Study.

(i) Matthew 8. 16: *Foretold in Scripture.* "When the even was come, they brought unto Him many that were possessed with devils: and He cast out the spirits with His word, and healed all that were sick: that it might be fulfilled which was spoken by Esaias the prophet, saying, Himself took our infirmities, and bare our sicknesses" (Isa. 53. 4).

(ii) Matthew 11. 2-6: *John the Baptist satisfied.* "Now when John heard in prison the works of Christ, he sent two of his disciples, and said unto Him, Art Thou He that should come, or look we for another? Jesus answered and said unto them, Go and show John again those things which ye do hear and see: the blind receive their sight, and the lame walk, the lepers are cleansed, and the deaf hear, the dead are raised up, and the poor have the gospel preached unto them. And blessed is he, whosoever shall not be offended in Me."

(iii) Acts 10. 38: *Peter's Testimony in the Home of Cornelius.* "God anointed Jesus of Nazareth with the Holy Ghost and with power: Who went about doing good, and healing all that were oppressed of the devil; for God was with Him."

(iv) John 14. 11: *Our Lord's Own Appeal.* "Believe Me that I am in the Father, and the Father in Me: or else believe Me for the very works' sake."

IV. The Character of Our Lord's Miracles.

1. THE LORD DID NOT PURPOSE TO BANISH SICKNESS, DISEASE, TYRANNY AND DEATH AT HIS FIRST COMING.

Although He refused none who came to Him, yet He did not proclaim *universal* healing or liberty to all captives; nor resurrection of *all* the dead.

For example:

He went to the Pool of Bethesda, where was a "multitude of impotent folk, blind, halt and withered," but the Lord healed only one.

When He stood by the grave of Lazarus He called, "Lazarus, come forth," but left the rest of the dead in their graves.

He came to set the prisoner free, yet He left His own cousin after the flesh to languish and die a cruel death in Herod's dungeon.

The reason is threefold:

(a) *The redemption of the body* is not yet; we still wait for it. See Rom. 8. 23.

(b) *The day of millennial blessing* and righteous government is not yet. Tyrants still hold their cruel sway.

(c) *The day when those in their graves* shall come forth is not yet. See John 5. 28-29.

These—sickness, tyranny, and death—are still permitted of God, and are overruled to serve His purpose. The wrath of man is made to praise Him; the remainder is restrained (Psa. 76. 10).

2. HIS MIRACLES BORE NO RESEMBLANCE TO THE LYING WONDERS OF ROME, which are often grotesque displays of magical tricks, as liquefying blood, nodding and winking madonnas, and such-like follies.

Nor are the uncertain, indefinite, and unreliable cures of neurotic cases so much in evidence today anything like the miracles of our Lord. They differ in these points:

(a) He cured *all* who came.

(b) He cured them *instantly.*

(c) He cured them *perfectly*.

(d) He cured them *permanently*.

(e) He cured them *without charge*.

3. His Wondrous Works had a Threefold Value:

(a) They were "*signs*" attesting His claim to be the Messiah,

(b) They were *acts of compassion* and *deeds of benevolence*, and

(c) They were *enacted parables*, each of them having some spiritual lesson to teach.

They were examples in the physical realm of what He came to do in the spiritual realm, and of what one day He will do universally when He comes to put things right on this troubled earth.

4. Yet We May Make Known our Requests in Prayer subject to His will, and He will always answer as shall be most to His glory and for our blessing.

That some saints are called to lifelong suffering is a well-known and undeniable fact. To suggest that they are not in the will of God, or are lacking in faith, is ignorant and wanton cruelty.

That many are raised up in answer to prayer is also beyond all question.

Let those who suffer continue in the prayer of faith, and accept joyfully the answer He gives them, whether it be relief or recovery or the ministry of patient suffering.

V. **Some Other Lessons** from the Study.

1. The Motive for the Mighty Works was always for the Glory of God.

Never (a) *for His own advantage*. In this He sought not His but always the good of others. He could have called for more than twelve legions of angels to deliver Him, but would not (Matt. 26. 53).

(b) *Never in revenge or judgment* on His enemies. He had not come to judge the world, and moreover He loved His enemies and prayed for them (Luke 23. 34).

(c) *Never to make a display or show*. When Satan invited Him to do this by casting Himself down from the

pinnacle of the Temple, He refused to tempt the Lord
His God.

(d) *Never to satisfy curiosity*, as when Herod hoped to
see a miracle wrought by Him He refused.

(e) *Not expecting them to convert His enemies*. They
strengthened the faith of His disciples, and they left the
opposers without excuse, only adding to their guilt in
rejecting His claim. They were just additional appeals
to those willing to hear.

(f) They were done " *that the works of God should be
made manifest* " (John 9. 3). So the Lord said when they
asked why the man had been born blind. They were
evidence of God's interest in man's happiness.

(g) They were " *for the Glory of God*." The Lord said
when Lazarus died (John 11. 4), " *that the Son of
man might be glorified thereby*." That is that His true
character might be known—His compassion, love and
power.

(h) They were *that we might believe*, as when the blind
man whose eyes had been opened said: " Who is He, Lord,
that I might believe on Him ? " So the mighty works
are given as a confirmation and ground of our faith (John
10. 25 and 14. 11).

2. THE BEAUTY AND GRACE OF THE MIGHTY WORKS.
They were the result of *the Divine Compassion* (Matt. 15.
32), as when He fed the fainting multitude, as when He
raised the widow's son (Luke 7. 13), as when He touched
the eyes of the blind (Matt. 20. 34). In each case we read
" He had compassion " (see Mark 1. 41, 6. 34).

They were *Good and Beneficent Actions*. Lepers
cleansed, sick healed, demons cast out, the blind made to
see, the lame to walk, the dead raised. No fanciful or
spectacular show marred their simplicity and tenderness.

3. " GREATER WORKS SHALL YE DO." This promise has
no doubt reference to the fact that the Lord's miracles
were wrought in the physical realm, but those who are
filled with the Spirit effect greater works than those
because by their ministry the spiritually dead are raised
to eternal life; the morally lame are made to walk in newness

of life; the defiled with the leprosy of sin made " clean every whit " in the sight of a holy God.

The spiritual is greater than the natural.

VI. Application.

Let us ponder the mighty works and learn of the Lord's ways and wisdom.

Let us seek His power that we may do greater works than these.

Let us blaze His Name abroad as the great Miracle-worker.

OUTLINES

Seven Various Works

Work of Sin in our members (Rom. 7. 5).
Work of the Law (Rom. 2. 15).
Work of God (John 6. 29).
Work of Christ (Phil. 2. 30).
Work in the Lord (1 Cor. 9. 1).
Work of Faith with Power (2 Thess. 1. 11).
Work and Labour of Love (Heb. 6. 10).

Kinds of Works

Wicked works (Col. 1. 21).
Dead works (Heb. 6. 1).
Deceitful works (Dan. 11. 23).
Devilish works (1 John 3. 8).

Good works (1 Tim. 6. 18).
Abiding work (1 Cor. 3. 14).
Faith works (Jas. 2. 18).
Love works (1 Cor. 13. 7).

A Simple Outline

Get Good—Be Good—Do Good.

His Parables as Self-Revelations

I. **Text.** " *Why speakest Thou unto them in parables* ?"
(Matt. 13. 10).

II. **Main Lesson.** The reply the Lord gave to the above
question revealed:

(*a*) *That truth is a privilege* for those who are willing to
obey it only (Matt. 13. 11). " Unto you (disciples) it is
given to know the mysteries of the Kingdom of Heaven,
but to them (the careless) it is not given." Parables hide
it from the latter and disclose it to the former.

(*b*) *That the Parables were Self-revelations*, many of them
representing Christ to us in different aspects of His office
and work. By studying them we shall get to know Him
better (Matt. 13. 16-17).

III. **Scripture to Study** (Matt. 13. 10-17).

v. 10. *The Disciples Ask why He Spoke in Parables.*
" The disciples came and said unto Him, Why speakest
Thou unto them in parables ?"

v. 11. *The Answer—Truth is for the Disciple Only.*
" He answered and said unto them, Because it is given
unto you to know the mysteries of the Kingdom of Heaven,
but to them it is not given."

v. 12. *The True Learner and the Willing Heart ever
gains more.* " For whosoever hath, to him shall be given,
and he shall have more abundance: but whosoever hath
not, from him shall be taken away even that he hath."

v. 13. *There are those Blind and Deaf who will not See or
Hear.* " Therefore speak I to them in parables: because
they seeing see not; and hearing they hear not, neither
do they understand."

v. 14. *This was as Foretold in Scripture.* " In them is
fulfilled the prophecy of Esaias, which saith, By hearing
ye shall hear, and shall not understand; and seeing ye shall
see, and shall not perceive."

v. 15. *Such had Closed their Eyes and Ears lest they should be Converted.* " For this people's heart is waxed gross, and their ears are dull of hearing, and their eyes they have closed; lest at any time they should see with their eyes, and hear with their ears, and should understand with their heart, and should be converted, and I should heal them."

v. 16. *The Blessedness of Opened Hearts.* " But blessed are your eyes, for they see: and your ears, for they hear."

v. 17. *The Appearance of Christ had been longed for by many Prophets and Righteous Men.* " For verily I say unto you, That many prophets and righteous men have desired to see those things which ye see, and have not seen them; and to hear those things which ye hear, and have not heard them."

IV. Reasons for Speaking in Parables.

1. The Mystery of Election. " My sheep (those given to the Lord by the Father) hear My voice " (John 10. 27); others did not hear " because ye are not of My sheep " (John 10. 26).

We are never in the Scriptures far away from the truth of Sovereign Grace—

> " Why was I made to hear His voice
> And enter while there's room ?"

Because it pleased God—" to you it is given " (v. 11).

2. The Responsibility of Man to Hear. All down the ages the prophets have cried, " Hear ye the word of the Lord." This truth is the complement of the former. All who have ears to hear are invited, entreated, and, indeed, commanded and warned to hear. To refuse is to incur guilt.

3. Yet the Mystery is only for Those who Hear. It is a " state secret " that none may know but those to whom the Lord is pleased to reveal it. The secret of the Lord is with them that fear Him. It is often revealed to babes, but hidden from the wise and prudent.

Pride cannot wrest it from God; the wisdom of the wise is but foolishness without it.

4. TO THE REBEL IT IS REFUSED.   "It is wise and reasonable to draw a veil, which, however, is willingly removed
whenever any faithful one wishes to join himself more
nearly to the King " (Stier).

Pearls are not cast before swine. The condition is
plainly stated by the Lord in John 7. 17: " If any man
will do His will, he shall know of the doctrine."

5. TRUTH WONDERFULLY BALANCED. God's truth is so
balanced that it forces no man, but leaves every man
without excuse.

Parables are truths so wrapped up that they meet the
need of the willing hearer and pass unknown and unvalued
over the mind of the unwilling.

" A Parable is like the pillar of cloud and fire which
turned the dark side to the Egyptians, the bright side to the
people of the Covenant; it is like a shell which keeps the
precious kernel as well *for* the diligent as *from* the indolent "
(von Gerlach).

V. Characters Assumed by the Lord in His Parables.

1. A SOWER (Matt. 13. 3). This is the first and the
outstanding parable, for Jesus said, " Know ye not this
parable ? and how then will ye know all parables ?"

It discloses the way in which the Lord intended to do
His great Salvation work in the world. It was as a
sower sowing seed. In other words, " It pleased God
by the foolishness of preaching to save them that
believe."

The Lord was the Great Sower of the Seed of the Word.
A variation of the same figure is in Matthew 13. 24, where
the Sower sows " the children of the Kingdom."

2. A SHEPHERD (Matt. 18. 12 and Luke 15. 4). A figure
used of the Lord all through the Bible. The Good Shepherd
Who gave His life for the sheep and sought the lost sheep
until He found it. The Shepherd and Bishop of our souls.

3. A MERCHANT MAN (Matt. 13. 45), seeking goodly
pearls Who, when He had found one pearl of great price,
went and sold all that He had and bought it. " Ye are
bought with a price."

4. A KING'S SON (Matt. 22. 2), for whom the king made a marriage.

5. A BRIDEGROOM (Matt. 25. 1), expected soon to come for His bride—the Church.

6. AN HOUSEHOLDER (Matt. 20. 1), Who hired labourers to work in His vineyard.

The GOODMAN OF THE HOUSE (20. 11), who gave to the last even as to the first.

7. A MAN TRAVELLING INTO A FAR COUNTRY (Matt. 25. 14), leaving His servants to trade for Him and coming again to reward them (see also Mark 13. 34).

8. A NOBLEMAN GOING INTO A FAR COUNTRY TO RECEIVE A KINGDOM (Luke 19. 12), and leaving His servants to occupy till He came again.

9. A CREDITOR who mercifully and frankly forgave His debtors (Luke 7. 41-42), and similarly,

10. A KING, taking account of His servants (Matt. 18. 23), Who compassionately forgave His debtor ten thousand talents, who proved to be an unmerciful and pitiless servant.

11. A GOOD SAMARITAN who rescued the man who had fallen among thieves and cared for him.

12. A LORD RETURNING FROM A WEDDING (Luke 12. 36), Who expected His servants to be watching and ready for His coming.

13. A CERTAIN MAN WHO MADE A GREAT SUPPER (Luke 14. 16), and bade many who excused themselves, and then bade His servants go out into the highways and hedges and compel others to come in.

14. THE " BELOVED SON " of the certain man who planted a vineyard (Luke 20. 9) and let it out to wicked husbandmen, who said, " This is the Heir: come, let us kill Him."

15. THE JUDGE OF ALL THE EARTH (Matt. 25. 31), coming as the Son of Man in His glory to judge all nations, separating the sheep and the goats.

What a grand variety of figures of our Lord these make !

What a profitable study for those who love to know Him better !

He has graciously revealed Himself to us thus in many different characters.

VI. Other Lessons from the Parables.

1. THE LORD'S PARABLES AS EXAMPLES. Those who have spiritual discernment will find this visible world full of parables of the invisible.

This old creation is a porch to and parable of the new creation. It has many wonderful lessons to teach us. St. Bernard wrote to an old Archbishop of York (1091-1153): " Believe one who has had experience; you will find something more in woods than in books. Trees and stones will teach you what you cannot learn from masters." This thought Shakespeare long afterwards embodied in the well-known words,

> " And this our life, exempt from public haunt,
> Finds tongues in trees, books in the running brooks,
> Sermons in stones, and good in everything."

Let us have open eyes and teachable hearts.

2. TRUTH HIDDEN. Nothing worth while is ever either done or gained without trouble. God has nothing for the idle and slothful, therefore He hides Himself (Isa. 45. 15). " Verily Thou art a God that hidest Thyself, O God of Israel, the Saviour."

Yet He is ever found of them that seek Him with the whole heart.

Truth also is Hidden. It is called " the hidden wisdom " (1 Cor. 2. 7), and " the hidden riches of secret places " (Isa. 45. 3).

Truth is worth seeking for, and to those who are in earnest, even though babes, it is revealed (Matt. 11. 25).

3. THE BEAUTY OF PARABLES. There is no form of truth that is so delightful to listen to as the parable. When once the secret is gained it lives for ever unforgotten in the memory.

A parable is like a lovely picture on the wall—a joy for

ever. It is like a window overlooking a wide view, or like music played by a skilful hand.

For the parables we thank our gracious Lord, especially for those that form life-like portraits of Himself.

VII. Application.

Pray for opened eyes and discerning hearts to see the hidden wisdom. Study diligently to discover the full meaning of the parables.

Pass on the good things you discover to others.

OUTLINES

Five Figures of Our Lord

The SON, as in the Parable of the Vineyard.
The SEEKER, as in the Parable of the Lost Sheep.
The SOWER, as in the Parable of the Sower.
The SHEPHERD, as in John 10.
The SAMARITAN, as in the Parable of the Good Samaritan.

Eight Hidden Things

Hidden things of darkness (1 Cor. 4. 5).
Hidden things of dishonesty (2 Cor. 4. 2).
Hidden man of the heart (1 Pet. 3. 4).
Thy hidden ones (Psa. 83. 3).
A man hidden (Prov. 28. 12).
Hidden riches of secret places (Isa. 45. 3).
Hidden wisdom (1 Cor. 2. 7).
Hidden manna (Rev. 2. 17).

The Lord's Promises

I. Text. "For all the promises of God in Christ are Yea, and in Him Amen, unto the glory of God by us" (2 Cor. 1. 20).

II. Main Lesson. The great and precious promises of God in Christ are given to us that by them we may be partakers of the Divine nature (2 Pet. 1. 4).

Promises formed a great part of the ministry of Christ. They are such as no mere man could have made. They therefore evidence His deity and substantiate His claim to be the Christ, the Son of the Living God.

In Him is the "Yea"—that is, the affirmation—and in Him is the "Amen," the confirmation. He promises, assures, and fulfils them.

His people are every day proving the truth of them and becoming by them partakers of the new nature, the eternal life, the life more abundant, the life that is life indeed.

III. Some of the Outstanding Promises of Christ.

1. THE PROMISE OF ETERNAL LIFE.

John 3. 16: "For God so loved the world, that He gave His only begotten Son, that whosoever believeth in Him should not perish, but have everlasting life." (See also John 3. 36, 5. 24, 6. 47 and 58, etc.)

John 10. 28: "I give unto (My sheep) eternal life; and they shall never perish."

2. THE PROMISE OF THE HOLY GHOST.

John 14. 16: "I will pray the Father, and He will give you another Comforter, that He may abide with you for ever."

John 16. 7: "If I depart, I will send (the Comforter) unto you."

John 16. 13: "When He, the Spirit of Truth, is come, He will guide you into all truth." (See also John 14. 26, 15. 26, 16. 8-14; and Luke 12. 12.)

3. Living Water.

John 4. 10: "If thou knewest the gift of God . . . thou wouldst have asked of Him, and He would have given thee living water."

v. 14: "The water that I shall give him shall be in him a well of water springing up into everlasting life."

John 7. 38: "He that believeth on Me . . . out of his belly shall flow rivers of living water."

4. Salvation.

John 10. 9: "I am the door: by Me if any man enter in, he shall be saved."

Matthew 24. 13: "He that shall endure to the end, the same shall be saved."

John 6. 37: "All that the Father giveth Me shall come to Me; and him that cometh to Me I will in no wise cast out . . . this is the Father's will, that of all which He hath given Me I should lose nothing."

5. Never Die.

John 8. 51: "Verily, verily, I say unto you, If a man keep My saying, he shall never see death."

John 11. 25: "I am the Resurrection, and the Life: he that believeth in Me, though he were dead, yet shall he live: and whosoever liveth and believeth in Me shall never die."

6. Answer to Prayer.

Matthew 7. 7: "Ask, and it shall be given you; seek, and ye shall find; knock, and it shall be opened unto you: for everyone that asketh receiveth."

Matthew 21. 22: "All things, whatsoever ye ask in prayer, believing, ye shall receive."

(See also Matt. 6. 33; Luke 12. 31; Mark 11. 23; Luke 18. 8; John 14. 13.)

7. Reward for Confession and Service.

Matthew 10. 32: "Whosoever shall confess Me before men, him will I confess before My Father which is in Heaven."

Matthew 19. 29: "Everyone that hath forsaken houses, or brethren, or sisters, or father, or mother, or wife, or children, or lands, for My Name's sake, shall receive an hundredfold, and shall inherit everlasting life."

Matthew 10. 42: " Whosoever shall give to drink unto one of these little ones a cup of cold water only in the name of a disciple, verily I say unto you, he shall in no wise lose his reward."

(See also Matt. 24. 45-47; Luke 14. 14; Mark 9. 37, 10. 29; John 4. 36 and 12. 26.)

8. HIS PRESENCE WITH US.

Matthew 18. 20: " Where two or three are gathered together in My Name, there am I in the midst of them."

Matthew 28. 20: " Lo, I am with you alway, even unto the end of the world. Amen."

Hebrews 13. 5: " For He hath said, I will never leave thee, nor forsake thee."

9. HE WILL COME AGAIN.

John 14. 3: " I will come again, and receive you unto Myself; that where I am, there ye may be also."

(See also Matt. 25. 19 and 44; Luke 20. 30; Rev. 21. 7, 12 and 20.)

IV. Other Lessons from the Study.

1. THE OLD TESTAMENT SAINTS. " Died in faith, not having received the promises (that is, of the coming of Messiah), but having seen them afar off, and were persuaded of them, and embraced them."

Let us be fully persuaded that God is able to perform what He has promised. Let us " embrace " them—that is, lay them to heart and rejoice in them.

Abraham believed God, being fully persuaded of this (Rom. 4. 20-21).

Faith rests on and rejoices in the promises.

2. HOW TO INHERIT THE PROMISES. It is " by faith and patience " (Heb. 6. 12). Faith that depends on the faithfulness of the Promiser and patience that can wait His time and is not discouraged by delay.

It is, therefore, by faith that we " obtain promises " (Heb. 11. 33)—that is, make them our own—now in anticipation, and in God's time in realization.

3. THE PURIFYING EFFECT OF THE PROMISES. " Having these promises, dearly beloved, let us cleanse ourselves

from all filthiness of the flesh and spirit, perfecting holiness in the fear of the Lord " (2 Cor. 7. 1).

" Every man that hath this hope (of the Lord's return) set on Him purifieth himself, even as He is pure " (1 John 3. 3).

One who expects soon to see the Lord is not likely to go about with soiled garments, but will seek to keep himself unspotted so as to be found of Him in peace with loins girded and lamp trimmed.

V. Application.

1. Let us remember the promises are made by Him that cannot lie.

2. Let us not fail of them through unbelief.

OUTLINES

The Promises Include

Pardon (Heb. 10. 17), Power (Acts 1. 8), Presence (Matt. 18. 20).
Resurrection (John 14. 19).
Overcoming (John 16. 33).
Mercy (Luke 1. 72).
Indwelling Spirit (John 14. 17).
Salvation (Rom. 1. 2).
Eternal Life (Titus 1. 2).
Sanctification (John 17. 17).

NEVER in John's Gospel

Never Thirst (4. 14), never Hunger (6. 35), never See Death (8. 51), never Perish (10. 28), never Die (11. 26).

LESSON 13

The Personal Talks of the Lord Jesus

I. Texts. " He talked with the woman " (John 4. 27). " He talked with us by the way " (Luke 24. 32).

II. Main Lesson. The art of personal dealing with seekers is one that every soul-winner must learn.

If the servant of God is to be a successful fisher of men, he must know how to catch men with guile.

The best way to learn is to ponder the individual talks that our Lord had in His ministry on earth. From them we shall learn how the great Master Soul-Winner went to work.

It is the object of this lesson to show this.

The variety and beauty of these talks is wonderful, but there are underlying them some first principles common to them all, that we shall do well to observe and emulate.

III. Scripture to Study. John 3. 3-16: *The Talk with Nicodemus.*

v. 3. *The Lord Answers Nicodemus, that he must be Born Again.* " Jesus answered and said, Verily, verily, I say unto thee, Except a man be born again, he cannot see the Kingdom of God."

v. 4. *Nicodemus Asks how a Man can be Twice Born.* " Nicodemus saith, How can a man be born when he is old ? "

vv. 5-7. *Jesus Explains that it is a Spiritual Rebirth.* " Jesus answered, Verily, verily, I say unto thee, Except a man be born of water and of the Spirit, he cannot enter into the Kingdom of God. That which is born of the flesh is flesh ; and that which is born of the Spirit is spirit. Marvel not that I said unto thee, Ye must be born again."

v. 8. *By the Operation of the Spirit like the Wind.* " The wind bloweth where it listeth, and thou hearest the sound thereof, but canst not tell whence it cometh, and whither it goeth: so is every one that is born of the Spirit."

78

v. 9. *Nicodemus Again Asks How it Can Be.* "Nicodemus answered and said to Him, How can these things be ?"

v. 14. *The Lord Explains by Reference to Moses Lifting up the Serpent—Life came by a Look.* "And as Moses lifted up the serpent in the wilderness, even so must the Son of Man be lifted up: that whosoever believeth in Him should not perish, but have eternal life."

IV. Personal Talks of the Lord Jesus.

1. NICODEMUS (John 3. 3-16), as above. A talk about the New Birth and how it could be.

2. THE WOMAN OF SAMARIA (John 4. 7-26). A talk about satisfying water and spiritual worship.

3. THE RICH YOUNG RULER (Matt. 19. 16-26; Luke 18. 18-30). A talk on eternal life, and how it may be had; who can be saved, and the danger of riches.

4. THE LAWYER (Luke 10. 25-37). A talk on inheriting eternal life; the use of the Law; and as to who is my neighbour.

5. THE SCRIBE (Matt. 22. 34-40 and Mark 12. 28). A talk to one "not far from the Kingdom," on the great commandments.

6. THE CANAANITE WOMAN (Matt. 15. 21-28; Mark 7. 24-30). A talk with a Gentile who would claim the mercies of David; the faith that would not be denied.

7. THE PHARISEE who asked Him to dine (Luke 7. 40-47). A talk on the love of a forgiven sinner.

8. MARTHA (Luke 10. 38-42). A talk on being cumbered with much serving; the one thing needful; and the better part.

9. THE BLIND MAN (John 9. 35-38). A talk with one He had healed, on faith in the Son of God.

10. MARY AND MARTHA at the grave of Lazarus (John 11. 21-27, 32-40). A talk about resurrection and revelation of Himself as the Resurrection and the Life.

11. PETER, after His resurrection (John 21. 15-25). A talk with a backslider, resulting in his restoration.

12. THOMAS, after His resurrection (John 20. 26-29). A talk with a doubter, on the wisdom of faith without seeing.

13. MARY MAGDALENE, after His resurrection (John 20. 11-18). A talk about the ascension.

14. CLEOPAS AND ANOTHER on the walk to Emmaus (Luke 24. 13-31). A talk on the value of the Scriptures.

V. Other Lessons on Our Lord's Personal Talks.

1. PERSONAL AND INDIVIDUAL INTEREST IN MEN. The Lord was not a mere preacher, a doctor of law, a theologian, but a lover of the souls of men, with an individual interest in each case.

Even opponents He loved and answered graciously and patiently, " in meekness instructing those who opposed themselves," as Paul bade Timothy do (2 Tim. 2. 25).

This leads each of us to regard Him as the Lover of *MY* soul; to say " The Son of God loved *ME* and gave Himself for *ME*."

2. HIS MANNER OF DEALING WITH SEEKERS.

(a) *The first thing was always to show them their LOST condition as sinners.*

As the Apostle afterwards taught, " *that every mouth may be stopped* " (Rom. 3. 19).

So the Lord silenced each in turn, so that they stood before Him guilty sinners with nothing to say.

It was so with Nicodemus. " Ye must be born again." So Nicodemus stood dumbfounded and helpless before his Lord. He could not create himself anew. His mouth was stopped.

It was so with the Woman of Samaria. " Go, call thy husband," and in a moment her mouth was stopped and she stood a convicted sinner before her Lord, without excuse, without escape.

It was so with the Rich Young Ruler. " Go, sell what thou hast and give to the poor," and in a moment his covetous heart was exposed to himself, and he saw that his supposed keeping of the Law from his youth up was folly —he stood there a self-condemned idolater—his god his money.

It was so with the Lawyer. He would endeavour to justify himself, but when shown what a true neighbour was and bidden go and do likewise he must have known it was hopeless. He stood an exposed and self-condemned lawbreaker.

Man must know and take his true place as a guilty sinner before God, ere he can be saved.

(b) *Then the Lord revealed Himself as the Object of Faith.*

To Nicodemus as the Son of Man who, like the serpent in the wilderness, must be lifted up, that eternal life might be given to all who believed.

To the Woman of Samaria. " I that speak unto thee am He "—the Messiah that was to come.

To the Rich Young Ruler. " Come, and follow Me."

To the Lawyer. He sketched the true neighbour, the Good Samaritan, an evident portrait of Himself.

To the Blind Man. " Thou hast both seen Him, and it is He that speaketh with thee "—the Son of God.

(c) *He Grounded all He said on the Scriptures.* For faith must rest on the Word of God.

He referred the Rich Young Ruler, the Lawyer and the scribe to the Commandments—not as the way of life but as the Law of God, which gave the knowledge of sin and the holy requirements of God.

On the way to Emmaus He began at Moses and all the prophets, and in all the Scriptures He expounded unto them the things concerning Himself.

(d) *He Rewarded Faith,* often saying, " Thy faith hath saved thee, Go in peace "; requiring first a real repentance, without which all must perish.

Let the one who seeks to deal with enquirers study these points, that he may be an effective worker.

3. His Gracious Answers to the Difficulties that trouble the minds of men. He was a Greater than Solomon. The Queen of Sheba had all her hard questions answered by him, but our Greater than he satisfies our hearts' enquiries more perfectly.

The Gentile Sinner got some of the crumbs from the Master's table when she took the place of a little dog.

Martha was lovingly warned against serving too much, one dish was sufficient, and Mary had chosen a better part, to sit at His feet and listen.

And she and Mary had their doubts as to resurrection resolved by learning that He is the Resurrection and the Life.

Peter learned that love could cover a multitude of sins, swearing and disloyalty among them, and only asked for love in return.

Thomas was advised to believe, and not insist on physical demonstration.

Mary Magdalene was assured of her Lord's physical resurrection, but was bidden not to detain Him with displays of natural emotion.

Cleopas and his Companion were taught to have more confidence in the Word of God.

So each in turn were instructed, rebuked and comforted according to their respective needs.

There is no case too difficult for our Solomon.

VI. Application.

Let the *Sinner* take his true place before the Lord and find in Him a real Saviour.

Let the *Believer* bring all his doubts and difficulties to the Greater than Solomon.

Let the *Worker* learn the holy art of personal dealing.

THE LIPS
Wise Words from the Book of Proverbs

The Lips of the Righteous feed many (10. 21).

The Lips of the Righteous know what is acceptable (10. 32).

The Lips of the wise shall preserve them (14. 3).

The Lips of the wise disperse knowledge (15. 7).

Righteous Lips are the delight of kings (16. 13).

The Sweetness of the Lips increaseth learning (16. 21).

The Lips of Knowledge are a precious jewel (20. 15).

For the Grace of his Lips the king shall be his friend (22. 11).

Every man shall kiss his lips that giveth a right answer (24. 26).

Our Lord's Illustrations

I. Text. "Consider the lilies of the field, how they grow; they toil not, neither do they spin: And yet I say unto you, That even Solomon in all his glory was not arrayed like one of these " (Matt. 6. 28).

II. Main Lesson. The Lord was the Master of the Art of Illustration. In this, as in all else, He takes the pre-eminence over all others in the world's literature. His purpose was to show that the Earth is, if rightly understood, a Parable of Heaven; things seen and temporal, a shadow of things unseen and eternal. In this He set the example to His servants; let them in their ministry see that they let light into the minds of their hearers by apt illustration.

The Lord took His illustrations from three sources:

(i) *The Scriptures*, enforcing His points by the histories and wise sayings of the Old Testament ;

(ii) *Nature* and the common objects all around us; and

(iii) *Real Life* wrought into Parables or recorded as facts.

III. Scriptures to Study : Matthew 6. 24-30.

v. 24. *Serving Two Masters.* "No man can serve two masters: for either he will hate the one, and love the other; or else he will hold to the one, and despise the other. Ye cannot serve God and mammon."

v. 25. *The Life more than Meat and the Body than Dress.* "Take no thought for your life, what ye shall eat, or what ye shall drink; nor yet for your body, what ye shall put on. Is not the life more than meat, and the body than raiment ?"

v. 26. *Behold the Birds, how they Live.* "Behold the fowls of the air: for they sow not, neither do they reap, nor gather into barns; yet your Heavenly Father feedeth them. Are ye not much better than they ?"

v. 27. *Who can Add to his Height ?* "Which of you by taking thought can add one cubit to his stature ?"

vv. 28, 29. *Look at the Way the Lilies are Clad.* "Consider the lilies of the field, how they grow; they toil not, neither do they spin: And yet I say unto you, That even Solomon in all his glory was not arrayed like one of these."

v. 30. "Wherefore, if God so clothe the grass of the field, which to day is, and to morrow is cast into the oven, shall He not much more clothe you, O ye of little faith?"

Matthew 12. 5, 8, 40-42.

v. 5. *A Greater than the Temple.* "The priests in the Temple profane the Sabbath, and are blameless? But I say unto you, That in this place is one greater than the Temple."

v. 8. *Son of Man Lord of the Sabbath.* "For the Son of man is Lord even of the Sabbath."

vv. 40-41. *Jonah, a Type of the Greater than Jonas.* "As Jonas was three days and three nights in the whale's belly; so shall the Son of man be three days and three nights in the heart of the earth. The men of Nineveh . . . repented at the preaching of Jonas; and, behold, a greater than Jonas is here."

v. 42. *The Queen of the South and Solomon.* "The Queen of the South shall rise up in judgment with this generation, and shall condemn it: for she came from the uttermost parts of the earth to hear the wisdom of Solomon; and, behold, a greater than Solomon is here."

IV. Our Lord's Illustrations from Scripture.

(i) *The Death of Abel* (Matt. 23. 35), as showing the evil of the natural heart and the guilt of the nation.

(ii) *The Flood* (Luke 17. 26), as a warning of a more terrible judgment to come.

(iii) *The Destruction of Sodom* (Luke 17. 29): a warning of the sudden retribution to fall on the wicked.

(iv) *The Fate of Lot's Wife* (Luke 17. 32): an example of the folly of looking backwards.

(v) *Abraham* rejoicing to see the day of Christ (John 8. 56), Who before Abraham was could say, "I am."

(vi) *Moses and the Burning Bush*, when the Lord said, "I am the God of Abraham, Isaac, and Jacob"—used as a proof of resurrection.

(vii) *Moses' Writings* (John 5. 46). Had they believed Moses they would have believed Him; for Moses wrote of Him.

(viii) *Moses' Law Given* (John 7. 19). " Did not Moses give you the Law, yet none of you keepeth it ?"

(ix) *The Rite of Circumcision* (John 7. 22): first given to Abraham and enforced by Moses in the Law.

(x) *The Law as to Brother's Wife* (Luke 20. 28), from which the Lord taught that in Heaven they do not marry.

(xi) *The Manna in the Wilderness* (John 6. 31): the Lord teaching that He was the True Bread from Heaven.

(xii) *The Serpent Lifted up in the Wilderness* (John 3. 14-15), which the Lord used as a type of His own death.

(xiii) *David Eating the Shewbread* (Matt. 12. 3-4), which it was only lawful for the priests to eat.

(xiv) *Solomon in all his Glory* (Matt. 6. 28): not clothed so gloriously as a lily of the field.

(xv) *The Queen of Sheba's Visit to Solomon* (Matt. 12. 42): would condemn those who refused the greater than Solomon.

(xvi) *Elijah and the Woman of Sarepta* (Luke 4. 26): a Gentile blessed while the elect people were passed by.

(xvii) *Elisha's Cleansing of Naaman* (Luke 4. 27), enforcing the same lesson.

(xviii) *The Murder of Zacharias* (Luke 11. 51) the priest, the son of the good Jehoiada (2 Chron. 24. 21), an example of the apostasy of Israel.

(xix) *Jonah* (Matt. 12. 40-41), a sign to the nation, and illustration of Christ in His death and resurrection.

V. Our Lord's Illustrations from Nature.

These are so many that space forbids to do more than make a selection.

The following are used as illustrations in the *Sermon on the Mount* alone, as given in Matthew 5-7; they serve to show the Lord's wonderful versatility and the extensive use He made of natural objects as teaching us spiritual lessons.

Salt (5. 13); light (5. 14); candle (5. 15); city set on a hill (5. 14); hand, foot, and eye (5. 29-30); Heaven and earth (5. 34-35); hair (5. 36); cheek (5. 39); cloke and coat

(5. 40); sun and rain (5. 45); moth and rust (6. 19); thieves
(6. 20); the eye as the window of the body (6. 22); birds
(6. 26); lilies (6. 28); mote and beam (7. 5); bread, stone,
fish, and scorpion or serpent (7. 9-10); wolves (7. 15);
grapes, thorns, figs and thistles (7. 16); good and bad
trees, and fruit (7. 17-20); rock and sand (7. 25); wind, rain,
flood and storm (7. 25 and 27).

Truly a wonderful fund of illustrations from Nature in
a single sermon.

Is it any wonder they hung on His words and the common
people heard Him gladly ?

VI. Our Lord's Illustrations from Real Life.

The Parables are in almost every case illustrations of
this kind.

The Sower who went forth to Sow (Matt. 13. 2).
The Enemy Sowing Tares (Matt. 13. 24).
The Finding of a Treasure in a Field (Matt. 13. 44).
A Merchant Seeking Goodly Pearls (Matt. 13. 45).
Fishermen Casting a Drag Net (Matt. 13. 47).
Woman Putting Leaven in Meal (Matt. 13. 33).
Two Builders Building each a House (Matt. 7. 24).
The Shepherd Seeking the Lost Sheep (Matt. 18. 12).
The Woman Seeking Lost Silver (Luke 15. 8).
The Prodigal Son (Luke 15. 11).
The Two Debtors (Luke 7. 41).
The Unmerciful Servant (Matt. 18. 23).
Labourers in the Vineyard (Matt. 20. 1).
Marriage of the King's Son (Matt. 22. 2).
Ten Virgins at a Wedding (Matt. 25. 1).

And so on through almost the whole series of Parables.

VII. Other Lessons from Illustrations.

1. OUR LORD'S REVERENCE FOR THE SCRIPTURES. In
choosing illustrations from them He gave them His Divine
Authority. He never questioned the truth of their histories, nor that they were inspired of God.

The wonder of the Bible is that it is exhaustive. There
is no truth, moral, ethical, social, or spiritual, that is not
contained in it. No new truth has ever been discovered

or added to the Scriptures, and nothing has been discredited.

2. OUR LORD'S LOVE OF NATURE. I suppose our text is the most beautiful and perfect sentence in the world (Matt. 6. 28): the lovely imagery of the lily, the striking contrast with Solomon in all his glory, is profoundly grand. We may safely challenge any student of literature in the world to produce a better one.

Each natural object is a thought of Christ's put into being. As Creator He thought the lily, and gave it its clothing, and bade it be, and it was.

Can we wonder that He took delight in all the lovely creations of His own mind ?

3. THE NATURAL AND THE SPIRITUAL. Every natural object has a spiritual lesson to teach us, had we eyes to see it. Indeed, the things seen are made and intended to be parables of the unseen.

The first creation (physical) is a manifestation on the plane of natural vision of the character and blessings of the new creation (spiritual). The spiritual mind will find delight in observing these, and every " bush will be aflame with God."

4. OUR LORD'S DELIGHT IN THE SONS OF MEN. Everything affecting man's life interested the Lord, and from the ordinary affairs of human existence the Lord drew His illustrations. He sympathized with all and saw in all wonderful examples of heavenly things.

From Eternity His delights were with the sons of men, and when on earth everything that affected them—joys and sorrows, hopes and disappointments—all found an echo in His heart and a lesson from His lips.

5. OUR EXAMPLE. The Lord chose and made up His own illustrations. Let us also seek to do so.

If speakers would take more trouble to seek out acceptable words and pleasant similes, there would not be such dry sermons and drowsy listeners. The more heavenly-minded a man is, the more of Heaven he will see on earth.

A pudding is less heavy for having some plums in it.

A house is better furnished that has pictures on the walls.

A bride does not forget her ornaments; let not the servant of God neglect his.

VIII. Application :

Keep your eyes open.

Keep a spiritual mind and find the lessons in what is all around.

Serve up good food, but see that it has a pleasant taste.

OUTLINES

Things to Behold

Behold
{
The Lamb of God (John 1. 29).
The Lion of the Tribe of Judah (Rev. 5. 5).
The Love of the Father (1 John 3. 1).
The Lord cometh (Jude 14).
}

Seven Things to Behold in Revelation

Behold
{
" I am alive for evermore " (1. 18).
" I have set before thee an open door " (3. 8).
" I come quickly; hold fast " (3. 11).
" I stand at the door and knock " (3. 20).
" The tabernacle of God is with men " (21. 3).
" I make all things new " (21. 5).
" I come quickly and My reward is with Me "
    (22. 7 and 12).
}

The Lord's Invitations

I. **Text.** " The Master is come, and calleth for thee " (John 11. 28).

II. **Main Lesson.** No study of Christ would be complete that omitted His loving invitations.

The difference between the Law and the Gospel is this: The Law said, " This do and thou shalt live," and left man to his own resources.

Jesus said, " Come unto Me," and becomes his Saviour. He is Salvation. To obtain it we must come to Him, for there is no Salvation in any other.

The Law said, " Thou shalt," and man failed.

Christ says, " I will," and men can through Him. It is to call sinners that He came. These calls are the study before us.

III. **Scriptures to Study.**

Matthew 11. 28: *The Loving Call of Christ to the Heavy Laden.* " Come unto Me, all ye that labour and are heavy-laden, and I will give you rest."

v. 29. *The Further Call to Discipleship.* "Take My yoke upon you, and learn of Me; for I am meek and lowly in heart: and ye shall find rest unto your souls."

v. 30. *The Yoke Easy.* " For My yoke is easy, and My burden is light."

John 7. 37: *The Invitation on the Last Day of the Feast of Tabernacles.* " In the last day, that great day of the feast, Jesus stood and cried, saying, If any man thirst, let him come unto Me, and drink."

v. 38. *The Rivers of Living Water.* " He that believeth on Me as the Scripture hath said, out of his belly shall flow rivers of living water."

v. 39. *He Spake of the Holy Spirit.* " But this spake He of the Spirit, which they that believe on Him should receive: for the Holy Ghost was not yet given; because that Jesus was not yet glorified."

Mark 1. 16: *The Lord Calls Simon and Andrew to Follow*

Him. " Now as He walked by the sea of Galilee, He saw
Simon and Andrew his brother casting a net into the sea:
for they were fishers."

v. 17. " And Jesus said unto them, Come ye after Me,
and I will make you to become fishers of men."

v. 18. " And straightway they forsook their nets, and
followed Him."

v. 19. *He Calls James and John also.* " And when He
had gone a little farther thence, He saw James the son of
Zebedee, and John his brother, who also were in the ship
mending their nets."

v. 20. " And straightway He called them: and they left
their father Zebedee in the ship with the hired servants,
and went after Him."

IV. Seven Outstanding Invitations of Christ.

(i) *COME and REST*, take the yoke and learn of
Him (Matt. 11. 28).

This invitation is threefold: " Come unto Me "; " Take
My Yoke "; " Learn of Me."

It invites to *Rest* from the burden of guilt and the
servitude of sin.

It invites to the *Submission of Faith.* " Take My
yoke "—that is, yield yourself to My obedience.

It invites to *Discipleship.* " Learn of Me." For the
Lord has three things in view in calling us to Himself:
Our Salvation, Our Obedience, and Our Character.

His Salvation includes *Rest for the Conscience* from the
guilt of sin.

Rest for the Mind from our doubts and fears and unbelief.

Rest for the Will and its restlessness in holy service
under His yoke.

Rest for the Heart in His Love.

He describes *Himself*, our Example: " I am meek and
lowly in heart."

He describes *His Service:* " My yoke is easy and My burden
is light."

> " His yoke is easy, His burden is light,
> I've found it so, I've found it so.
> He leadeth me by day and by night
> Where living waters flow."

(ii) *COME and DRINK* (John 7. 37). Here the Lord invites us to receive the Holy Spirit, the Gift that He freely gives to all who believe.

Receiving the Spirit by the hearing of faith (Gal. 3. 2) is likened to drinking of the living water. Water being the constant emblem of the Spirit, it is the water of life which Jesus gives. Believers are said all to have been made to drink into One Spirit (1 Cor. 12. 13).

(iii) *COME and FOLLOW* (Mark 1. 17): "Come ye after Me, and I will make you to become fishers of men."

While the first called to *Salvation* and the second to *Sanctification*, this invitation is a call to *Service*. "I will make you to become." No man can make himself a soul-winner, he must come to Christ, Who will equip and fit him to catch men.

(iv) *COME and SEE* (John 1. 30). Two of John's disciples (one of them was Andrew) follow Jesus and ask, "Master, where dwellest Thou?" He saith unto them, "Come and see."

This invitation He extends to all. We are blind and ignorant until we come to Him, and ask Him, as blind Bartimeus did, "Lord, that I may receive my sight." He ever answers, "Receive thy sight." Then, as He said to the disciples, "Blessed are your eyes, for they see" (Matt. 13. 16).

(v) *COME ye APART*, and rest awhile (Mark 6. 31). Here the Lord calls to separation. For the rush and turmoil of life wearies the servant of God. The Lord knows our need of rest and refreshment, and invites us to come apart that we may enjoy communion with Him and thus renew our strength.

(vi) *COME and DINE* (John 21. 12). This He said to the disciples who had toiled all the night and caught nothing.

It is a true picture of His invitation to all His children to sit down and sup with Him (Rev. 3. 20).

At their Lord's table they know what it is to eat of His bread and drink of the wine that He has mingled.

(vii) *COME, take up the Cross* (Mark 10. 21): "Come, take up thy cross, and follow Me."

The believer is called not only to believe on His Name but to suffer for His sake.

He is called to the fellowship of His sufferings, to bear His reproach, to suffer now that he may reign hereafter.

Such are some typical invitations of our Lord Jesus.

V. Other Lessons from the Study.

1. The Deity of Christ Revealed in the Invitations.

No one who was only a man could invite his fellow-men to come to him for rest, or to receive the Holy Spirit. The marvellous fact remains that One stood among us who could, and did, say, " Come unto Me . . . I will give you rest."

Who could ask men to hate father and mother and come and follow Him but One who was Divine ?

In other lips such words would be folly.

2. The Invitations Addressed to Sinners. "I came not to call the righteous but sinners." This astonishing fact makes the invitations all the more wonderful. Sinners do not receive many invitations to share in good things, but here is One inviting even the vilest of men to come to Him, for Love, Life, Liberty and Light.

3. Children are Included. " Suffer little children to come unto Me, and forbid them not."

None who can understand it are too young to accept the Saviour's gracious invitation.

Learning is not needed; the more simple and childlike the acceptance of the invitation the better.

4. The Invitation is " Come to the Marriage " (Luke 22. 4). For the Lord likens the Salvation He offers to those who accept His invitation to a feast—not to a funeral—for there is nothing but blessing for those who come.

5. Alas ! that Many Excuse Themselves. " Ye will not come unto Me that ye might have life."

VI. Application :

Let us accept the invitation.

Let us pass it on to others.

OUTLINE

The Seven " Comes "

Come and Rest=Salvation.
Come and Drink=Sanctification.
Come and Follow=Service.
Come and See=Sight.
Come Apart=Separation.
Come and Dine=Satisfaction.
Come, take up the Cross=Suffering.

J-E-S-U-S

Jesus Endured Silently Unjust Shame.
Jesus Expired Suffering Under Sin.
Jesus Exalted Secures Us Salvation.
Jesus Ever Seeks Unworthy Sinners.
Jesus Expected Soon Unto Salvation.

The REST Jesus gives is to (see IV. 1)—

The Conscience in Cleansing.
The Mind in Meditation.
The Will in Work.
The Heart in Himself.

Who are Invited ?

Sinners (Matt. 9. 13); Children (Matt. 19. 14); Labouring and Heavy Laden (Matt. 11. 28); Thirsty (John 7. 37; Isa. 55. 1); Whosoever will (Rev. 22. 17). *When?* " Come now " (Isa. 1. 18); make haste (Luke 19. 5).

Jesus and the Pharisees

I. Text. "Have any of the . . . Pharisees believed on Him?" (John 7. 48).

II. Main Lesson. The Pharisees were among the chief enemies and opponents of the Lord Jesus.

His manner of dealing with them is most instructive.

1. He Exposed their Folly and Rebuked them most Severely. No language is stronger than that He used toward them.

2. He Warned Them of the Woes that were coming upon them.

3. He Instructed them Carefully, answering all their questions and quibbles with great patience.

4. He Sought to Turn them to Repentance by speaking Parables exactly suited to their case, which set before them the Way of Salvation.

5. He Received and Saved those of them that believed on Him, as, for example, Nicodemus.

III. Scripture to Study: Matthew 23. 13-33. *The Lord Pronounces Eight Woes* (or seven if with the R.V. we omit verse 14) *on the Pharisees.*

v. 13. *For Shutting up the Kingdom of Heaven.* "But woe unto you, scribes and Pharisees, hypocrites! for ye shut up the Kingdom of Heaven against men: for ye neither go in yourselves, neither suffer ye them that are entering to go in."

v. 14. *For Devouring Widows' Houses.* "Woe unto you, scribes and Pharisees, hypocrites! for ye devour widows' houses, and for a pretence make long prayers."

v. 15. *For Proselytizing.* "Woe unto you, scribes and Pharisees, hypocrites! for ye compass sea and land to make one proselyte, and when he is made, ye make him twofold more the child of Hell than yourselves."

vv. 16-22. *For Foolish Teaching as to Swearing.* "Woe unto you, ye blind guides, which say, Whosoever shall swear by the Temple, it is nothing; but whosoever shall swear by the gold of the Temple, he is a debtor! Ye fools and blind: for whether is greater, the gold, or the Temple that sanctifieth the gold?" etc.

vv. 23-24. *For Nicety in Tithing and Omitting Judgment, Mercy and Faith.* "Woe unto you, scribes and Pharisees, hypocrites! for ye pay tithe of mint and anise and cummin, and have omitted the weightier matters of the Law, judgment, mercy, and faith. . . . Ye blind guides, which strain at a gnat, and swallow a camel."

vv. 25-26. *For Making the Outside only Clean.* "Woe unto you, scribes and Pharisees, hypocrites! for ye make clean the outside of the cup and of the platter, but within they are full of extortion and excess," etc.

vv. 27-28. *Are like Whited Sepulchres, full of Dead Bones.* "Woe unto you, scribes and Pharisees, hypocrites! for ye are like unto whited sepulchres, which indeed appear beautiful outward, but are within full of dead men's bones, and of all uncleanness," etc.

vv. 29-31. *For they Build Tombs to the Old Prophets and Kill their own.* "Woe unto you, scribes and Pharisees, hypocrites! because ye build the tombs of the prophets . . . and say, If we had been in the days of our fathers, we would not have been partakers with them in the blood of the prophets. Wherefore ye be witnesses unto yourselves, that ye are the children of them which killed the prophets."

vv. 32-33. *He Denounces them as a Generation of Vipers.* "Fill ye up then the measure of your fathers. Ye serpents, ye generation of vipers, how can ye escape the damnation of hell?"

IV. Who were the Scribes, Pharisees, etc.?

1. The Pharisees were a reforming sect among the Jews. Their strictness, however, was in outward observance rather than inward holiness, as the Lord pointed out. The name means "separatists" or "exclusives," their great aim being to preserve themselves from legal contamination by a scrupulous avoidance of what they regarded as

unholy.   Their language was that of Isaiah 65. 5: " Stand
by thyself, come not near to me; for I am holier than thou,"
of whom the prophet adds, " These are a smoke in my nose."

They acquired in this way a high self-esteem and self-
righteousness, as witness the prayer of the Pharisee in the
Parable (Luke 18. 11-12).

2. THE SCRIBES (who were often Pharisees and Lawyers
also—Matt. 22. 34-35, Mark 12. 28) were the professional
students of the law, who copied it and taught it to the
people, and their own ideas with it.

3. THE LAWYERS were much the same, except that they
would attend the courts and act as advocates.

4. THE SADDUCEES were a sect, generally rivals of the
Pharisees (Acts 23. 6-9), who were often of the priestly
order (Acts 5. 17).   Their name is possibly derived from
Zadok, a priest who was their founder—the word means in
its verbal form " to be righteous."

They were the *modernists* of their day, denying what
their natural reason did not commend to them.   It was
said of them, " *Their theology might be called religion within
the limits of mere sensation.*"   Their denial of any spiritual
world and of the resurrection of the dead (Acts 23. 8)
marked them as practical sceptics, although professing
submission to the Law of God.

We never read of any conversions from among them,
but often from among the Pharisees.

V. Other Lessons from the Pharisees.

1. THE SINS OF THE PHARISEE are among those that
God is said to hate; that is why the words of Christ are
so strong against them.

For sins that are the result of weakness, of folly and
ignorance, He was ever compassionate, but those of the
Pharisee were not of this kind.

PRIDE, especially Pride of Piety or Religion, is one of
the seven things the Lord is said to hate and abominate
(Prov. 6. 16-17), as are a high look and a proud heart
(Prov. 21. 4).

DISPLAY in Religion (Matt. 23. 4).   Perhaps no form of
pride is more hateful.   All dressed-up religion is merely

gratifying to the flesh, covering as it does a poor sinner. The more showy the religious garb, the less is the wearer to be trusted.

LOVE OF PRAISE (John 12. 43), which is always unmerited, for the very desire of it shows a man to be unworthy. Man is nothing (2 Cor. 12. 11), and should give all praise to God.

DECEIT (Matt. 23. 25-28), covering up sin with an outside piety, whited sepulchres full of dead bones.

PROFESSION (Matt. 23. 29-31) without possession—pretended holiness with secret sinning.

DESPISING OTHERS (Luke 18. 11) and separating from them as being superior in holiness.

OPPRESSION of the poor (Matt. 23. 14)—robbing widows while making long prayers.

SUPPRESSION of the truth (Matt. 23. 13)—hindering those who are seeking it.

Let us remember that by nature we are all Pharisees, having hearts deceitful above all things. Only grace can overcome these innate tendencies.

2. IT WAS THE PHARISEES AND SADDUCEES WHO PUT THE LORD TO DEATH. For there is nothing more cruel than religion without the love of God in the heart. History teaches us this. The record of Rome is the outstanding example. Ever since Cain slew his brother Abel because "his own works were evil and his brother's righteous," the religious bigots have murdered the true servants of God.

Saul of Tarsus was a Pharisee of the Pharisees. He persecuted the Church of God, verily thinking he was doing God service, yet gloried in his own righteousness and fleshly religion at the same time; till Christ arrested him on the way to Damascus and showed him he was a blasphemer, an injurious persecutor, in the very front rank of sinners.

3. YET THERE IS MERCY FOR THE PHARISEE. *Nicodemus* needed to be born again, and by his after conduct showed that he was indeed a new creature.

Saul of Tarsus became Paul the Apostle, a slave of Jesus Christ, whose life and writings have affected more lives than those of any other man.

In Acts 15. 5 we read of "certain of the sect of the Pharisees which believed," and in Acts 6. 7 that "a great company of the priests were obedient to the faith."

So that our text, "Have any of the Pharisees believed on Him?" is answered in the affirmative.

4. UNCONSCIOUS HYPOCRISY. It is more than likely that many Pharisees, like Saul of Tarsus, were unconscious of their hypocrisy, verily thinking they were right when they were wrong.

It is possible to be such. Men assent to certain professions or beliefs, and take vows with all good intention, which place them in a false position; the profession, though good in theory, is *false in fact*; the vows, though pious in intention, are *impossible to the flesh*.

Men thus find themselves saying and professing what a little self-examination would discover to them to be false.

5. THE REMEDY FOR HYPOCRISY is to renounce all self-righteousness and trust only in Christ; to abandon our own ideas and rest only on the Word of God; to search our own hearts lest we say what is not true or profess what is not fact.

Let our prayer be, "Search me, O God, and see if there be any wicked way in me"; and when anything that will not bear the light is discovered let us judge it and put it away.

The believer never professes anything before a sinful world but that he is *a sinner who has found mercy*, a grace he invites every other sinner to share. He entreats them not to look at him, but at Christ.

VI. Application.

Mistrust thine own heart: it is a hypocrite.
Look to Christ for the sincerity and simplicity of faith.
Beware of glorying in the flesh: it is an incurable evil.

Our Lord's Warnings

I. **Text.** "Fear Him Who is able to destroy both body and soul in Hell" (Matt. 10. 28).

II. **Main Lesson.** A great part of our Lord's ministry was devoted to warning. The great Apostle in this followed His example, "I ceased not to warn everyone night and day with tears" (Acts 20. 31).

It has been well said that only a friend warns. The Lord, knowing our true condition and the deceitfulness of our hearts, the power and enmity of the spiritual forces against us, warned us of many dangers within and around us, bidding us time after time to "Beware," "Take Heed," "Watch and Pray," and "Look to ourselves," that we be not deceived or taken unawares. Some of these warnings are set out below (IV.).

In preaching Christ we shall need to pass on to others these solemn warnings, seeking to do so with the fearlessness and grace that He displayed when warning those who were in danger of eternal death in rejecting Him and refusing the Salvation He offered them in the Gospel.

III. **Scripture to Study** (Luke 12. 1-15).

v. 1. *The Lord Warns of the Leaven of the Pharisees.* "Beware ye of the leaven of the Pharisees, which is hypocrisy."

vv. 2-3. *The Truth will come out.* "For there is nothing covered that shall not be revealed. . . . Therefore whatsoever ye have spoken in darkness shall be heard in the light; and that which ye have spoken in the ear in closets shall be proclaimed upon the housetops."

v. 4. *Fear not Men, who can only Kill the Body.* "Be not afraid of them that kill the body, and after that have no more that they can do."

v. 5. *Whom to Fear.* "But I will forewarn you whom ye shall fear: Fear Him, which after He hath killed hath power to cast into Hell; yea, I say unto you, Fear Him."

v. 6. *God's Care for His Own.* " Are not five sparrows sold for two farthings, and not one of them is forgotten before God ? "

v. 7. " But even the very hairs of your head are all numbered. Fear not therefore: ye are of more value than many sparrows."

v. 15. *In Answer to One who asked Him to Speak to his Brother to Divide the Inheritance.* " Take heed, and beware of covetousness: for a man's life consisteth not in the abundance of the things which he possesseth."

Read also the Parable of the Rich Fool (vv. 16-21).

IV. **The Dangers of which the Lord Warned.** Although they are very many, they can for the most part be gathered under the following heads:

1. BEWARE OF LIVING AND DYING IN SIN. The Lord left us no doubt of our lost and ruined condition as sinners.

He told the rich young ruler, " *There is none good.*" He warned those who told of Herod's cruelty to the Galilæans they were not to think they were specially guilty above others because they suffered thus. Twice He added, " *Except ye repent, ye shall all likewise perish.*" He told Nicodemus, " *Ye must be born again,*" or he could never see or enter the Kingdom; and told all, " *Except ye be converted . . .* ye cannot enter the Kingdom."

He warned us that " our righteousness must exceed that of the scribes and Pharisees "; that it were better to cut off an offending hand or foot and pluck out a wicked eye than risk hell fire.

He warned those who committed sin that they were the servants of sin, and that unless they believed upon Him they *would die in their sins.*

When the disciples enquired, " Who then can be saved ? " He replied, " *With man it is impossible.*"

But He had come to seek and to save that which was lost; to call sinners to repentance; to preach good news.

2. BEWARE OF REJECTING CHRIST. He proclaimed Himself as *the Way, the Truth, and the Life,* and that no man could come to the Father but by Him. If they refused Him, they refused Life.

He said He was *the Door*, through which we must enter
to be saved. To turn from Him would be to find the Door
shut when it was too late.

He was *the Bread* of which if a man eat he should live
for ever; but "except ye eat . . . ye have no life in you"
(John 6. 52).

He assured those who believed on Him that they should
not perish, but have eternal life, but that unbelievers would
never see life, but the wrath of God abode on them (John
3. 36).

He was *the Light*; the condemnation of the sinner lay
in this, that the Light is come, and men love darkness
rather than light. The unbeliever, He said, was "condemned already" (John 3. 18).

He bade the sinner " Come unto Me," but warned those
who refused, " Ye will not come unto Me that ye might
have life."

3. BEWARE OF REFUSING TO HEAR AND OBEY THE WORD
OF GOD. Perhaps this was the most frequent warning
of all from the Lord's lips.

In the Sermon on the Mount He warned us against
saying "Lord, Lord," and not doing what He said; He
likened the man who heard but did not do His words
to a foolish man who built his house on the sand.

In the Parable of the Sower He spoke of the good seed
being devoured by birds (snatched away by the Devil),
withered by the sun because it had no root, or choked by
thorns.

In the Parable of the Rich Man in Hades, He told how
he was answered when he prayed for his five brethren:
" They have Moses and the prophets; let them hear them."

He told His opponents " they erred, not knowing the
Scriptures," and that the words He spoke would judge
them in the last day.

After His resurrection He rebuked the two disciples on
the walk to Emmaus thus: " O fools, and slow of heart to
believe all that the prophets have spoken."

4. BEWARE OF FALSE PROPHETS and of the leaven of
the scribes and Pharisees, for they perverted the Scriptures

and made them of none effect by their traditions, teaching
for doctrines the commandments of men (Mark 12. 38).

There were, He said, blind leaders of the blind, both of
whom fell into the ditch (Matt. 15. 14).

False prophets came disguised like wolves in sheep's
clothing. They deceived many. They were to be known
by their fruits.

5. BEWARE OF SELF-DECEPTION—of being satisfied with
an outside performance, while the heart remained unclean.
Cleansing the outside of the cup and platter, being out-
wardly religious, while inside was full of extortion and
excess.

It is surprising with what constancy the Lord returned
to this subject.

Many would say to Him in that day, " Lord, Lord, have
we not prophesied in Thy Name, cast out demons, and done
many mighty works ?" and He would say, " I never knew
you !" They could say, "We have eaten and drunk in Thy
presence, and Thou hast taught in our streets " ; yet,
alas ! they had continued workers of iniquity.

Often the Lord spoke of those who made *a False Start*, a
profession that failed (alas ! so common today).

The man who began to build and was not able to finish.

The three who would follow, but failed to do so (Luke
9. 57-68).

The man who built on the sand, whose house fell.

The man out of whom the unclean spirit went, but
returned with seven worse than himself (Luke 11. 24).

The five foolish virgins who had no oil in their lamps.

The man who came to the marriage without a wedding
garment (Matt. 22. 12).

The servant who was unprofitable and cast out (Matt.
25. 30).

In most of these cases the mistake was found out too
late. Beware, then, of self-deception.

6. BEWARE OF COVETOUSNESS (Luke 12. 15). Of this
particular danger the Lord often warned us.

The love of money is a root of all evil, and the Lord
spoke plainly about the danger of riches.

He told us it was easier for a camel to go through the eye of a needle than for a rich man to enter the Kingdom of God.

He told us that we cannot serve God and mammon.

He warned us that we might gain the whole world and lose the soul.

He spoke several parables of those who were ruined by riches. The rich man and Lazarus lying at his gate, who lifted up his eyes in torment. The rich fool who would pull down his barns and build bigger, whose soul was that night required of him.

The rich young ruler went away " very sorrowful " because the love of money held him in its power.

Of the many dangers besetting the path, this is the one the Lord specially warned against.

7. BEWARE OF HELL. No one ever spoke so often and so terribly of Hell as the Lord Jesus.

He alone knew its horrors, for He Himself as the Maker and Upholder of all things has appointed it.

He bade us fear Him Who is able to destroy both body and soul in Hell.

He spoke again and again of the fire that cannot be quenched and of the worm that dieth not.

He spoke of the impossibility of escaping from it (Luke 16. 26), and of the torment of the flame.

He, moreover, described it as everlasting punishment (Matt. 25. 46).

It was better, He said, to lose an eye, a hand or a foot than have to be cast into hell-fire.

He says of Judas, " It were better for that man that he had never been born."

V. Other Lessons on the Lord's Warnings.

1. THE GRACE OF THE WARNINGS. When collected as in IV. above, the warnings of the Lord seem many and terrible. Yet our impression of His teaching is not that of denunciation or harsh judgment. On the contrary, we marvel at the gracious words that proceeded out of His mouth. His warnings are so true, so reasonable, and carry such conviction with them, that they appear gracious

—the solemn, kindly cautions of One Who loves our souls and would save us from fatal mistakes.

2. HEEDING THE WARNINGS. Beware of thinking the warnings are unnecessary in our case, of putting up a moral umbrella and passing them off to others, to whom perhaps we think they apply more than to us.

We all need them all. Our hearts are all alike capable of the grossest sin and the most desperate folly.

Let him that thinketh he standeth take heed lest he fall.

3. WARNINGS AND PROMISES. Let the two go together. No sorrow but has its remedy in Christ; therefore never warn without preaching Christ.

Let the Rainbow of Promise illumine the Dark Cloud of Threatening Danger.

It is said that a dock always grows near a nettle and is a remedy for its sting. So let the promises abound where the dangers are thickest.

4. HEED TAKEN TOO LATE. In most of the illustrations the Lord used the warning was neglected until it was too late. Caution the hearers of this.

Some years ago a noted preacher preached on a second chance after death. A lady had taken a godless, worldly man to hear him, promising him that he would hear a great preacher. The result was that the man said, " Well, if that's true, I'll take my chance," and went away un-awakened to continue his godless life. Oh, the guilt of such preaching !

5. WITHOUT EXCUSE. A man who has been warned is without excuse if he give no heed. He is doubly guilty.

He who knew his Lord's will and did it not, we are told, would be beaten with many stripes. The son who said, " I go, sir," and went not, is without any excuse.

Noah's carpenters were without excuse when they were swept away by the Flood.

Lot's wife was without excuse for looking back to the Sodom from which angels had dragged her.

VI. Application.

To the Sinner—" You have been warned."

To the Seeker—" Beware of false prophets."

To the Professor—" Look to your foundation: it may be only sand."

To the Child of God—" Take heed that no man take thy crown."

OUTLINES

Beware

BEWARE lest thou forget the Lord (Deut. 6. 12).

BEWARE lest He take thee away (Job 36. 18).

BEWARE of false prophets (Matt. 7. 15).

BEWARE of men (Matt. 10. 17), of dogs (Phil. 3. 2), of evil workers (Phil. 3. 2).

BEWARE of the leaven of the Scribes (Mark 12. 38).

BEWARE of coveteousness (Luke 12. 15).

BEWARE lest any man spoil you (Col. 2. 8).

Seven Take Heeds

What ye hear (Mark 4. 24).

How ye hear (Luke 8. 18).

That ye despise not one little one (Matt. 18. 10).

That the light in thee be not darkness (Luke 11. 35).

How he buildeth (1 Cor. 3. 10).

Lest he fall (1 Cor. 10. 12).

To the ministry (Col. 4. 17).

The Lord's Call to Full Surrender

I. Text. "So likewise, whosoever he be of you that forsaketh not all that he hath, he cannot be My disciple" (Luke 14. 33).

II. Main Lesson. No man ever did or could rightly have made so tremendous a claim as did the Lord Jesus.

That a man must hate his father and mother, children, brethren and sisters (Luke 14. 26).

Must forsake all that he hath (14. 33).

Must surrender "his own life also."

Must take up his cross daily and follow Christ.

As Canon Liddon says, "*How fearful is such a claim, if the Son is only human; how natural, how moderate, how just if He is in very deed Divine.*"

The wonder is not merely that the claim has been made, but that millions ever since have gladly yielded to it and laid life and all at the feet of Jesus, only to prove, as He promised, that in losing the life they have found it.

III. Scripture to Study (Luke 14. 25-35).

v. 25. *A Great Multitude follow Christ.* "And there went great multitudes with Him: and He turned and said unto them . . ."

v. 26. *He Declares the Price of Discipleship.* "If any man come to Me, and hate not his father, and mother, and wife, and children, and brethren, and sisters, yea, and his own life also, he cannot be My disciple."

v. 27. *The Cross must be taken up.* "And whosoever doth not bear his cross, and come after Me, cannot be My disciple."

v. 28. *He Illustrates the Need of Counting the Cost.* "For which of you, intending to build a tower, sitteth not down first, and counteth the cost, whether he have sufficient to finish it?"

vv. 29-30. *The Man Unable to Finish Mocked at.* "Lest haply, after he hath laid the foundation, and is not able

106

to finish it, all that behold it begin to mock him, Saying,
This man began to build, and was not able to finish."

vv. 31-32. *Another Illustration—a King making War.*
" Or what king, going to war against another king, sitteth
not down first, and consulteth whether he be able with
ten thousand to meet him that cometh against him with
twenty thousand ? Or else . . . desireth conditions of
peace."

v. 33. *So all must be Forsaken for Christ.* " So likewise, whosoever he be of you that forsaketh not all that he
hath, he cannot be My disciple."

vv. 34-35. *Another Illustration from Salt.* " Salt is good:
but if the salt have lost his savour, wherewith shall it be
seasoned ? It is neither fit for the land, nor yet for the
dunghill; but men cast it out. . . . He that hath ears to
hear, let him hear."

IV. Some Who Left All.

1. *Simon Peter and Andrew* (Matt. 4. 20) left their nets
and followed Jesus.

2. *James and John* (Matt. 4. 22) left their ship and their
father Zebedee and followed Christ.

3. *Matthew the Publican* (Matt. 9. 9; Luke 5. 28) " left
all, rose up and followed Him."

4. *The Woman of Samaria* (John 4. 28) left her water-
pot to tell the men, " Come, see, is not this the Christ ?"

5. *Blind Bartimæus* (Mark 10. 50) cast away his garment
to come to Jesus.

6. *The Man in the Parable* who found a *Treasure hid
in a field* (Matt. 13. 44) sold all that he had to buy the
field.

7. *The Merchantman* seeking *Goodly Pearls* (Matt. 13. 46)
sold all that he had to buy the pearl of great price.

8. *Paul the Apostle* (Phil. 3. 8) suffered the loss of all
things to win Christ.

9. *Barnabas, the Levite of Cyprus* (Acts 4. 36), having
land sold it and brought the money and laid it at the
Apostles' feet.

10. *The Hebrew Christians* (Heb. 10. 34) took joyfully
the spoiling of their goods.

11. *Moses* (Heb. 11. 25) esteemed the reproach of Christ greater riches than the treasures in Egypt.

12. *The Early Believers* (Acts 2. 44-45) sold their possessions and goods and parted them to all men, as every man had need.

V. Other Lessons on Full Surrender.

1. The Claim of Christ shows Him to be the Son of God, for no other had the right to demand so great a sacrifice from men.

Although unseen, the Love of Christ still compels men to yield Him their all in full and glad obedience.

2. Impossible to the Flesh. The natural man will never make this surrender. He regards it as losing his life; the world would regard him as a fool for doing it. The example of the Rich Young Ruler shows this; even to gain Eternal Life he could not make the sacrifice.

But when the Love of Christ constrains, the believer says with Mephibosheth, "Yea, let Him take all" (2 Sam. 19. 30).

3. False Starts. Many have set out to be Christians who have not continued.

So the Lord bids us sit down and count the cost if we be able. The answer, of course, will be, "We are not sufficient of ourselves." Then let there be a full surrender to Christ.

But to start in the strength of the natural man and in the energy of the flesh is to fail.

4. Half-Hearted Service will not Avail. There must be a submission to the obedience of Christ in everything. To obey in some things only is not true obedience. The obedience of faith covers the whole realm of life.

" Half heart can never be My disciple."

A mother and son who had been long praying for father were glad to see him go out to the penitent form at a Salvation Army meeting.

" Do you think he is really saved ?" asked the anxious mother of her boy. To which the boy replied," I'm afraid not, mother; father only went down on one knee."

5. BUILDING A TOWER. Our Lord's illustration of a man building a tower reminds us that the Christian sets out to *build a godly character*.

Can he finish ? Not without fully yielding to Christ.

How many have "decided" for Christ, and filled up decision cards, who have not gone on !

Others mock at them, saying, "This man began to build, and was not able to finish."

One such felt the reproach, and when asked to yield to Christ said bitterly, "No, thanks; I made a fool of myself once."

6. MEETING AN ENEMY. The Lord's other illustration was of a king going to war. So the professor sets out to fight and overcome sin.

Can he get the victory ?

Not unless there is a full yielding to Christ in heart obedience; then and then only can the mighty power of Christ be known in his life.

What general could lead half-hearted soldiers to victory ?

7. SAVOURLESS SALT is good for nothing—not even for the dunghill ! (35).

So an empty professor is worthless. Let him be one thing or the other. To be lukewarm is to be thrown out of the mouth (Rev. 3. 16).

8. KEEP YOURSELVES IN THE LOVE OF GOD. This is the only way to continue. It is the Love that constrains. Without the constraining Love of Christ the professor is like a watch with its mainspring broken.

But when the Holy Spirit sheds that Love abroad in the heart, then life springs up like a well of water.

VI. Application.

To the Seeker. Count the cost. Can you, without a full submission to Christ, ever live to the glory of God or overcome sin ?

To the Christian. Be wholehearted. Half-heart will neither build the tower, overcome the enemy, nor be as salt.

To the Preacher. See that you make this clear: The whole heart or none.

The Lord Jesus as Prophet

I. Text. " Moses truly said unto the fathers, A Prophet shall the Lord your God raise up unto you like unto me " (Acts 3. 22).

II. Main Lesson. Three terms are used of Christ, all of which have much the same meaning.

The *Apostle* (Heb. 3. 1), the *Prophet* (Acts 3. 22), and the *Faithful Witness* (Rev. 1. 5).

For the Lord came forth from the Father, as One sanctified and sent by Him (Apostle) to bear witness to the truth, speaking as the mouthpiece of God (Prophet).

A Prophet is one who speaks from or on behalf of God, as an Oracle of God, an inspired revealer of truth and faithful witness to it. Such was our gracious Lord.

" God, who at sundry times and in divers manners spake in times past unto the fathers by the prophets, hath in these last days spoken unto us by His Son " (Heb. 1. 1-2).

All that are of the truth hear Him.

III. Scripture to Study (Deut. 18. 15-19).

v. 15. *Moses Foretells of a Prophet.* " The Lord thy God will raise up unto thee a Prophet from the midst of thee, of thy brethren, like unto me."

vv. 15-16. *He must be hearkened to.* " Unto Him ye shall hearken."

v. 16. *They had felt their need of such an one.* " According to all that thou desiredst of the Lord God in Horeb saying, Let me not hear again the voice of the Lord my God, neither let me see this great fire any more, that I die not."

v. 17. *The Lord commends them for this.* " The Lord said unto me, They have well spoken that which they have spoken."

v. 18. *God promises a Prophet.* " I will raise them up a Prophet from among their brethren, like unto thee, and will put My words in His mouth, and He shall speak unto them all that I shall command Him."

v. 19. *Whoever will not hearken, it will be required.*
"And it shall come to pass, that whosoever will not
hearken unto My words which He shall speak in My Name,
I will require it of him."

IV. Other Lessons from the Study.

1. THE NEED OF A PROPHET. It is natural to the sinful
heart of man that he should not desire to hear the Voice
of God. At Sinai the people entreated that God would
cease to speak to them: "Let me not hear again the Voice
of the Lord my God" (Deut. 18. 16).

For the Voice of God is terrible to the guilty and distasteful to those who desire not the knowledge of His ways.
Yet God desires to speak to man, and has therefore spoken
to us in His Son.

2. THE WORK OF A PROPHET is not only to foretell the
future, but is various:

(*a*) *To Act as the Mouthpiece of God,* as Aaron was said to
be prophet to Moses (Exod. 7. 1). "Aaron thy brother
shall be thy prophet"—for Moses had pleaded that he was
not eloquent.

So Christ speaks from God, as the mouth of God: "The
words I speak are not Mine, but the Father's that sent Me"
(John 14. 24).

(*b*) *To Speak in the Authority and Power of God.* This
we read, "If any man speak, let him speak as the oracles
of God" (1 Pet. 4. 11). So Christ said, "I speak not of
Myself" (John 12. 49).

(*c*) *To Edify and Comfort.* As we read in 1 Cor. 14. 3,
"He that prophesieth speaketh unto men to edification,
and exhortation, and comfort." As one put it:

> EDIFY—to build up,
> EXHORT—to stir up, and
> COMFORT—to bind up.

(*d*) *To Look Back and to Speak of the Past,* as Moses did
when he wrote the story of Creation.

(*e*) *To Look Forward and Foretell Things to Come,* as our
Lord did in His great prophetic utterances in Matthew 24
and 25.

3. CHRIST AS A PROPHET WAS—

(a) *Ordained and Sent of God*, as was Jeremiah, to whom God said, " Before thou camest out of the womb I ordained thee to be a prophet unto the nations " (Jer. 1. 5).

(b) *Anointed for the Service*, as Elijah was bidden to anoint Elisha to be a prophet (1 Kings 19. 6). So we read of Christ, "God, even Thy God, hath anointed Thee" (Heb. 1. 9 and Acts 10. 38).

(c) *A Witness to the Truth*. As it is said, " To Him give all the prophets witness." So Christ Himself was " The Faithful and True Witness." He told Pilate, " To this end was I born . . . that I should bear witness unto the truth. Every one that is of the truth heareth My voice " (John 18. 37).

(d) *An Expounder of the Scriptures*. The Lord confirmed the words of the prophets who had gone before (Heb. 1. 1), as we read in Luke 24. 27: " Beginning at Moses and in all the prophets, He expounded unto them in all the Scriptures the things concerning Himself."

(e) *An Enlightener of the Understanding*. " Then opened He their understanding, that they might understand the Scriptures " (Luke 24. 45).

(f) *A Builder of His Church*. It was built upon the foundation of the Apostles and Prophets (that is, upon the Truth they were given to reveal), Jesus Christ (as the Greatest of all the Prophets) being the Chief Corner-stone (Eph. 2. 20).

4. THE RESPONSIBILITY TO HEAR THIS PROPHET. " Whosoever will not hearken unto My words which He shall speak in My Name, I will require it of him." This is what the Lord emphasized when He said, " The Words that I speak unto you, they shall judge you in that day." It is a solemn thing to refuse to hear God: " If they escaped not who refused him that spake on earth, much more shall not we escape, if we turn away from Him that speaketh from Heaven " (Heb. 12. 25).

5. THE SUPERIORITY OF CHRIST TO ALL THE PROPHETS. They had partial revelation and passed off the scene:

" Your fathers, where are they ? and the prophets, do they live for ever ?" asked Zechariah (1. 5).

As the Pharisees said to Christ, " Art thou greater than our father Abraham, which is dead ? and the prophets are dead: Whom makest Thou Thyself ?" (John 8. 53).

He is the One Who liveth and was dead, but is now alive again for evermore.

V. Application.

Let us hear and believe this Great Prophet that we may be established. " Believe His prophets, so shall ye prosper " (2 Chron. 20. 20).

Let us remember that His words will judge us at that day.

OUTLINES

Some who are called Prophets

Abraham (Gen. 20. 7).   David (Acts 2. 30).
Moses (Deut. 34. 10).   Elijah (1 Kings 18. 36).
Samuel (Acts 3. 24).   Elisha (2 Kings 6. 12).

Prophets of Judah

Isaiah, Jeremiah, Hosea, Amos, Micah, Zephaniah.

Prophets of the Captivity

Ezekiel and Daniel.

Prophets of the Restoration

Haggai, Zechariah, Malachi.

Undated Prophets

Joel, Obadiah, Jonah, Nahum, Habakkuk.

Behold My Servant

I. Text. "Behold My Servant, whom I uphold; Mine elect, in Whom My soul delighteth; I have put My Spirit upon Him: He shall bring forth judgment to the Gentiles" (Isa. 42. 1).

II. Main Lesson. The Lord Jesus humbled Himself to become the Obedient and Dependent Servant of Jehovah. Found in fashion as a Man, "*He took upon Him the form of a servant*" (Phil. 2. 7).

He is called "*Thy Holy Child* (R.V., Servant) *Jesus*" (Acts 4. 30).

He came to do the Will of God, and delighted to do it; He won the approval of the Father, who twice bore Witness from Heaven, "*This is My Beloved Son in Whom I am well pleased.*"

His walk and work as the Servant of Jehovah is described in the Gospel of Mark specially, and His submission to death as the Sinless Substitute in Isaiah 53. "Behold, My Servant shall deal prudently. . . . His visage was so marred more than any man, and His form more than the sons of men" (Isa. 52. 13-14).

III. Scriptures to Study (Isa. 42. 1-7).

v. 1. *God Bids us Behold His Servant.* "Behold My servant, whom I uphold; Mine elect, in whom My soul delighteth."

v. 1. *He has put His Spirit on Him.* "I have put My Spirit upon Him: He shall bring forth judgment to the Gentiles."

v. 2. *He will not Strive nor Cry.* "He shall not cry, nor lift up, nor cause His voice to be heard in the street."

v. 3. *He will not Break the Bruised Reed.* "A bruised reed shall He not break, and the smoking flax shall He not quench: He shall bring forth judgment unto truth."

v. 4. *He will not be Discouraged.* "He shall not fail nor be discouraged, till He have set judgment in the earth: and the isles shall wait for His law."

vv. 5-6. *God will Uphold Him and give Him for a Covenant.* "Thus saith God the Lord. . . . I the Lord have called thee in righteousness, and will hold thine hand, and will keep thee, and give thee for a covenant of the people, for a light of the Gentiles."

v. 7. *His Works of Mercy.* " To open the blind eyes, to bring out the prisoners from the prison, and them that sit in darkness out of the prison house. I am the Lord: that is My name: and my glory will I not give to another."

Isaiah 52. 13-15. *The Suffering Servant.* " Behold, My servant shall deal prudently, He shall be exalted and extolled, and be very high. As many were astonied at Thee; His visage was so marred more than any man, and His form more than the sons of men: So shall He sprinkle many nations; the kings shall shut their mouths at Him: for that which had not been told them shall they see; and that which they had not heard shall they consider."

Read the whole of Isaiah 53.

IV. The Servant of Jehovah in Isaiah.

1. Who is This Servant ? No name is given and all the critical surmises fail. It cannot be Israel, as the servant dies to bear Israel's sins (Isa. 53. 5).

The believer finds no difficulty, since the answer to the eunuch's question, " Of whom speaketh the prophet this ? Of himself, or of some other man ?" (Acts 8. 34), is given in the following Scriptures.

Luke 22. 37, R.V. *The Lord Himself* speaks: "I say unto you, that this which is written must be fulfilled in Me, And he was reckoned with transgressors" (Isa. 53. 12)— "for that which concerneth Me hath fulfilment." Thus the Blessed Lord claims this 53rd of Isaiah as speaking of Himself (see also Isa. 61. 1-3 and Luke 4. 21 below).

Seven other quotations of the 53rd of Isaiah in the New Testament, all of which ascribe it to Jesus.

Acts 8. 32. " Philip . . . began at the same Scripture, and preached unto him (the eunuch) Jesus."

Matthew 8. 17. " That it might be fulfilled which was spoken by Esaias the prophet, saying, Himself took our infirmities, and bear our sicknesses " (Isa. 53. 4).

Matthew 12. 17. " That it might be fulfilled which was
spoken by Esaias the prophet, Behold My servant whom I
have chosen," etc. (Isa. 42. 1-4).

Mark 15. 28. At the crucifixion: " And the Scripture
was fulfilled which saith, And He was numbered with the
transgressors " (Isa. 53. 12).

John 12. 38. " They believed not on Him: that the
saying of Esaias the prophet might be fulfilled, which he
spake, Lord, who hath believed our report ? and to whom
is the arm of the Lord revealed ?" (Isa. 53. 1).

2 *Corinthians* 5. 21. " He hath made Him to be sin
for us, Who knew no sin " (Isa. 53. 6 and 10).

1 *Peter* 2. 22. " Who did no sin, neither was guile found
in His mouth " (Isa. 53. 9).

So we have the testimony of the Lord Himself, all
four evangelists, and the Apostles Peter and Paul,
that Christ is the servant of Jehovah of whom Isaiah
spoke.

2. THE FIVE " SERVANT " PASSAGES IN ISAIAH.

Chap. 49. 1-9. The servant in His gracious ministry as
set out in III. above.

Chap. 49. 1-12. The servant as the Redeemer of Israel
and the Light to the Gentiles, introducing the great day
of Salvation.

Chap. 50. 4-11. The servant in perfect subjection,
hearing and obeying the Voice of the Lord.

Chap. 52. 13–53. 12. The servant as the substitute,
suffering for the sins of His people.

Chap. 61. 1-3. The servant as the Preacher of Good
Tidings—quoted by the Lord as of Himself in the Synagogue
at Nazareth with the words, " *This day is this Scripture
fulfilled in your ears* " (Luke 4. 21).

V. Other Lessons on the Servant of Jehovah.

1. THE DUTIES OF A SERVANT.

(1) *Attention* (Psa. 123. 2). " Behold, as the eyes of
servants look unto the hand of their masters." So the
Lord had the ear of an instructed One (Isa. 50. 4).
He was wakened morning by morning to hear.

(2) *Obedience.* "I was not rebellious, neither turned away back" (Isa. 50. 5). "He became obedient unto death, even the death of the Cross" (Phil. 2. 8).

For the first time on earth God beheld a perfectly obedient Man.

(3) *Willing for even the Lowliest Service.* So He washed the disciples' feet and set us an example of loving service to others.

(4) *Delight in the Master's Will.* No grudging service, but the Lord said, "Lo, I come: in the volume of the book it is written of Me, I delight to do Thy Will, O My God; yea, Thy law is within My heart."

(5) *Winning the Favour of His Master.* Proverbs 14. 35: "The King's favour is toward a wise servant."

Proverbs 29. 21 is expressive of the reward of a good servant, "He that delicately bringeth up his servant from a child shall have him become a son at last."

2. THE DIGNITY OF SERVICE. The Lord often emphasized the fact that it was noble to serve. All service is, of course, not dignified—there is slavery, and cruel bondage; there are some necessary duties that are ignominious and only expected of "vessels unto dishonour," but *willingly to serve others in anything is honourable.* The spirit of humility which will wash another's feet is highly regarded in God's sight.

Many passages teach this (Matt. 20. 17, 23. 11; John 13. 12-17).

So the Lord tells us, He "came not to be ministered unto, but to minister, and to give His life a ransom for many."

3. EXHORTATION TO SERVANTS. Our Lord's example in becoming a servant is a great encouragement to those whose lot it is to be servants. To them special advice is given:

Ephesians 6. 5-8 calls them to obey, as unto Christ, not with eye service as men pleasers, but as to the Lord, and promises them a reward.

Colossians 3. 22-25 repeats this, and adds, "Whatsoever ye do, do it heartily," and adds a warning that wrong-

doing will be visited; that God is no respecter of persons.
See also 1 Timothy 6. 1, Titus 2. 9 and 1 Peter 2. 18.

Specially "not answering again," not " purloining," but
showing "all good fidelity," and that not only to the good
and gentle, but to the froward also, are commended.

4. THE PRIVILEGE OF SERVICE TO THE LORD. "If any
man serve Me, Him will My Father honour." No greater
honour can any man have than to be called a servant of
the Most High God.

Paul was glad to call himself the slave of Jesus Christ.

By and by in the Kingdom His servants shall serve
Him.

VI. Application.

Let us fear the pride that desires to be first or greatest.

Let us be ashamed of the self-indulgence that desires
to be served.

Let us seek to follow the example of Him who washed the
disciples' feet.

Let servants be obedient, willing and faithful to their
masters, good or bad, for Christ's sake.

Their godly conduct may win the master to Christ.

OUTLINE

Seven Notable Servants

ELIEZER (Gen. 15. 2), Abraham's servant and steward.

JACOB (Gen. 29. 15), who served for love.

JOSEPH (Gen. 41. 12), who became lord of Egypt.

MOSES (Exod. 3. 1), the shepherd who became the shepherd
of Israel.

PHURAH (Judges 7. 10), Gideon's brave servant, who went
with him to the Midianite camp.

GEHAZI (2 Kings 8. 4), the lying servant of Elisha, smitten
with leprosy.

PHEBE (Rom. 16. 1), servant of the Church at Cenchrea.

The Good Physician

1. Text. " Jesus said unto them, They that be whole need not a physician, but they that are sick. . . . I am not come to call the righteous, but sinners to repentance " (Matt. 9. 12-13).

II. Main Lesson. The Lord came as a Doctor for the sin-sick.

> " The worst of all diseases
> Is light compared with sin.
> On every part it seizes
> And rages most within;
> 'Tis leprosy and fever
> And palsy all combined,
> And none but the believer
> The least relief can find."—J. Newton.

Sin is not a disease, but is likened to one. Sin is a *guilty* thing, which suffering often is not. Our Lord did not come to banish disease or death, since these still have their place in this present order, while our body is still waiting for its redemption (Rom. 8. 23).

The cures He wrought were signs and parables of the great work He came to do as the Great and Good Physician of the Soul.

(For a discussion of this subject, see 70 *Less Known Bible Stories* under the heading "Signs and Wonders," pp. 227-8.)

III. Scriptures to Study.

1. Prophecy. Isaiah 61. 1-3:

v. 1. *Christ Anointed.* " The Spirit of the Lord God is upon me; because the Lord hath anointed me to preach good tidings to the meek; He has sent me to bind up the brokenhearted, to proclaim liberty to the captives, and the opening of the prison to them that are bound."

v. 2. *To Proclaim the Day of Salvation.* " To proclaim the acceptable year of the Lord, and the day of vengeance of our God; to comfort all that mourn."

v. 3. *To give Joy for Mourning.* " To appoint unto them that mourn in Zion, to give unto them beauty for ashes, the oil of joy for mourning, the garment of praise for the spirit of heaviness; that they might be called trees of righteousness, the planting of the Lord, that He might be glorified."

2. FULFILMENT. Luke 4. 16-21.

v. 16. *Jesus in the Synagogue at Nazareth.* " And He came to Nazareth, where He had been brought up: and, as His custom was, He went into the synagogue on the Sabbath day, and stood up for to read."

vv. 17-19. *He reads Isaiah 61. 1-2.* " And there was delivered unto Him the book of the prophet Esaias. And when He had opened the book, He found the place where it was written, The Spirit of the Lord is upon me," etc. (as above).

v. 20. *He Applies it to Himself.* " And He closed the book, and He gave it to the minister, and sat down. And the eyes of all them that were in the synagogue were fastened on Him."

v. 21. " And He began to say unto them, This day is this Scripture fulfilled in your ears."

IV. Our Lord's Miracles of Healing.

The Blind.   Matthew 9. 27, Mark 8. 22, Luke 18. 35, John 9. 1.

The Deaf and Dumb.   Matthew 12. 22, Mark 7. 31.

The Lame.   Matthew 11. 5, 15. 30-31, 21. 14.

The Leper.   Matthew 8. 2, Luke 14. 1.

The Crooked.   Luke 13. 11.

The Withered.   Matt. 12. 10.

The Demon-possessed.   Matthew 8. 28, Mark 1. 23, Luke 9. 38.

Issue of Blood.   Matthew 9. 20.

Fever.   Matthew 8. 14.

Palsy.   Matthew 9. 2.

Dead Raised.   Matthew 9. 23, Luke 7. 11, John 11. 43.

The Great Physician:

   (*a*) Never sent any away unhealed.
   (*b*) Healed immediately with a word.
   (*c*) Healed all who came.
   (*d*) Healed permanently.
   (*e*) Healed without charge.
   (*f*) Healed without medicine or operation,

though He sometimes used means, as spittle, clay or washing, with the laying on of His hands, or a touch or lifting up by the hand.

V. Other Lessons on Healing.

1. PHYSICIANS OF NO VALUE (Job 13. 4).   Just as there are many quack doctors and pretended healers about, so in the spiritual realm there are, as Job called them, " forgers of lies " and " physicians of no value."

Of these the Apostle warns often:

Dr. Law, who professes, by the efforts of the flesh to keep the commandments, to heal the sin-sick soul. John Bunyan describes him well in *Pilgrim's Progress*.

Mr. Worldly Wiseman directs the Pilgrim to Sinai, where he lives; his name is Legality, of the town of Morality.   But the law only inflames and discovers sin, and can never cure it.

Dr. Philosophy (Col. 2. 8), whose medicine is " vain deceit " after the tradition of men, turning men's thoughts to their own crude notions (rudiments) and cunning follies, that only land them deeper in sin because of their pride and unbelief.

Dr. Religion (Col. 2. 16-18), whose remedies for sin consist of voluntary humility, worshipping of angels, keeping feasts and observing days.   A round of piety that the flesh enjoys, but which never changes the heart nor arrests the plague of sin.

Dr. Ascetic (Col. 2. 20-23), who prescribes fasts and the neglecting of the body and strict man-made ordinances and will worship, which, the Apostle says, " *are not of any avail against indulgence of the flesh* " (23, R.V.).

One thing these quack doctors have in common: they turn men's thoughts from Christ to occupy them with things that cannot profit.

2. SPIRITUAL DISEASES HEALED BY THE GREAT PHYSICIAN.

The Blind are those who suffer from unbelief. They cannot see the truth. They are sceptics, agnostics and self-willed thinkers because they are blind. There is only one hope for such. It is to cry with Blind Bartimæus, " Lord, that I may receive my sight."

The Deaf and Dumb are those who never hear the Shepherd's voice (as do all the true sheep—John 10. 27), and therefore can never speak for Christ nor testify to Him. The Lord alone can say " Ephphatha " to such dead ears and lips.

The Lame are those who cannot walk in God's ways, nor keep in the path of holiness. Their legs are not equal: they cannot walk in newness of life, and never will till the Lord gives them power.

The Lepers are the unclean by reason of sin, whose whole nature is defiled and corrupt, even their thoughts being so vile that nothing is pure. Only One can say to such, " I will, be thou clean."

The Crooked and the Withered and the Palsied all tell the same story. Their infirmities have paralysed all their efforts. They are useless in God's service, for sin has rendered them without strength. The Good Physician alone can bid them Arise and Walk.

The Fever and the Issue of Blood tell of the unrest and unabated passion of sin. Nothing will avail to stay it till He rebukes the fever and staunches the issue of blood.

The Demon-possessed are those in whom sin, passion, and lust rage with unrestrained fury, a curse to themselves and a danger to others. Only Jesus can cast out the foul demons so that they will be found in their right mind, clothed and seated at His feet.

The Dead in Trespasses and Sins are those who, being dead towards God, are dead while they live. Only One voice can call the dead to eternal life (John 5. 25).

3. THE MEDICINES USED BY THE GOOD PHYSICIAN.

The Balm of Gilead (Jer. 8. 22 and 51. 8) is one.   Another is *Oil and Wine*, that the Good Samaritan poured into the wounds of the man fallen among thieves.

There are also *Leaves from the Tree of Life*, which have always proved effective for the healing of the nations (Rev. 22. 2).

Bunyan makes Dr. Skill employ pills compounded " Ex Carne et Sanguine Christi," to be taken with a proportionable quantity of salt in half a quarter of a pint of the tears of repentance.

These signify the Word of God applied by the Spirit of God with the Efficacy of the Blood of Christ received with true repentance and faith, as the remedy for all spiritual ills.

4. "THEY THAT BE WHOLE."   Are there any such in this sin-stricken world ?   No, there is none righteous, no, not one. Alas ! there are many, and it is to these the Lord referred, who have never seen their true state, as sinners guilty and sin-stricken.   Because they are unawakened they think they are whole, and have therefore no need of Christ.

They are the same as the " ninety and nine that went not astray " in the Parable of the Lost Sheep.   There are really none such, for all have gone astray (Isa. 53. 6, Rom. 3. 12).   Alas ! some are self-righteous, and so never come to the Physician.

5. "THEY THAT ARE SICK."   Not only sick in sin, but sick of sin, weary of it, longing to be free from it.   It is such that will gladly turn to the Great Healer: " Blessed are they that hunger and thirst after righteousness, for they shall be filled."

> " The Great Physician now is near,
>   The sympathizing Jesus.
> He speaks the drooping heart to cheer:
>   O hear the voice of Jesus."

VI. Application :

There is a Physician for the sin-sick — One Who can save us from sin.   Go to Him.

Bring no price: He heals for nothing.

Come at once, for diseases neglected mean death.   " Sin when it is finished bringeth forth death."

The Friend of Sinners

I. Text. "The Son of man came eating and drinking, and they say, Behold a man gluttonous, and a winebibber, a friend of publicans and sinners" (Matt. 11. 19).

II. The Main Lesson. Sinners have few friends. They have companions in evil who encourage them in their sins, but forsake them when they are in trouble.

The Lord Jesus is the True Friend of all sinners in that He desires their good, seeks their salvation, and never changes in His love to them, nor will until He brings them home to glory.

What His enemies reproached Him with He glories in. He is the Friend of Sinners.

III. Scriptures to Study : Luke 7. 39-50.

v. 39. *The Pharisee Objects to the Sinful Woman Touching Christ.* "When the Pharisee which had bidden Him saw it, he spake within himself, saying, This man, if He were a prophet, would have perceived who and what manner of woman this is which toucheth Him: that she is a sinner."

vv. 40-42. *Jesus Asks the Pharisee a Question.* "And Jesus answering said unto him, Simon, I have somewhat to say unto thee. And he saith, Master, say on. There was a certain creditor which had two debtors: the one owed him five hundred pence, and the other fifty. And when they had nothing to pay, he frankly forgave them both. Tell me therefore which of them will love him most."

v. 43. *The Pharisee Answers Rightly.* "Simon answered, I suppose that he to whom he forgave most. And He said unto him, Thou hast rightly judged."

vv. 44-46. *Jesus Calls Attention to the Woman's Devotion.* "And He turned to the woman, and said unto Simon, Seest thou this woman? I entered into thine house, thou gavest Me no water for My feet: but she hath washed

My feet with tears, and wiped them with the hairs of her head. Thou gavest Me no kiss: but this woman since the time I came in hath not ceased to kiss My feet. My head with oil thou didst not anoint: but this woman hath anointed My feet with ointment."

v. 47. *Jesus says it was because she was Forgiven much.* "Wherefore I say unto thee, Her sins, which are many, are forgiven; for she loved much: but to whom little is forgiven, the same loveth little."

vv. 48-50. *He Pronounces her Forgiven and Saved, and bids her go in Peace.* "And He said unto her, Thy sins are forgiven. . . . Thy faith hath saved thee; go in peace."

IV. Some Sinners the Lord Befriended.

1. THE WOMAN WHO WAS A SINNER (Luke 7. 37-50, as above). Recognizing her tears of repentance and devotion to His person, He pronounces her remission and salvation and sends her away in peace.

2. THE WOMAN TAKEN IN SIN (John 8. 3-11). Bidding those without sin cast the first stone at her and thus calling down judgment on those who called for judgment on her, He tells her he does not condemn her, for He had not come to judge but to save, and bids her go and sin no more.

3. MARY MAGDALENE. "A certain woman which had been healed of evil spirits and infirmities . . . out of whom went seven devils" (Luke 8. 2), who stood by the Cross (John 19. 25), and who was the first to whom the Lord Jesus appeared in resurrection (Mark 16. 9).

4. THE WOMAN OF SAMARIA, who had had five husbands, and was living with another not her husband (John 4. 18), to whom He gave the living water.

5. THE THIEF ON THE CROSS, who confessed the justice of his condemnation and appealed to the Lord, "Lord, remember me when Thou comest into Thy Kingdom." To whom the Lord replied, "This day shalt thou be with Me in Paradise" (Luke 23. 43).

*   *   *   *   *

The Lord seemed to show special compassion to women who had the reputation of being immoral, as in the above cases.

Was it that He knew their frailty; the strength of passion; the fierceness of temptation and the awful cruelty and selfishness of lustful men ?

At any rate, He befriended them when all others, with hypocritical self-righteousness, despised them.

V. Marks of a True Friend.

(1) *He shows Pity to his Friend* (Job 6. 14).

(2) *He Loves at all Times* (Prov. 17. 17).

(3) *And is Born for Adversity* (Prov. 17. 17).

(4) *Sticketh Closer than a Brother* (Prov. 18. 24).

(5) *Is Faithful to Rebuke* (Prov. 27. 6: " Faithful are the wounds of a friend ").

(6) *Is Sweet in Hearty Counsel* (Prov. 27. 9), like ointment and perfume, rejoicing the heart.

(7) *Sharpens his Countenance* (Prov. 27. 6), as iron sharpeneth iron.

(8) *Shows himself Friendly* (Prov. 18. 24), and so maintains the friendship.

(9) *The Greatest Love to a Friend is to Die for Him* (John 15. 13).

(10) *Friendship to Christ* shown by obedience to His commands (John 15. 14).

(11) *A Friend is Admitted to Secrets* (John 15. 15) that servants are not allowed to hear (Gen. 18. 17, Psa. 25. 14).

(12) *Gives his Friend of his Best*, as Jonathan did to David (1 Sam. 18. 1-4), and stands up for him (19. 4).

(13) *Loves to the End* (John 13. 1), for Love never faileth.

VI. Other Lessons on Friendship.

1. BROTHER, NEIGHBOUR AND FRIEND. All these titles are assumed by the Lord Jesus. He is not ashamed to call us brethren (Heb. 2. 11). He was neighbour to us who fell among thieves (Luke 10. 36), and He calls us His friends (John 15. 15). Let us see to it that we show ourselves friendly to this our Lover and Friend.

2. THE LORD EATING WITH SINNERS. We must not think He was a companion with them in their ribaldry and foolish talking and jesting. He would never have gone among them to encourage them in folly or sin.

He was there to rebuke (as He did Simon, so gracefully and tenderly), to teach and to win.

He was among them as a doctor is among patients in a hospital—not as one of them, but there to do them good and heal them.

3. IN FOLLOWING HIS EXAMPLE let none make it an excuse to join in the feasting, frivolity and vanity of the worldly. If you are bidden to a feast and are disposed to go, see that you are about your Master's business; that you go as a Christian and witness for Christ; that you do not demean yourself to join in anything unworthy of the Name you bear.

Christ, though the friend of sinners, was holy and so separate from sinners in *Character*, and ever about His Father's business, and so separate from them in *Conduct and Conversation*. Yet their truest friend.

4. THE LORD NEVER EXCUSED SIN or apologized for it in any case. Though compassionate to the sinner, He always treated sin as the abominable thing which God hates. It was always " Go, and sin no more."

One who sympathizes with sin is never the true friend of the sinner.

" Faithful are the wounds of a Friend."

5. A FRIEND IS A HELPER. Sympathy is not enough. So the Lord is the True Friend in that He holds out the helping hand to the fallen, so that they may recover themselves. He gives them repentance to the acknowledgment of the truth to this end.

So that the sinner can say:

> " He lifted Me, He lifted Me—
> From sin and shame He lifted me."

6. A FRIEND IS A CONFIDANT. One to whom we may entrust the secrets of the heart; may uncover our deepest shame and sorrow; knowing that he will give true and

faithful counsel, not sparing in love, yet abundant in sympathy and wise advice.

And the friend tells of his plans too. So the Lord said, " I have called you friends; for all things that I have heard of My Father I have made known unto you " (John 15. 15).

7. A FRIEND IS GOOD COMPANY. Like ointment and perfume, he rejoices the heart; and as iron sharpens iron, so he sharpens the countenance of his friend.

That is a poor man who has no such friend.

One learns more of spiritual things by godly conversation with a friend than in any other way.

8. A FRIEND LOVES AT ALL TIMES RIGHT TO THE END. When adversity comes he does not desert nor turn traitor. When all men turn against his friend he stands by him to the end.

A man charged wrongfully with a crime had three friends.

The first, on hearing of his disgrace, deserted him.

The second went to the court door and wished him a successful issue.

The third went in with him, pleaded his cause, testified to his character and brought him out in happiness, against all accusers.

VII. Application.

Seek the Friend of sinners.

Cultivate His friendship.

Be the friend of sinners, too, as much as in you lies.

OUTLINE

Our Friend
{
Feels for our infirmities and is
Faithful to His promises.
Forgives our transgressions.
Fights our battles.
Forgets our backslidings.
Furnishes our table.
Feasts with us.
Frees us from bondage.
Fulfils His word.
Finishes the work.
}

SECTION III.

Our Lord Jesus Christ:
His Testimony to the Truth

BEHOLD THE MAN !

Tune G.B. 529

They platted Thee a crown of thorn,
And placed it on Thy head;
A purple robe with bitter scorn,
Thy sceptre was a reed.
" Behold the Man !   Behold your King !"
Was Pilate's mocking cry, Lord;
" Thou hast redeemed us," loud we sing,
And own Thee King most High, Lord.

They led Thee from the judgment hall,
And nailed Thee to the tree;
They gave Thee mingled wine and gall,
And mocked Thine agony.
" Father, forgive them," was Thy prayer,
" 'Tis finished," was Thy cry, Lord.
Thou hast redeemed us dying there,
And art gone upon high, Lord.

Now seated on Thy throne to reign,
Thy shame and suffering past,
Thou soon wilt surely come again,
The hour approaches fast.
" Behold, I come," will be Thy call,
" Behold the Bridegroom nigh," Lord.
Thy saints who love Thee, one and all,
Shall meet Thee in the sky, Lord.

O ye who turn away from light,
For that great day prepare,
Lest coming as a thief by night
It take you unaware.
" Behold the Lamb " for sinners slain.
What grace to us is shown, Lord !
When Thou at length shalt come again,
We too shall share Thy throne, Lord !

Our Lord's Testimony to His Death

I. **Text.** " Except a corn of wheat fall into the ground and die, it abideth alone: but if it die, it bringeth forth much fruit " (John 12. 24).

II. **Main Lesson.** The Lord anticipated His death. It was for that cause He had come into the world, to put away sin by the sacrifice of Himself. He announced beforehand its character, its value, and the blessed results that would flow from it.

He taught all that was afterwards written in the Epistles concerning His death.

III. **Scripture to Study.** Psalm 22, which is the Lord speaking in prophecy. It may be said to be *the account of the Crucifixion by the Crucified One Himself*. We are allowed to see what passed through His mind as He hung there.

Some think He repeated the whole of the Psalm on the Cross. His cry, " My God, My God, why hast Thou forsaken Me ?" was the first verse. His later cry, " It is finished," follows the last verse, " He hath done it " (R.V.).

vv. 1-2. *He Complains of God Forsaking Him and being Silent to His Prayer.* " My God, My God, why hast Thou forsaken Me ? . . . far from helping Me . . . I cry . . . Thou hearest not."

v. 3. *He Justifies God.* " But Thou art holy, O Thou who inhabitest the praises of Israel."

vv. 4-5. *The Fathers Cried and were Delivered.* " Our fathers trusted in Thee . . . and Thou didst deliver them. They cried . . . and were not confounded."

vv. 6-8. *He is a Worm—a Reproach and Despised— Mocked.* " But I am a worm, and no man; a reproach of men, and despised of the people. All . . . laugh me to

131

scorn . . . saying, He trusted on the Lord . . . let Him
deliver Him, seeing He delighted in Him."

vv. 9-11. *Yet He had Hoped from Birth in God.* "Thou
didst make Me hope when I was upon My mother's breasts.
I was cast upon Thee from the womb."

vv. 12-13. *He is Surrounded by Enemies.* "Many bulls
have compassed Me. . . . They gaped on Me . . . as a
roaring lion."

vv. 14-15. *His Physical Distress.* "I am poured out
like water . . . My heart is like wax . . . melted in the
midst of My bowels. My strength is dried up . . . tongue
cleaveth to My jaws . . . brought into the dust of
death."

vv. 16-17. *Hands and Feet Pierced.* "Dogs have compassed Me . . . they pierced My hands and My feet.
I may tell all My bones: they look and stare upon Me."

v. 18. *Garments Parted among Them and Lots Cast.*
"They part My garments among them, and cast lots upon
My vesture."

vv. 19-21. *He Prays for Deliverance.* "Be not far from
Me, O Lord. . . . Deliver My soul. . . . Save Me from
the lion's mouth."

v. 22. *The Triumph after Death—in Ever-widening
Circles.* "I will declare Thy Name unto My brethren:
in the midst of the congregation will I praise Thee."

v. 25. "My praise shall be in the great congregation."

v. 27. "All the ends of the world shall remember and
turn to the Lord . . . all kindreds worship."

v. 28. The Kingdom is the Lord's; He is Governor among
the nations."

v. 30. "A seed shall serve Him."

v. 31. *A People to be Born Shall Hear of His Righteousness and Finished Work.* "They shall come, and shall
declare His righteousness unto a people that shall be born,
that He hath done this."

IV. What the Lord said as to His Death.

1. It was NECESSARY to the accomplishment of His
work of Salvation.

John 3. 14. "The Son of Man must be lifted up."

John 12. 24. " Verily, verily, I say unto you, Except a corn of wheat fall into the ground and die, it abideth alone: but if it die, it bringeth forth much fruit."

2. It was PREDETERMINED of God.

John 10. 18. " No man taketh (My life) from Me, but I lay it down of Myself. I have power (authority) to lay it down, and I have power to take it again. This commandment have I received of My Father."

This bears out what the Apostles afterwards taught: that His death was by the determinate counsel and fore-knowledge of God (Acts 2. 23, 4. 28).

3. It was in FULFILMENT OF SCRIPTURE.

Luke 24. 25. " O fools and slow of heart to believe all that the prophets have spoken: Ought not Christ to have suffered these things, and to enter into His glory ?" Verse 46: " Thus it is written, and thus it behoved Christ to suffer, and to rise from the dead the third day."

(See Acts 13. 27, 29 and 33.)

4. It was A RANSOM.

Matthew 20. 28. " The Son of Man came . . . to give His life a ransom for many."

(See also Mark 10. 45 and 1 Tim. 2. 6.)

That is, a price paid for the release of the captive.

5. It was for THE REMISSION OF SINS.

Matthew 26. 28. " This is the Blood of the New Testament, which is shed for many for the remission of sins."

It is on this ground we are said to be " Justified by His Blood."

6. It was to BRING US LIFE.

John 10. 10-11. " I am come that they might have life, and that they might have it more abundantly. I am the Good Shepherd: the Good Shepherd giveth His life for the sheep."

John 3. 16. " For God so loved the world that He gave His Only Begotten Son, that whosoever believeth in Him should not perish, but have everlasting life."

7. It was to Cleanse from Sin.

John 13. 8. " If I wash thee not, thou hast no part with Me."

John 13. 10. " He that is washed . . . is clean every whit."

This agrees with 1 John 1. 7—" The Blood of Jesus Christ His Son cleanseth us from all sin "; and Hebrews 10. 14— " By One offering He hath perfected for ever them that are sanctified."

8. It was the Blood of the Covenant.

Mark 14. 24. " This (cup) is My Blood of the New Covenant, which is shed for many."

9. It is the Drawing Power of the world.

John 12. 32. " I, if I be lifted up from the earth, will draw all men unto Me. This He said, signifying what death He should die."

10. He described in advance the Manner of Death He would die.

Matthew 20. 18. " Behold, we go up to Jerusalem; and the Son of Man shall be betrayed unto the chief priests and unto the scribes, and they shall condemn Him to death, and shall deliver Him to the Gentiles to mock, and to scourge, and to crucify Him; and the third day He shall rise again." (See also Matt. 17. 22-23.)

V. **Other Lessons** from the Study.

1. Modern Ideas Refuted. The suggestion that the Lord never taught the subjective theory of the Atonement is refuted by the above Scriptures, as also is the modern theory that redemption by Blood is Pauline theology. Nothing of what the Epistles teach is without its foundation in the teaching of the Lord. Jesus taught that His death was a ransom by which forgiveness and life come to the believer.

2. Death before Fruit. The Lord taught this plainly. The corn of wheat must fall into the ground and die ere it brought forth fruit. So in the Psalm. There the sufferer was brought into the dust of death (or as some think it means " the ashes of the sacrifice ") before there is

" a seed to serve Him " (Psa. 22. 30).   But after His death
the blessing extends in ever-widening circles: " My
brethren " (22), " the great congregation " (25), and then
" all the ends of the earth " (27) tell the Kingdom is the
Lord's (28).

It is so in Isaiah 53, which the Lord said applied to Himself (Luke 22. 37).   Until the Suffering Substitute has died
and been buried (9) no fruit appears, but after that He sees
of the travail of His soul and is satisfied in the many who
are justified (11).

3. The Drawing Power. Nothing attracts the heart
of the sinner like the story of Calvary.   All sorts and conditions of men are won from sin to holiness by the fact that
the Son of God loved them and gave Himself for them.

John Newton describes how he was attracted:

> " Till a new object met my sight
> And stopped my mad career.
> I saw One hanging on a tree
> In agonies and blood."

It was this sight that turned the profligate slave-owner
into a witness for Christ and winner of souls.

Let us see that we preach Christ crucified.

VI. Application.

To the Sinner. " Behold the Lamb of God that beareth
away the sin of the world."

To the Saint. Let the love of Christ constrain you to
live unto Him Who died for you and rose again.

To the Preacher. Preach no worldly wisdom, but Christ
crucified, the wisdom of God.

Seven Figures of Christ in His Death

A Sheep before her shearers.
A Lamb led to the slaughter.
The Shepherd smitten for the sheep.
A Corn of wheat falling into the ground.
A Serpent lifted up.
Bread corn bruised.
Wine poured out.

Our Lord's Witness to His Resurrection and Coming Again

I. Text. " Why seek ye the living among the dead ? He is not here, He is risen: remember how He spake unto you when He was yet in Galilee, saying, The Son of Man must be delivered into the hands of sinful men, and be crucified, and the third day rise again " (Luke 24. 5-7).

II. Main Lesson. The Resurrection of Christ is the foundation truth of our Christian faith. " If Christ be not raised, your faith is vain " (1 Cor. 15. 17).

The Lord taught this, and again and again assured His disciples that He would rise again the third day. This He did.

Then after His resurrection He assured them He would come again and receive them to Himself. As the first was literally and physically fulfilled, so will the second be.

III. Scripture to Study : Acts 2. 22-36. Peter preaches on the day of Pentecost, the theme being the Resurrection of the Lord Jesus from the dead, the truth of which he confirms by quotations from the Old Testament Scriptures.

vv. 22-23. *He calls Israel to hear concerning Jesus.* " Ye men of Israel, hear these words; Jesus of Nazareth, a man approved of God . . . Him, being delivered by the determinate counsel and foreknowledge of God, ye have taken, and by wicked hands have crucified and slain."

v. 24. *God had Raised Him from the Dead.* " Whom God hath raised up, having loosed the pains of death: because it was not possible that He should be holden of it."

vv. 25-28. *He quotes David in Psalm 16 in Confirmation.* " For David speaketh concerning Him, I foresaw the Lord always before my face . . . therefore did my heart rejoice . . . because Thou wilt not leave my soul in Hell (R.V.

136

Hades), neither wilt Thou suffer Thine Holy One to see corruption."

vv. 29-32. *He Shows that David could not be Speaking of Himself* (since he died and saw corruption), *but of Christ.* "Men and brethren . . . the patriarch David . . . is both dead and buried, and his sepulchre is with us unto this day. Therefore being a prophet, and knowing that God had sworn . . . that He would raise up Christ to sit on his throne; he seeing this before spake of the resurrection of Christ, that His soul was not left in Hell, neither His flesh did see corruption."

v. 32. *They were Witnesses of the Fact.* "This Jesus hath God raised up, whereof we all are witnesses."

vv. 33-36. *David was not ascended, but Christ was, and had been made both Lord and Christ.* "David is not ascended into the Heavens: but he saith himself, The Lord said unto my Lord, Sit Thou on My right hand. . . .

"Therefore let all the house of Israel know assuredly, that God hath made that same Jesus, Whom ye crucified, both Lord and Christ."

IV. The Lord's References to His Resurrection.

1. Nine Times He is Reported as assuring His disciples He would rise again the third day after death—twice in Matthew (20. 19, 27. 63), three times in Mark (8. 31, 9. 31, 10. 34), three times in Luke (18. 33, 24. 7, 24. 46), and once in John (20. 9).

So that we have four independent witnesses to the fact that He foretold His resurrection—a thing no other man has or ever could do. It caused fear (Mark 9. 32) and wonder (Mark 9. 10) in the disciples, who questioned what it could mean.

2. He used Jonah as a Type of His Resurrection (Matt. 12. 40). "The sign of the prophet Jonah" was that he, coming as one risen from the dead to warn Nineveh, was a figure of Him Who would rise from the dead.

"For as Jonah was three days and three nights (part of three "day-night" periods) in the whale's belly; so shall the Son of Man be three days and three nights in the heart of the earth" (see also Luke 11. 29-30).

3. HE SPOKE OF THE TEMPLE OF HIS BODY (John 2. 18-21).
"The Jews said unto Him, What sign showest Thou unto
us . . . ? Jesus answered, Destroy this Temple, and in
three days I will raise it up. Then said the Jews, Forty
and six years was this temple in building, and wilt Thou
rear it up in three days ? But He spake of the Temple of
His body." (See also Matt. 27. 40.)

4. HE CLAIMED HIMSELF TO BE THE RESURRECTION
(John 11. 25). " I am the Resurrection and the Life: he
that believeth in Me, though he were dead, yet shall he
live: and whosoever liveth and believeth in Me shall
never die." It was He who would call the dead from their
graves (John 5. 28-29).

5. HE WOULD ALSO BE THE JUDGE IN THE GREAT DAY
(John 5. 22). "The Father judgeth no man, but hath
committed all judgment unto the Son."
Matthew 7. 22. "Many will say to Me in that day,
Lord, Lord, have we not prophesied in Thy Name . . . ?
Then will I profess unto them, I never knew you: depart
from Me, ye that work iniquity."

6. HE WOULD COME AGAIN TO RECEIVE HIS OWN (John
14. 3). " If I go and prepare a place for you, I will come
again and receive you unto Myself; that where I am, there
ye may be also."

7. AND COME IN MANIFESTATION TO HIS PEOPLE ISRAEL
(Matt. 26. 64). "Hereafter ye shall see the Son of Man
sitting on the right hand of power, and coming in the
clouds of Heaven."

(See also the great prophetic chapters, Matthew 24 and
25.)

V. Other Evidences of the Resurrection.

1. THE SCRIPTURES FORETOLD IT (John 20. 9). "As
yet they did not know the Scripture, that He must rise
again from the dead."

2. THE ANGELS REMINDED THE WOMEN OF IT (Luke 24.
6-7). " Remember how He spake unto you when He

was in Galilee, saying, The Son of Man must be . . . crucified, and the third day rise again.''

3. The Enemy Remembered It (Matt. 27. 63). '' Sir,
we remember that that deceiver said, while He was yet alive,
After three days I will rise again.''

This was in striking contrast to the disciples, who did
not remember it, and could scarce believe it when it was
announced to them.

4. The Tomb was Found Empty (Luke 24. 2-3). '' They
found the stone rolled away from the sepulchre, and they
entered in, and found not the body of Jesus.''

5. He Appeared for Forty Days after His Resurrection to Many Witnesses Chosen of God (see 1 Cor.
15. 4-8 and the Gospel accounts).

Acts 10. 40. '' Him God raised up the third day, and
showed Him openly; not to all the people, but unto witnesses chosen before of God, even to us, who did eat and
drink with Him after He rose from the dead.''

6. Both Stephen and Saul of Tarsus saw Him in
Heaven after His ascension.

Acts 7. 56. '' Behold, I see the Heavens opened, and the
Son of Man standing on the right hand of God.''

Acts 9. 5. '' And Saul said, Who art Thou, Lord ?   And
the Lord said, I am Jesus Whom thou persecutest.''

VI. **Other Lessons** from the Study.

1. A Unique Fact.   Men who are dying do not speak
of rising again in the body on the third day afterwards.
But the Lord constantly affirmed it.   The fact that He
did so is historically established beyond question, and the
fact that He rose as promised is a glorious indisputable
truth.

2. Physical Proofs.   The Lord took every occasion
to prove beyond doubt His bodily resurrection.

He ate and drank with them.

He let them handle His Body, and see the nail prints,
and feel that He had bones and flesh, and was not a mere
apparition or spirit.

He walked with them, and had long and intimate talks with them—such holy conversations that none could invent.

He rose up into the Heavens in sight of them all.

3. Paul's Unanswered Question before King Agrippa. "Why should it be thought a thing incredible with you that God should raise the dead?"

No one has ever replied to this challenge.

4. No Relics. The Buddhist has a glorious temple in which they keep a tooth of Buddha. The Mohammedan has a coffin in which is enclosed the dust of their prophet. We have a living Saviour.

5. The Glorious Hope of His Return. He who kept His promise to rise the third day from the dead actually and literally will surely keep His promise to come again in like manner as He was seen to go.

"Yet a little while, and He that shall come will come, and will not tarry."

VII. Application.

Our Saviour lives. Let us rejoice in Him and seek His face.

Our Lord is coming. Let us be as men that wait for Him.

Seven Old Testament Characters that speak of Resurrection

Seth (appointed instead of Abel slain) (Gen. 4. 25).
Enoch was not, for God took him.
Noah brought through the flood.
Isaac given back as from death (Heb. 11. 19).
Joseph raised from prison to power.
Elijah caught up without dying.
Jonah (2. 10) a type of Christ (Matt. 12. 40).

Our Lord's Testimony to the Scriptures

I. Text. "Sanctify them through Thy Truth: Thy Word is Truth " (John 17. 17).

II. Main Lesson. Our Lord Jesus sets His seal upon the Scriptures of the Prophets, what we know now as the Old Testament.

He asserted its *accuracy* and its Divine *authority*.

He quoted no other authority, and silenced His opponents by referring to it.

He confirmed its histories and recognized its typical and prophetical value.

" It is written " was to Him an end of all strife.

III. Scriptures to Study :

Matthew 5. 17. *He Came to Fulfil the Law and the Prophets*. "Think not that I am come to destroy the Law or the Prophets: I am not come to destroy, but to fulfil."

v. 18. *Not the Least of them can Fail*. "For verily I say unto you, Till Heaven and earth pass, one jot or one tittle shall in no wise pass from the Law, till all be fulfilled."

v. 19. *The Solemn Responsibility of Breaking Them*. "Whosoever therefore shall break one of these least commandments, and shall teach men so, he shall be called the least in the Kingdom of Heaven: but whosoever shall do and teach them, the same shall be called great in the Kingdom of Heaven."

Luke 24. 25-26. *Jesus after His Resurrection Attests the Scriptures*. "Then He said to them (the two disciples on the Emmaus road), O fools, and slow of heart to believe all that the prophets have spoken: Ought not Christ to have suffered these things, and to enter into His glory ?"

v. 27. *He Expounds the Old Testament* and its testimony
to Himself. "Beginning at Moses and all the prophets,
He expounded unto them in all the Scriptures the things
concerning Himself."

v. 44. *He Acknowledges the Authority of the Old Testament
Canon.* "All things must be fulfilled, which were written
in the Law of Moses, and in the Prophets, and in the Psalms,
concerning Me."

v. 45. *He Enlightens their Minds to Understand.* "Then
opened He their understanding, that they might understand the Scriptures."

IV. Our Lord's Sevenfold Attitude to the Scriptures.

1. As to the *NATURE* of them.

(*a*) They are TRUTH. John 17. 17: "Thy Word is
Truth." Notice, not merely true, but truth.

(*b*) They proceeded FROM THE MOUTH OF GOD. Matthew
4. 4: "Man shall not live by bread alone, but by every
Word that proceedeth out of the mouth of God."

(*c*) They are therefore FOOD FOR THE SOUL. It is through
the medium of them we feed upon Christ the Living Bread
(John 6. 63).

(*d*) They are ONE and INDIVISIBLE. John 10. 35: "The
Scriptures cannot be broken." This must also mean that
they are UNASSAILABLE as to their truth and accuracy.

(*e*) They are ETERNAL. Matthew 5. 18 (as above): "It
is easier for Heaven and earth to pass away than for one
tittle of the Law to fall."

(*f*) They are LIVING. [Luke 8. 11: "The seed is the
Word," having inherent life.

"The words that I speak unto you, they are spirit, and
they are life" (John 6. 63).

(*g*) They are HOLY and sanctifying in power. John
17. 17: "Sanctify them through Thy truth."

(*h*) They bring BLESSING. Luke 11. 28: "Blessed are
they that hear the Word of God, and keep it."

2. *He CONFIRMED its HISTORIES.*

He spoke of *Adam and Eve* (Matt. 19. 4; Mark 10. 6);
Abel (Matt. 23. 35); *Abraham* (John 8. 56-58); *Lot* (Luke

17. 28-29); *Lot's wife* (Luke 17. 32); *Moses* (John 5. 46);
the Israelites (Matt. 10. 6; Luke 22. 30); *Manna* (John 6. 49);
Brazen Serpent (John 3. 14); *Giving of Law* (John 7. 19);
David (Luke 20. 42); *Solomon* (Luke 11. 31, 12. 27);
Zacharias (Matt. 23. 35); *Jonah* (Matt. 12. 41); *Daniel*
(Matt. 24. 15); and others.

3. He *APPEALED to its AUTHORITY*.

" Have ye never read ?" (Mark 12. 10).

" Ye do err, not knowing the Scriptures " (Matt. 22. 29).

No less than twenty times is He reported as saying " *It
is written*," and that in a manner that showed He regarded
the fact of its being written as sufficiently establishing a
truth and settling a question.

The following quotations are introduced with the words
" It is written ":

At His Temptation He quenched all the fiery darts of
the Wicked One with these words.

Matthew 4. 4. " Man shall not live by bread alone, etc."

Matthew 4. 7. " Thou shalt not tempt the Lord thy
God."

Matthew 4. 10. " Thou shalt worship the Lord thy God."

Matthew 21. 13. " My house shall be called a house of
prayer."

Matthew 26. 24. " The Son of Man goeth as it is written
of Him."

Mark 7. 6. " This people honoureth Me with their lips."

Mark 9. 12. " The Son of Man must suffer."

Mark 9. 13. " Have done as it is written."

Luke 22. 37. " He was reckoned with the transgressors."

John 6. 31. " He gave them bread from Heaven to
eat."

John 6. 45. " Ye shall all be taught of God."

John 8. 17. " The testimony of two men is true."

John 10. 34. " I said, Ye are gods."

4. He was *ZEALOUS of their FULFILMENT*.

Seven times we read that He acted as He did "that the
Scripture might be fulfilled."

In Nazareth Synagogue (Luke 4. 2).

In choice of Judas (John 13. 18).

In submitting to arrest (Matt. 26. 54, and again in Mark 14. 49).

In allowing the disciples to escape (John 17. 12).

" I thirst " on the Cross (John 19. 28).

In foretelling the days of vengeance (Luke 21. 22).

5. He *CLAIMED to be the SUBJECT* of them.

John 5. 39. " These are they which testify of Me."

John 8. 56. " Abraham saw My day and was glad."

John 5. 24. " Moses wrote of Me."

Luke 24. 27. " The things concerning Himself."

6. He *PUT HIS OWN WORDS on an EQUALITY* with them.

John 6. 63. " The words that I speak unto you, they are spirit and they are life."

Matthew 7. 24. " Whosoever heareth these sayings of Mine and doeth them, I will liken him unto a wise man which built his house upon a rock."

John 8. 51. " Verily, verily, I say unto you, If a man keep My saying, he shall never see death."

7. He *WARNED of the FATE of those who DIS-OBEYED* them.

John 12. 48. " The Word that I have spoken unto you, the same shall judge you in the last day."

Luke 16. 31. " They have Moses and the prophets: let them hear them . . . lest they also come into this place of torment."

V. Other Lessons from the Study.

1. BEWARE OF MODERNISM. That is the teaching that disparages and makes light of the Old Testament Scriptures. Do not believe the foolish suggestion that the God of the Old Testament is different in character from Him Whom Christ manifested in the flesh. Often the most tender passages of love are in the Old Testament, and certainly the most awful words are in the New Testament. No place of torment is revealed in the Old Testament. Almost all we know of Hell comes from the lips of our Blessed Lord.

2. THE LIVING WORD AND THE WRITTEN WORD. There is a striking analogy between the Written Scriptures and Christ the Living Word.

(*a*) *Each has a Divine and a Human Nature.* The human element in the Bible is evident in that we recognize John's writings to be quite distinct from Peter's and, again, Paul's from James's—yet each is God-breathed.

A musician plays several instruments. Each has its distinctive tone and quality, but it is the same breath through each.

(*b*) Each has its part in—

Regeneration. We are born of the Spirit, yet it is by the Word of God.

Sanctification. We are sanctified by the Spirit, yet it is by the Word of God.

Liberty. Where the Spirit is there is liberty, yet Jesus said the truth shall set you free.

Peace is the fruit of the Spirit, yet it is written, " Great peace have they that love Thy Law."

(*c*) Each is *Eternal* and will never pass away.

3. THE WRITTEN WORD REVEALS THE LIVING WORD. It is in the Scriptures that we find the full-length portrait of the Lord Jesus.

We know nothing of Him except what is revealed there by the Spirit to faith.

4. THE LIVING WORD SPEAKS TO US THROUGH THE WRITTEN WORD. It is thus the sheep hear the Shepherd's voice and follow Him.

VI. Application.

Let us study the Written Word, that we may get to know the Living Word.

Let us Obey the Shepherd's voice as He speaks to us through the Scriptures.

Let us Keep the Faith, holding fast to it as the Revelation of God to men.

The Lord's Witness to the Gospel

I. Text. " Go ye into all the world and preach the Gospel to every creature " (Mark 16. 15).

II. Main Lesson. It has been well said: The Lord Jesus came not so much to preach the Gospel, but *that there might be a Gospel to preach*.

Until He had died and risen again and shed forth the Holy Ghost from Heaven, the Gospel could not be fully proclaimed to all men.

But we are told that salvation began to be spoken by the Lord (Heb. 2. 3), but only to the lost sheep of the House of Israel; but after His resurrection He bade His disciples go and preach the Gospel to every creature, waiting first for the Gift of the Holy Ghost at Pentecost.

This Gospel was that which the Apostle Paul afterwards called "My Gospel." The object of this Lesson is to prove this by showing that Paul's doctrine was precisely what the Lord Himself taught.

III. Scriptures to Study:

Luke 4. 16. *The Lord goes into the Synagogue at Nazareth.* " And He came to Nazareth, where He had been brought up: and, as His custom was, He went into the Synagogue on the Sabbath day, and stood up for to read."

v. 17. *He Reads from Isaiah* 61. 1-2. " There was delivered unto Him the book of the prophet Esaias. And when He had opened the book, He found the place where it was written (v. 18): The Spirit of the Lord is upon Me, because He hath anointed Me to preach the gospel to the poor; He hath sent Me to heal the brokenhearted, to preach deliverance to the captives, and recovering of sight to the blind, to set at liberty them that are bruised, to preach the acceptable year of the Lord " (v. 19).

v. 21. *He Announces its Fulfilment that Day.* " He began to say unto them, This day is this Scripture fulfilled in your ears."

Luke 24. 46. *The Preaching Defined.* "Thus it is written, and thus it behoved Christ to suffer, and to rise from the dead the third day: and that repentance and remission of sins should be preached in His Name to all nations."

John 3. 36. *The Responsibility of the Hearers.* "He that believeth on the Son hath everlasting life: and he that believeth not the Son shall not see life; but the wrath of God abideth on him."

IV. **What was Paul's Gospel?** Let us see what he preached, and then we shall consider if this was what the Lord Jesus taught.

Paul's Gospel as set out in the Epistle to the Romans may be stated under seven heads:

1. MAN IS A GUILTY SINNER under the judgment of God. No exception, no excuse, and no escape (Rom. 1-3).

2. HE CANNOT BE JUSTIFIED BY THE LAW, which could give the knowledge of sin, but not save (3. 20).

3. THAT A RIGHTEOUSNESS OF GOD is now revealed, apart from the Law, but witnessed by it (3. 21-22).

4. THAT SALVATION IS FOUND IN CHRIST ALONE, and in none other (5. 8-9).

5. THAT JUSTIFICATION IS BY GRACE—"Justified by Grace" (3. 24).

6. ON THE GROUND OF BLOOD—"Justified by Blood" (5. 9).

7. THROUGH FAITH IN CHRIST—"Justified by Faith" (5. 1).

V. **Did the Lord Teach These Things?** In other words, was the Lord's way of Justification and Salvation the same as that proclaimed by the Apostle? Let us take the seven points one by one.

1. DID CHRIST PRONOUNCE MAN A GUILTY SINNER UNDER JUDGMENT—without exception, excuse or escape? Without doubt He did.

To the Young Ruler He said: "*There is none good*" (Matt. 19. 17). This the Apostle seems to have had in mind when he wrote, " There is none righteous, no, not one." " There is none that doeth good."

When they told Him of the Galileans whom Herod had slaughtered and of those on whom the tower of Siloam fell, He said twice (Luke 13. 3 and 5): " *I tell you, Nay : but, except ye repent, ye shall all likewise perish.*"

His first public ministry was *Repent* (Matt. 4. 17).

His first recorded discourse to Nicodemus said: " *Except a man be born again, he cannot see the Kingdom of God* " (John 3. 3).

He said that those who did not believe were " *condemned already* " (John 3. 18).

He told us, " *Out of the heart proceed evil thoughts, murders, adulteries, fornications, thefts, false witness, blasphemies : these are the things which defile a man* " (Matt. 15. 19).

He said, " If ye, *being evil*, know how to give, etc." Moreover, He said He had come "Not to call the righteous, but *sinners*," " to seek and to save that which was *lost*."

He told the three Parables in Luke 15 of lost things —the Sheep, the Silver, and the Son, and of the Good Shepherd who sought until He found.

All these leave us in no doubt as to the Lord's teaching of man's lost estate.

2. DID CHRIST SAY THAT MAN COULD NOT BE JUSTIFIED BY THE WORKS OF THE LAW ? He certainly used the Law to give the knowledge of sin, both to the Rich Young Ruler (Matt. 19. 17) and to the Lawyer (Luke 10. 28), and the other Lawyer (Matt. 22. 37). In each of these cases He brought conviction on the heart by appealing to the Commandments.

When the Rich Young Ruler had gone away sorrowful, the disciples asked, "*Who then can be saved ?*" The Lord replied, " *With men this is impossible* " (Matt. 19. 26).

In the Sermon on the Mount the Lord said (Matt. 5. 20), "*Except your righteousness shall exceed the righteousness of the scribes and Pharisees,* ye shall in no case enter into the Kingdom of Heaven."

In Luke 17. 10 He told us, " When ye shall have done all those things which are commanded you, say, *We are unprofitable servants.*"

In the Parable of the Publican and the Pharisee, the Pharisee who boasted of his self-righteousness went away unblessed; the Publican who sought for mercy found it.

3. DID THE LORD SPEAK OF A RIGHTEOUSNESS FROM GOD UPON ALL THEM THAT BELIEVE ? He told the story of the Prodigal returning to the father, upon whom was put "*the Best Robe*" (Luke 15. 22). If this is taken with Isaiah 61. 10, "*He hath covered me with the Robe of Righteousness,*" it certainly implies a Gift of Righteousness.

He told the story of the man who came into the wedding *without a Wedding Garment* (Matt. 22. 12) and was cast out. This certainly suggests Isaiah 64. 6, "*All our righteousnesses are as filthy rags*"; that in them we cannot appear before God, but must receive at His hand "a wedding garment."

Moreover, He bade us: "Seek ye first the Kingdom of God and *His Righteousness*" (Matt. 6. 33), and promised a blessing on those who "*Hunger and Thirst after Righteousness*" (Matt. 5. 6).

4. DID THE LORD TEACH THAT SALVATION WAS IN HIMSELF ALONE ? Yes, most definitely.

"*I am the Way, the Truth, and the Life : no man cometh unto the Father but by Me*" (John 14. 6).

"I am the Door: *by Me* if any man enter in, *he shall be saved*" (John 10. 9).

"*Come unto Me, all ye that labour and are heavy laden, and I will give you rest*" (Matt. 11. 28).

"*He that eateth Me even he shall live by Me*" (John 6. 56), and "Except ye eat . . . ye have no life in you" (53).

It is unnecessary to multiply quotations; there are so many (John 3. 14-16, 36, 5. 24, etc.).

5-7. WHAT OF THE GREAT PAULINE DOCTRINE OF JUSTIFICATION—by Grace—by Blood—by Faith ? Did the Lord teach it ?

It will be sufficient to take the Parable of the Publican and the Pharisee, and to note what is said as to the Publican, of whom the Lord said, "*He went down to his house justified*" (Luke 18. 14).

It was certainly a case of God justifying the ungodly (see Rom. 4. 5).

It was of Grace—for he had no merit to plead and had done no good works. He was admittedly "the sinner," who pleaded no excuse or extenuating circumstances.

It was on the Ground of Blood—for the Publican's prayer was "God *be propitiated* to me the sinner" (13, R.V.M.) (Greek *hilasthēti*). It was the time of evening sacrifice. No doubt the Publican watched the lamb slain and its blood sprinkled, and put in his plea on that ground.

It was by Faith. He believed and rejoiced. That Salvation is *by Grace through faith* the Lord constantly taught.

The woman who was a sinner was "frankly forgiven" (gratuitously); her faith had saved her.

We need only recall the Lord's frequent repetition of the words, "Thy faith hath saved thee; go in peace."

And His constant emphasis on the words "Whosoever believeth on Him" should not perish—and the dictum, "All things are possible to him that believeth."

He definitely affirmed, "*This is the work of God, that ye believe on Him Whom He hath sent*" (John 6. 29).

VI. Other Lessons from the Study.

1. ALL THE TEACHING OF THE APOSTLE PAUL has its foundation in that of the Lord. He taught no doctrine the seed-thought of which is not found in the teaching of Christ.

Beware of those false prophets who talk of Pauline doctrine as in conflict with the supreme morality of the Lord's Sermon on the Mount. It is the result of prejudice and ignorance; a close study of the Lord's teaching does not bear it out.

2. THE GOSPEL IS GOOD NEWS. There is no good news in legal teaching. The Law made nothing perfect: to preach it to sinners is to deprive them of all hope, for by the works of the Law shall no flesh be justified. The ministry of the Law is a ministry of condemnation and death (2 Cor. 3. 7 and 9).

The good news is that the Son of God loved me and gave Himself for me, and lives to be my Lord, Saviour, High Priest and Friend.

3. GRACE—BLOOD—FAITH. These are the greatest words in the Bible; to understand their meaning aright is to know the Salvation of God.

They are the true ringing notes of the Gospel bells. An address that does not sound them is not a Gospel address. Nor does it obey the command of the Lord, " Go and preach the Gospel to every creature."

VII. Application.

Ponder the Lord's teaching closely lest a superficial reading of it should mislead us.

Compare the Apostle's teaching with that of the Master, that it may be rightly understood.

Seek first " His righteousness."

OUTLINE

The GOSPEL is

G   Good news of
    God's Grace to
    Guilty men.
O   Offered to all and
    Obeyed by faith.
S   Salvation by a
    Substitutionary Sacrifice.
P   Peace and Pardon proclaimed through
    Propitiation.
E   Eternal Life given to
    Everyone that believeth, with
L   Light, Liberty and Love.

Our Lord's Teaching as to the Christian Life

I. Text. "Abide in Me and I in you. As the branch cannot bear fruit of itself, except it abide in the vine; no more can ye, except ye abide in Me " (John 15. 4).

II. Main Lesson. The Christian life must be guided by the teaching of Christ.

To live as a true Christian one must follow Christ—that is, hear and obey Him.

This Lesson is an attempt to give a broad general outline of the character of the life that the Lord sets before His disciples.

That it is exactly similar to that afterwards unfolded in detail in the Epistles goes without saying.

It is a contrast to that under Law, since the Christian is not under the Law, but under Grace.

It is spiritual rather than legal.

Its true characteristic is holiness or likeness to Christ inwrought by the operation of the Holy Spirit as we abide in Christ.

III. Scripture to Study.

1. THE DESCRIPTION OF THE BLESSED MAN (Matt. 5. 1-12).

vv. 3-5. *The Poor in Spirit—Mourners and Meek.*
" Blessed are the poor in spirit: for their's is the kingdom of Heaven.

" Blessed are they that mourn: for they shall be comforted.

" Blessed are the meek: for they shall inherit the earth."

vv. 6-9. *The Hungry after Righteousness—Merciful, Pure in Heart and Peacemakers.* " Blessed are they that do hunger and thirst after righteousness: for they shall be filled.

" Blessed are the merciful: for they shall obtain mercy.

" Blessed are the pure in heart: for they shall see God.

" Blessed are the peacemakers: for they shall be called the children of God."

vv. 10-12. *The Persecuted are to Rejoice.* " Blessed are they which are persecuted for righteousness' sake: for their's is the kingdom of Heaven.

" Blessed are ye when men shall revile you . . . for My sake. Rejoice, and be exceeding glad: for great is your reward in Heaven."

2. THE SOURCE OF THE NEW LIFE (John 15. 4).

v. 4. " Abide in Me, and I in you. As the branch cannot bear fruit of itself, except it abide in the vine; no more can ye, except ye abide in Me."

v. 5. *Without Christ we can do Nothing.* " I am the Vine, ye are the branches: he that abideth in Me, and I in him, the same bringeth forth much fruit: for without Me ye can do nothing."

v. 7. *The Words of the Lord to be Observed.* " If ye abide in Me, and My words abide in you, ye shall ask what ye will, and it shall be done unto you."

v. 8. *The Father Glorified in our Fruitfulness.* " Herein is My Father glorified, that ye bear much fruit; so shall ye be My disciples."

v. 9. *We must Abide in His Love.* " As the Father hath loved Me, so have I loved you: continue ye in My love."

v. 10. *Obedience is Abiding.* " If ye keep My commandments, ye shall abide in My love; even as I have kept My Father's commandments, and abide in His love."

IV. The Nature of the New Life as Taught by Christ.

1. HE REPUDIATED ALL THE WORLD'S IDEALS.

(*a*) *The Warrior in Shining Armour* (Matt. 5. 38-48) finds no place in His teaching. It is the meek who inherit the earth—those who resist not evil and do not seek their own, or avenge themselves. The ideal of the Roman is rejected.

The Crusades were not only a hopeless failure, but were the result of a false conception of Christianity. They that take the sword perish by it.

(b) *The Pursuit of Wealth* (Matt. 6. 19). The Lord showed the folly of it in the Parables of the Rich Fool (Luke 12. 16), Dives and Lazarus (Luke 16. 19), and by His teaching after the Rich Young Ruler had gone away sorrowful (Luke 18. 24), and His warning, "What shall it profit a man if he gain the whole world and lose his own soul?" (Matt. 16. 26).

(c) *The Vain Ambition of Life* (Matt. 20. 20-28, John 5. 44). Those who seek place and honour of men are rebuked. To be great is to be the lowly servant of all.

(d) *Piety and Religion* (Matt. 6. 1-7, 7. 22) as an end in themselves. To be seen of men, to be called Rabbi, to become professional religionists either for gain or power or praise. True piety is a means to an end, not an end in itself. The "religious," as they are called, err in this. All dressed-up religion is offensive.

2. Christian Life is Founded on Redemption. It must begin with *Reconciliation* to God by the precious Blood of Christ.

The Lord came to give His life a Ransom for many. He must die that we might live (see Lesson 12).

In His Name *Remission* is preached (Luke 24. 47), and until a sinner has been purged from sin he has no part or lot with Christ (John 13. 8).

3. The New Life Begins with the New Birth. This the Lord taught in unmistakable terms (John 3. 3). "Verily, verily, I say unto you, Except a man be born again, he cannot see the Kingdom of Heaven."

The Lord promised the Holy Spirit, the Comforter, and those who believed in Him would receive that Gracious Gift and be quickened to new life.

This was what Peter proclaimed on the Day of Pentecost: "Repent and be baptized, every one of you, for the remission of sins, and ye shall receive the Gift of the Holy Ghost." All who receive Christ receive the Spirit, so that every true believer is born of the Spirit.

4. The New Life is Lived by Faith. Faith that *abides in Christ*. The Lord constantly called for Faith.

When the Pharisees asked, "What shall we do that we

might work the works of God?" He replied, "This is the work of God, that ye believe in Him whom He hath sent."

He said, " Ye believe in God, believe also in Me."

He told us that nothing was impossible to faith, but warned us that without Him we could " do nothing." He represented Faith as a *continuing principle*, a life-long attitude. His great illustration was the Vine and its branches. Fruit—that is, spiritual life, the Fruit of the Spirit—can be produced only by the branch abiding in the Vine. He is the Vine, we are the branches.

5. THE IMPORTANT THING IN LIFE IS CHARACTER. It is not in possessions, not what a man has, but what he is. Purity, Truth, Humility and Love are the things that please God.

> " O God of Truth, for Whom we long,
>   Thou who wilt hear our prayer,
> Do Thine own battle in our heart,
>   And slay the falsehood there."

6. TRUE NOBILITY LIES IN SACRIFICE AND LOWLY SERVICE. This He enforced by His example.

He set a child in the midst, and bade us humble ourselves as that little child.

He washed the disciples' feet, and taught us thus by love to serve one another.

He laid down His life a Ransom for us, and the Apostle John tells us we ought to lay down our lives for the brethren.

7. WE MUST ALL APPEAR BEFORE HIM. We must all be manifested at the Judgment Seat of Christ, and give an account of ourselves and our deeds.

Again and again the Lord warned us that He would come and take account of His servants, and that His reward or censure would be given to each of His servants as he deserved.

So He taught the solemn responsibility and accountability of life.

Such, then, is the Teaching of Christ on the manner of the Christian's life.

V. Other Lessons from the Study.

1. KIND, NOT DEGREE. The Christian life is not a *better* life, but a *different* kind of life. It is a new creation,

a different nature—not an *improved* man, but a *new* man.

A Child of God is not like other men, only kinder and more moral; he is utterly other than they in species (1 John 5. 19).

Therefore a *moral* change does not make a man a Christian, nor does *religion* make him one. Wicked and unregenerate men have often been very pious. Many of the Popes were vile and immoral men, while at the head of the world's religion.

The new birth is the entrance upon a new creation.

2. Not Effort, but Faith. A man cannot, then, become a Christian by effort. It is the work of God in him.

He cannot blot out his sin, or cover his guilt; only God can justify and remit sin.

Faith brings us to God, Who for Christ's sake forgives, and gives the Spirit whereby we are born from above.

3. The Work of Faith. While Salvation is "*not of works*," it is "*unto good works*." God created us unto good works (Eph. 2. 9-10).

Even our works after regeneration must be faith-works —that is, wrought in God—the result of the obedience of faith in Christ.

The energy of the flesh will produce no good fruit. Good works flow from abiding in Christ.

4. The Beauty of the Christian Life. The Beauty lies in this, that Christ is formed in us.

> " Let the Beauty of Jesus be seen in me,
>   All His wondrous compassion and purity."

It is not copying Christ, but His likeness reproduced in us by the Spirit.

Holiness is Christlikeness.

When the work is complete, we shall be like Him, the purpose being to fit us to be His companions throughout eternity.

VI. Application.

Let us see that we are not satisfied with a mere moral and religious change, but are truly born again.

Let us walk by faith in love, self-denial and good works.

OUTLINES

What is a Christian ?

A New Creature because of his second birth (2 Cor. 5. 17).
A Child of God by Adoption (Rom. 3. 16).
A Son of God by Separation (2 Cor. 6. 18).
An Heir of God by Inheritance (Rom. 8. 17).
A Saint because of his holiness (Rom. 1. 7).
A Believer because of his Faith (Acts 5. 14).
A Brother because of his Love (Phil. 16).
A Servant because of his Labour (Rom. 6. 22).
A Friend because of his Obedience (John 15. 14).
A Witness because of his Testimony (Acts 1. 8).
A Branch because of his Fruitfulness (John 15. 5).
A Temple because of the Indwelling Spirit (2 Cor. 6. 16).
A Pilgrim because not of this world (1 Pet. 2. 11).
A Steward because put on trust (1 Pet. 4. 10).
A Living Stone because on the Rock (1 Pet. 2. 5).
A Priest because of his Worship (1 Pet. 2. 5 and 9).
A Christian because of his Confession (1 Pet. 4. 6).

How does He Live ?

By Faith in the Son of God (Gal. 2. 20).
By every Word from God (Matt. 4. 4).
By feeding upon Christ (John 6. 57).
In the Spirit (Gal. 5. 25).
By mortifying the deeds of the body (Rom. 8. 13).
By being spiritually minded (Rom. 8. 6).
To the Will of God (1 Pet. 4. 2).

Christ's Witness to the Church

I. Text. " I will build My Church " (Matt. 16. 18).

II. Main Lesson. Christ made known His purpose to build a Church. He used the word only three times (Matt. 16. 18 and 18. 17), but gave the keynote, the full truth of which was afterwards developed by the Apostle Paul by special revelation (Eph. 3. 1-10).

Some of the underlying principles of it were enlarged upon in the three chapters of Matthew (16-18) which we are considering.

III. Scriptures to Study :

Matthew 16. 13-20. *The Lord Announces His Purpose to Build a Church.*

v. 13. *At Cæsarea He asks Whom Men said He was.* " When Jesus came into the coasts of Cæsarea Philippi, He asked His disciples, saying, " Whom do men say that I the Son of Man am ? "

v. 14. *The Disciples Name Various Persons.* " They said, Some say, John the Baptist: some, Elias; and others Jeremias, or one of the prophets."

v. 15. *Jesus asks, Whom do ye say?* " He saith unto them, But whom say ye that I am ? "

v. 16. *Peter Confesses Jesus as Christ.* " And Simon Peter answered and said, Thou art the Christ, the Son of the Living God."

v. 17. *Jesus Blesses Peter for his Confession.* Jesus said, " Blessed art thou, Simon Bar-Jona: for flesh and blood hath not revealed it unto thee, but My Father which is in Heaven."

v. 18. *He Promises to Build His Church.* " I say also unto thee, That thou art Peter, and upon this rock I will build My Church; and the gates of Hell shall not prevail against it."

v. 19. *He gives Peter the Keys of the Kingdom.* " And

I give unto thee the keys of the kingdom of Heaven; and whatsoever thou shalt bind on earth shall be bound in Heaven: and whatsoever thou shalt loose on earth shall be loosed in Heaven."

Matthew 18. 15-20. *The Lord Instructs as to a Local Church.*

v. 15. *A Trespassing Brother is to be Gained.* "If thy brother shall trespass against thee, go and tell him his fault between thee and him alone: if he shall hear thee, thou hast gained thy brother."

v. 16. *If he will not Hear, others to Go.* "But if he will not hear thee, then take with thee one or two more, that in the mouth of two or three witnesses every word may be established."

v. 17. *If he Neglect this, the Church to be Told.* "And if he shall neglect to hear them, tell it unto the Church: but if he neglect to hear the Church, let him be unto thee as a heathen man and a publican."

v. 18. *The Promise Repeated.* "Verily, I say unto you, whatsoever ye shall bind on earth shall be bound in Heaven: and whatsoever ye shall loose on earth shall be loosed in Heaven."

v. 19. *Where Two Agree the Request is Granted.* "Again I say unto you, That if two of you shall agree on earth as touching anything that they shall ask, it shall be done for them of My Father which is in Heaven."

v. 20. *The Lord is Present with Two or Three.* "For where two or three are gathered together in My Name, there am I in the midst of them."

IV. The Discourses of the Gospel of Matthew.

There are *Five Discourses* in this Gospel, each of which is terminated with the expression, "*When Jesus had ended these sayings*" (see 7. 28, 11. 1, 13. 53, 19. 1 and 26. 1).

These discourses may be described as follows:

1. THE TEACHER AND HIS DISCIPLES. Chapters 5-7, called the "Sermon on the Mount."

2. THE MASTER AND HIS SERVANTS. Chapter 10, showing the cost of discipleship.

3. THE KING AND HIS SUBJECTS. Chapter 13, the Seven Parables of the Kingdom.

4. THE HEAD OF THE CHURCH AND HIS MEMBERS. Chapters 16-18, teaching how they should act.

5. THE JUDGE AND HIS CREATURES. Chapters 24 and 25, telling of the last days.

It is of the fourth of these that we are now writing.

V. **Our Lord's Teaching as to the Church.** The word Church (*Ecclesia*) means an outcalling. The Lord purposed " *to take out a people for His Name* " (Acts 15. 14), a people for His own possession (Titus 2. 14, R.V.), from Jew and Gentile, and form them into One Body, of which He Himself is the Head.

He likens it to a Temple built of Living Stones, of which He Himself is the Foundation (1 Cor. 3. 11, 2 Pet. 2. 4-6). Let us notice—

1. PETER'S CONFESSION. "Thou art the Christ, the Son of the Living God."

This confession was inspired, the Father having revealed the truth to the Apostle.

The Deity of Christ is the Great Foundation Truth on which Christianity rests. If Jesus be not God, our faith falls to the ground.

2. THE ROCK ON WHICH THE CHURCH IS BUILT. Christ Himself is the Foundation (see above).

The Apostles and Prophets were those through whom the Foundation of Truth was laid. "(We) are built upon the foundation of the Apostles and Prophets, Jesus Christ Himself being the chief corner-stone " (Eph. 2. 20).

Some think that this " rock " referred to Peter himself as one of those through whom the truth was first made known. Others that the rock was the great foundation truth he had confessed—the Deity of Christ.

That Christ is the Rock on which the Church is built is clear from 1 Corinthians 3. 11, " Other foundation can no man lay than that is laid, which is Jesus Christ."

3. THE KEYS OF THE KINGDOM. Keys represent knowledge (Luke 11. 52), authority and power (Rev. 1. 18).

The Apostle Peter had the privilege of opening the Door of Faith first to the Jews (at Pentecost), then to the Gentiles (in the house of Cornelius). He describes the privilege thus: " *Ye know how that a good while ago God made choice among us, that the Gentiles by my mouth should hear the Word of the Gospel, and believe* " (Acts 15. 7).

These keys are now placed in the hands of all Spirit-filled men for the work to which God has called them.

No caste of priests (a thing unknown in the New Testament) has a monopoly of them.

4. BINDING AND LOOSING. This privilege, first given to Peter (16. 19) and then to all the disciples (18. 18), is now the privilege of all believers, who may exercise it under the guidance of the Holy Spirit only, whether personally, or as elders in an Assembly, or as preachers declaring the remission of sins and liberty to all who believe in the Lord Jesus Christ.

5. THE REBUKE TO PETER. "Get thee behind Me, Satan " (22) shows that Peter, acting after the flesh, was no privileged person. So long as he " savoured the things of men " he was but the instrument of the enemy.

6. THE THREE INCIDENTS OF CHAPTER XVII.

The Transfiguration of Christ (vv. 1-13),

The Failure of the Disciples to cast out the demon from the lunatic boy (14-21), and

The Payment of Tribute (24-27).

Each has its lesson to teach to the Churches:

" *To Hear Him* " (5) who was there transfigured before them.

To know that *apart from Him they could do nothing.* Faith in Him alone could enable them (20).

To be *subject to the powers that be* (27).

These were necessary lessons for all the Churches.

7. THE LESSONS FROM CHAPTER XVIII.

(*a*) *The Great Lesson of Humility* to be learned from a child (4).

(*b*) *The Responsibility to Receive the Child* (5) and the solemn warning against stumbling or despising one such.

(c) *The Manner of Settling Disputes* (15-18). First going to the offended brother alone to win him if possible; then taking two or three others to establish the truth; and then to bring the matter before the Local Assembly.

(d) The *Simple Definition of a Local Assembly*—one of the Churches of the Saints (20): " *Where two or three are gathered together in My Name, there am I in the midst of them.*"

(e) *The Grace of Forgiveness*—even to seventy times seven (21-22).

(f) *The Solemn Parable*, enforcing the importance of a forgiving spirit (23-35).

VI. Other Lessons from the Study.

1. THE USE OF THE WORD CHURCH. The word is used sometimes of *the Invisible Body of Christ*, that election of Grace, consisting of every true believer, past, present and future, whose unseen Head is the Lord in Heaven, whose unseen bond of union is the Holy Spirit, who share a common life and form a Mystic Organism. This union is formed as soon as the sinner believes. To him is given the Holy Spirit by the hearing of faith (Gal. 3. 2; Acts 2. 38, 10. 44), and by that same Spirit he is baptized into the One Body (1 Cor. 12. 13).

The word is also used of the Local Gatherings of Believers in the Name of the Lord Jesus. These are called " *the Churches* (or Assemblies) *of the Saints* " (1 Cor. 14. 33), or *Churches of God* (1 Cor. 11. 16, 1 Thess. 2. 14, 2 Thess. 1. 4) —as, for example, the Seven Churches of Asia (Rev. 1. 20), amid which the Lord Jesus walked (2. 1).

The Lord used the word in its first meaning in Matthew 16. 18, and in the second sense in Matthew 18. 16-17.

2. THE NEW THING. The disciples might have asked, " Lord, what is a Church ?" for hitherto the Lord had not spoken of such a thing. He had told of a kingdom, but never of an Outcalling or Election of Grace called a Church. It was a new thing.

Yet He called it " My Church." He Himself would build it. It would be His Bride, for whom He would come. It would be hated and persecuted down the ages, but the gates of Hell would not prevail against it.

3. The Wonder of History. All has come true. The lowly man of Nazareth who foretold it was despised and rejected of men, and at last hanged on a tree and slain. But the miracle has come to pass. The Mystic Church, His Body, exists in fact. Tens of thousands of millions have been gathered home. Millions still confess His Name on earth, and there are yet more to be called out.

How glorious will be the completed Church when, perfected and glorified, He presents it to Himself as a chaste virgin (2 Cor. 11. 2), perfect (Col. 1. 28), holy and unblameable, His Bride !

The last pages of the Bible picture the great manifestation when the Bride, the Lamb's wife, is seen descending out of Heaven, and adorned to meet her Heavenly Bridegroom.

4. The Universal, Invisible Church is described in glowing terms in Hebrews 12. 22-24. To this we have come by faith. It is into this that we were baptized by the Spirit on believing.

VII. Application.

See that we belong to the True Church, the Mystic Body of Christ. Let us make our calling and election sure.

Let us walk holily and take our place in the Assembly, accepting its responsibility and enjoying its privileges.

Churches in Private Houses

Priscilla and Aquila (Rom. 16. 3 and 1 Cor. 16. 19).
Nymphas (Col. 4. 15).
Philemon (2).

Christ's Teaching as to the Kingdom

I. Text. "Art Thou a King then? Jesus answered, Thou sayest that I am a King" (John 18. 37).

"My Kingdom is not of this world" (John 18. 36).

II. Main Lesson. The Lord Jesus claimed to be a King, and spoke of "My Kingdom."

It was to be a "*Kingdom of Heaven*," not a kingdom of earth. It was the "*Kingdom of God*," Who has set Christ as King upon His holy hill of Zion (Psa. 2. 6), and will one day proclaim Him "King of kings and Lord of lords" (1 Tim. 6. 15).

The Kingdom of God will then include the whole universe. When Christ shall have put down all rule and all authority and power and subdued all enemies, He will then deliver the Kingdom to God, even the Father (1 Cor. 15. 24).

The Church, the Bride of Christ, will reign with Him in the Kingdom. The Church and the Kingdom must not be confused.

The Kingdom is where the King reigns. At present it is established only in the hearts of His people. It will one day be set up on earth in the Millennium, and when all that offends has been taken out of it it will be universal over all creation.

III. Scriptures to Study.

1. THE KINGDOM IN PROPHECY.

Daniel 2. 44. Nebuchadnezzar's image is destroyed by a stone cut out without hands, that became a great moun-tain and filled the whole earth (2. 31-35). *Daniel interprets it thus.*

v. 44. "In the days of these kings shall the God of Heaven set up a Kingdom, which shall never be destroyed: and the Kingdom shall not be left to other people, but it shall break in pieces and consume all these kingdoms, and it shall stand for ever."

Daniel 7. 13. *The Son of Man Comes in the Clouds of Heaven and Receives an Everlasting Kingdom.* " I saw in the night visions, and, behold, One like unto the Son of Man came with the clouds of Heaven, and came to the Ancient of Days, and they brought Him near unto Him. And there was given unto Him dominion, and glory, and a Kingdom, that all peoples, nations, and languages should serve Him: His dominion is an everlasting dominion, which shall not pass away, and His Kingdom that which shall not be destroyed."

2. THE LORD'S WORDS AS TO THE KINGDOM.

Luke 17. 20. *The Pharisees Demand to Know when the Kingdom of God should Come.* " And when He was demanded of the Pharisees when the Kingdom of God should come, He answered them and said, The Kingdom of God cometh not with observation: neither shall they say, Lo here! or, Lo there! for, behold, the Kingdom of God is within you."

John 18. 33. *Jesus before Pilate Speaks of His Kingdom.*

v. 33. " Pilate entered into the judgment hall again, and called Jesus, and said unto Him, Art Thou the King of the Jews ?"

v. 36. " Jesus answered, My Kingdom is not of this world: if My Kingdom were of this world, then would My servants fight, that I should not be delivered to the Jews: but now is My Kingdom not from hence."

v. 37. " Pilate therefore said unto Him, Art Thou a King then ? Jesus answered, Thou sayest that I am a King. To this end was I born, and for this cause came I into the world, that I should bear witness unto the truth. Every one that is of the truth heareth My voice."

Luke 21. 31. *The Lord Foretold the Signs of His Coming,* and added: "So likewise ye, when ye see these things come to pass, know ye that the Kingdom of God is at hand."

Luke 22. 18. *At the Institution of the Lord's Supper.* " I say unto you, I will not drink of the fruit of the vine, until the Kingdom of God shall come."

v. 29-30. " And I appoint unto you a Kingdom, as My Father hath appointed unto Me; that ye may eat and drink at My table in My Kingdom, and sit on thrones judging the twelve tribes of Israel."

IV. Other Lessons from the Study.

1. DEFINITION OF THE KINGDOM. The Ordered Rule of Christ established in the hearts of His people; on the earth in the Millennial Kingdom; in the whole universe at length.

Where that Rule is recognized, there is the Kingdom.

2. TITLES OF THE KINGDOM. It is called " *the Kingdom of Heaven* " in the Gospel of Matthew, because the Jews expected an earthly Kingdom to be set up, and the Lord emphasized that the Kingdom would be a Kingdom of Heaven, where " the Heavens do rule " (Dan. 4. 26). It is called " *the Kingdom of God*," for the God of Heaven will rule. The terms are synonymous (*e.g.*, Matt. 19. 4; Luke 18. 16).

It is spoken of as " *the Heavenly Kingdom* " (2 Tim. 4. 18); " *The Kingdom of His dear Son* " (Col. 1. 13); and " *of Christ* " (Eph. 5. 5).

3. "THE KINGDOM OF GOD IS WITHIN YOU." No one enters the Kingdom until the Kingdom enters him.

Christ must be received as Lord in the heart in order to enter the Kingdom.-

The Lord made this clear in Matthew 18. 3: " *Verily I say unto you, Except ye be converted, and become as little children, ye shall not enter into the Kingdom of Heaven* "; and again in John 3. 3: " *Verily, verily, I say unto thee, Except a man be born again, he cannot see the Kingdom of God.*"

4. THE PRESENT AGE OF THE KINGDOM. The Lord's many illustrations and parables of the Kingdom show how the Kingdom, now said to be " in mystery " or hidden, is progressing.

Again and again the Lord said, " Unto what shall I liken the Kingdom of Heaven ?" The Seven Parables in Matthew 13, for example, show that it grows by the preaching of the Gospel; those who receive the good seed of the Word into good and honest hearts being the children of the Kingdom.

5. THE LORD'S PRAYER teaches us to pray " Thy Kingdom come," and the following petition may be taken as an explanation of the nature of the Kingdom: " Thy will be done on earth as it is in Heaven " ; when that is fulfilled the Kingdom will be realized.

6. THE COMING OF THE KINGDOM in manifestation will not be by the world gradually becoming better, but by the Coming of the Lord to set up His Kingdom—when the stone hewn out without hands falls upon the kingdoms of the world and destroys them, and becomes a great mountain and fills the earth, as foretold by Daniel.

7. MISTAKEN VIEWS OF THE KINGDOM. Augustine, in his famous book *De Civitate Dei*, represented the Kingdom of God as a Visible Church on earth (a conception unknown in the Bible; the Church which is the Body of Christ is an *invisible* organism, not an earthly organization), while all outside the " church " was the kingdom of Satan; but in this he confused the Church with the Kingdom, a mistake which largely contributed to the false claims of the Roman hierarchy.

8. THE FINAL TRIUMPH is described in Revelation 11. 15. " The kingdoms of this world are become the kingdoms of our Lord and of His Christ, and He shall reign for ever and ever." Of that day the Psalmist sings: " The Lord hath prepared His throne in the Heavens; and His Kingdom ruleth over all " (Psa. 103. 19).

" They shall speak of the glory of Thy Kingdom, and talk of Thy power: to make known to the sons of men . . . the glorious majesty of His Kingdom. Thy Kingdom is an everlasting Kingdom, and Thy dominion endureth throughout all generations " (Psa. 145).

The Lord shall reign for ever and ever.

V. Application.

Let us see that we enter the Kingdom by conversion and new birth.

Let us pray, " Thy Kingdom come."

Let us anticipate the Coming of the King with holy preparation.

OUTLINES

Ten Titles of our King

King of Glory (Psa. 24. 7).
King for Ever (Psa. 29. 10).
King of Old (Psa. 74. 12).
King of Israel (John 1. 49).
King of the Jews (John 19. 19).
King Eternal, Immortal, Invisible (1 Tim. 1. 17).
King of Kings and Lord of Lords (1 Tim. 6. 15).
King of Righteousness (Heb. 7. 2).
King of Peace (Heb. 7. 2).
King of Saints (Rev. 15. 3).

The Kingdom

His Kingdom ruleth over all (Psa. 103. 19).
The Glorious Majesty of His Kingdom (Psa. 145. 12).
An Everlasting Kingdom (Psa. 145. 13).
Set up by the God of Heaven (Dan. 2. 44).
From Generation to Generation (Dan. 4. 34).
The Kingdom of Heaven (Matt. 3. 2).
The Kingdom of God (Matt. 12. 28).
The Kingdom of their Father (Matt. 13. 43).
Kingdom of Our Father David (Mark 11. 10).
Kingdom not of this world (John 18. 36).
His Heavenly Kingdom (2 Tim. 4. 18).
The Kingdom of His dear Son (Col. 1. 13).

SECTION IV

Our Lord Jesus Christ: The Great "I Am"

Gloria Agni

Where the Lamb is all the Glory
  And the Light of all the place,
Where they need no solemn Temple
  Who behold Him face to face;
Thither guided by Thy Spirit
  We may enter by the Blood,
And upon our faces falling
  Worship Thee our Father God.

Leaving all of earthly glory
  As no longer living here,
Partners of a holy calling
  In the Heavenlies we appear;
There we worship and adore Thee,
  There extol the wondrous grace
Of the Lamb once slain for sinners,
  See the glory of His face.

Feeble are our highest praises.
  Could our lips an angel touch,
Then might we express with rapture
  All the love we feel so much.
Call we on our souls within us
  Now to bless Thy Holy Name,
Magnify Thy wondrous mercy,
  Now and evermore the same.

G. G.

The Lord as the "I Am"

I. Text. "If ye believe not that I AM, ye shall die in your sins" (John 8. 24).

II. Main Lesson. God revealed Himself to Moses at the burning bush as "*I AM THAT I AM*," and bade him tell the children of Israel that the " I AM " had sent him to deliver them.

The meaning of that mystic name is given below.

The Lord Jesus claimed to be the I AM.

Indeed, it was He Who appeared to Moses in the bush as "the Angel of the Lord" (Exod. 3. 2), in one of the Christophanies or pre-appearances of Christ before His incarnation.

(For a lesson on these, see *Seventy Less Known Bible Stories*, No. 6, pp. 43-48.)

Thus the Lord thought it not robbery to be equal with God, but asserted His claim thus to be " God manifest in the flesh " (1 Tim. 3. 16).

III. Scriptures to Study:

Exodus 3. 1-2. *The Angel of the Lord appears to Moses in a Burning Bush.* " Now Moses kept the flock of Jethro his father in law, the priest of Midian: and he led the flock to the backside of the desert, and came to the mountain of God, in Horeb. And the Angel of the Lord appeared unto him in a flame of fire out of the midst of the bush: and he looked, and, behold, the bush burned with fire, and the bush was not consumed."

vv. 3-4. *Moses Turns Aside to See the Great Sight.* " And Moses said, I will now turn aside, and see this great sight, why the bush is not burnt. . . . And God called to him out of the midst of the bush, and said, Moses, Moses. And he said, Here am I."

vv. 5-6. *God Reveals Himself as the God of the Fathers.* " And He said, Draw not nigh hither: put off thy shoes from off thy feet, for the place whereon thou standest is holy ground. Moreover He said, I am the God of Abraham, the God of Isaac, and the God of Jacob. And Moses hid his face; for he was afraid to look on God."

v. 14. *God Reveals Himself further as the I AM.* "And God said unto Moses, *I AM THAT I AM.* . . . Thus shalt thou say unto the children of Israel, *I AM* hath sent me unto you."

Our Lord Claims the Title.

John 8. 52, 53. *The Jews Oppose Christ.* "The Jews said unto Him, Now we know that Thou hast a devil. Abraham is dead, and the prophets; and Thou sayest, If a man keep My saying, he shall never taste of death. Art Thou greater than our father Abraham, which is dead ? . . . Whom makest Thou Thyself ?"

v. 56. *The Lord Claims to be before Abraham.* "Jesus answered, . . . Your father Abraham rejoiced to see My day; and he saw it, and was glad. . . . Verily, verily, I say unto you, Before Abraham was, I AM."

IV. **The Meaning of the Name**. It may be read as " I am what I am " or " I am (to you) what I am (in Myself)." It was no doubt intended as an explanation of the Name JEHOVAH, which means the One who was, is, and will be—that is, the Eternal One. Some suggest the title would be more correctly rendered " I will be what I will be," or " I am because I am," as given in the R.V. margin; but these do not seem to have the dignity and majesty of the simple I AM.

The Name suggests:

1. The Self-Existent One, the Absolute Essential Deity—an ascription of which to Christ is found in John 1. 1: " In the beginning was the Word, and the Word was with God, and the Word was God "; and in Col. 2. 9: " In Him dwelleth all the fulness of the Godhead bodily."

2. The Eternal One. He is the One Who inhabits eternity, "having neither beginning of days nor end of life " (Heb. 7. 3).

3. The Inscrutable. " Whose ways are past finding out."

4. The Unchangeable. "I am Jehovah, I change not." "Jesus Christ is the same yesterday, and today, and for ever."

5. The Ever-Present One. The wonder of this is fully described in Psalm 139. It is borne out in the words of the Lord, "Lo, I am with you always, even unto the end of the age."

6. The All-Embracing One. The Lord described Himself as the First and the Last; the Beginning and the Ending; the Alpha and Omega.

The twenty-six letters of the English alphabet include all that is written in that language. Think of the British Museum Library and realize the wonder of it—all included within the Alpha and Omega, the A and Z of the alphabet.

7. The All-Sufficient One. The Lord Jesus claimed this: " All power is given unto Me in Heaven and in earth."

8. The Only One. " Look unto Me and be ye saved, all the ends of the earth: for I am God, and there is none else "; and, as Jesus said: " I am the Way, the Truth, and the Life: no man cometh unto the Father, but by Me."

V. Our Lord's Claim. Two things are to be noticed as to the use of the words " I am " by the Lord.

1. In the passages quoted below there is no " He " added after the words " I am." The " He " has been put in in the a.v. (and also r.v., but see the margins). It might well read " I am," and not " I am He."

2. The " I " is emphasized in each case, so that it might well read " I, even I, am," following the language of Isaiah 43. 11, " *I, even I, am* Jehovah "; and verse 25, " *I, even I, am* He that blotteth out thy transgressions "; 48. 15, " *I, even I,* have spoken "; 51. 12, " *I, even I, am* He that comforteth you."

The usual unemphasized " I am " is εἰμι, but the Lord always used ἐγώ εἰμι—" I, even I, am."

The occasions when the Lord used the expression are as follows:

(1) John 8. 24. " *If ye believe not that I AM, ye shall die in your sins.*"

The Jews seemed to understand Him, for they said, "Who art Thou?" His reply may fairly be rendered "The One from the beginning (τὴν ἀρχήν), He of Whom I am telling you"—words which forcibly remind us of the opening verse of the Gospel, "In the beginning was the Word."

To refuse the Lord His claim to be the Son of God, the Christ, is to "die in your sins."

(2) John 8. 28. "*Then said Jesus unto them, When ye have lifted up the Son of Man, then shall ye know that I AM.*"

They would find out too late Who it was that they with wicked hands had crucified and slain.

(3) John 8. 57-58. "*Thou art not yet fifty years old, and hast Thou seen Abraham? Jesus said unto them, Verily I say unto you, Before Abraham was, I AM.*"

It is impossible to resist the truth of this. The Lord claimed to be the I AM before Abraham had been born. As Dr. F. Godet says:

"Jesus says '*I am,*' not '*I was.*' This latter expression would have designated mere priority with respect to Abraham, while the former expression places the existence of the subject who thus speaks in the rank of the Absolute, the Eternal, the Divine. It recalls the words of Psalm 90. 2: 'Before the mountains were brought forth, or ever Thou hadst formed the earth and the world, even from everlasting to everlasting, Thou art God.'"

(4) John 13. 19. "*Now I tell you before it come to pass that, when it is come to pass, ye may believe that I AM.*"

It was the challenge of Isaiah to the false prophets to show their inspiration if they could by telling what should come to pass in the future.

"Let them bring them forth, and show us what shall happen: . . . or declare us things for to come. Show the things that are to come hereafter, that we may know that ye are gods" (Isa. 41. 22-23).

The Lord seems to accept the challenge, and tells what shall come to pass, thus showing Himself to be indeed God, Who knows the end from the beginning.

(5) John 18. 4-5. "*Jesus . . . went forth* [in the Garden of Gethsemane], *and said unto them, Whom seek ye? They*

answered Him, Jesus of Nazareth. Jesus saith unto them, I AM. . . . As soon then as He had said unto them, I AM, they went backward, and fell to the ground."

This extraordinary incident seems to suggest that the Lord allowed, for the moment, His Divine dignity as the I AM to be seen, and thus overawe His assailants.

The reasons for this may have been:

(a) *That Judas and those with him might know* the exceeding sinfulness of their crime.

(b) That He might let them know that, *had He not submitted to be taken,* they could have had no power against Him. This He had told Pilate at His trial (John 19. 11).

(c) That He might *sufficiently overawe* them so that they would let the disciples go (John 18. 8).

(d) That the *Scripture might be fulfilled* (John 18. 9).

(e) That they might know that He had *no recourse to carnal weapons* (v. 11).

(f) That the disciples might see *His perfect obedience* to His Father: "The cup which My Father hath given Me, shall I not drink it?" (v. 11).

*   *   *   *   *

In addition to these, we have the seven I AM's of the Gospel of John, which we shall consider one by one (Lessons 31-37).

VI. Other Lessons from the Study.

1. REVERENCE DUE TO THE NAME. If we appreciate Who the Lord Jesus was, the I AM, we shall not take His Name lightly upon our lips, remembering that the Third Commandment applies to Him: "Thou shalt not take the Name of the Lord thy God in vain; for the Lord will not hold him guiltless that taketh His Name in vain" (Exod. 20. 7).

Therefore let us speak of "the Lord Jesus," which is equivalent to "Jehovah Jesus," and not too familiarly of "Jesus."

2. THE MIGHTY POWER OF THAT NAME. Peter stressed this when he told the High Priests: "Be it known unto you all . . . that by the Name of Jesus Christ of Nazareth, Whom ye crucified, Whom God raised from the dead, even by Him doth this man stand here before you whole. . . .

Neither is there Salvation in any other: for there is none other Name under Heaven given among men, whereby we must be saved " (Acts 4. 10-12).

3. The Value of the Name. To His people the Name tells of One Who is to them all that He is in Himself.

The constant repetition of the Lord, " I am the Bread of Life, the Light, the Door, the Good Shepherd, the Resurrection, the Way, the Truth, and the Life, the True Vine," teaches us that He is not only all in all to His people, but ever present to meet their every need.

4. The Claim Involved. The repetition of the " I am " meant a definite claim on the part of the Lord Jesus to full Deity—a claim which He summed up in the words " I and My Father are One." "He that hath seen Me hath seen the Father."

> " Jehovah, Great I Am,
> By earth and heaven confessed;
> We bow and bless the sacred Name,
> For ever blessed."

VII. Application.

Let us learn to appreciate the Majesty and Glory of our Saviour Lord.

Let us avail ourselves of all He says He is to us.

Seven Old Testament " I am's "

I am thy Shield and thy Exceeding Great Reward (Gen. 15. 1).

I am the Almighty God (Gen. 17. 1).

I am the God of Bethel (Gen. 31. 13).

I am the Lord which sanctifieth you (Lev. 20. 8).

I am thy Salvation (Psa. 35. 3).

I am the Lord your Holy One (Isa. 43. 15).

I am the First, I also am the Last (Isa. 48. 12).

LESSON 31

"I Am the Bread of Life"*

I. Text. "I am the Living Bread which came down from Heaven: if any man eat of this Bread, he shall live for ever" (John 6. 51).

II. Main Lesson. In this the first of the seven I am's in the sixth chapter of the Gospel of John the Lord represents Himself as "the Bread of God" (33), "the Bread of Life" (48), "the Living Bread" (51), and "the True Bread from Heaven" (32).

He is the One Who must be received by faith, as a starving man eats bread to live, and must be eaten habitually that life may be sustained.

He is the Food of the Soul—the Life-Giving and the Life-Sustaining One. There is no Spiritual Life apart from Him. Faith must feed on Him or else "ye have no life in you" (John 6. 53).

III. Scripture to Study. John 6. 31-63 should be prayerfully pondered; only the salient verses are given here.

vv. 32-33. *The Lord Jesus Declares Himself to be the Bread from Heaven.* "Verily, verily, I say unto you, Moses gave you not that bread from Heaven; but My Father giveth you the True Bread from Heaven. For the Bread of God is He which cometh down from Heaven, and giveth life unto the world."

vv. 34-35. *They Ask for the Bread, and He Tells them how it is Received—by Coming and Believing.* "Then said they unto Him, Lord, evermore give us this Bread. And Jesus said unto them, I am the Bread of Life: he that cometh to Me shall never hunger; and he that believeth on Me shall never thirst."

v. 41. *The Jews Murmur at the Saying.* "The Jews then

---

* For a Lesson on the Manna as a type of Christ, see *Seventy Best Bible Stories*, No. 13, pp. 59-61. This part of the subject is omitted here

177

murmured at Him, because He said, I am the Bread which came down from Heaven."

v. 47. *The Lord Explains Again.* " Verily, verily, I say unto you, He that believeth on Me hath everlasting life."

vv. 48-51. *He Repeats the Truth Again.* " I am that Bread of Life. Your fathers did eat manna in the wilderness, and are dead. This is the Bread which cometh down from Heaven, that a man may eat thereof, and not die. I am the Living Bread which came down from Heaven: if any man eat of this Bread, he shall live for ever: and the bread that I will give is My flesh, which I will give for the life of the world."

v. 52. *The Jews Complain Again.* " The Jews therefore strove among themselves, saying, How can this Man give us His flesh to eat ?"

vv. 53-58. *The Lord insists upon our Eating His Flesh and Drinking His Blood.* " Verily I say unto you, Except ye eat the Flesh of the Son of Man, and drink His Blood, ye have no life in you. Whoso eateth My Flesh, and drinketh My Blood, hath eternal life; and I will raise him up at the last day. For My Flesh is meat indeed, and My Blood is drink indeed. He that eateth My Flesh and drinketh My Blood, dwelleth in Me, and I in him. As the living Father hath sent Me, and I live by the Father: so he that eateth Me, even he shall live by Me. This is that Bread which came down from Heaven: not as your fathers did eat manna, and are dead: he that eateth of this Bread shall live for ever."

vv. 61-63. *Some Disciples being Offended, the Lord Explains His Meaning Again.* " Doth this offend you ? What and if ye shall see the Son of Man ascend up where He was before ? It is the Spirit that quickeneth; the flesh profiteth nothing: the words that I speak unto you, they are spirit, and they are life."

IV. **The Eating and Drinking Explained.** It is not the Lord's Supper in view here, for the following reasons:

1. The Supper had not been instituted.

2. We do not come to the Lord's table to get life, but because we have been born again; no one else has a right

to be there. We must have eaten of Christ and obtained life before we can eat of His Supper. The fact must precede the figure.

3. If it were so, those who are too young or too distant to come to the Lord's table would have no life in them (53).

4. We do not feed on Christ on certain ceremonial occasions only, but should do so always and habitually.

5. Because the Lord explains that " He that believeth on Me hath everlasting life " (47), and " He that cometh to Me shall never hunger, and he that believeth on Me shall never thirst." The eating, then, is coming to and believing upon Christ.

THE EXPLANATION IN VV. 62-63 tells us:

1. *The Lord in His Body would Ascend Up where He was before.* It could not be that we eat that Body.

2. *The Holy Spirit is the Life Giver :* no ceremonial eating could bring life.

3. *The Flesh Profiteth Nothing.* Could we actually eat it, such a fleshly and material effort would not profit.

4. *The Words that I speak unto you, they are Spirit and they are Life.* Faith is fed upon the words of God; as they are received they quicken (1 Pet. 1. 23) and sustain the soul. As Augustine says, "Believe, and thou hast eaten."

As Jeremiah said, " Thy words were found, and I did eat them; and Thy word (the Living Word) was unto me the joy and rejoicing of mine heart " (15. 16).

V. How is Christ the Bread of Life ?

1. HE BRINGS US LIFE BY HIS DEATH. " The Bread that I will give is My flesh, which I will give for the life of the world " (51).

He was the corn of wheat that fell into the ground and died so that it might bring forth much fruit (John 12. 24). " Bread corn is bruised in order to make bread " (Isa. 28. 28), so was He " bruised for our iniquities " (Isa. 53. 5), that through His stripes we might be healed.

2. HE MINISTERS LIFE TO THOSE WHO BELIEVE. A man dying of starvation eagerly eats the proffered bread, that he may not perish.

So whosoever believeth on Him shall not perish, but have everlasting life.

The eating of verse 53 is "PHAGETE." It is the initial coming to Christ, to receive Him as our Life, our Living Bread, so that we pass out of death into life.

3. HE SUSTAINS OUR SPIRITUAL LIFE as we continue to feed by faith upon Him. " He that eateth My Flesh and drinketh My Blood dwelleth (abideth) in Me, and I in him " (56).

The word to eat this time is " TROGON," and has the meaning of habitual eating in order that the life received may be sustained and maintained.

4. HE STRENGTHENS AND INVIGORATES OUR SPIRITUAL BEING BY THE LIVING BREAD. He is our Melchisedec High Priest who brings out bread and wine to refresh us in the conflict (Gen. 14. 18)—the " wine that maketh glad the heart of man . . . and bread that strengthens man's heart " (Psa. 104. 15), so that our courage is nerved and our strength renewed.

5. HE SATISFIES OUR SPIRITUAL APPETITES. Just as of old the Lord fed the five thousand by multiplying the loaves, so He says, " Come, eat of My bread, and drink of the wine which I have mingled."

Like David, who bade Mephibosheth eat bread continually at his royal table, so the Lord bids us eat: " Eat, O friends ; drink, yea, drink abundantly, O beloved " (S. of Sol. 5. 16).

VI. Other Lessons from the Study.

1. VARIOUS KINDS OF BREAD mentioned in the Bible.

Memorial Bread (Lev. 24. 7), or Shewbread (Presence Bread), upon the Table of Shewbread in the Tabernacle; called *Hallowed* Bread (1 Sam. 21. 4).

Unleavened Bread (Exod. 12. 17), eaten at the Feast of the Passover.

The Bread of thy God (Lev. 21. 6 and 8), specially reserved for the priests, the sons of Aaron.

Bread of the Firstfruits (2 Kings 4. 42), made from the firstfruits of the harvest and given to the priests.

The Bread of Mourners (Hosea 9. 4), eaten at funerals.

Pleasant Bread (Ezek. 10. 3), eaten at feasts.

Polluted Bread (Mal. 1. 7), defiled and unfit to be offered on the altar.

Bread of Affliction (Deut. 16. 3, 1 Kings 22. 27), given to prisoners and captives.

Bread of Tears (Psa. 80. 5), a figure of sorrow.

Bread of Sorrows (Psa. 127. 2), the same figure.

Bread of Adversity (Isa. 30. 20), a similar figure.

Bread of Wickedness (Prov. 4. 17).

Bread of Idleness (Prov. 31. 27).

Bread of Deceit (Prov. 20. 17).

All these serve to show what frequent use is made of the figure of bread as the staff of life, and indicating the manner of its use in the Scriptures.

2. THE BREAD AND WINE ON THE LORD'S TABLE. These speak to us of Fellowship in the Body and Blood of Christ. "The Cup of Blessing which we bless, is it not fellowship (κοινωνία) in the Blood of Christ ? The bread which we break, is it not fellowship in the Body of Christ ? " (1 Cor. 10. 16).

Eating and drinking are manifestations of participation in the realities for which the symbols stand.

Because I have my part in the finished work (Blood) of Christ, I can drink of the Memorial Cup; because I am a member of the Body of Christ, I may eat of the Memorial Bread.

Eating is fellowship—Faith rejoicing in its participation of the blessings.

> " Only bread and only wine,
>   But to faith the solemn sign
>   Of the Heavenly and Divine:
>   We give Thee thanks, O God.—H. BONAR.

3. THE BREAD (LOAF) A SYMBOL OF THE CHURCH. The Bread is a figure of the Body of Christ, not only of the sinless body in which He bore our sins, but of the mystic body (the Church) of which He is Head and we are all members. Thus we read in 1 Corinthians 10. 17, " For we being many are one bread, and one body: for we are all

partakers of that one bread " (loaf). The Unity of the Church is set forth in this figure.

4. THE SHEWBREAD ON THE GOLDEN TABLE IN THE HOLY PLACE, called also " The Bread of the Presence " and "Continual Shewbread," consisted of twelve loaves of bread renewed every Sabbath. The priests ate the loaves when taken off the table, in the holy place.

They were thin cakes, and were covered with frankincense.

They represented the Twelve Tribes presented before the Lord and continually in His presence. On our table there is but One loaf; for we are all One in Christ—one bread, one body.

VII. Application.

Let us see to it that we have our part in Christ, that we have so eaten that we have life.

Let us eat habitually by faith of the Living Bread.

Let us rejoice to take our place at the Lord's Table.

OUTLINE

The LIVING BREAD

" He that eateth Me shall live by Me."

Bread corn is bruised and baked in the oven.
Broken also for us and to us.

Received with meekness and
Rejoiced in.

Eaten by Faith and
Enjoyed.

Appropriated and
Assimilated by Meditation and Communion.

Distributed and
Dealt out to others.

"I Am the Light of the World"

I. Text. "I am the Light of the World; he that followeth Me shall not walk in darkness, but shall have the Light of Life" (John 8. 12).

II. Main Lesson. The Lord Jesus is the True Light that lighteth every man coming into the world (John 1. 9).

Wherever His Name is known darkness flees away.

Upon every country that once sat in darkness He has arisen, a Great Light, the Sun of Righteousness, with healing in His wings.

What is true nationally is true individually. Those who receive Christ no longer walk in darkness, but have the light of life.

Sin, Despair and the Fear of Death all fly at His presence.

Life and Immortality come to light wherever His Name is known.

III. Scriptures to Study:

John 1. 4. *He is the Light of Life.* "In Him was Life, and the Life was the Light of men. And the Light shineth in darkness; and the darkness comprehended it not."

v. 9. *The True Light.* "That was the True Light which lighteth every man that cometh into the world."

John 9. 5. "As long as I am in the world, I am the Light of the world."

John 3. 19. *Man's Responsibility to come to the Light.* "This is the condemnation, that Light is come into the world, and men loved darkness rather than light, because their deeds were evil. For everyone that doeth evil hateth the light, neither cometh to the light, lest his deeds should be reproved. But he that doeth truth cometh to the light, that his deeds may be made manifest, that they are wrought in God."

Ephesians 5. 8-14. *Walk as Children of Light.*

v. 8. "Ye were sometimes darkness, but now are ye light in the Lord: walk as children of light."

v. 11. "Have no fellowship with the unfruitful works of darkness, but rather reprove them."

v. 13. "But all things that are reproved are made manifest by the Light: for whatsoever doth make manifest is light. Wherefore He saith, Awake, thou that sleepest, and arise from the dead, and Christ shall give thee light."

IV. The Functions of Light.

1. AT CREATION. God's first spoken word was "Let there be light" (Gen. 1. 3).

The Light was said to be for five purposes:

v. 14. To DIVIDE—that is, to separate from darkness.

v. 15. To ILLUMINE—to give light upon the earth.

v. 16. To RULE over the day (the Sun) and over the night (the Moon).

v. 14. For SIGNS or witnesses for God (Psa. 19).

v. 14. For SEASONS, to regulate day and night, summer and winter, for the comfort and happiness of men.

It is easy to spiritualize these and show how Christ, the True Light, exercises all these offices in the spiritual realm.

2. LIGHT IS KNOWLEDGE. "The Light of the knowledge of the glory of God in the face of Jesus Christ" (2 Cor. 4. 6).

Ignorance is darkness. Those who sit in darkness are those who are without the knowledge of the True God Who has revealed Himself in Christ.

To come to the Light is to come to the knowledge of God and His Salvation.

3. LIGHT IS RIGHTEOUSNESS, as contrasted with sin, which is darkness (men love darkness because their deeds are evil). "Light is sown for the righteous" (Psa. 97. 11).

I will "bring forth *thy righteousness as the light*" (Psa. 37. 6). A sinner justified is called out of darkness into His marvellous light (1 Pet. 2. 9).

4. LIGHT IS TRUTH. "Thy Word is a Light;" "The law is Light" (Prov. 6. 23). Every lie is darkness.

5. LIGHT IS ARMOUR (Rom. 13. 12). "Let us put on the armour of light." A man is open to sudden and

unexpected attack in the dark, but the believer, walking in light, is forewarned. The light is his defence against the powers of darkness.

6. LIGHT IS FOR GUIDANCE. Those who follow Christ do not walk in darkness, but have the Light of life. His word is a lamp to their feet and a Light to their path.

7. LIGHT IS FOR FRUITFULNESS. We read of the unfruitful works of darkness, but light shall produce the fruit. The believer, walking in the light, will bear the fruit of righteousness, and the gracious fruit of the Spirit.

8. LIGHT IS TESTIMONY. "Let your light so shine before men that they may see your good works, and glorify your Father which is in Heaven" (Matt. 5. 16). As Christ who is our Light shines upon us, so we reflect His Light and in our turn become the Light of the world.

9. LIGHT IS FOR JOY AND PLEASURE. "Truly the Light is sweet, and a pleasant thing it is for the eyes to behold the Sun" (Eccles. 11. 7).

We rejoice in the light. The saints are said to be "in light" and "children of light."

They pray, "Lord, lift Thou up the light of Thy countenance upon us."

V. How Christ is the Light.

1. AS THE ONLY SOURCE OF THE KNOWLEDGE OF GOD. He is the Effulgence of the Glory of God, the Shining forth of His Majesty.

Only in Christ is God, Who is Light, known. "No man hath seen God at any time; the Only Begotten Son, which is in the bosom of the Father, He hath declared Him" (John 1. 18).

2. AS THE SUN OF RIGHTEOUSNESS to the Believer, rising on his darkness, dispelling the gloom and bringing light, peace and gladness into his soul.

As He caused the blind to see when He was on the earth, so He opens the blind eyes of the heart of the natural man, and shines in with knowledge of Salvation.

3. AS THE GUIDE OF THE CHILD OF GOD INTO TRUTH. He is Himself the Truth, and by His Spirit, which He gives to all who believe, He guides into all the Truth.

4. AS THE JOY OF HIS LIFE. The believer can truly say of Christ, "Truly the Light is sweet, and a pleasant thing it is to behold the Sun." He finds in Christ spiritually all and far more than the natural finds in the light and sunshine.

5. AS THE TEACHER OF HOLINESS. Holiness is likeness to Christ, and it results from walking in His light and obeying His word. Purity, Truth and Love are the ingredients of Holiness, and these are all light from Him.

VI. Other Lessons from the Study.

1. THE LIGHTS IN THE HEAVENS ALL SPEAK OF CHRIST. He is the Sun. The Church (having no inherent light) is like the moon: it shines by the reflection of His light. As long as He was in the world, He was the light of the world, but the world refused and put out the light. It is the world's night now, and He is seen only by reflection of the lesser light to rule the night.

The stars are individual Christians (Dan. 12. 3), each shining in his own sphere.

2. THE PILLAR OF FIRE that led the Israelites through the wilderness and was to give them light by night (Exod. 13. 21) is another picture of Christ as the Light of Life guiding His people by His Spirit through the darkness of this world.

3. THE GOLDEN LAMPSTAND in the Tabernacle is a figure of the Lord as the Light of His people.

Their testimony is maintained and their light shines only as He supplies the oil of His grace—His Holy Spirit.

The same figure is found in Zechariah 4. 2-3, 11-14, and in Revelation 1. 12-20.

4. WE MUST BELIEVE IN THE LIGHT AND WALK IN THE LIGHT (John 12. 35-36)—that is, exercise faith and yield obedience to the Lord Jesus and the truth of His word and conviction of His Spirit.

This is the Obedience of Faith. If we do so, we shall never miss the Light on our path. We shall have the Light of Life.

VII. Application.

" Awake, thou that sleepest, and arise from the dead, and Christ shall give thee light " (Eph. 5. 14).

" Walk in the Light, as He is in the Light " (1 John 1. 7).

OUTLINES

"LIGHT"

LIGHT is for
- Life (John 1. 4).
- Illumination (Gen. 1. 15).
- Guidance and Government (IV. 6 and Gen. 1. 16).
- Happiness and Holiness (V. 4 and 5).
- Testimony and Truth (IV. 8 and 4).

SEVEN THINGS said to be LIGHT

GOD is LIGHT (1 John 1. 5).

CHRIST (John 8. 12).

SAINTS (Matt. 5. 14).

WORD of GOD (Psa. 119. 105).

GOSPEL (2 Cor. 4. 4).

PATH of the JUST (Prov. 4. 18).

CHURCHES (Rev. 1. 12, Golden Lampstands).

"I Am the Door"

I. Text. " I am the Door: by Me if any man enter in, he shall be saved, and shall go in and out, and find pasture " (John 10. 9).

II. Main Lesson. The Lord Jesus here represents Himself as the Door into Salvation—the Only Way of Safety.

Salvation is not something we receive *from* Christ, but something we have *in* Him.

To have Salvation we must be " found *in* Him " (Phil. 3. 9). Neither is there Salvation in any other.

To be found in Him we must *enter in*, by an act of faith that is like crossing the threshold of a door.

There is " no condemnation to them that are *in* Christ Jesus " (Rom. 8. 1). " If any man be *in* Christ, he is a new creature: old things are passed away; behold all things are become new " (2 Cor. 5. 17).

III. Scriptures to Study :

John 10. 7. *Christ Represents Himself as the Door of the Sheep.* " Then said Jesus unto them again, Verily, verily, I say unto you, I am the Door of the Sheep."

v. 8. *Others who came Professing to be Christ were Thieves and Robbers.* " All that ever came before Me were thieves and robbers: but the sheep did not hear them."

v. 9. *He is the Door into Salvation.* " I am the Door: by Me if any man enter in, he shall be saved, and shall go in and out, and find pasture."

v. 10. *The Purpose of His Coming.* " The thief cometh not, but for to steal, and to kill, and to destroy: I am come that they might have life, and that they might have it more abundantly. "

v. 11. *As the Good Shepherd He Died for the Sheep.* " I am the Good Shepherd: the Good Shepherd giveth His life for the sheep."

v. 12. *The Hireling Described.* "But he that is an hireling, and not the shepherd, whose own the sheep are not, seeth the wolf coming, and leaveth the sheep, and fleeth: and the wolf catcheth them, and scattereth the sheep. The hireling fleeth, because he is an hireling, and careth not for the sheep."

v. 14. *The Shepherd's Care for the Sheep.* "I am the Good Shepherd, and know My sheep, and am known of Mine."

IV. **Some Notable Doors** or Gates in the Bible.

1. THE DOOR OF THE ARK (Gen. 6. 16), the entrance into the one place of safety from the coming flood.

2. THE BLOOD-SPRINKLED DOOR on Passover night when the blood on the lintel and side posts saved the first-born from the Destroyer.

3. THE DOOR OF THE TABERNACLE (Exod. 27. 16 and 29. 4), the entrance into the Court and to the Holy places.

4. THE DOOR OF RAHAB'S HOUSE (Josh. 2. 19), within which her household was safe.

5. THE DOOR OF THE CITY OF REFUGE (Josh. 20. 4), into which the manslayer fled for refuge.

6. THE DOOR INTO THE WEDDING (Matt. 25. 10), in the Parable of the Ten Virgins, shut against the five foolish ones.

7. THE DOOR OF MERCY (Luke 13. 25), opened in this Day of Grace, but which the Lord will one day rise up and shut.

8. THE DOOR OF THE SEPULCHRE (Matt. 27. 60), from which the stone had been rolled away when the Lord rose from the dead.

9. THE DOOR OF THE PRISON (Acts 12. 6), which opened to let Peter and the Angel out.

10. THE GREAT AND EFFECTUAL DOOR (1 Cor. 16. 9), opened for the Gospel—"a door of utterance" (Col. 4. 3), "an open door" (Rev. 3. 8), set before the servant of God.

11. THE DOOR OF THE HEART (Rev. 3. 20), before which the Lord stands knocking for admission.

12. THE DOOR OF FAITH opened to the Gentiles (Acts 14. 27).

13. THE DOOR IN HEAVEN (Rev. 4. 1) that John saw in vision, into which the righteous enter, who have washed their robes and made them white in the Blood of the Lamb (Rev. 7. 14).

14. THE DOOR OF THE BOTTOMLESS PIT, into which Satan and his angels were cast (Rev. 20. 1-2 and 10).

V. The Value and Uses of a Door.

1. IT IS THE ENTRANCE.   The way into that of which it is the door—as of the Ark, or the Tabernacle, or Mercy, or Salvation, or Heaven.

2. IT IS THE ONLY WAY into a house or other place. To attempt to climb in some other way is to be a thief or a robber (John 10. 1).

3. IT HAS TWO SIDES, outside and inside.   One must be either within to enjoy what is there, or outside to be excluded from the privileges and blessings.

> " Only one Door, and yet its sides are two.
> Outside or inside—on which side are you ?"

4. IT IS BUT ONE STEP OVER THE THRESHOLD.   It may take a long time to get to the Door; it takes only one step to pass from the outside to the inside.   So it is:

> " Only a step to Jesus,
> Then why not take it now ?"

5. IT IS CONTROLLED BY THE MASTER OF THE HOUSE.   No one may force his way in without permission. One must *knock* to obtain entrance.
Our Lord promises to open to all who do so.

6. IT IS USED BY ALL ALIKE.   Kings and Emperors, or beggars, masters and servants, old or young—there is no difference.   To get in there is but one way for all alike.
A Door is no respecter of persons.

7. IT SHUTS OUT UNDESIRABLES. ' So the sinner is excluded from Heaven (Rev. 21. 27).

8. THOSE WITHIN ARE SAFE. Whether from the Storm, or the Enemy, or the Avenger of Blood—safe as was Noah and Rahab and as is every sinner who flees for refuge to Christ.

9. THOSE WHO ARE OF THE HOUSEHOLD GO IN AND OUT (John 10. 9). They have the freedom of the children of the family.

VI. Other Lessons on Christ as the Door.

1. THE OPENING OF THE DOOR. The " New and Living Way " was " consecrated " (dedicated or made new) for us through the shedding of the precious Blood of Christ.

The way into the Holiest was through the rent Veil— that is, the Body broken, the Blood shed. So He became the Door.

2. ENTERING THE DOOR. " By Me if any man enter in " means that to go into life and salvation we must enter by faith in Christ.

It is called the " Door of Faith " for this reason.

Faith is entering into Christ.

We believe " into Him " (John 3. 16: εἰς αὐτόν).

Confidence is reposed in Him, followed by Submission and Obedience. He is our Lord.

3. THE SAFETY INSIDE. " Him that cometh unto Me [that is, enters the door] I will in no wise cast out [or eject again] " (John 6. 37).

Once received into the Household of Faith, we are never given up again. Once in Christ, we are eternally in Him. There is no condemnation to them that are in Christ Jesus (Rom. 8. 1).

"The Name of the Lord is a Strong Tower: the righteous runneth into it and is safe."

4. THE JOY AND PEACE INSIDE. " In Thy Presence is Fulness of Joy." " He brought me into His banqueting house, and His banner over me was Love."

In Revelation 3. 20 the figure is reversed. There the

heart's door is opened to receive the Lord. " If any man hear My voice, and *open the door*, I will come in to him, and will sup with him, and he with Me."

The communion represented here is the same. As we come unto Christ we enter into holy and happy fellowship with Him and all His household of saints.

5. THE DOOR SHUT. More than once the Lord warned us that the door would one day be shut—that is, the day of Grace end, mercy's offer be closed.

It was so in the Parable of the Ten Virgins. The five foolish ones came too late. " The door was shut." One day the Master of the House will rise up to shut the door. It will then be too late to knock and find an entrance.

> " Too late, too late, will be the cry,
> Jesus of Nazareth has passed by."

VII. Application.

To the Sinner.   Beware lest thou knock too late.

To the Seeking.   Knock, and it shall be opened unto you.

To the Fearful.   Fear not: if you are in Christ, you are with Him eternally shut in.

To the Saint.   Rejoice in the liberty of the children to enjoy all the privileges of the household of faith.

OUTLINES

The Door

I am the
- Divine="the Lord."
- Open=" by the Blood."
- Only=no Salvation in any other.
- Refuge=from the wrath to come.

A Door

A Door
- Divides those in and out.
- Offers a refuge to all.
- Opens to those who knock.
- Receives those who enter into Rest.

LESSON 34

"I Am the Good Shepherd"

I. Text. "I am the Good Shepherd: the Good Shepherd giveth His Life for the sheep" (John 10. 11).

II. Main Lesson. The Lord represents Himself to us as a Shepherd. The Good (John 10. 11), the Great (Heb. 13. 20), and the Chief (1 Pet. 5. 4) Shepherd of the sheep—that is, His own redeemed people, those whom God has given to Him, those who have believed on Him.

He is the Shepherd and Bishop of our Souls (1 Pet. 2. 25).

Those who have returned to Him can say with David, "The Lord is My Shepherd: I shall not want."

He exercises all the offices of a Shepherd to tend His people.

III. Scriptures to Study:

Ezekiel 34. 11. *After a Stern Rebuke to the Unfaithful Shepherds of Israel (1-10), the Shepherd of Israel Speaks of His Care for the Sheep.*

vv. 11-12. "Thus saith the Lord God: Behold, I, even I, will both search My sheep, and seek them out. As a shepherd seeketh out his flock in the day that he is among his sheep that are scattered, so will I seek out My sheep, and will deliver them . . ."

v. 14. "I will feed them in a good pasture, and upon the high mountains of Israel shall their fold be: there they shall be in a good fold, and in a fat pasture shall they feed . . ."

v. 15. "I will feed My flock, and I will cause them to lie down, saith the Lord God."

v. 16. "I will seek that which was lost, and bring again that which was driven away, and will bind up that which was broken, and will strengthen that which was sick: . . ."

vv. 22-23. "Therefore will I save My flock, and they shall no more be a prey . . .; and I will set up One Shepherd over them, and He shall feed them, even My Servant David: He shall feed them, and He shall be their Shepherd."

John 10. 1-10. *The Shepherd Enters the Fold and Calls His Own Sheep by Name and Leads them out.*

v. 2. " He that entereth in by the door is the Shepherd of the sheep."

v. 3. " The sheep hear His voice: and he calleth His own sheep by name, and leadeth them out."

v. 4. " When He putteth forth His own sheep, He goeth before them, and the sheep follow Him: for they know His voice. And a stranger they will not follow. . . ."

The Shepherd Dies for the Sheep.

v. 11. " I am the Good Shepherd: the Good Shepherd giveth His life for the sheep."

v. 14. " I am the Good Shepherd, and know My sheep, and am known of Mine."

v. 15. " As the Father knoweth Me, even so know I the Father: and I lay down My life for the sheep."

v. 16. *He has other Sheep not of the Jewish Fold : them He Gathers so that both Form One Flock and One Shepherd.* " And other sheep I have, which are not of this fold: them also I must bring, and they shall hear My voice; and there shall be One Flock (R.V.), and One Shepherd."

v. 26. *Only Believers are His Sheep.* " But ye believe not, because ye are not of My sheep."

vv. 27-30. *His Sheep Receive Eternal Life and Cannot Perish.* " My sheep hear My voice, and I know them, and they follow Me: and I give unto them Eternal Life; and they shall never perish, neither shall any man pluck them out of My hand. My Father, which gave them Me, is greater than all: and no man is able to pluck them out of My Father's hand. I and My Father are One."

IV. Some Shepherds of the Bible.

1. ABEL (Gen. 4. 2), who brought of the firstlings of the flock the more acceptable sacrifice to God than Cain, his brother.

2. JACOB, who describes his work of a shepherd to Laban thus: " This twenty years have I been with thee; thy ewes and thy she goats have not cast their young, and the rams of thy flock have I not eaten. That which was torn of beasts I brought not unto thee; I bare the loss

of it; of my hand didst thou require it, whether stolen by day, or stolen by night. Thus I was; in the day the drought consumed me, and the frost by night; and my sleep departed from mine eyes " (Gen. 31. 38-40).

3. JOSEPH (Gen. 37. 2), whom the wicked shepherds, his brethren, sold as a slave, but whom God seated on the right hand of power in Egypt, and who became their Saviour.

4. MOSES (Exod. 3. 1), to whom God appeared in the burning bush while he fed his flock in Horeb.

5. DAVID (1 Sam. 16. 11), who in defence of the sheep slew a lion and a bear, who sang the Shepherd Psalm, " The Lord is my Shepherd " (Psa. 23. 1).

6. AMOS (7. 15), whom the Lord took from following the flock and said unto him, " Go, prophesy unto My people Israel."

7. THE SHEPHERDS OF BETHLEHEM, TO whom the Angel of the Lord announced the good tidings of great joy to all nations: " Unto you is born this day in the City of David a Saviour, which is Christ the Lord."

V. The Work of a Good Shepherd.

1. To GATHER THE FLOCK. Sheep readily go astray and follow one another into danger, like the lost sheep of the Parable (Luke 15. 4; Matt. 18. 12).

We were " as sheep going astray," and can say, " I have gone astray like a lost sheep; seek thy servant " (Psa. 119. 176).

The first duty of the shepherd is to seek out the lost and gather the scattered sheep together.

2. To KNOW THEM ALL. A good shepherd calleth his own sheep by name; they know his voice and follow him.

This personal and individual interest is the work of a good shepherd as contrasted with a hireling.

3. To DEFEND THEM EVEN AT THE COST OF HIS LIFE. So David faced the lion and the bear, risking his own life in order to save the sheep.

So the Lord gave His life to save the sheep.

4. To SEEK PASTURE FOR AND FEED THEM (1 Chron. 4. 39-41). He must find green pastures and quiet waters for them, so that they may lie down contented and be well nourished.

5. To LEAD THEM. The Eastern shepherd did not drive, nor use a dog to the sheep, but went before them and called any straying ones by name, or used the crook or staff to bring them back to himself if they strayed.

6. To BIND UP THE BROKEN (Ezek. 34. 4 and 16). Sheep sometimes fall and break their legs on the steep or treacherous mountain sides. It is the shepherd's duty to rescue them and bind up the broken.

7. To HEAL THE SICK. Sheep are not free from diseases, and suffer from cold and heat and even from overdriving. Such must be tended and healed.

8. To GO GENTLY WITH THOSE WITH YOUNG. In the lambing season this is imperative; to overdrive the ewes may mean that they will cast their young.

9. To CARRY THE LAMBS. Either the older sheep upon the shoulders when they are wounded, sick or wearied, or the lambs in his bosom.

10. To ACCOUNT TO THE OWNER FOR THEM. A good shepherd will not lose his sheep. So our Good Shepherd says to His Father of His sheep, " Not one of them is lost " (John 17. 12).

VI. Other Lessons from Christ as the Shepherd.

1. THE TITLES OF THE SHEPHERD.

(1) The *Good* Shepherd—that is, both *efficient* (good at His work) and *kind* (good and loving at heart). It was love that led Him to die for the sheep.

(2) The *Great* Shepherd (Heb. 13. 20), Whom God brought again from the dead. Great in Majesty, in Power, and in Wisdom.

(3) The *Chief* Shepherd (1 Pet. 5. 4), Who will at His coming reward under-shepherds who have fed and tended the flock.

(4) The *Bishop* Shepherd (1 Pet. 2. 25), Who oversees
the flock, receiving them as they come and preserving
them.

(5) *The Shepherd of Israel* (Psa. 80. 1), Who feeds and
leads Israel like a flock, Who will yet gather the scattered
people and be to them in their own land One Shepherd of
One Flock (Ezek. 34. 22).

(6) *God's Shepherd.* "Awake, O sword, against My
Shepherd" (Zech. 13. 7). The One Whom God spared not,
but was pleased to bruise for our iniquities, Who will one
day bring all the sheep entrusted to Him of the Father
home safely to God. The Shepherd Who will stand before
God (Jer. 49. 19 and 50. 44).

2. THE LORD'S CLAIM TO BE THE SHEPHERD. When
the Lord said, " I am the Good Shepherd," He evidently had
Psalm 23. 1 in mind: " Jehovah is My Shepherd." It was
an application of the Psalm to Himself, a claim to be
Jehovah, the Lord. The Jews so understood it (John
10. 33), for they took up stones to stone Him because, as
they said, " Thou, being a Man, makest Thyself God."

3. THE LORD MARKS HIS SHEEP (Rev. 7. 3-4). As
shepherds in our land do, either by painted or branded
signs of ownership upon them.

> " Then on each He setteth
> His own secret sign;
> They that have My Spirit,
> These, saith He, are Mine."

It is with the Spirit that He seals His sheep as a mark
of possession, an assurance of eternal life and a firstfruit
of future blessing.

4. THE LORD SEEKS THE LOST. In the simple and
lovely Parable of the Lost Sheep the Lord assures us that
He goes after the lost sheep *" until He find it."* He then
brings it home on His shoulders. He *rejoices over* the sheep
with all the household of faith. Even the Heavens rejoice.
So we learn His Love for, His Faithfulness to, and His
Joy in His own.

5. THE LORD PROVIDES A HOME FOR THE FLOCK.
Not like the Jewish fold, surrounded by a wall of partition

contained in ordinances, but a Church—a Flock, an Assembly, the Household of Faith, where there is mutual love and care each for the other, while He Himself is in their midst, the Shepherd of the sheep.

6. THE LORD WILL SEPARATE THE SHEEP FROM THE GOATS (Matt. 25. 32), taking from among His people those who, while they may be meeting with them, are not truly of them.

7. THE CHIEF SHEPHERD IS SOON TO COME AGAIN. "Surely," He says, "I come quickly." His reward is with Him, to give each according to his deeds. Then those who have been faithful under-shepherds will "receive a crown of glory that fadeth not away" (1 Pet. 5. 4).

VII. Application.

Let us follow our Shepherd, hearing His voice and yielding gladly to His control.

Let those who are under-shepherds act with a due sense of their responsibility to the Chief Shepherd.

OUTLINE

A Wonderful Text

John 10. 27-28 *revealing Christ as :*
SHEPHERD AND OWNER="My sheep."
OMNIPRESENT="Hear My voice."
OMNISCIENT="I know them."
LEADER AND COMMANDER="They follow Me."
LIFE GIVER="I give unto them eternal life."
PRESERVER="They shall never perish."
PROTECTOR="Neither shall any man pluck them out of My hand."

"I Am the Resurrection and the Life"*

I. Text. "I am the Resurrection, and the Life: he that believeth in Me, though he were dead, yet shall he live: and whosoever liveth and believeth in Me shall never die" (John 11. 25-26).

II. Main Lesson. Both physical and spiritual resurrection are to be known only in Christ. It is by association with Him that we have hope of life hereafter. "The life existing in Him and passing from Him to all believers is the cause and sure principle of all resurrection" (Stier). Thus He is both the Resurrection and the Life that effects it. He is the Resurrection because He is the Life.

Those who believe in Him receive a life that never dies. So the dead will live again and the living will never die.

III. Scriptures to Study :
John 11. 23-44.

v. 23. *The Lord Tells Martha that her Brother will Rise Again.* "Jesus saith unto her, Thy brother shall rise again."

v. 24. "Martha saith unto Him, I know that he shall rise again in the resurrection at the last day."

vv. 25-26. *Jesus Reveals Himself as the Resurrection and the Life.* "Jesus said unto her, I am the Resurrection, and the Life: he that believeth in Me, though he were dead, yet shall he live: and whosoever liveth and believeth in Me shall never die. Believest thou this ?"

v. 27. *Martha Protests her Faith in Christ.* "She saith unto Him, Yea, Lord: I believe that Thou art the Christ, the Son of God, which should come into the world."

1 Corinthians 15. 20-23, 42-49: *Christ Risen is the Firstfruits.*

---

* A Lesson on the Raising of Lazarus is to be found in *Seventy Best Bible Stories*, No. 63, pp. 229-231.

v. 20. " Now is Christ risen from the dead, and become the firstfruits of them that slept."

v. 21. *As in Adam all Die, so in Christ all Rise.* " For since by man came death, by man came also the resurrection of the dead."

v. 22. "For as in Adam all die, even so in Christ shall all be made alive."

v. 23. *Each will Rise in his own Order.* " But every man in his own order: Christ the firstfruits; afterward they that are Christ's at His coming."

vv. 42-44. *The Body Sown Rises a Spiritual Body.* " So also is the resurrection of the dead. It is sown in corruption; it is raised in incorruption: it is sown in dishonour; it is raised in glory: it is sown in weakness; it is raised in power: it is sown a natural body; it is raised a spiritual body. There is a natural body, and there is a spiritual body."

vv. 45-47. *The Two Adams: the First and Second Man.* " So it is written, The first man Adam was made a living soul; the last Adam was made a quickening spirit. Howbeit that was not first which is spiritual, but that which is natural; and afterward that which is spiritual. The first man is of the earth earthy: the second Man is the Lord from Heaven."

v. 49. *We shall Bear the Image of the Heavenly.* " As we have borne the image of the earthy, we shall also bear the image of the Heavenly."

IV. Some Different Aspects of Resurrection.

1. TEMPORARY RECALL to physical life. When the Lord said, "Thy brother shall rise again," He no doubt promised in the first instance that He would recall Lazarus to a prolongation of his life on earth, as He did.

There are seven outstanding cases of this in the Bible:

(1) *Elijah* called the widow of Zarephath's son to life again.

(2) *Elisha* called the Shunamite's son to life.

Our Lord Jesus recalled to life—

(3) Jairus' daughter.

(4) The widow of Nain's son.

(5) Lazarus.

(6) *Peter* brought back Dorcas to life.

(7) *Paul* restored Eutychus to life.

But resurrection in its full meaning is more than a temporary recall to the present existence.

2. Universal Resurrection. "As in Adam all die, so in Christ shall all be made alive " (1 Cor. 15. 22).

When Adam sinned the pronouncement was, "Thou shalt surely die." So death passed on him and all his seed. "In Adam all die."

That is to say, the whole human race passes by death into Hades, the realm of the dead.

Nothing was said to Adam of resurrection from the dead, nor of a second death after such resurrection.

But Christ brought resurrection to all.

All mankind—good and bad, righteous and wicked—all are called out of death.

Christ having then paid the penalty due to them for Adam's transgression, those who die *the second death* do so for their own sin, the rejection of Christ and the Light and Salvation He offers in the Gospel. None die the second death for Adam's transgression.

3. Present Resurrection Life. "If ye then be risen with Christ, seek those things which are above " (Col. 3. 1).

The believer in Christ is seen by God as having died with Christ and risen with Him.

The death and resurrection of His Divine Substitute is his death and resurrection. He can say, "I have been crucified with Christ: nevertheless I live; yet not I, but Christ liveth in me " (Gal. 2. 20).

This the believer reckons to be so (Rom. 6. 11), and henceforth regards himself as dead indeed unto sin and alive unto God.

His ambition thenceforth is to know Christ and the power of His resurrection (Phil. 3. 10) and to attain to the resurrection of the dead, a life entirely delivered from the things of the old dead life.

4. To Depart and be with Christ at death. "To depart and to be with Christ; which is far better " (Phil. 1. 23).

At death this body is dissolved (2 Cor. 5. 1), and the spirit departs to be with Christ, awaiting the redemption of the body (Rom. 8. 23) at the Coming of Christ. Till then the believer anticipates the "house from Heaven" with which he will be clothed when the Lord comes. It is described as "a building of God, an house not made with hands, eternal in the Heavens."

5. THE COMING OF CHRIST (the Parousia). This is fully described in 1 Thess. 4. 13-18.

The Lord will descend from Heaven and His saints be caught up in the clouds to meet the Lord in the air.

Then we shall be clothed upon with the resurrection body—the spiritual body, the house from Heaven, like to the Lord's glorified body—and be for ever with Him.

6. THE RESURRECTION OF CONDEMNATION (John 5. 29). This is fully and fearfully described in Rev. 20. 11-15. It will be a judgment of them that have done evil, according to the secrets of men, and to their works.

The Christ-rejecter who has died in his sins will be punished with everlasting destruction from the presence of the Lord.

V. The Hope of Resurrection in the Old Testament.

Very little was revealed in the Old Testament as to resurrection and the life beyond.

The Prophets were chiefly occupied with the earthly prosperity and the millennial blessing of the Elect People. They anticipated the Coming of Messiah, but chiefly as the Hope of Israel.

Yet there are glimpses of resurrection. The following are some:

Job 19. 25. "For I know that my Redeemer liveth, and that He shall stand at the latter day upon the earth: and though after my skin worms destroy this body, yet in my flesh shall I see God: Whom I shall see for myself, and mine eyes shall behold, and not another." (R.V. renders it "*from* my flesh," with margin "*without*.")

Hosea 6. 1-3. We give a striking translation by a Hebrew Christian, Mr. D. C. Joseph:

"Come, and let us return to the Lord: for He is torn,

and we are healed; He is smitten, and we are bound up. He revives after two days; on the third day He rises, and we shall live in His presence. Then we shall know if we follow on to know the Lord."

Daniel 12. 2. "Many of them that sleep in the dust of the earth shall awake, some to everlasting life, and some to shame and everlasting contempt. And they that be wise shall shine as the brightness of the firmament; and they that turn many to righteousness as the stars for ever and ever."

Psalm 17. 15. "As for me, I will behold Thy face in righteousness: I shall be satisfied, when I awake, with Thy likeness."

VI. Other Lessons from Christ the Resurrection and Life.

1. THE RESURRECTION OF CHRIST introduced Christianity to the world. It was "Jesus and the Resurrection" that the Apostles preached.

It became the great fact upon which the Christian faith is based. "If Christ be not raised, your faith is vain" (1 Cor. 15. 17).

2. CHRIST WAS THE FIRSTFRUITS. The first sheaf of a mighty harvest. His followers rejoiced in His assurance, "Because I live, ye shall live also."

The type of this is found in Leviticus 23. 11, when the third day after the Passover (the morrow after the Sabbath) *the sheaf of the firstfruits* was waved before the Lord.

The Gift of the Spirit was the *seal* and *firstfruits* (Rom. 8. 23), the earnest of the resurrection and fulness of life to follow (Eph. 1. 14).

3. LIFE IN CHRIST ASSURES RESURRECTION. We are "raised with Him." Until we have by faith become joined to the Lord, and become sharers with Him of a common life—even Eternal life—we have no hope of a glorious resurrection. In this sense He is to us the Resurrection and the Life—the Life which, being Eternal in principle, assures us of resurrection and eternity with Him.

4. HE IS THE RESURRECTION AND LIFE NOW TO HIS PEOPLE. Risen with Him, they live unto Him and in the power of His resurrection while here below.

As those that are " alive from the dead " (Rom. 6. 13), they yield themselves to Him and their members as instruments of righteousness unto holiness.

This resurrection life is an evidence that they will share in His glorious resurrection at the great day of His coming.

5. THE TWO CLASSES. " He that believeth in Me, though he were dead, yet shall he live " (John 11. 24). " He that liveth and believeth in Me shall never die " (25). That is, the believing dead and the living believers will alike share His resurrection life—death will not be death to them.

Another meaning may perhaps be inferred. When He comes, the dead will live, the living will never die, for both together (1 Thess. 4. 17) will be caught up to meet Him in the air.

VII. Application.

Let us see to it that we are found in Him; only such have Eternal life.

Let us live the resurrection life down here.

Let us anticipate His coming with holy joy.

OUTLINE

The Resurrection Life

The Believer is

- Risen with Christ.
- Indwelt by the Spirit.
- Seated in the Heavenlies.
- Entering into the Holiest.
- Never to see death.

"I Am the Way, the Truth, and the Life"

I. Text. "I am the Way, the Truth, and the Life: no man cometh unto the Father but by Me" (John 14. 6).

II. Main Lesson. The Lord Jesus not only claimed to be the Door into Salvation and Life, but the Way upon which the believer enters when he crosses the threshold of the door, and the Truth by which he is guided in the Way, and the Life by which he is invigorated and maintained as he pursues his journey along the way that leads to the Father. The three are one:

> Without the Way there is no Going.
> Without the Truth there is no Knowing.
> Without the Life there is no Growing.

Christ is all and in all to the believer.

III. Scriptures to Study :

John 14. 1-7.

vv. 1-3. *The Lord Comforts His Disciples by a Promise to Come Again.* "Let not your heart be troubled: ye believe in God, believe also in Me. In My Father's house are many mansions: if it were not so, I would have told you. I go to prepare a place for you. And if I go and prepare a place for you, I will come again and receive you unto Myself; that where I am, there ye may be also."

v. 4. *He Tells Them They Know the Way.* "And whither I go ye know, and the way ye know."

v. 5. *Thomas Asks how They can Know the Way.* "Thomas saith unto Him, Lord, we know not whither Thou goest; and how can we know the way ?"

v. 6. *The Lord replies that He is the Way.* "Jesus saith unto him, I am the Way, the Truth, and the Life: no man cometh unto the Father but by Me."

v. 7. *To Know Christ is to Know the Father.* "If ye had known Me, ye should have known My Father also: and from henceforth ye know Him, and have seen Him."

Hebrews 10. 19-22. *The New and Living Way.* " Having therefore, brethren, boldness to enter into the Holiest by the Blood of Jesus, by a New and Living Way, which He hath consecrated for us, through the veil, that is to say, His flesh."

v. 21. *The High Priest over the Household of God.* " And having an High Priest over the House of God."

v. 22. *How to Draw Near.* " Let us draw near with a true heart in full assurance of faith, having our hearts sprinkled from an evil conscience, and our bodies washed with pure water."

IV. Some Ways Mentioned in the Bible.

1. JACOB'S LADDER. Seen in his dream set up on earth, the top whereof reached to Heaven. This type the Lord applied to Himself in John 1. 51: " Hereafter ye shall see Heaven open, and the angels of God ascending and descending upon the Son of Man."

2. THE WAY INTO THE HOLIEST. The Holy of Holies, wherein was the Ark of the Covenant with the Mercy Seat, was shut off by a Veil. No one entered save the High Priest once a year, on the Day of Atonement (the tenth day of the seventh month). " The Way into the Holiest of all was not yet made manifest " (opened). But when Christ died He opened that way.

3. THE WAY OF HOLINESS (Isa. 35. 8). An highway, only for the cleansed, but the wayfaring men, though fools, shall not err therein. The ransomed of the Lord walk it with songs and everlasting joy.

4. THE NEW AND LIVING WAY. Opened in the Death of Christ, so that we draw near by the Blood of Jesus.

It is " through the Veil "—that is, the Body of Christ.

For we have been sanctified by the offering of the Body of Christ, once for all (Heb. 10. 10), and thus as purged worshippers we can come into the presence of God.

5. THE WAY OF GOD is described by many expressions:

" The Way of His steps " (Psa. 85. 13).

" A Perfect Way " (Psa. 10. 12).

" The Right Way " (Psa. 107. 7).

" The Way of Thy Testimonies " (Psa. 119. 14).

" The Way of Truth " (Psa. 119. 30).

" The Way Everlasting " (Psa. 139. 24).

" The Way of His Saints " (Prov. 2. 8).

" The Way of Good Men " (Prov. 2. 20).

" The Way of Righteousness " (Prov. 8. 10).

" The Way of Life " (Prov. 15. 24).

" The Way of the Ransomed " (Isa. 51. 10).

" The Way of Peace " (Isa. 59. 8).

" The Way of Salvation " (Acts 16. 17).

6. THE WAY OF THE WICKED is also described in many ways:

" Dark and Slippery " (Psa. 35. 6); " Hard " (Prov. 13. 15); " The Way of Death " (Jer. 21. 8); " False "(Psa. 119. 104); " Wicked " (Psa. 139. 24); " Lying " (Psa. 119. 29); " Folly " (Psa. 49. 13); " Darkness " (Prov. 4. 19); " The Way to Hell " (Prov. 7. 27); " The Way of a Fool " (Prov. 12. 15); " The Way to His Anger " (Psa. 78. 50).

V. Other Lessons on Christ the Way-Truth-Life.

1. NOT THREE, BUT ONE. The Lord is not telling us He is three separate things, but *three in one*. Just as He is the Resurrection because He is the Life, so He is the Way *because He is the Truth and the Life*. Only by His death and resurrection could He bring us to the Father, but having risen He becomes the Way. Having dealt with sin, He becomes our Righteousness. So that Grace and Truth and Life are ours through His finished work and risen power. He is the Way, Truth, and Life.

2. CHRIST IS HIMSELF THE WAY. " No man cometh unto the Father but *by Me*." He does not point out the Way as a Teacher, nor show us the Way as our example merely. *He is the Way*. I must have Christ if I am ever to be brought to the Father. I must *receive* Him (John 1. 12) and be *found in Him* (Phil. 3. 9), or I shall miss the Way.

3. CHRIST IS THE ONLY WAY. The law proved a way of condemnation and death. It made nothing perfect.

It could not justify or give me a righteous standing in God's sight. Only Christ can do this. Peter boldly asserted this before the High Priests (Acts 4. 12): " Neither is there salvation in any other: for there is none other Name under Heaven given among men whereby we must be saved."

4. THE TRUTH SEEN ONLY IN CHRIST. The natural man receiveth not the things of God: they are foolishness to him. But when he receives Christ his eyes are opened; he sees the truth, all becomes clear. No man knows truth apart from Christ. He is the Wisdom of God—the Truth. Earthly wisdom gropes in the dark until He, the Sun of Righteousness, enlightens.

5. PILATE'S QUESTION : WHAT IS TRUTH ? The Lord told Pilate, " Thou sayest that I am a king. To this end was I born, and for this cause came I into the world, that I should bear witness unto the truth. Every one that is of the truth heareth My voice " (John 18. 37).

Then Pilate asked, " What is Truth ?"

The Truth was there before Him.

6. A CURIOUS ANAGRAM. Pilate asked " QUID EST VERITAS ?" (" What is Truth ?"). Someone has put the answer into the form of an anagram, " EST VIR QUI ADEST " (" It is the Man Who is before thee ").

7. LET US DRAW NEAR (Heb. 10. 22). We must avail ourselves of the Way. To know the Way is not the same as taking it. We often speak of a way *leading* somewhere; this is actually true of only one Way. Christ the Way does lead us to the Father. The qualification is fourfold: *A True Heart*, no insincerity; *Full Assurance* of faith; *a clean heart*—that is, sprinkled from an evil conscience; *a pure body*, washed from outward defilement.

VI. Application.

To the Sinner. If we miss Christ we miss the only way to Heaven.

To the Saint. Let us see to it that we draw near in worship and walk in holiness.

To the Servant of God. See that we preach Christ, the Only, New, and Living Way.

"I Am the True Vine"

I. Text. "I am the Vine, ye are the branches: He that abideth in Me, and I in him, the same bringeth forth much fruit: for without Me ye can do nothing " (John 15. 5).

II. Main Truth. Israel had proved to be a "degenerate plant of a strange vine," although God had planted it "a noble vine, wholly a right seed " (Jer. 2. 21).

There was therefore no hope in being of the natural seed of Abraham (Matt. 3. 9; Rom. 2. 29, 9. 8; Gal. 3. 29).

But now Christ has come, the True Vine. It is by association with Him, by abiding in Him and He in us, as a branch in a Vine, that fruitfulness is realized. There is no fruit apart from Christ. Without Him we can do nothing.

The secret of abiding in Christ, the great secret of the Christian life, is taught us here.

III. Scripture to Study : John 15. 1-10.

v. 1. *The Lord Calls Himself the True Vine.* "I am the True Vine, and My Father is the Husbandman."

v. 2. *Fruitful Branches are Pruned to Bring More Fruit.* "Every branch in Me that beareth not fruit He taketh away: and every branch that beareth fruit He purgeth it, that it may bring forth more fruit."

v. 3. *He had already Cleansed the Disciples.* "Now ye are clean through the Word which I have spoken unto you."

v. 4. *They must therefore Abide in Him.* "Abide in Me, and I in you. As the branch cannot bear fruit of itself, except it abide in the Vine; no more can ye, except ye abide in Me."

v. 5. *He Repeats the Illustration.* "I am the Vine, ye are the branches: He that abideth in Me, and I in him, the same bringeth forth much fruit: for without Me ye can do nothing."

v. 6. *Men Burn Fruitless Branches.* "If a man abide

not in Me, he is cast forth as a branch, and is withered; and men gather them, and cast them into the fire, and they are burned."

v. 7. *Prayer is answered if we Abide in Him.* " If ye abide in Me, and My words abide in you, ye shall ask what ye will, and it shall be done unto you."

v. 8. *The Father Glorified by Fruit-bearing.* " Herein is My Father glorified, that ye bear much fruit; so shall ye be My disciples."

v. 9. *We must Abide in His Love.* " As the Father hath loved Me, so have I loved you: continue ye in My love."

v. 10. *We must Keep His Commands to Abide in Him.* " If ye keep My commandments, ye shall abide in My love; even as I have kept My Father's commandments, and abide in His love."

v. 11. *It is the Way of Joy.* " These things have I spoken unto you, that My joy might remain in you (*My joy in you might continue*), and that your joy might be full."

IV. Other Lessons from the Study.

1. THE VINE A TYPE OF ISRAEL. The Vine is one of the three trees used as figures or types of the Elect Nation—the Vine, the Olive (Rom. 11. 17), and the Fig (Luke 13. 7, 21. 29). The Vine is constantly so employed. The prophets Isaiah (5. 2), Jeremiah (2. 21, 6. 9), Ezekiel, (15. 2, 17. 6), Hosea (10. 1), and Joel (1. 7), all use it—all complaining that though God had planted His people in a good land, with a perfect law, a Divine religion, and every privilege, they had miserably failed to bring forth fruit unto Him.

2. CHRIST, THE TRUE VINE, had taken the place of Israel in the purposes of God. He was the Vine whose branches would bear fruit to the Glory of God, the Father Himself being the Husbandman.

To be a fruitful branch in the True Vine one must be *joined to the Lord.*

It is a similar idea to that of the head and the body. The nourishment of the body as well as its direction is from the head. So with the vine; the life and the vital force is in the vine, and passes through the branches. The branch has but to remain in vital union to be fruitful.

3. WHAT IS "ABIDING IN CHRIST"? The whole depends on this. We must abide in Christ, and He in us, if there is to be fruit. The word "abide" is found twelve times in this chapter (John 15), but is variously translated "abide," "remain," "continue," and elsewhere "dwell," "tarry," "stand" (Rom. 9. 11), and "endure" (1 Pet. I. 25), and "being present" (John 14. 25). The value of the word can be gathered from these various renderings.

What, then, does it mean?

Dr. F. Godet explains it: "The continuous act by which the Christian lays aside all that he might draw from his own wisdom, strength or merit, to derive all from Christ by the inward aspiration of Faith. . . . It is by constantly remembering and meditating on the words of Jesus (v. 7) that the disciple remains united to Him, and that He can continue to act on and by His disciple."

Dr. Westcott says: "The disciple must set his life in Christ and let Christ live in him. . . . Effect by God's help this perfect mutual fellowship, your abiding in Me and My abiding in you."

Dr. J. C. Ryle puts it: "Abide in Me. Cling to Me. Stick fast to Me. Live the life of close and intimate communion with Me. Get nearer and nearer to Me. Roll every burden on Me. Cast your whole weight on Me. Never let go your hold on Me for a moment. Be, as it were, rooted and planted in Me. Do this and I will never fail you. I will ever abide in you."

May we suggest more simply that abiding is *continuing in the unbroken communion of faith and love to Christ,* loyal always to Him, dependent always on Him?

4. THE ABIDING IS MUTUAL. "Abide in Me, and I in you."

As a sponge is in the water and the water is in the sponge.

As the light is in the air and the air is in the light.

As the Vine is in the branch and the branch is in the Vine.

Our hand is clasped in His and His hand is clasped in ours. Each holds the other.

So we find our joy in Him and He finds His joy in us (see verse 11 above).

His love is in us and our love in Him.

5. The Conditions of Abiding.

(1) *His Words must Abide in Us* (7). All the blessings that come to us from Christ are ministered through His Word. If His words abide in us richly, we shall be enriched by Him.

(2) *We must Abide in His Love* (9 and 10). That is, " Keep yourselves in the love of God " (Jude 21), allowing that love to constrain us (2 Cor. 5. 14).

(3) *We must Keep His Commandments* (10), for then we shall continue in His love, and there is special blessing for those who do so (John 14. 23).

6. The Results of Abiding.

(1) *There will be much Fruit*, and in this God will be glorified (8).

(2) *The Fruit will Remain* (16). It will be no passing effort.

(3) *We shall be Disciples indeed* (8, and compare 8. 31)— that is, true learners and followers.

(4) *Our Prayers will be Answered* (7), and we shall have great liberty in asking what we will.

(5) *The Lord will have Joy in Us still* (11). " That My joy in you may continue " (cf. Heb. 10. 38).

(6) *Our Joy will be Full* (11); for in His presence is fulness of joy, and at His right hand pleasures for ever-more.

(7) *God's Love will Dwell in Us* (10, and see 1 John 3. 17).

(8) *We shall not Sin* (1 John 3. 6). " Whosoever abideth in Him sinneth not."

(9) *We shall Walk in Light* (John 12. 46 and 1 John 2. 10).

(10) *We shall have Confidence* when our Lord returns (1 John 2. 28).

V. Application.

Let us see that we are true branches of the True Vine.

Let us beware lest we be put away as unfruitful branches.

Let us bear patiently the pruning, that we may bear more fruit.

Let us abide in Him and He will abide in us.

Let us fear all that would break our communion and thus hinder fruit-bearing.

OUTLINES

Seven things in which we must Abide

His Word (John 8. 31).

His Love (John 15. 10).

His Joy (John 15. 11).

The Faith (1 Tim. 2. 15).

Brotherly Love (Heb. 13. 1).

In the Light (1 John 2. 10).

In the Doctrine (2 John 9).

If we do so our

Righteousness will abide (2 Cor. 9. 9).

Fruit will remain (John 15. 16).

Work will abide (1 Cor. 3. 14).

Joy will be full (John 15. 14).

Love will abound (Phil. 1. 9).

We have an

ABIDING {
Priest (Heb. 7. 3).
City (Heb. 13. 14 and 11. 16).
Substance (Heb. 10. 24).
}

To Abide is to

" Always Be In Daily Enjoyment " of Christ.

The Crucifying

Described by Alfred Edersheim, D.D., in his " Life and Times of Jesus the Messiah "

" First the upright wood was planted in the ground. It was not high, and probably the Feet of the Sufferer were not above one or two feet from the ground.

" Thus could the communication described in the Gospels take place between Him and others; thus also might His sacred lips be moistened with the sponge attached to a short stalk of hyssop.

" Next the transverse wood (antenna) was placed on the ground and the Sufferer laid on it, when His arms were extended, drawn up and bound to it. Then (this not in Egypt, but in Carthage and in Rome) a strong sharp nail was driven first into the right, then into the left hand (the clavi trabales).

" Next the Sufferer was drawn up by means of ropes, perhaps ladders; the transverse either bound or nailed to the upright and a rest or support for the body (the cornu or sedile) fastened on it. Lastly, the feet were extended and either one nail hammered into each or a larger piece of iron through the two. And so might the crucified hang for hours, even days, in the unutterable anguish of suffering till consciousness at last failed."

SECTION V

Our Lord Jesus Christ:
The Cross in Type and Fact

"Him There"

" And sitting down they watched Him there "

" Him there !"   The Prince of Life and Love
Upon a Cross stretched out to die.
No eye to pity, arm to save.
Men wag the head as they pass by.

" Him there !"   The Sinless Son of God,
Who while He lived did only good,
Now mocked and put to open shame,
Despised, unloved, misunderstood.

" Him there !"   They taunt with ribald jest:
" Others He saved," and " trusted God."
" Come down from thence and save Thyself !"
Silent He hears, but speaks no word.

" Him there !" we see with grateful eyes
Bearing our sins upon the tree—
A Substitute for sinful men,
A Ransom paid to set us free.

" Him there !" a Willing Sacrifice,
Yielding Himself to wicked hands.
They take His life and yet fulfil
The counsel of Eternal plans.

" Him there !" we see and hear His cry,
As in the dark, with latest breath,
He yields His spirit up to God,
And passes to the realm of death.

No longer there, we see Him crowned
With glory on the throne above,
And know our sins are all forgiven,
And yield ourselves in faith and love.

G. G.

BOURNEMOUTH,
   March 17, 1939.

LESSON 38

Types and Shadows of the Cross

I. **Text.** "The Law having a shadow of good things to come, and not the very image of the things, can never with those sacrifices which they offered year by year continually make the comers thereunto perfect" (Heb. 10. 1).

II. **Main Lesson.** The Death of Christ for our sins was the Great Hour of the World's History. It was anticipated in the Garden of Eden (Gen. 3. 15), and all down the ages prophets have foretold the sufferings of Christ and the Glory that should follow (1 Pet. 1. 11), testifying that through the Name of Jesus "whosoever believeth in Him should receive remission of sins" (Acts 10. 43).

One form prophecy took was that of Typology, a remarkable foreshadowing in actual history of the truths of the Gospel.

Typology is Peculiar to the Bible. No other book has or could have anything of the kind.

Our Lord recognized it by using the types as pictures of Himself. As, for example, the Manna (John 6. 33, 48-51), the Brazen Serpent (John 3. 14) and Jonas (Matt. 12. 41). Our study is to discover some of the types of the Cross of our Lord Jesus Christ foreshadowing His sacrificial death.

III. **Scripture to Study :** Hebrews 9. 11-14, 22-28.

vv. 11-12. *Christ came to Fulfil all the Types of the Law.* "Christ being come an High Priest of good things to come, by a greater and more perfect tabernacle, not made with hands, that is to say, not of this building; neither by the blood of goats and calves, but by His own Blood He entered in once into the holy place, having obtained eternal redemption for us."

vv. 13-14. *The Animal Sacrifices compared with the One Sacrifice of Christ.* "For if the blood of bulls and of goats, and the ashes of an heifer sprinkling the unclean, sanctifieth to the purifying of the flesh: how much more shall the

217

Blood of Christ, Who through the eternal Spirit offered Himself without spot to God, purge your conscience from dead works to serve the living God ?"

v. 22. *Under the Law Purging was always by Blood.* " Almost all things are by the Law purged with blood: and without shedding of blood is no remission."

vv. 23-24. *Better Blood was needed to put away Sin.* " It was therefore necessary that the patterns of things in the heavens should be purified with these; but the heavenly things themselves with better sacrifices than these. For Christ is not entered into the holy places made with hands, which are the figures of the true; but into Heaven itself, now to appear in the presence of God for us."

vv. 25-26. *Nor was it necessary to Repeat the Offering of Christ.* " Nor yet that He should offer Himself often, as the High Priest entereth into the Holy Place every year with blood of others; for then must He often have suffered since the foundation of the world: but now once in the end of the world hath He appeared to put away sin by the sacrifice of Himself."

vv. 27-28. *He will come again.* " And as it is appointed unto men once to die, but after this the judgment: So Christ was once offered to bear the sins of many; and unto them that look for Him shall He appear the second time without sin unto Salvation."

The subject is continued in Chapter 10, which should also be studied.

IV. **Outstanding Types of the Cross.** We learn many lessons from the Cross; therefore many types of it are given.

Our part is to discern the distinctive lesson from each of these, so that we may have a full-orbed view of the glory and grace of the Cross—that is, the death of the Son of God for our sins.

1. ABEL'S LAMB is perhaps the earliest shadow of the Death of Christ. Of him we read that " by it he being dead yet speaketh." It remains for ever a type of Christ, but we read that the Blood of Sprinkling speaketh better things than did Abel by his type (Heb. 11. 4 and 12. 24).

For " The Lamb of God," see Lesson 50.

2. THE ARK is a type of Christ, since, when the judgment (the flood) fell, it fell on the Ark instead of on those inside. They were saved by being found in the Ark. So there is now no condemnation for them that are in Christ Jesus (Rom. 8. 1).

For the Story of the Ark see *Seventy Best Bible Stories*, No. 4, pp. 29-33.

3. THE PASSOVER is perhaps the outstanding type of Salvation by the Sprinkling of Blood.

This is dealt with separately in Lesson 42.

4. THE PASSAGE OF THE RED SEA teaches how by association with Christ by faith the believer passes through death and resurrection. Noah's Ark teaches a similar lesson. The sinner found in Christ passes through the storm of judgment and comes out into a new creation. He died with Christ by baptism into death, and is risen with Him to newness of life. In 1 Cor. 10. 1-2 we read: " Our fathers . . . all passed through the sea; and were all baptized unto Moses in the cloud and in the sea."

As they were associated with Moses and with him passed through the sea, so the believer associated with Christ passes through death and judgment.

5. THE SMITTEN ROCK teaches us that Christ was made a curse for us—Moses, the type of the Law, smiting the Rock. Living Waters (the Gift of the Holy Spirit) flowed from the Rock after it had been smitten.   John 7. 39 explains this: " This spake He of the Spirit, which they that believe on Him should receive: for the Holy Ghost was not yet given; because that Jesus was not yet glorified."

For a Lesson on the Smitten Rock, see *Seventy Best Bible Stories*, No. 14, pp. 62-64. For a Lesson on the Rock Smitten the Second Time, see *Seventy Less Known Stories*, No. 14, pp. 85-88.

6. THE BLOOD OF THE COVENANT. Exodus 24. 3-8 (referred to in Heb. 9. 18-22) illustrates to us how a Covenant had to be ratified by blood. After the Covenant had been read both the people and the book were sprinkled with blood, and thus solemnly pledged to obedience to its terms.

Our Lord Jesus ratified the new Covenant by His own blood (Matt. 26. 38).

For a Lesson on Christ as the Mediator of the Covenant, see No. 51.

7. THE TABERNACLE is full of Lessons on the Value of the Blood of Christ, the whole speaking of Him, and each item of it having some distinct glory of Him to teach. So wide is this subject that it cannot be gone into here. Its great lesson is the Way of a Sinner's approach to God —coming by the Gate, the Altar, the Laver, and through the Holy Place to the Very Presence of God in the Holiest through the rent Veil. Only by the Blood of Jesus can we do this (Heb. 10. 19-20). (The Ark of the Covenant is discussed in Lesson 43.)

8. THE FIVE LEVITICAL OFFERINGS. Each of these has a different aspect of the Cross to teach us. Shortly, the Offerings set forth:

The Burnt Offering (Lev. 1) speaks of *the Perfect Obedience of Christ* in doing the whole Will of God.

The Meat Offering (Lev. 2) of the Perfect Sinless Character of Christ as qualifying Him to become the Lamb of God.

The Peace Offering (Lev. 3) sets forth Christ as our Peace (see Lesson 40), Who, having made Peace through the Blood of His Cross, speaks Peace to every believer.

These three offerings were *Sweet Savour Offerings*, and typified the acceptability of Christ to God as offering Himself for us as an offering and a sacrifice to God for a sweet-smelling savour.

The next two typified Christ under judgment. *The Sin Offering* (Lev. 4)—differing according to the status of those for whom it was offered: the priest (v. 3), the whole congregation (v. 13), a ruler (v. 22), or one of the common people (v. 27)—shows us Christ bearing judgment for our lost estate as " all under sin."

The Trespass Offering (Lev. 5) tells us of our trespasses, and how they are forgiven on the ground of the blood.

9. THE RED HEIFER (Num. 19). This peculiar offering was for those who defiled themselves by contact with the dead. It consisted of a young cow entirely red, whose

blood was first offered and then its body reduced to ashes
on a heap of wood outside the camp.

The ashes were preserved and used as occasion demanded,
being sprinkled with the water of separation on the offender
on the third and on the seventh day.

It typifies the believer who has defiled his conscience
and needs to be restored to the joy and fellowship of God's
salvation.   It is discussed in Lesson 41.

10. THE LEPER'S TWO BIRDS (Lev. 14. 1-8).   This offering
that the leper who had been healed was to offer for his
cleansing is one of the simplest and most beautiful of the
types of Christ in death and resurrection.

The one bird was slain over running water and its blood
put upon the leper's right ear, right thumb, and right
great toe, the other bird, dipped in the blood and water,
was released in the open field.   The two birds are one,
setting forth Christ dying, then risen and ascended, and
so bearing away our sin.

11. THE DAY OF ATONEMENT (Lev. 16) is perhaps the
fullest and most wonderful of all the types of the death of
Christ.   It portrays for us in striking imagery the double
aspect of the work of Christ.   First the blood of the one
goat being taken into the Holiest and sprinkled on the
Mercy Seat so that *God was satisfied*; then the sins laid
upon the scapegoat and borne away into the wilderness
so that the *sinner was satisfied*, and his soul rejoiced to see
the curse removed.

For a Lesson on this subject, see *Seventy Familiar Bible
Stories*, No. 16, pp. 79-82.

12. THE BRAZEN SERPENT (Num. 21. 4-9).   This type has
the honour of having been chosen by Christ Himself as
a figure of His death.   " As Moses lifted up the serpent
in the wilderness, even so must the Son of Man be lifted
up: that whosoever believeth in Him should not perish,
but have eternal life " (John 3. 14-15).

There are many more; the student can look them out
and study them.   These suffice for the purpose of this
Lesson to show how the Cross was typified down the ages.

V. Other Lessons from the Types of the Cross.

1. GROUPS OF TYPES.   The types concerning the death of Christ may be divided into three principal groups. They may for convenience be called:

(a) *The Earlier Types*—those in Genesis and Exodus. They show the value of the death of Christ to the *sinner seeking salvation*.   Two things distinguish them from the second class, the Levitical types.   There is no laying on of hands and no priesthood.

In other words, they are the death of Christ as seen by one not yet identified by faith with his Lord: the Ark, the refuge from the coming storm; the Passover, shelter from the destroyer; and so on.

(b) *The Levitical Types* are the death of Christ as seen by the saved sinner, *the saint, the worshipper*.   He has been identified with Christ; he has a great priest in Christ, and can speak in terms of substitution.   He delights to contemplate the death of Christ in its varying aspects, each showing him more of its wonders and filling him with worship.

(c) *The Numbers Types* reveal Christ as meeting the need of the pilgrim in his wilderness journey and conflict down here below.

The Brazen Serpent brings him " life for a look," that new life which alone fits him for his walk and work; the Red Heifer makes provision for the purging of the conscience should it become defiled again by contact with the dead things of the past; the crossing of the Jordan teaches him his position as dead and risen with Christ, so that he can enter the Promised Land—that is, the Land of Promises —and enjoy all the blessings in the Heavenlies in Christ.

2. THE TYPES AS EVIDENCE OF INSPIRATION.   Anyone who studies the types, those foreshadowings of good things to come, will find in them a wonderful evidence of the inspiration of Scripture.

Who could have anticipated, 1,500 years before the event, the Deliverance effected by Christ our Passover dying for us, as does that marvellous type ?

That the types are there, none but the most obstinate can deny; that they exactly forecast the events any spiritual

man can see. Who could have done this thing but He
Who knows the end from the beginning ?

3. INTERPRETING THE TYPES. We are not left to guess
their meaning. Almost all of them are interpreted for
us in the New Testament. Not only are we told " all these
things happened for ensamples " (types) (1 Cor. 10. 11),
and that the Holy Ghost signified certain things by them
(Heb. 9. 8), but both the Lord and the Apostles used them
and told us their meaning. Christ is our Passover; He
must be lifted up as was the Brazen Serpent; He is the
Bread that came down from Heaven; the Rock that was
smitten was Christ; and so on.

No one may challenge the value of the types after this.

4. THE TYPES ONLY SHADOWS. We are told they were
not the very image of the things (Heb. 10. 1); for shadows
are only outlines. Shadows do not give details or colours
or perspective, so that we must not press the types too far
or attempt to make types where none are intended. Some
dear brethren once discussed what the six water-pots of
stone at the wedding in Cana meant, until after an hour's
discussion a simple brother said, "Maybe they were just
pots !"

Truths plainly taught in the New Testament are often
twisted from incidents in the Old Testament more ingeni-
ously than helpfully or convincingly.

5. FORWARDS AND BACKWARDS. The Old Testament
believers looked forwards to the death of Christ and were
justified thereby; the New Testament saints look back to
Calvary and are at peace with God. The one anticipated
it by observing the Passover, the other remember it in the
Lord's Supper.

It has been likened to the bunch of grapes that the spies
carried on a pole from Eshcol. The one in front saw it
not, but knew it was coming; the other saw it plainly as he
walked behind.

VI. Application.

Let us ponder the types, for in them many a light will
be thrown on the Great Event of the Ages.

Let us be simple and sincere in handling them, not treating them cunningly to display our skill.

Let us use them to open the eyes of such as yet do not know the value of the Cross.

Let us, above all, learn to worship as we remember our Lord, and show His death till He come.

The Message of the Cross

In the Cross of Christ I see,
  All the Love of God to me;
He it was who loved and gave,
  Guilty, sinful men to save.

In the Cross of Christ I know
  Something of my Saviour's woe.
I may surely read therein,
  All the sinfulness of sin.

In the Cross of Christ I learn
  Righteous judgment to discern;
See the Substitute for me
  Cursed and smitten on the Tree.

There I see my Surety die
  For a sinner such as I,
There my broken heart can trace
  All the riches of His grace.

At the Cross my soul finds peace,
  From its burden full release;
There I may be reconciled,
  And confessed by God His child.

G. G.

Meaning of the Great Words used in Scripture of the Death of Christ

1. ATONEMENT: to be at one, or at-one-ment. "The reconciliation or restoration of friendly relations between God and sinners" (Oxford Dictionary).

But the Hebrew word (*kaphar*) means a covering, and

the thought in the Old Testament is that God covered the sins of His people by the blood of sacrifice, putting them out of sight (behind His back, in the depths of the sea).

The word is not used in the New Testament (Rom. 5. 11 should have " reconciliation " as in the R.V.).

2. MEDIATION: the work of an intermediary, one who acts between two persons. God wrought our Salvation through Christ, who was therefore our Mediator. He is called the Mediator of the New Covenant, because He secured for us by His death the better promises made by God in that Covenant.

3. "MADE SIN " (2 Cor. 5. 21) means that Christ was made a Sin Offering, having our sins imputed to Him and suffering for them as our Substitute that we might have righteousness imputed to us. He was made sin that we might become righteousness.

4. "MADE A CURSE " (Gal. 3. 13): by having our sins imputed to Him He involved Himself in the curse due to them. He bore it and so redeemed us from it. The just penalty of the law was discharged.

5. PROPITIATION (1 John 2. 2 and 4. 10). The word in Romans 3. 25 is the same as " mercy seat " in Hebrews 9. 5. It is the place where the sinner can meet God because of the Blood sprinkled there. Propitiation means Satisfaction. Christ has satisfied God on our behalf. He is now our Propitiation before God (1 John 2. 2), the One in Whom God has been and is satisfied.

6. RECONCILIATION means to make peace. The Lord " made peace by the Blood of His Cross."

7. REDEMPTION is deliverance by a price paid. The Price is the Ransom; the redemption, the liberty following on it.

8. SUBSTITUTION is not a Bible word but a great Bible truth. It means one taking the place of another, being substituted for the other—a blessed exchange. So Christ was the substitute for all who believe, the Head dying instead of all the members.

9. SURETY. One who makes himself responsible for the liability of another. The Lord Jesus became surety for all His saints and discharged on the cross all their liability.

The Burnt Offering

I. Texts. " Walk in love, as Christ also hath loved us, and hath given Himself for us, an offering and a sacrifice to God for a sweet-smelling savour " (Eph. 5. 2).

" Lo, I come (in the volume of the book it is written of Me,) to do Thy will, O God " (Heb. 10. 7; Psa. 40. 7).

II. Main Lesson. The Burnt Offering was peculiar in that the whole of it was consumed upon the altar. No part was eaten by either priest or offerer, as in the case of the other Levitical Offerings.

It therefore typified the death of Christ as being a complete and perfect act of obedience to the Will of God. " He was obedient unto death, even the death of the Cross " (Phil. 2. 8).

No study of Christ would be complete without considering the Perfect Submission of Christ to the Will of God. He was the whole Burnt Offering.

The Burnt Offering was a Sweet Savour offering, and set forth in type the satisfaction and love of God to the Son in that He died for sinners. In this, as in all else, He was the Well-Beloved Son in Whom the Father was well pleased. As the Lord Himself said, " Therefore doth My Father love Me, because I lay down My life " (John 10. 17). He was an offering and a sacrifice to God for a sweet-smelling savour (Eph. 5. 2).

III. Scripture to Study : Leviticus 1. 2-9.

v. 2. *The Lord's Command as to the Burnt Offering.* " Speak unto the children of Israel. If any man of you bring an offering unto the Lord, ye shall bring your offering of the cattle, even of the herd, and of the flock."

v. 3. *A Burnt Sacrifice of the Herd.* " If his offering be a burnt sacrifice of the herd, let him offer a male without blemish : he shall offer it of his own voluntary will [R.V. that he may be accepted before the Lord] at the door of the Tabernacle."

v. 4. *He must lay his Hand on its Head as his Substitute.* " He shall put his hand upon the head of the burnt offering; and it shall be accepted for him to make an atonement for him."

v. 5. *He must then Kill it.* " And he shall kill the bullock before the Lord."

v. 5. *The Priests then Sprinkle its Blood.* " The priests, Aaron's sons, shall bring the blood, and sprinkle the blood round about upon the altar."

v. 6. *He then Cuts it to Pieces.* " He shall flay the burnt offering and cut it into his pieces."

vv. 7-9. *The Whole Laid in Order on the Altar and Burnt.* " Aaron's sons shall put fire upon the altar, and lay the wood in order upon the fire . . . and shall lay the parts, the head, and the fat, in order upon the wood. . . . But his inwards and his legs shall he wash in water: and the priest shall burn all on the altar, to be a burnt sacrifice, an offering made by fire, of a sweet savour unto the Lord."

IV. Some Burnt Offerings.

1. THE FIRST MENTIONED IN SCRIPTURE (Gen. 8. 20). Noah took of every clean beast and fowl and offered them as burnt offerings on the altar he built on coming out of the Ark after the flood. It is said, " And the Lord smelled a sweet savour."

2. ABRAHAM (Gen. 22. 2) was commanded to take his only son Isaac and offer him for a burnt offering. It was then that he made the wonderful prophecy, " God will provide Himself the Lamb for a burnt offering " (8, R.V.).

The ram caught in the thicket that was offered up instead of Isaac was a burnt offering (13).

3. GIDEON (Judg. 6. 26) cut down the grove and altar to Baal, and offered his father's second bullock for a burnt offering.

4. JEPHTHAH (Judg. 11. 31) rashly promised to give to the Lord whatever came forth to meet him on his return from the battle, or offer it up for a burnt offering.

5. MANOAH (Judg. 13. 16-20) offered a burnt offering, in the flame of which the Angel of the Lord ascended.

6. SAMUEL (1 Sam. 8. 9) offered a suckling lamb as a burnt offering when the Philistines threatened Israel, so that the Lord thundered upon them and they fled.

7. DAVID (2 Sam. 6. 17) offered burnt offerings on the occasion of his bringing the Ark to Jerusalem, and again when the plague broke out (2 Sam. 24. 25), on which occasion the Lord answered with fire from Heaven (1 Chron. 21. 26).

8. SOLOMON (1 Kings 8. 64) offered many burnt offerings at the dedication of the Temple, when again fire came from Heaven and consumed the burnt offering (2 Chron. 7. 1), and the glory of the Lord filled the Temple.

9. ELIJAH (1 Kings 18. 38) offered a burnt offering when he challenged the prophets of Baal. The fire again fell from Heaven and consumed it.

10. EVERY MORNING AND EVENING on Sabbaths and new moons, and on almost all special occasions, burnt offerings were offered.

V. Other Lessons from the Burnt Offering.

1. SWEET SAVOUR OFFERINGS, while they set forth the death of Christ, had not propitiation so much in view as homage, devotion, and thanksgiving.

They were *voluntary*, whereas the propitiatory offerings (sin and trespass) were compulsory.

This would appear from the cases of Isaac and Jephthah's daughter (who were certainly not propitiations for sin, but voluntary gifts to God).

The burnt offering was a sweet savour to God in that it made atonement for sin, and in this God rejoiced.

The death of Christ was acceptable and well-pleasing to God and drew out His Love (John 10. 17), because of the grace, self-sacrifice, and perfect obedience displayed in it; and that atonement was thereby made, and man redeemed was a further sweet savour to God.

2. GOD'S PART IN THE DEATH OF CHRIST. It must ever be remembered that God is the Saviour; He mediated our

salvation through His Only Begotten Son, Who is therefore
also called our Saviour.

But we must beware of speaking as if Christ had to save
us from God. " *He did not die to save us from God, but to
bring us to God.*"

God Purposed it.   It was He Who in love devised means
whereby His banished ones be not expelled from Him.

God's Grace Planned it.   He commends His Love to us,
in that Christ died for us (Rom. 5. 8).

> " Grace first contrived the plan
> To save rebellious man."

The Cross revealed the Love of God.

God was in Christ reconciling the world to Himself
(2 Cor. 5. 19). He had chosen this way to put away
sin.

God Saves those who come through Christ (Heb. 7. 25).
It is He Who justifies them (Rom. 8. 33), Who gives the
seal of the Holy Spirit and accepts as His children those
who come by Christ to the Throne of Grace.

3. OUR LORD'S PERFECT SUBMISSION TO THE WILL OF
GOD. It was this that made the Burnt Offering a sweet
savour, a sacrifice well-pleasing to God.

His Obedience began at His coming into the world,
when He said, " Lo, I come to do Thy will."

His First Utterance as a boy was: " Wist ye not that I
must be about My Father's business ?" (Luke 2. 49).

His Purpose was, " I must work the works of Him that
sent Me."

His Meat was to do the will of Him that sent Him, and
to finish His work (John 4. 34).

The Temptation manifested that He would not act
independently nor tempt the Lord His God.

In the Garden of Gethsemane, when the dread hour was
come, He prayed, "Nevertheless, not My will, but Thine
be done."

Twice the Father Testified from Heaven, " This is My
Beloved Son in Whom I am well pleased."

The Lord Himself Testified, " I do always those things

which please the Father," and in the prayer in the upper room, " I have glorified Thee on the earth, I have finished the work which Thou gavest Me to do."

On the Cross He offered Himself without spot to God, not by compulsion; no man took His life from Him: He laid it down of Himself.

So He was obedient unto death, even the death of the Cross.

This was the Burnt Offering that was a sweet savour to God.

4. THE ONLY OBEDIENT MAN. Never had God been able to look down on earth upon a perfectly obedient man. He had to conclude all in disobedience (Rom. 11. 32, R.V.). There was none righteous. But now, as His eyes rested on Christ, He beheld one who was obedient from the heart, perfect in every iota of the Law. It was He, without spot or blemish, Who could become a whole burnt sacrifice.
> " There was none other good enough
> To pay the price of sin."

5. THE OBEDIENCE OF JOY. Obedience that is forced is not obedience from the heart. Here the Law failed, for compulsion and obedience under threat of sanctions could never please God.

But the Lord Jesus rejoiced to obey. " I delight to do Thy will, O My God: yea, Thy Law is within My heart."

Even in dying it was *for the Joy set before Him* that He endured the Cross, despising the shame.

He could truly say, " Oh, how I love Thy Law: it is My meditation all the day long."

6. OUR EXAMPLE. In this He is our Perfect Exemplar.

Those who are born again exhibit the same spirit. They love the Will of God as He did; they rejoice in the Law of God as He did; they yield themselves unto God " a living sacrifice, holy, acceptable unto God " (Rom. 12. 1).

For the Eternal Life that was manifested on earth in Him (1 John 1. 1-2) has been given to them.

Let us see that we lay hold of it, and, living in the power of it, walk even as He walked.

VI. Application.

Let us see in the Will of God our highest happiness.
Let us follow our Lord in His delight to do it.
Let us yield our bodies a Living Sacrifice.
Let us seek to walk as He walked.

OUTLINE

Peter a Witness of the Sufferings of Christ (5. 1)
Seven References in 1 Peter

1. We have been redeemed by the precious Blood of Christ (1. 19).
2. Christ suffered, leaving us an example (2. 21).
3. He bore our sins in His body on the Tree (2. 24).
4. He suffered for sins, the Just for the unjust, to bring us to God (3. 18).
5. He suffered in the flesh; arm yourselves with the same mind (4. 1).
6. We may be partakers of His sufferings (4. 13).
7. Be not ashamed of suffering as a Christian (4. 16).

Let us

O { Open our hearts.
    Offer ourselves.
    Obey in faith.

B { Believe the Word.
    Behold the Example.
    Beware of sinning.

E { Enter the Holiest.
    Enjoy Communion.
    Eschew all evil.

Y { Yield our bodies.
    Yearn after holiness.
    Yoke ourselves to Christ.

"He is Our Peace"

I. Texts. "For HE is our Peace, Who hath . . . broken down the middle wall of partition between us . . . for to make in Himself of twain one new man, so making peace" (Eph. 2. 14).

"And having made peace through the Blood of His Cross, by Him to reconcile all things unto Himself" (Col. 1. 20).

II. Main Lesson. The Lord Jesus is our Peace in the following ways:

1. HE MADE PEACE through the Blood of His Cross, so that He is *our Peace Offering*.

2. HE CAME AND PREACHED PEACE—to the Jew who was " near " by Covenant relationship, and to the Gentile who was " afar off," having no hope (Eph. 2. 17).

3. He is Himself THE PRINCE OF PEACE (Isa. 9. 6), and will one day establish peace on this warring and troubled earth.

4. HE IS OUR PEACE—that is, between Jew and Gentile, who were separated by "a wall of partition contained in ordinances " (the Mosaic law). Having " abolished in His flesh the enmity " by taking both into the one body by the Cross (Eph. 2. 16), He has slain the enmity and reconciled them—both to God and to one another—making One New Man.

5. HE BEQUEATHED HIS PEACE TO HIS DISCIPLES BEFORE HE LEFT THEM. " Peace I leave with you, My Peace I give unto you: not as the world giveth give I unto you " (John 14. 27).

6. HE BRINGS FORTH THE FRUIT OF PEACE in His people by the Spirit, for " the Fruit of the Spirit is Love, Joy, Peace " (Gal. 5. 22).

7. HIS PEACE GARRISONS OUR HEARTS AND MINDS so that nothing can disturb or rob us of that Peace (Phil. 4. 7).

III. **Scripture to Study** : Eph. 2. 11-19.

vv. 11-12. *The Gentiles were Aliens, Strangers, having no Hope.* " Wherefore remember, that ye being in time past Gentiles in the flesh . . . that at that time ye were without Christ, being aliens from the commonwealth of Israel, and strangers from the covenants of promise, having no hope, and without God in the world."

v. 13. *But now are Made Nigh by the Blood of Christ.* " But now in Christ Jesus ye who sometimes were far off are made nigh by the Blood of Christ."

v. 14. *He is our Peace.* " For He is our Peace, Who hath made both One, and hath broken down the middle wall of partition between us."

v. 15. *The Enmity between Jew and Gentile Abolished.* " Having abolished in His flesh the enmity, even the law of commandments contained in ordinances; for to make in Himself of twain one new man, so making peace."

v. 16. *They are Reconciled in One Body.* " And that He might reconcile both unto God in one body by the Cross, having slain the enmity thereby."

v. 17. *He Came and Preached Peace.* " And came and preached peace to you which were afar off, and to them that were nigh."

v. 18. *Both have Access now to the Father.* " For through Him we both have access by One Spirit unto the Father."

v. 19. *Now we are Fellow-Citizens with the Saints.* " Now therefore ye are no more strangers and foreigners, but fellow-citizens with the Saints, and of the Household of God."

IV. **Christ our Peace Offering.** Of all the Levitical Offerings, none is so full of instruction as the Peace Offering. It brings before us the Work of Christ as making Peace through the Blood of the Cross, reconciling us to God and bringing us into holy fellowship with Him.

It is most like the Lord's Supper of all the types, for the worshipper ate of the sacrifice as well as the priest.

The account of the Peace Offering is in Leviticus 3. 1-17, and the Law of the Peace Offering in Leviticus 7. 11-21, 29-34.

Let us observe the *Seven Steps in the Offering of the Peace Offering* (R.V.M.), also called the *Salvation Offering* (LXX).

1. IT COULD BE EITHER A CALF (male or female), A LAMB (male or female), OR A GOAT, and must be accompanied by its meal offering—cakes made with oil and leavened bread —and its drink offering of wine. The offerer brought the animal and tied it to the horns of the altar (Psa. 118. 27).

2. THE OFFERER THEN PUT HIS HANDS UPON THE HEAD OF THE ANIMAL (Lev. 3. 8). This was a figure of identification and substitution. The man became, for the purpose of the sacrifice, one with the animal, so that it could be accepted for him, dying instead of him. It is thus that we by faith become identified with Christ—

> " My faith would lay her hand
> On that dear Head of Thine,
> While like a penitent I stand,
> And there confess my sin."

It was, moreover, a symbolic transfer of the offerer's sins to the sacrificial animal, as in the case of the scapegoat it is said, " *all their sins, putting them on the head of the live goat* " (Lev. 16. 21).

3. THE OFFERER THEN HIMSELF SLEW THE ANIMAL. For we have to confess the fact that it was our sins for which Christ died, that we were guilty of the murder of Calvary. Our sins were imputed to Him, so that " Christ died for our sins according to the Scriptures."

4. THE PRIEST THEN SPRINKLED THE BLOOD UPON THE ALTAR ROUND ABOUT. This was an evidence of death to be seen of all.

For without shedding of blood is no remission.

So Christ, our Great Priest, has passed through the Heavens and now appears in the Presence of God, bearing in His Body the evidences of His death.

He is there for us, both as our Advocate and our Propitiation (1 John 2. 1-2).

5. THE FAT WAS THEN BURNT UPON THE ALTAR. That is, the excellency of the Offering was to be God's portion.

For the death of Christ was " *an offering and a sacrifice to God for a sweet-smelling savour* " (Eph. 5. 2). The Peace Offering was a " sweet savour " unto the Lord (Lev. 3. 5), and the word used for burning is not "consume," but " *cause to ascend,*" as if it were incense.

So we think of God finding delight in that One Offering that evidenced the perfect obedience of the One Beloved Son, but brought to the many sons Eternal Redemption. "Therefore," Jesus said, "doth My Father love Me, because I lay down My life."

6. THE PRIESTS THEN RECEIVED THE WAVE BREAST AND THE HEAVE SHOULDER AS THEIR PORTION (Lev. 7. 34), for those who serve the altar are partakers and eat of the sacrifices (1 Cor. 10. 18).

7. THE OFFERER ALSO ATE OF THE SACRIFICE—the Peace offering being the only one of the Levitical offerings of which this was true.

Here, then, we have a beautiful type of fellowship, the reconciled sinner enjoying fellowship with the Father and with His Son Jesus Christ over the finished work of the Cross (1 John 1. 3).

Like the prodigal at the father's table enjoying the fatted calf (the peace offering might be a calf).

Either male or female being allowed as a peace offering suggests that in Christ that distinction is abolished (Gal. 3. 28).

The leaven in the bread reminds us that there is still sin in the believer, though reconciled and at peace with God through the Blood.

The solemn injunction of Leviticus 7. 20 should be borne in mind:

" *The soul that shall eat of the flesh of the sacrifice of peace offerings which pertain unto the Lord, having his uncleanness upon him, even that soul shall be cut off from His people.*"

Let us, then, come to the Lord's table "with a true heart, in the full assurance of faith, having our hearts sprinkled from an evil conscience, and our bodies washed with pure water" (Heb. 10. 22).

V. Other Lessons on Christ our Peace.

1. CHRIST THE CENTRE is the ground of Peace. Where men gather to some party name (see 1 Cor. 1. 12-13, the beginning of Exclusivism), or to a creed, or a man-made organization calling itself "the Church," there will always be strife, pride, and dissension. Only as Christ is recognized as the Head of the One Body, and all hold the Head, will there be peace among Christians.

2. OBEDIENCE THE PRACTICAL WAY OF PEACE. So it is written, "Great peace have they that love Thy Law, and nothing shall offend them" (Psa. 119. 165). Our troubles arise, not from obedience to, but departure from, the truth of the Bible. Those who yield to their Lord the Obedience of Faith and Love know and enjoy the Peace that passeth understanding.

3. THE GOSPEL IS CALLED THE GOSPEL OF PEACE (Rom. 10. 18) because it brings the message of Peace with God on the ground of Peace made by the Cross and received by faith (Rom. 5. 1).

There is no peace to the wicked (Isa. 48. 22), but the Gospel is the proclamation of peace. Its reception at once speaks peace to the sinner.

4. PRAYER IS THE MEANS OF RETAINING OUR PEACE. "Be careful for nothing, but in everything by prayer and supplication, with thanksgiving, let your requests be made known unto God: and the Peace of God, that passeth all understanding, shall keep your hearts and minds through Christ Jesus."

Prayer casts the burden on the Lord.
Prayer changes things.
Prayer is the language of faith.
Prayer brings the soul into Peace.

VI. Application.

Let us see to it that, being justified by faith, we have peace with God.

Let us seek peace and pursue it in all our relationships.

Let us walk in the obedience of faith to Christ, that our peace be made to flow as a river.

OUTLINES

PEACE from the PRINCE of PEACE
- Purchased (Col. 1. 20).
- Promised (John 14. 27).
- Preached (Eph. 2. 17).
- Prayed for (1 Tim. 2. 2).
- Perfect (Isa. 26. 3).
- Passing understanding (Phil. 4. 7).
- Pursued (1 Pet. 3. 11; 2 Tim. 2. 22).

The Seven Steps in the Offering of the Peace Offering
(IV. 1-7)

1. Chosen and tied to Horns of Altar=CHOSEN AND DEVOTED.
2. Hands laid on Head=IDENTIFICATION.
3. Slain by the Offerer=CONFESSION.
4. Blood Sprinkled on Altar=ATONEMENT.
5. Fat burnt=GOD'S PORTION.
6. Breast and Shoulder given to Priest=PRIESTS' PORTION.
7. Offerer eats of it=SINNER'S PORTION.

The Red Heifer

I. Text. " For if . . . the ashes of an heifer sprinkling the unclean, sanctifieth to the purifying of the flesh; how much more shall the Blood of Christ . . . purge your conscience from dead works to serve the Living God?" (Heb. 9. 13-14).

II. Main Lesson. The Offering of the Red Heifer is unique among the various sacrifices as being the only one where *the continuing efficacy of the death of Christ* is typified.

The preservation of the ashes for future use suggests the *abiding virtue of the death of Christ*, as John puts it in his first Epistle: " The Blood of Jesus Christ His Son cleanseth us from all sin " (continually avails to cleanse).

There is, therefore, no need for Christ to die a second time (Heb. 9. 25) or for the offering to be repeated, as in the blasphemy of the Mass.

The ashes are the remembrance of a death that once took place.

The one defiled by contact with the dead is the Christian whose conscience has become defiled by the things that belong to his unregenerate days—by sin and by turning again to folly.

The ashes mingled with the water of separation were sprinkled upon him on the third day and on the seventh day.

The water of separation (or " water of impurity " or " waters of sprinkling ") represents the Word of God (Ezek. 36. 25; Eph. 5. 26) applied in the Power of the Holy Spirit to the heart, so that sin is judged, separated from and purged.

The defiled conscience is relieved and the sinning believer restored to fellowship and peace.

III. Scripture to Study : Numbers 19. 2-22.

v. 2. *A Red Heifer without Spot Chosen.* "This is the ordinance of the Law. . . . Speak unto the children of Israel, that they bring thee a Red Heifer without spot, wherein is no blemish, and upon which never came yoke."

v. 3. *Eleazer to Take it without the Camp and Slay it.* "Ye shall give her unto Eleazer the priest, that he may bring her forth without the camp, and one shall slay her before his face."

v. 4. *The Blood Sprinkled before the Tabernacle.* "Eleazer . . . shall take of her blood with his finger, and sprinkle of her blood directly before the tabernacle of the congregation seven times."

v. 5. *The Body Burned.* "One shall burn the heifer in his sight; her skin, and her flesh, and her blood, with her dung shall he burn."

v. 6. *Cedar Wood, Hyssop, and Scarlet cast into it.* "The priest shall take cedar wood, and hyssop, and scarlet, and cast it into the midst of the burning of the heifer."

vv. 7 and 8. *The Priest and the Man Unclean until Even.* "The priest shall wash his clothes, and bathe his flesh . . . and be unclean until the even. He that burneth her shall wash . . . and be unclean until the even."

v. 9. *The Ashes Laid up for a Purification for Sin.* "A man that is clean shall gather up the ashes of the heifer, and lay them up without the camp in a clean place, and it shall be kept . . . for a water of separation: it is a purification for sin."

v. 10. *The Man who does so to be Unclean.* "He that gathereth the ashes . . . shall wash his clothes, and shall be unclean until the even."

vv. 11-12. *Anyone Touching the Dead to Purify Himself therewith.* "He that toucheth the dead body of any man shall be unclean seven days. He shall purify himself with it on the third day, and on the seventh day he shall be clean."

vv. 17-18. *How the Ashes were Sprinkled.* "For an unclean person they shall take of the ashes of the burnt heifer of purification for sin, and running water shall be put thereto in a vessel: and a clean person shall take hyssop, and dip it in the water, and sprinkle it upon the tent, and upon all the vessels, and upon the persons that were there, and upon him that touched a bone, or one slain, or one dead, or a grave."

v. 19. *On the Third and Seventh Day.* " The clean person shall sprinkle upon the unclean on the third day, and on the seventh day: and on the seventh day he shall purify himself, and wash his clothes, and bathe himself in water, and shall be clean at even."

IV. Particulars as to the Heifer.

1. IT WAS A FEMALE. Usually in sacrifice a male was required. But in the peace offering (Lev. 3. 1), the sin offering for the common people (Lev. 4. 28), the purification of the leper (Lev. 14. 10), the trespass offering (Lev. 5. 6), the case of a man found slain (Deut. 21. 3), and at the end of the Nazarite's vow (Num. 6. 14), a female was employed.

2. IT MUST BE RED. If two hairs black or white were found it was disqualified under the Rabbinical Law. Matthew Henry quaintly says on this: " Christ as man was the Son of Adam—red earth; and we find Him red in His apparel, red with His own blood, and red with the blood of His enemies."

3. IT MUST NEVER HAVE HAD YOKE UPON IT. If even a cloth had been laid on it, the Rabbi disqualified it.

The same requirement is found in Deuteronomy 21. 38; 1 Samuel 6. 7.

4. CEDAR, AND HYSSOP, AND SCARLET were cast into the burning. It is difficult to say why.

Cedar and Hyssop were regarded as having medicinal qualities.

The Scarlet was, we learn from Hebrews 9. 19, scarlet wool, but its significance has never been discovered.

5. THE HEIFER WAS NEVER OFFERED ON THE ALTAR, but burnt outside the camp, the blood being sprinkled towards the Tabernacle seven times. This gave it a peculiar significance as rather a memorial than an actual sacrifice.

6. THOSE WHO HAD TO DO WITH IT WERE RENDERED UNCLEAN, which was not the case with the Levitical offerings. That the same things should render unclean and purify was a thing the Jews said even Solomon himself could not understand.

7. THE WHOLE CEREMONY TOOK PLACE " OUTSIDE THE CAMP," the place of judgment, where we read in Hebrews 13. 12 Jesus suffered for us, the place of separation whither we go out to Him (13).

8. THE WATER OF PURIFYING was used when the Levites were consecrated (Num. 8. 7). It is called the " water of expiation " in the R.V.

It was also used to cleanse things taken as spoil in battle (Num. 31. 23): they were to be " purified with the water of separation."

9. THE THIRD AND SEVENTH DAYS—the Days of Resurrection and Completion.

10. THE SPRINKLING OF THE BLOOD WITH HYSSOP reminds us of David's prayer, " Purge me with hyssop, and I shall be clean; wash me, and I shall be whiter than snow."

Hyssop, the meanest of the herbs, that sprang out of the wall (1 Kings 4. 33), may speak of humiliation, as did the bitter herbs at the Passover of sincere repentance.

11. THE NEGLECT OF CLEANSING meant that the one who failed to purify himself had his uncleanness upon him, and was to be cut off from the congregation as having defiled the sanctuary (20).

V. Other Lessons from the Red Heifer.

1. THE CLEANSING BY BLOOD IS ONCE FOR ALL. Justification by the Remission of Sins is once for all. One does not need to be Redeemed by Blood more than once. He is " perfected for ever " by the One offering (Heb. 10. 14). He is " clean every whit," Jesus said, if once bathed (John 13. 10).

2. THE BELIEVER WHO HAS SINNED needs to use the ashes of the Heifer—that is, to remember the One offering

and its eternal efficacy and plead it before the Father, knowing that if we confess our sins He is faithful and just to forgive us our sins, and to cleanse us from all unrighteousness.

3. "CLEANSE US FROM ALL UNRIGHTEOUSNESS" (1 John 1. 9) suggests the sprinkling of the ashes with the water of separation.

The believer must not allow sin to remain on his conscience, or, like water allowed to remain on steel, it will rust, but must judge and put away everything unrighteous by the application of the Word of God to his life in the energy and power of the Spirit of God.

"If through the Spirit ye do mortify the deeds of the body, ye shall live" (Rom. 8. 13).

4. UNJUDGED SIN IN A BELIEVER will lead to judgment. "For if we would judge ourselves we should not be judged, but when we are judged we are chastened of the Lord, that we should not be condemned with the world" (1 Cor. 11. 31-32).

The "cutting off from the congregation" suggests that if a believer continues in his uncleanness the Lord will put him away from His assembly and the fellowship of His people around the Lord's Table.

VI. Application.

Let us rejoice in our Eternal Redemption through the Blood.

Let us avail ourselves of the provision made in Christ for the sins of believers.

Let us beware of continuing either with a bad conscience or in the practice of any evil.

Things that must be CLEAN

The Conscience (Heb. 9. 14, 10. 22).
The Hands (Jas. 4. 8).
The Ways (Psa. 119. 9).
The Heart (Jas. 4. 8; Psa. 51. 10).
The Vessel (Isa. 66. 20; 2 Tim. 2. 21).
The Garments (Eccles. 9. 8; Rev. 7. 14).
The Body (Heb. 10. 22).

Christ Our Passover*

I. Text. " Even Christ our Passover is sacrificed for us: therefore let us keep the feast, not with old leaven, neither with the leaven of malice and wickedness; but with the unleavened bread of sincerity and truth " (1 Cor. 5. 7-8).

II. Main Lesson. The incident recorded in Exodus 12 is generally called the Passover because then the Lord passed over the houses of those who had sprinkled the Blood, to protect the Firstborn from the Destroyer; but in the account the Lamb is called " *the Lord's Passover* " (11) and " *the Sacrifice of the Lord's Passover* " (27), and this is confirmed by the text above, " Christ our Passover hath been sacrificed for us."

Christ is our Passover (as the Lamb was Israel's) in the following particulars:

1. HE WAS THE SACRIFICE ON THE GROUND OF WHICH GOD PASSES OVER the guilty sinner when he believes that is, the Sacrifice of the Lord's Passover.

2. HE WAS GOD'S FIRSTBORN given for the life of Israel's firstborn. God said of Israel (Exod. 4. 22), " Israel is My Firstborn." We have here, then, a figure of substitution.

3. HE WAS QUALIFIED TO BE A SACRIFICE OF PASSOVER in that He was without blemish.

Other qualifications are given below.

III. Scripture to Study : Exodus 12. 3.

v. 3. *The Lamb for the Passover Described.* " In the tenth day of this month they shall take to them every man a lamb, according to the house of their fathers, a lamb for an house."

v. 5. *It must be without Blemish.* " Your lamb shall be

---

* For a Lesson on the Story of the Passover, see *Seventy Best Bible Stories*, No. 12, pp. 56-58, and " Behold the Lamb of God," No. 50 in this volume. This Lesson is directed to the Person rather than the history.

without blemish, a male of the first year: ye shall take it out from the sheep, or from the goats."

v. 6. *It must be Kept till the Fourteenth Day.* "And ye shall keep it up until the fourteenth day of the same month."

v. 6. *It must be Killed in the Evening.* "And the whole congregation of Israel shall kill it in the evening."

v. 7. *The Blood must be Sprinkled.* "And they shall take of the blood, and strike it on the two side posts and on the upper door post of the houses, wherein they shall eat it."

v. 8. *Its Body must be Eaten.* "And they shall eat the flesh in that night, roast with fire, and unleavened bread; and with bitter herbs they shall eat it."

v. 9. *Not Raw, but Roast with Fire.* "Eat not of it raw, nor sodden at all with water, but roast with fire . . . and with the purtenance thereof."

v. 10. *Nothing to Remain until the Morning.* "And ye shall let nothing of it remain until the morning; and that which remaineth of it until the morning ye shall burn with fire."

v. 11. *Eaten in Haste with Loins Girt.* "Thus shall ye eat it; with your loins girded, your shoes on your feet, and your staff in your hand; and ye shall eat it in haste: it is the Lord's Passover."

IV. Other Lessons on Christ our Passover.

1. SEVEN TITLES FOR THE PASSOVER in Exodus 12:

(1) The *Lord's Passover* (11).

(2) The *Sacrifice* of the Lord's Passover (27).

(3) This *Service* (26).

(4) *A Token* upon the houses (13).

(5) *A Memorial* (14).

(6) *A Feast* (14).

(7) *An Ordinance for ever* (14).

It was to be celebrated yearly on the fourteenth day of the first month by *a Holy Convocation* (16), followed by *the Feast of Unleavened Bread,* lasting for seven days.

2. OUR PASSOVER CHOSEN. "They shall take to them every man a Lamb " (3); "Every man . . . shall make your count for the Lamb " (4).

None can be saved without Christ. There is a personal responsibility upon each to take or receive Christ for himself, for to be without Him is to perish by the Destroyer.

3. OUR PASSOVER MUST BE WITHOUT BLEMISH. A sinner must die for his own sins; he could never be a substitute for another's guilt.

So Christ was without spot or blemish before God, or He could not have been our Passover (1 Pet. 1. 19).

4. OUR PASSOVER must be slain. For without the *shedding* of blood there is no remission. "The Son of Man must be lifted up." "Except a corn of wheat fall into the ground and die, it abideth alone."

5. OUR PASSOVER'S BLOOD must be sprinkled on the heart's door. Faith must make a personal application of the Sacrifice to its own case.

This is by "faith in His Blood" (Rom. 3. 25).

6. OUR PASSOVER MUST BE EATEN. So Christ said, "He that eateth Me shall live by Me."

He becomes our soul's food. *Roast with fire* indicates that He has passed through judgment for us.

7. OUR PASSOVER MUST BE EATEN WITH BITTER HERBS. That is, Christ must be received with genuine repentance. Unless there is a true renouncing of the hidden things of darkness there will be no true appropriating faith.

We believe with a view to ceasing from all sin.

8. OUR PASSOVER MUST BE EATEN IN HASTE. For there is danger in delay. We must seek the Lord while He may be found; we must call upon Him while He is near. He calls, as He did to Zacchæus, "Make haste."

9. OUR PASSOVER MUST BE EATEN WITH LOINS GIRT AND WITH STAFF IN HAND: for we become pilgrims when we receive Christ. We turn our backs on Egypt (the world) and escape from Pharaoh's tyranny (the Devil) when we receive Christ to follow Him.

10. OUR PASSOVER IS FOLLOWED BY THE FEAST OF UN-LEAVENED BREAD. "Let us keep the feast" means let us

live unsinning lives ever afterwards, putting away all leaven of malice and wickedness.

For those Redeemed by Blood must cease to sin.

11. OUR PASSOVER MUST BE CELEBRATED by a Memorial Feast. As Israel of old never forgot that great Redemption day, so on the first day of each week believers love to keep the Passover in memory by a Memorial, a Feast, a Service and an Ordinance for ever—that is, till He shall come again.

So around their Lord's Table they remember Him Who was their Passover and show His death.

V. Application.

Let the Sinner make haste lest the Destroyer find him without any protection.

Let the Believer rejoice in the sprinkled Blood that speaks his safety.

Let the Saint feed upon the Lamb by meditation and worship.

Let the Children of God assemble at their Lord's Table to remember Him and show His death till He come.

OUTLINE

CHRIST our PASSOVER

was
- Chosen of God.
- Holy and without spot or blemish.
- Roast with fire (under judgment).
- Instead of the sinner (Substitute).
- Sprinkled us by His Blood (faith availing itself of His death).
- Taken as Food (eaten).

The Passover Feast was a (see IV. 1)
- Passover (the Lord's).
- Assembly (Holy Convocation).
- Service.
- Sacrifice.
- Ordinance for ever.
- Victory (celebrated).
- Eating (Feast).
- Remembrance of the Exodus.

Christ, the Ark of the Covenant

I. Text. " Whom God hath set forth to be a propitiation (*hilastērion*=Mercy Seat, Heb. 9. 5) through faith in His Blood " (Rom. 3. 25).

II. Main Lesson. The Ark of the Covenant which stood within the Holy of Holies was a type of Christ.

It was the symbolic Throne of God, and reminds us that God is enthroned in Christ. It is " in Christ " that He meets the sinner, who, now that Christ has died and the Veil been rent and the Blood been sprinkled on the Mercy Seat, is bidden to draw near (Heb. 10. 22), to come boldly to the Throne of Grace, that he may obtain mercy and find grace to help in time of need (Heb. 4. 16).

The various parts of the Ark shall have our attention.

III. Scripture to Study : Exodus 25. 10-22.

v. 10. *The Size of the Ark.* " And they shall make an Ark of shittim wood: two cubits and a half shall be the length thereof and a cubit and a half the breadth thereof, and a cubit and a half the height thereof."

v. 11. *It must be Overlaid with Gold.* " And thou shalt overlay it with pure gold, within and without shalt thou overlay it, and shalt make upon it a crown of gold round about."

v. 12. *Rings to Carry it.* " And thou shalt cast four rings of gold for it, and put them in the four corners thereof; and two rings shall be in the one side of it, and two rings in the other side of it."

vv. 13-15. *Staves of Shittim Wood Overlaid with Gold.* " And thou shalt make staves of shittim wood, and overlay them with gold. And thou shalt put the staves into the rings by the sides of the ark, that the ark may be borne with them. The staves shall be in the rings of the ark: they shall not be taken from it."

v. 16. *The Ark to Contain the Law.* " And thou shalt put into the ark the testimony which I shall give thee."

v. 17. *A Mercy Seat of Pure Gold.* "And thou shalt make a mercy seat of pure gold: two cubits and a half shall be the length thereof, and a cubit and a half the breadth thereof."

vv. 18-19. *Two Cherubims of Beaten Gold.* "And thou shalt make two cherubims of gold, of beaten work shalt thou make them, in the two ends of the mercy seat. And make one cherub on the one end, and the other cherub on the other end: even of the mercy seat shall ye make the cherubims on the two ends thereof."

v. 20. *The Cherubims Look Toward the Mercy Seat.* "And the cherubims shall stretch forth their wings on high, covering the mercy seat with their wings, and their faces shall look one to another; toward the mercy seat shall the faces of the cherubims be."

v. 21. *The Mercy Seat upon the Ark.* "And thou shalt put the mercy seat above upon the ark; and in the ark thou shalt put the testimony that I shall give thee."

v. 22. *It is the Place of Communion with God.* "And there I will meet with thee; and I will commune with thee from above the mercy seat, from between the two cherubims which are upon the ark of the testimony, of all things which I will give thee in commandment unto the children of Israel."

IV. The Parts of the Ark and their Symbolism.

1. THE TABERNACLE. The whole of this wonderful Tent in the Wilderness was a Type of Christ. Each part has a distinct lesson to teach of Him.

We read in John 1. 14 that "The Word was made flesh and tabernacled [*eskenōsen*] among us."

And in Hebrews 8. 2 Christ is said to be "a Minister of the Sanctuary and of *the True Tabernacle*, which the Lord pitched, and not man." This no doubt refers to the Sinless Body that God prepared for Him, and in which He fulfilled all the types in the Tabernacle.

The "Temple of His Body," as He Himself called it (John 2. 21).

In Hebrews 9. 11 He is said to have come "by *a greater*

and more perfect Tabernacle, not made with hands, that is to say, not of this building " (R.V. " creation ").

Space does not permit us to enlarge on this the most perfect and complete type of Christ.

2. THE ARK OF THE COVENANT consisted of the following parts:

(*a*) *The Box* of shittim wood covered with pure gold, 2½ by 1½ by 1½ cubits.

(*b*) *The Mercy Seat* above it, and forming the lid or covering: 2½ by 1½ cubits.

(*c*) *The Two Cherubims* upon the ends of the Mercy Seat, spreading their wings over it and looking down upon it, of beaten gold; no dimensions given.

(*d*) *The Golden Crown* round the Ark.

(*e*) *Golden Rings* upon the four corners, with *staves* of shittim wood by which to carry the Ark on the shoulders of the Kohathites, the sons of Levi, when it journeyed.

The whole, as we saw in the main lesson above, formed a Symbolic Throne of God.

3. THE ARK OR CHEST was a box of shittim wood overlaid with gold. It was constructed to contain the Two Tables of Stone on which the Ten Commandments were written. Later two other things were put into it:

The Pot of Manna (Exod. 16. 33-34).

The Rod that Budded (Num. 17. 10).

These are all referred to as being in the Ark in Hebrews 9. 4; but later the two last were removed, for we read in 1 Kings 8. 9, " There was nothing in the ark save the two tables of stone which Moses put there at Horeb."

4. THE THREE THINGS IN THE ARK. The Ark may be regarded as the Heart of Christ, for it is written, " Thy law is within My heart."

It indicates, too, that the Throne of God is based upon Righteousness, the Law of God being the Foundation of the Government.

The Manna speaks of Christ as the Food of His people —He Himself claiming to be the Bread which came down from Heaven of which if a man eat he shall never die (John 6. 50).

The Rod speaks of His Authority as the High Priest and the Fruitful Branch.

There is, however, another way of regarding those things in the Ark. Each of them was a memorial of the rebellion of the people; each recalled the sin of the people, for the occasions of their being put therein were those of the Golden Calf, the Murmuring of the People, and the Rebellion of Korah, Dathan and Abiram.

The Mercy Seat with the Sprinkled Blood covered these memorials of their iniquity, illustrating the truth of the New Covenant, "Their sins and their iniquities will I remember no more."

5. THE MERCY SEAT. The *hilastērion* or Propitiatory is expressly said to be a Type of Christ in Romans 3. 25, for there we read, "Whom God hath set forth to be a Mercy Seat through faith in His Blood."

It was on the tenth day of the seventh month each year that the High Priest, on the Great Day of Atonement, dressed, not in robes of glory and beauty, but in his white linen robes (Lev. 16. 4), entered into the Holy of Holies with the Blood of the Sin Offering that had been offered outside, and sprinkled it upon and seven times before the Mercy Seat.

The evidence of the finished sacrifice was thus brought into the Presence of God, and on the ground of it the people were reconciled to God.

Christ, we read, "by His own Blood entered once ["once for all," R.V.] into the Holy Place, having obtained Eternal Redemption for us."

6. THE CHERUBIMS overshadowing the Mercy Seat. There is much enquiry as to the exact meaning of these wonderful living creatures.

Some regard them as representing all creation; others as the executive power of God.

Perhaps more simply they may be looked upon as those spiritual beings or intelligences that attend upon the Deity, beautiful angels who go and return as a flash of light to do the Will of God.

The first mention of them is in Genesis 3. 24, keeping

the way to the Tree of Life; they seem to be supporters
of the Throne of God: " He rode upon a Cherub " (Psa. 18.
10) and " He that sitteth [enthroned] above the Cherubims "
(Psa. 80. 1; 1 Sam. 4. 4).

That these angelic beings are interested in the Great
Mystery of Godliness we know, from their joy at the birth
of Christ (Luke 2. 13), their ministry to the Lord, and from
1 Peter 1. 12, where we read, " Which things the angels
desire to look into " (and see Eph. 3. 10).

Their presence on the Mercy Seat looking down on the
Blood-sprinkled Propitiatory suggests this interest in the
matter of man's Salvation.

7. THE CROWN OF GOLD suggests the dignity of our Lord
Jesus. " We see Jesus crowned with Glory and Honour,"
and one day He will wear " many diadems."

8. THE RINGS AND STAVES were provided that the priests,
the sons of Kohath, might carry the Ark upon their
shoulders. It was the failure to observe this that brought
about the breach of Uzzah, when David essayed to bring
the Ark to Jerusalem (2 Sam. 6. 6-7; see 1 Chron. 15. 13).

V. Some Other Lessons from the Ark.

1. THE WAY INTO THE HOLIEST was not yet made manifest
(Heb. 9. 8) until Christ died, but now, the Veil (that is,
His flesh) having been rent, all may come boldly to the
Throne of Grace (Mercy Seat or Throne, Heb. 4. 16).

2. THE DIVINE PRESENCE over the Mercy Seat. The
Shekinah Glory filled the Tabernacle at its dedication
(Exod. 40. 34-35), and appears to have rested over the
Mercy Seat; for God is said to dwell between the Cherubims
(Psa. 99. 1).

When Nadab and Abihu presumed to enter that Holy
Presence with strange incense and probably in a drunken
condition, they were struck dead for their folly.

3. " THERE WILL I MEET WITH THEE AND COMMUNE
WITH THEE." It is the highest privilege of the believer
to draw near to God in Christ, to enter the Holiest of all
by the Blood of Jesus, and to have fellowship with God.

" In the secret of His Presence how my soul delights to hide;
    Oh, how precious are the moments that I spend at Jesus' side !"

" Of all things which I will give thee in commandment."
It is in the presence of our God that we learn the joy of
the obedience of faith, finding His law our delight.

> " Within the Holiest of all,
>   Cleansed by His Precious Blood,
> Before Thy throne Thy children fall,
>   And worship Thee, O God " (J. G. DECK).

VI. Application.

Let us meditate on the Glories of Christ as discovered
in this Type.

Let us avail ourselves of drawing near and communing
with God.

Let us rejoice that the Throne is Blood-sprinkled and
becomes a Mercy Seat.

OUTLINES

The Three ARKS

1. Noah's Ark (Gen. 6. 14).
2. The Ark of Bulrushes (Exod. 2. 3).
3. The Ark of the Covenant (Exod. 25. 10).

The ARK in Seven Scenes

1. In the Holy of Holies (Heb. 9. 4).
2. On the wilderness journey (Num. 10. 35).
3. Crossing the Jordan (Josh. 3. 15).
4. Carried round Jericho (Josh. 6. 6).
5. On the battlefield (1 Sam. 4. 4).
6. In Dagon's temple (1 Sam. 5. 2).
7. In Heaven (Rev. 11. 19).

Five Aspects of the Cross

I. Text. " God forbid that I should glory save in the Cross of our Lord Jesus Christ, by Whom the world is crucified unto me, and I unto the world " (Gal. 6. 14).

II. Main Lesson. The Cross of Christ, which means both the death of Christ and the reproach attaching to those who confess the Crucified One as Lord and Saviour, may be viewed from different aspects.

There are five expressions used of it, as follows:

1. AS ENDURED BY THE LORD JESUS=The *DEATH* of the Cross—that is, with its pain and shame.

2. AS SEEN BY GOD=The *BLOOD* of the Cross. For it is He who says, " When I see the Blood I will pass over you."

3. AS PREACHED TO THE SINNER=The *WORD* (or preaching) of the Cross, in which is offered Eternal Life.

4. AS SUFFERED BY THE BELIEVER=The *OFFENCE* of the Cross: the reproach he bears.

5. AS ACKNOWLEDGED BY THE DISCIPLE=The *GLORY* of the Cross. In it he glories as being by it crucified to the world, and the world to him.

III. The Scriptures in which the expressions occur.

1. THE DEATH OF THE CROSS (Phil. 2. 8). " Being found in fashion as a man, He humbled Himself, and became obedient unto death, even the death of the Cross."

And Hebrews 12. 2: " Who for the joy set before Him endured the Cross, despising the shame."

2. THE BLOOD OF HIS CROSS (Col. 1. 20). " Having made peace through the Blood of His Cross, by Him to reconcile all things unto Himself."

3. THE WORD OF THE CROSS (1 Cor. 1. 18). " For the Preaching (R.V., " Word ") of the Cross is to them that

perish foolishness, but unto us which are saved it is the power of God."

4. THE OFFENCE OF THE CROSS (Gal. 5. 11). "I, brethren, if I yet preach circumcision, why do I yet suffer persecution ? then is the offence of the Cross ceased."

5. THE GLORY OF THE CROSS (Gal. 6. 14). "But God forbid that I should glory, save in the Cross of our Lord Jesus Christ, by Whom the world is crucified unto me, and I unto the world."

IV. Other Lessons from the Cross.

1. THE CROSS AS A SYMBOL. The wearing of crosses or the bowing to or adoration of them is a great mistake. The Cross was the Roman gibbet upon which the world murdered the Lord of Glory; to choose it as an ornament or use it as a fetish is to forget that it represents the hatred of wicked men, and to overlook the fact that *Christ is risen*. There is no Cross now: it is a long-past event; only the efficacy of the death of the Saviour Who died thereon remains, with the reproach attaching to all who confess the Holy One Who died, but is now crowned with glory and honour.

2. THE DEATH OF THE CROSS. Two things are involved in this expression—the physical pain and the shame or indignity of it. Of these we read that the Lord " *endured the Cross.*" He died as any brave man would without any shadow of cowardice or craven fear. Though dying in the vigorous strength of full manhood, pure and noble, yet He withheld not His Holy Body from the suffering; He endured the Cross.

The Shame He Despised, not with any bitterness or contempt for His enemies, but treating it as nothing for the joy of saving sinners.

The Suffering of the Cross lay in its sacrificial character. His soul was made an offering for sin; He was made sin for us; he was made a curse for us: in this lay the bitterness and grief.

Of the suffering He endured we gather something from

the Messianic Psalms (see Psa. 22, Lesson 45), such as Psalm 69. 1-4 and 17-21.

3. THE BLOOD OF THE CROSS. The expression " Blood " means " the Blood shed," for without *Shedding* of Blood is no remission (Heb. 9. 22).

The Life is in the Blood, so that the Shedding of Blood means the Life laid down, the Soul poured out unto death.

" The Blood " is another way of saying the Sacrificial Death of Christ for our sins.

It is a Past Event, a Finished Work. All expressions that speak of the Blood as if it were flowing now, or as if material blood existed now, must be carefully avoided as offending against the Finished Work of Christ.

The Blood, the Evidence of Death, was sprinkled on the Mercy Seat, a memorial of a Sin Offering already offered on the Burnt Altar.

So God sees the Finished Work of Christ, since He appears in the Presence of God for us with the marks of His death on Him, " *as a Lamb slain* "; and on the ground of that Perfect Offering receives, justifies, sanctifies, and perfects for ever those who draw near to Him by the Blood of Jesus.

4. THE WORD (OR PREACHING) OF THE CROSS. The Word of the Cross is the Proclamation to Sinners of a full and free Salvation on the ground of the Finished Work of Christ.

The Cross tells of Reconciliation made, for God was in Christ reconciling the world unto Himself; and because of it the sinner is invited, even entreated, to be reconciled to God.

(a) *This Preaching Sweeps aside all Man's Pretensions*. The Cross, being the murder by man of the Son of God, leaves man without excuse, guilty and utterly condemned. His sin is seen in its true light at the Cross. It is the rejection of the Love, Law, Authority, and Rule of Christ. It is man in his self-will saying, " Away with Him. We will not have this man to reign over us."

Where the Cross is faithfully preached man will see himself a hopelessly guilty murderer.

(b) *The Preaching of the Cross Reveals the Grace of God.*
If God showed no Grace, then man's case was desperate.
But when man was seen at his worst, God's Grace appeared
at its best.

The day of Calvary was the day of man's crime, but
became the day of God's compassion, the day of man's
ruin, and the day of God's redemption.

On that day, when sin abounded, Grace did much more
abound.

(c) *The Preaching of the Cross Shows the Way of Salvation.*
Not by merit, for it was man's guiltiest day; not by works,
for man's works were the worst possible; but by free gift
to whomsoever believeth on Him.

(d) *The Cross Divides the World.* Those who reject
Christ side with His murderers and will share their awful
judgment: those who receive Christ will be saved with an
eternal redemption.

5. THE OFFENCE OF THE CROSS. The preaching above
described gives offence to men. *Their pride is offended* at
having all their merit rejected; by being accounted guilty
of the Body and Blood of Christ; by having their righteousnesses described as filthy rags.

Their Religion is Insulted by being told that it was the
religious who crucified Christ, that all religion, unless
confessing Christ crucified as the only hope of salvation
and life, is mockery and a sham performance of no value
in God's sight.

This offence is revenged by the world on those who
preach Christ crucified. Such will suffer persecution for
the Cross of Christ.

They may avoid this offence by compromise.

Let the Galatians be circumcised and the Judaizing
professors will cease to trouble them.

But the faithful—they that *will* live godly, trusting in
the Death of Christ and denying their own works or merit
—will suffer persecution.

6. THE GLORY OF THE CROSS. While the Jew stumbled
at the Cross—Salvation by the Death of the Sinless
Substitute—and the Greek regarded it as foolishness, the

believer glories in it, and finds in it peace and power and blessing.

It has with him *a separating effect*. He is cut off absolutely from the world by it, and the world utterly rejects him because of it.

Moreover, the Cross not only separated him from worldly men, but *weaned his affections* from all of earth. It is as though he had been crucified to the world, the world giving him the outcast's place of total rejection and even ascription to death; and he treating the world in the same way: it is dead, rejected, as far as he is concerned.

V. Application.

To the World. See in the Cross your sin at its consummation, your guilt, your condemnation.

To the Seeker. See in the Cross your only way of escape from the wrath to come and hope of Salvation.

To the Believer. See in the Cross the resting-place of your faith and the glory of your life.

OUTLINE

Five Crucifixions in Galatians

1. JESUS CHRIST " evidently set forth crucified " (3. 1).
2. THE SINNER, believing, says, " I have been crucified with Christ " (2. 20).
3. THE FLESH: " they that are Christ's have crucified the flesh " (5. 24).
4. THE WORLD " is crucified unto me " (6. 14).
5. THE SAINT: " and I unto the world " (6. 14).

Christ on the Cross*

Psalm 22 and the Seven Utterances

I. Text. " The Son of God loved me, and gave Himself for me " (Gal. 2. 20).

II. Main Lesson. We have learned from our Lord's Testimony to His own death (Lesson 12) how He regarded it as necessary to the accomplishment of His salvation work. This present Lesson is to show what was in His holy mind while He was hanging on the Cross. We gather this from two sources:

1. The Messianic Psalms, where He expresses His feelings on the subject in prophetic anticipation; specially in Psalm 22, which may be called *The Crucifixion described by the Crucified One Himself.*

2. His Seven Utterances from the Cross, for in these He reveals all that was in His heart. They tell of His thought for others—His murderers, His mother, the penitent thief—and then reveal the sacrificial character of His death in the three hours of darkness.

III. Scripture to Study : Psalm 22.

vv. 1-2. *The Lord Cries out of being Forsaken.* " My God, My God, why hast Thou forsaken Me ? why . . . so far from helping Me . . . ? O My God, I cry . . . but Thou hearest not. . . ."

v. 3. *He Justifies God.* " But Thou art Holy, O Thou that art enthroned upon the praises of Israel " (r.v.).

v. 4. *The Fathers Trusted and were Delivered.* " Our fathers trusted in Thee: they trusted, and Thou didst deliver them. . . ."

vv. 5-8. *His Case is Different : He cannot Deliver if*

---

* For Lessons on the Crucifixion, see *Seventy Best Bible Stories*, No. 64, pp. 232-237, and *Seventy Less Known Stories*, " They watched Him there," No. 61, pp. 277-280.

Delivered. " But I am a worm, and no man; a reproach of men, and despised of the people. All they that see Me laugh Me to scorn: they shoot out the lip, they shake the head, saying, He trusted on the Lord that He would deliver Him: let Him deliver Him, seeing He delighted in Him."

vv. 9-10. *From the Womb He was Cast on God.* " I was cast on Thee from the womb: Thou art My God from My mother's belly."

v. 11. *He Prays for Help.* " Be not far from Me . . there is none to help."

vv. 12-13. *The Strong Enemy Compasses Him about.* " Many bulls of Bashan have beset Me round. They gaped on Me with their mouths, as a roaring lion."

vv. 13-15. *His Pitiful Physical State.* " I am poured out like water, and all My bones are out of joint: My heart is like wax. . . . My strength is dried up like a potsherd; My tongue cleaveth to My jaws; Thou hast brought Me into the dust of death."

vv. 16-17. *His Hands and Feet Pierced.* " For dogs have compassed Me . . . the wicked have inclosed Me: they pierced My hands and My feet. I may tell all My bones: they look and stare upon Me."

v. 18. *They Divide and Cast Lots for His Clothes.* " They part My garments among them, and cast lots upon My vesture."

vv. 19-21. *He Cries again for Help.* "Be not Thou far from Me, O Lord: O My strength . . . deliver My soul . . . My darling from the power of the dog. Save Me from the lion's mouth. . . ."

vv. 22-31. *The Rest of the Psalm is of the Glory that shall Follow the Sufferings, in an Ever-widening Circle.*

v. 22. " I will declare Thy Name unto *My brethren*."

vv. 22 and 25. "In the midst of *the great congregation*."

v. 27. "*All the ends of the earth* . . . all the kindreds of the nations shall worship before Thee."

The Kingdom is the Lord's. . . . *A seed*—a generation —*a people that shall be born*, shall testify, "He hath done it " (R.V.); or in His own words on the Cross, "It is finished."

IV. Thoughts on Psalm 22.

1. NO CONFESSION OF SIN OR FAILURE is found in this Psalm. He was the Sinless One suffering for the sin of others.

2. HE JUSTIFIES GOD. "Thou art holy." He never complained of God's will. It was perfect. He had come to do it, and in doing it to sanctify us (Heb. 10. 10).

3. THE DETAILS OF THE CRUCIFIXION ARE PERFECT. The first verse was cried on the Cross (Matt. 27. 46).

The laughing of the crowd, shooting out the lip, shaking the head (Matt. 27. 39-43).

The very words used to reproach Him: "He trusted" and "let Him deliver Him" (Matt. 27. 43).

"They pierced My hands and My feet" (Matt. 27. 35).

"They part My garments, and cast lots for My vesture" (John 19. 24).

4. There is in this Psalm (as in Isa. 53) *no work effected till after death.* He must die ere He can save. But after death the work begins.

5. NOTE THE EVER-WIDENING CIRCLE OF BLESSING. My brethren (22); in the great congregation (25); all the ends of the earth (27); in the kingdom (28); a holy seed among those yet unborn (31).

V. The Seven Utterances : Three in Luke, three in John, and one in Matthew and Mark.

1. FATHER, FORGIVE THEM, THEY KNOW NOT WHAT THEY DO (Luke 23. 34). In this prayer for His murderers the Lord showed:

(a) *His Compassion for Sinners.* "Father, forgive them."

(b) *His Absence of Revenge or Malice.* This was never in His heart. He loved too well.

(c) *His Recognition of their Ignorance.* As the Apostle says, "Had they known they would not have crucified the Lord of Glory" (1 Cor. 2. 8).

(d) *An Anticipation of the Fruit of His Agony.* Forgiveness would be righteously possible on the ground of

His death. " Beginning at Jerusalem " was His command later. Let His murderers first hear the good news.

2. TO THE PENITENT THIEF. " *Verily I say unto thee, Today shalt thou be with Me in Paradise* " (Luke 23. 43). Here we note:

(*a*) *Something of the Joy set before Him.* This poor wretch was to be the first of thousands of millions who have been saved from sin and shame.

(*b*) *The Assurance that His Prayer was Heard.* He was not to fail. The Cross would certainly be followed by the Glory.

(*c*) *Paradise is Identified with the Third Heaven* in 2 Corinthians 12. 2 and 3. So that the poor thief entered with his Lord that day into blessedness.

3. WOMAN, BEHOLD THY SON. SON, BEHOLD THY MOTHER (John 19. 26-27). Here we have:

(*a*) *Tender Thought for the Suffering Mother.* A sword was that day piercing her soul (Luke 2. 35). He knew it, and would have her removed from the sad scene.

(*b*) In doing so the Lord had regard to the fifth commandment, " *Honour thy . . . mother,*" thus again setting His seal to the Word of God.

4. ELI, ELI, LAMA SABACHTHANI ? (Matt. 27. 46; Mark 15. 34). The darkness had now covered the scene. It is the sacrificial hour, when God laid on Him the iniquity of us all.

(*a*) *He Addresses God,* not now as Father, for it is in the capacity of the Judge of all the earth that God is dealing with Him to Whom our sins were imputed. Righteousness was vindicated.

(*b*) *It was not Ignorance* that asked the " Why ?" for the Lord had told His disciples that He was to give His Life a Ransom for many.

(*c*) *He was Forsaken* in that hour that we might never be forsaken for all eternity.

5. I THIRST (John 19. 28). We are expressly told that this utterance was " that the Scripture might be fulfilled." We notice then:

(*a*) *His Refusal of a Drugged Drink* offered to deaden His pain (Matt. 27. 34).

(*b*) *The Scripture referred to was probably Psalm* 69. 21: "They gave Me also gall for My meat; and in My thirst they gave Me vinegar to drink."

(*c*) *One Scripture Remaining Unfulfilled* (only one word, *dipsc*), He would not die until it had been regarded. Such was His reverence for and desire to do all the Word of God.

6. It is Finished (John 19. 30). Again only one word, *tetelestai*. It was the triumph over death and Hell as He bowed His head and gave up the ghost.

(*a*) *Our Redemption* was perfected completely. The Price paid, the Ransom made, the sinner may go free.

(*b*) *The Earthly Course of Suffering* was ended. No more the Man of sorrows, He would after the triumph of resurrection be the "Living One," never again to die.

(*c*) *The Will of God Fully Done.* All that He came to do He had wondrously effected. God was glorified, man redeemed.

(*d*) *The Types and Shadows* ended.

> "Finished all the types and shadows
> Of the ceremonial law."

The substance having come, the sun having risen, the shadows flee away.

(*e*) *The Veil is Rent* in the Temple, the way into the Holiest is opened for all to come boldly to the Throne of God, to find mercy and grace to help in time of need.

7. Father, into Thy Hands I Commend My Spirit. Then, bowing His head, He yielded up His Spirit.

(*a*) *He Reverts to the Name "Father,"* for the Sacrifice is finished as He dies. It remains only to commit Himself to His Father, Who had "made Him to be sin for us."

(*b*) *He did not Die by Force,* but yielded up His Spirit.

He had said, "No man taketh it from Me: I lay it down

of Myself." He commanded His Spirit to depart, and
commended it to His Father.

> "And so He died, and this is why
> He came to be a man and die:
> The Bible says He came from Heaven
> That we might have our sins forgiven."

VI. Other Lessons from the Cross.

1. THE DEATH OF CHRIST is given by far the greater
part in each of the Gospels, almost one-third being devoted
to the scenes of the last week.

This shows the prominent place given by the Holy
Spirit to His death.

He came into the world to die: He came to give His
life a Ransom; He appeared to put away sin by the
sacrifice of Himself; He came to save sinners, and could
do so only by being made sin for them.

The life was the prelude to the death; the death the
consummation and purpose of the life.

2. THE HEART OF CHRIST is revealed in the Messianic
Psalms and the Utterances from the Cross.

We notice in them that His thoughts were occupied with
the Glory of God, ever His first purpose in life and death;
His *Sorrow for Sinners* as He looks down from the Cross
at their ribald mockery and taunting blasphemies; *His
horror at Sin*, seeing it led to His being forsaken; *His desire
to save* in His prayer for His murderers; *His Willing Submission to death* in yielding up His Spirit; *His Anticipation
of the Glory* to follow.

3. FORSAKEN. The horror of this to the Lord can be
realized only as we remember that through all eternity
there had been perfect love and unbroken fellowship with
the Father. Nothing had ever come between. Now the
awful guilt and shame of sin cause a separation, a forsaking,
the fearfulness of which causes the agony and bloody
sweat and the loud cry.

4. THE FINISHED WORK. So complete that we read,
" There is no more offering for sin " (Heb. 10. 18).

God has been Satisfied; the sin question can be raised no

more now. "Who shall lay anything to the charge of God's elect?"

The Believer can Rest Satisfied, for the great word "Finished" silences all fears and gives him assurance of eternal redemption.

VII. Application.

To the Sinner. How shall we escape if we neglect so great salvation, bought at such a cost?

To the Doubter. Look steadfastly at the Crucified One, and hear the great word "Finished."

To the Believer. Live in the light of the Cross, and the world and sin will lose their power.

To the Preacher. Remember your first duty is to preach Christ crucified.

OUTLINE

Four Finished Things

SIN. "When it is finished . . . death" (Jas. 1. 15).
SALVATION. "It is finished" (John 19. 30).
SERVICE. "I have finished my course" (2 Tim. 4. 7).
SUFFERING. "The Mystery of God" (Rev. 10. 7).

Preaching Christ Crucified

WE PREACH CHRIST
- Crucified through weakness.
- Risen in Power.
- Up-taken to Heaven (or uplifted).
- Coming again.
- Inviting all to Himself.
- Faithful to promises.
- Indwelling His people.
- Eternally saving His own sheep.
- Delighting in their service and Delivering them from Sin's Power.

Christ as a Ransom

I. Texts. " The Son of Man came not to be ministered unto, but to minister, and to give His life A RANSOM for many " (Matt. 20. 28; Mark 10. 45).

" Who gave Himself A RANSOM for all, to be testified in due time " (1 Tim. 2. 6).

II. Main Lesson. The Death of Christ was not merely an example of suffering wrongfully (it was that also, 1 Pet. 2. 21), nor the martyrdom of a great hero: it was a voluntary sacrifice, a life laid down as a Ransom.

The Lord Himself asserts it and the Apostle confirms it. It was a Ransom " for all " (conditionally) and " for many " (absolutely)—a Ransom *sufficient* for all, but *efficient* only for the many who believe.

III. Scripture to Study : Matt. 20. 20-28.

vv. 20-21. The Sons of Zebedee Seek a Preference Over the Other Disciples. " Then came to Him the mother of Zebedee's children with her sons, worshipping Him, and desiring a certain thing of Him. And He said unto her, What wilt thou ? She saith unto Him, Grant that these my two sons may sit, the one on Thy right hand, and the other on the left, in Thy Kingdom."

v. 22. The Lord Rebukes their Desire, and asks them if they can Drink of His Cup. " But Jesus answered and said, Ye know not what ye ask. Are ye able to drink of the cup that I shall drink of, and to be baptized with the baptism that I am baptized with ? They say unto Him, We are able."

v. 23. He Tells them they will Share His Sufferings, but that to Grant their Request is not His. " And He saith unto them, Ye shall drink indeed of My cup, and be baptized with the baptism that I am baptized with: but to sit on My right hand, and on My left, is not Mine to give, but it shall be given to them for whom it is prepared of My Father."

v. 24. *The Ten are Indignant.* " When the ten heard it, they were moved with indignation against the two brethren."

v. 25. *The Lord Bids them not Seek Dominion or Authority.* " But Jesus called them unto Him, and said, Ye know that the princes of the Gentiles exercise dominion over them, and they that are great exercise authority upon them. But it shall not be so among you."

v. 26. *True Greatness Lies in Service to Others.* " Whosoever will be great among you, let him be your minister; and whosoever will be chief among you, let him be your servant."

v. 28. *The Gracious Example of Christ.* " Even as the Son of Man came not to be ministered unto, but to minister, and to give His life a Ransom for many."

IV. The Nature of a Ransom.

1. *Definition.* It is a Price paid to secure the release of a man under sentence of death or a slave in bondage, or for the repurchase of a forfeited inheritance.

The *Ransom* is the Price paid.

The *Redemption* is the Freedom resulting.

So that it may be described as *a Price paid for Redemption*, a satisfaction by sacrifice.

The Ransom Price for our Redemption was the Blood of Christ—that is, His Life laid down, His atoning sacrifice.

As sinners we were (1) *under sentence* of death, (2) in *bondage* to sin, and (3) our *birthright lost* and forfeited by sin.

From all these the Ransom Price paid in the Death of Christ redeemed us.

2. *Illustrations.*

(1) At the Numbering of the People (Exod. 30. 12): " When thou takest the sum of the children of Israel after their numbers, then shall they give every man *a RANSOM for his soul unto the Lord* . . . that there be no plague among them, when thou numberest them."

It was the neglect of this by David when he numbered the people that incurred the plague by which seventy thousand died (1 Sam. 24. 25).

As all were guilty, all needed to recognize their need of redemption by paying half a shekel as a Ransom price for their souls.

> " Ye were not ransomed with a price of gold,
> But with the precious Blood of God's dear Son;
> Ye were not ransomed with a sum untold,
> But with the precious Blood of Christ."

(2) WHEN A MAN'S OX KILLED A MAN (Exod. 21. 28-32). If the man knew his ox was dangerous his life was forfeited, and he had to pay *" for the ransom of his life "* (30) such a sum as was laid upon him by the judges.

(3) NO RANSOM (satisfaction) WAS TO BE ACCEPTED FOR A WILFUL MURDERER (Num. 35. 31). " Ye shall take no satisfaction for the life of a murderer, which is guilty of death: but he shall surely be put to death."

Even though he had fled to the City of Refuge, he was to be given up to the Avenger of Blood.

Hebrews 10. 26-31 is the spiritual counterpart of this.

(4) NO MAN CAN GIVE A RANSOM TO REDEEM ANOTHER (Psa. 49. 7-9). " None of them can by any means redeem his brother, nor give to God a Ransom for him: for the redemption of the soul is precious (costly), and must be let alone for ever (R.V.): that he should live for ever, and not see corruption."

Under the Law an earthly price was allowed for an earthly temporal deliverance, but it cannot be for the salvation and eternal redemption of the soul.

(5) ELIHU INSTRUCTS JOB as to God's grace (Job 33. 23-24). " If there be a Messenger with him, an Interpreter; . . . Then He is gracious unto him, and saith, Deliver him from going down to the pit: I have found a Ransom."

When Abraham said to Isaac, " The Lord will provide Himself the Lamb," it was to the same effect. Here God speaks: " I have found a Ransom "; and the Lord says He gave His life a Ransom.

(6) ELIHU SPEAKS AGAIN TO JOB (36. 18). " Beware lest He take thee away with His stroke: then a great Ransom cannot deliver thee."

He intends to remind Job that he cannot magnify Himself against God; He must fear, and look alone to God for redemption.

(7) TO WHOM WAS THE RANSOM PAID ? *Not to Satan,* as Origen and others thought, for though man had sold himself to the enemy who held him in bondage all his lifetime (Heb. 2. 14-15), the Lord did not recognize his claim. Man had no right to sell nor Satan to buy. Satan was the strong man armed whom the Stronger than he overcame (Luke 11. 21-22) and spoiled, setting his captives free.

The Ransom was always spoken of as being paid " *unto the Lord* " (Exod. 30. 12, and see Heb. 9. 14), because His holy Law demanded the death of the transgressor. " *The Ransom price was paid to the Guardian of that Holy Law, the Administrator of Eternal Justice* " (*International Standard Bible Encyclopædia*, p. 2532).

V. Other Lessons from the Study.

1. THE VALUE OF THE RANSOM. " Ye know that ye were not redeemed with corruptible things, as silver and gold . . . but with the Precious Blood of Christ " (1 Pet. 1. 18-19)—the Blood always meaning the Shed Blood, or the Life of Christ laid down for us.

In old times large sums in gold were paid to ransom those taken in battle.

Richard I. was ransomed for £100,000, David Bruce of Scotland for 100,000 marks, and King John of France for £500,000. But these immense sums were nothing compared with the price of our Ransom.

2. THE EFFECT OF THE RANSOM we shall consider under " Christ our Redeemer," for our redemption is the result of the Ransom.

But shortly we may view it thus. It bought us *Life,* so that we are no longer under Condemnation and Sentence of Death. It purchased us *Liberty,* so that Sin shall not have dominion over us. It gave us in Christ far more than we lost in Adam:

> " In Christ the sons of Adam boast
> More than their first forefather lost."

3. THE JOY OF THE RANSOMED. This is described in several passages in Isaiah. These relate in the first instance to Israel, but all the true Israel of God rejoice in them.

Isaiah 35. 10: " The Ransomed of the Lord shall return, and come to Zion with songs and everlasting joy upon their heads: they shall obtain joy and gladness, and sorrow and sighing shall flee away " (and see also Isa. 51. 10-11; Jer. 31. 11-12).

4. FOR WHOM WAS THE RANSOM? The Apostle says " For all "—that is, " on behalf of all." He uses the preposition *huper*.

The Lord says " *Instead of* many," using the preposition *anti*.

This rightly explains the position. Christ offered Himself a Ransom for all in the sense that the invitation based upon His finished work is given to all, but those who reject Him find no blessing from it. Christ offered Himself a Ransom instead of many, for all who receive Him are so joined to the Lord that they can speak of Him as their Substitute.

As Calvin expressed it, " His death was *sufficient* for all: it was *efficient* in the case of many."

VI. Application.

Let us see to it that we come to Christ, so that the Ransom sufficient for us may become efficient in our case.

Let us live as Ransomed ones, rejoicing in our blood-bought liberty.

Let us proclaim the Ransom far and wide.

OUTLINE

Our Liberty by Ransom

GOD in GRACE—SOUGHT IT.
CHRIST by BLOOD—BOUGHT IT.
The SPIRIT by the WORD—TAUGHT IT.
The PREACHER of the GOSPEL—BROUGHT IT.
FAITH in PRACTICE—WROUGHT IT.

Christ Our Redeemer

I. Text. " I the Lord am thy Saviour and thy Redeemer, the Mighty One of Jacob " (Isa. 49. 26).

II. Main Lesson. Redemption is the result of a Ransom paid (see last Lesson). It is the effect given to the Ransom. The Price being paid, the liability discharged, satisfaction made, the Ransomed one goes free. Life and Liberty are his.

This Redemption on the ground of the Ransom paid *is enforced by Power*; so we read: " Thou hast redeemed by Thy great power, and by Thy strong arm " (Neh. 1. 10), and " Thou hast with Thine arm redeemed Thy people " (Psa. 77. 15).

So while the Price paid was Blood, the Deliverance was given effect to by the Mighty Power of God. We are Ransomed by a Great Price and Redeemed by Mighty Power.

Where redemption is spoken of as by Blood (1 Pet. 1. 18) it refers, of course, to the Price of Redemption—that is, the Ransom. Christ was our Ransom. He is our Redeemer.

Those He ransomed He has redeemed.

III. Scripture to Study : Ruth 4. 1-11.

v. 1. *Boaz, the Kinsman of Naomi, Purposes to Redeem the Inheritance of Elimelech.* " Then went Boaz up to the gate, and sat him down there: and, behold, the kinsman of whom Boaz spake came by; unto whom he said, Ho, such a one ! turn aside, sit down here. And he turned aside, and sat down."

v. 2. *Ten Witnesses are Chosen.* " And he took ten men of the elders of the city, and said, Sit ye down here. And they sat down."

v. 3. *He States the Case.* " And he said unto the kinsman, Naomi, that is come again out of the country of Moab, selleth a parcel of land, which was our brother Elimelech's:"

v. 4. " And I thought to advertise thee, saying, Buy it before the elders of my people. If thou wilt redeem it, redeem it: but if thou wilt not redeem it, then tell me, that I may know: for there is none to redeem it beside thee; and I am after thee."

v. 4. *The Next-of-Kin Offers to Redeem.* " And he said, I will redeem it."

v. 5. *A Condition Imposed.* "Then said Boaz, What day thou buyest the field of the hand of Naomi, thou must buy it also of Ruth the Moabitess, the wife of the dead, to raise up the name of the dead upon his inheritance."

v. 6. *The Kinsman cannot do this.* " And the kinsman said, I cannot redeem it for myself, lest I mar mine own inheritance: redeem thou my right to thyself; for I cannot redeem it."

v. 7. *The Manner of Redemption.* " Now this was the manner concerning redemption . . . a man plucked off his shoe, and gave it to his neighbour: and this was a testimony in Israel."

v. 8. *Boaz Gives his Shoe.* " Therefore the kinsman said unto Boaz, Buy it for thee. So he drew off his shoe."

v. 9 *Boaz Calls the Elders to Witness.* " And Boaz said unto the elders, . . . Ye are witnesses this day, that I have bought all that was Elimelech's, and all that was Chilion's and Mahlon's, of the hand of Naomi."

v. 10. *He also Takes Ruth to his Wife.* "Moreover, Ruth the Moabitess, the wife of Mahlon, have I purchased to be my wife. . . . Ye are witnesses."

v. 11. *The Witnesses Bear Testimony.* " And all the people that were in the gate, and the elders, said, We are witnesses."

IV. From what We are Redeemed.

1. FROM THE CURSE OF THE LAW (Gal. 3. 13). For the Law pronounced a curse on everyone who continued not in all things that were written in the Book of the Law to do them.

Christ was made a Curse for us, and, the Ransom being paid, we are rescued from the curse.

2. FROM DEATH AND THE GRAVE (Hosea 3. 14). "I will ransom them from the power of the grave; I will redeem them from death: O death, I will be thy plagues; O grave, I will be thy destruction " (*cf.* 1 Cor. 15. 54-57).

Henceforth death is but a falling asleep to the believer.

3. FROM DESTRUCTION (Psa. 103. 4). The Life is delivered from the destroying power of sin. The believer will never perish.

4. FROM OUR ENEMIES (Psa. 107, 2; 136. 24; Jer. 15. 21). These include Satan and the " terrible "; the wicked who plot against the just; the lusts and powers within. "For Sin shall not have dominion over you: for ye are not under the law, but under grace " (Rom. 6. 14).

5. FROM ALL OUR INIQUITIES (Psa. 130. 8; Titus 2. 14). The sins which so easily beset us. Having blotted out the guilt by BLOOD, He breaks the chain by His POWER, and changes the heart by His LOVE.

> " He breaks the power of cancelled sin,
> He sets the prisoner free."

6. FROM THE HOUSE OF BONDMEN (Deut. 7. 8). The Slaves of Sin are set free. They rejoice in the Liberty that has been purchased for them by a Great Ransom. For if the Son shall set you free, ye shall be free indeed.

7. FROM ADVERSITY (2 Sam. 4. 9), DISTRESS (1 Kings 1. 29), and AFFLICTION (Psa. 34. 19). The Believer is not exempt from these, but is brought triumphantly through them all.

V. Other Lessons from the Study.

1. THE KINSMAN-REDEEMER, OR " GOEL." This word Goel is variously translated as follows: *Kinsman* (Num. 5. 8), *Avenger* (Num. 35. 12), *Redeemer* (Lev. 25. 25; Isa. 60. 16; Jer. 50. 34), *Revenger* (Num. 35. 24).

It was the one who, because of his near kinship, had the right to redeem; the responsibility to raise up seed to a deceased brother; the solemn duty to slay the murderer of his kinsman.

It is beautifully illustrated in the Story of Ruth (see III. above).

The Lord Jesus, because He was our near kinsman, having been made like unto His brethren (Heb. 2. 10-18), had the right to redeem us. He was neighbour to us who had fallen among thieves.

2. ILLUSTRATIONS OF REDEMPTION.

The Children of Israel (Exod. 6. 6). Having been ransomed by the sprinkled blood, they were saved from the Destroyer, and then brought out of Egypt and from under the slavery of Pharaoh " with a stretched out arm."

Every Firstborn of Man (Exod. 13. 13) among the children of Israel had to be redeemed with a lamb.

Every Firstling of an Ass had also to be redeemed with a lamb, or, " if thou wilt not redeem it, then thou shalt break its neck " (Exod. 34. 20).

The Poor Brother's Possession which he had had to sell might be redeemed by any of his kin (Lev. 25. 25).

The One who had Sold Himself might be redeemed. " One of his brethren may redeem him " (Lev. 25. 48-49), or " any nigh of kin unto him "; or, if he were able, he might redeem himself at a fit price (v. 49).

The Firstborn were redeemed each by one of the Levites, who were taken as the Lord's, instead of the firstborn. Of these, 273 were over (that is, more than the Levites), and these had each to be redeemed for five shekels (1,365 shekels in all), and the price given to Aaron and his sons (Num. 3. 45-51).

3. AN ILLUSTRATION FROM CHINA. Some missionaries in China were greatly distressed for a little girl who had been sold by her parents as a slave. They appealed to friends at home and raised enough money to ransom her. The price was duly paid, but the one who had bought her still refused to hand her over to her parents. So the missionaries went to demand her, threatening the strong arm of the law if refused. This prevailed; the ransom paid, they had a right to rescue.

4. THE UNBELIEVER'S FOLLY. Many through unbelief still remain under the curse, and in cruel bondage when they might go free.

It is said that when the rioters, in the Gordon riots,

destroyed Newgate prison, some of the prisoners refused to go free, but remained in the ruins until they were taken again.

VI. **Application.** The Ransom having been paid, let all the " prisoners of hope " avail themselves of it, and call upon the Mighty Redeemer to rescue them by His great power.

OUTLINES

Eight Notable Prisoners Released

Joseph (Gen. 41. 14).
Simeon (Gen. 43. 23).
Manasseh (2 Chron. 33. 13).
Jehoiachin (2 Kings 25. 29).
Jeremiah (38. 13; 39. 14).
Peter (Acts 12. 5-11).
Paul (2 Tim. 4. 17).
Timothy (Heb. 13. 23).

Redeem

Only One could
{
Redeem us by a Blood Ransom.
Endure the Cross.
Die as Substitute.
Engage Himself as Surety.
Enter into Covenant for us.
Mediate our Salvation.
}

Christ Our Substitute

I. Text. " He hath made Him to be sin for us, Who knew no sin; that we might be made the righteousness of God in Him " (2 Cor. 5. 21).

II. Main Lesson. The words Substitute and Substitution do not occur in the Bible, but the Truth of Vicarious Suffering is clearly taught.

The Lord Jesus died not only for all, but in a special sense " instead of " those who believe.

He is thus said to be the Saviour of the World—that is, the World's One and Only Saviour (John 4. 42; 1 John 4. 14)—and " *The Saviour of all men, specially of those that believe* " (1 Tim. 4. 10).

When the sinner flees to Christ he is said to be " joined to the Lord," and as one with Christ, a member of His Body, he enjoys all that the Head suffered for the members. He can then use the language of substitution and say, "I was crucified," "I am risen," for what the Divine Substitute did is reckoned to him.

His sin was imputed to Christ and laid to His charge, and when he believes he " becomes righteousness " by the imputation of righteousness to him. So Christ was made sin for us that we might become righteousness in Him.

The Just One became the Substitute for the unjust.

III. Scripture to Study :

2 Corinthians 5. 17-21. *A Man in Christ is a New Creation*. " Therefore if any man be in Christ, he is a new creature: old things are passed away; behold, all things are become new."

v. 18. *God hath Reconciled us to Himself*. " And all things are of God, Who hath reconciled us to Himself by Jesus Christ, and hath given to us the ministry of reconciliation."

v. 19. *The Ministry of Reconciliation Defined.* " To wit, that God was in Christ, reconciling the world unto Himself, not imputing their trespasses unto them; and hath committed unto us the word of reconciliation."

v. 20. *We are therefore Ambassadors Beseeching Men to be Reconciled.* " Now then we are ambassadors for Christ, as though God did beseech you by us; we pray you in Christ's stead, be ye reconciled to God."

v. 21. *The Reconciled are Made the Righteousness of God.* " For He hath made Him to be sin for us, Who knew no sin; that we might be made (R.V. become) the righteousness of God in Him."

IV. Illustrations of Substitution.

1. SETH. " God," said Eve, " hath appointed me another seed instead of Abel, whom Cain slew " (Gen. 4. 25).

2. ISAAC. " And Abraham lifted up his eyes, and looked, and behold behind him a ram caught in a thicket by his horns: and Abraham went and took the ram, and offered him up for a burnt offering in the stead of his son " (Gen. 22. 13).

3. JACOB. Laban substituted Leah for Rachel, whom Jacob loved (Gen. 29. 23).

4. THE LEVITICAL SACRIFICES. In all these offerings the idea of substitution is prominent. The laying of the hands on the Sacrifice meant that the offerer identified himself with the animal, so that it was " *accepted for him to make atonement for him* " (Lev. 1. 4).

The substitute's death was accepted in the stead of the offerer's.

So the Five Great Levitical Offerings are substitutionary, and may be stated thus:

The Burnt Offering typified Christ for what we *should have done*—perfect obedience.

The Meat Offering, Christ for what we *should have been*—perfect in character.

The Peace Offering, Christ for what we *should have enjoyed*—perfect peace with God.

The Sin Offering, Christ *for what we were*—sinful and guilty.

The Trespass Offering, Christ for *what we have done—* sinned and trespassed.

5. THE LAW DEMANDED IT (Exod. 21. 24; Lev. 24. 20; Deut. 19. 21; Matt. 5. 38). "If any mischief follow, then thou shalt give life for life, eye for eye, tooth for tooth, hand for hand, foot for foot, burning for burning, wound for wound, stripe for stripe." "Thine eye shall not pity."

6. HEROD. "When [Joseph] heard that Archelaus did reign in Judea in the room of his father Herod, he was afraid to go thither " (Matt. 2. 22).

7. FATHERS AND CHILDREN. "If a son shall ask bread of any of you that is a father, will he give him a stone ? or if he ask a fish, will he for [*anti*] a fish give him a serpent ?"

V. Other Lessons on Christ our Substitute.

1. SUBSTITUTION IN THREE ASPECTS. There are three ways of looking at Substitution, all of which are true of our Lord Jesus. They are:

(a) *One Suffering for Another*, in order that the one for whom he suffers may be blessed. Not necessarily " instead of," but "on behalf of," or for the sake of another.

This Christ did when He died to bring us salvation, life and peace.

It is a common rule of life, so common as to be a universal principle of life.

Nothing good comes to us but through another suffering.

Our mothers suffered to give us birth. They suffered to nurture and preserve us. Our instructors laboured that we might learn.

No piece of coal warms us but some miner went to the bowels of the earth to gain it for us. And so on in a thousand things.

No one can do good unless they are willing to suffer for others.

The analogy is perfect. Our highest good (our salvation) came through the Highest suffering for us.

Had He not died we must have died. He died that we might live.

(b) *One Acting as Representative for Another*. When Peace was made after the Great War, it was signed by the Prime Minister for the whole nation.

He acted as the Representative or Head for the body politic, the nation.

So Christ acted for all His members, as the Federal Head. He made peace for all by the Blood of His Cross.

As Adam, the Federal Head of the Human Race, sinned us all, so that in him we all sinned; so Christ, the last Adam, graced all who are found in Him. Each was what the old writers called a " *Common Man* "—that is, a Representative Man, One who acted not alone for himself, but for all with whom he had a common interest (see Heb. 2. 11-18).

(c) *One Taking the Place of Another*. As when the ram was bound to the altar instead of Isaac, actually taking his place and dying the death he would have died had no substitute been found.

So Christ not only died for us to bring us blessing; not only died as the Head or Representative of the body; but actually in the stead and in the place of us. Our sin was imputed to Him and He bore its penalty, so now God's righteousness is imputed to us, and we are treated as having died and risen again from the dead.

> " He knew how wicked man had been,
> He knew that God must punish sin;
> So out of pity Jesus said
> He'd bear the punishment instead."

2. Identification before Substitution. No one can speak of Christ as His Substitute (except in the general sense of His dying on behalf of all) until he has become identified with Christ by personal faith. The Christ rejecter has no substitute; only when the sinner receives Christ and is joined to the Lord, is by the Spirit baptized into His body, can he speak of Christ as having died " instead of him." So that there has been that blessed exchange—my sins and His righteousness.

I must hold the Head if as one of His members I can participate in the sufferings of the Head.

3. THE DAY OF ATONEMENT. Although the sin offering had been slain and its blood taken into the Holy of Holies and sprinkled " before and on the Throne," the Mercy Seat, yet the people were still in their sins until the priest laid his hands upon the scapegoat and put on it all their sins. Then the goat bore them away. So—

> " My faith would lay her hand
> On that dear Head of Thine,
> While as a penitent I stand
> And there confess my sin."

The laying on of hands was a figure of identification with the scapegoat; so faith in Christ brings us into union with Him, and we rejoice to see the load of guilt removed from us.

4. OUR OLD MAN CRUCIFIED (Rom. 6. 6). The wonder of Substitution is that as we look at Calvary we see not only Christ dying for our sins, but " our old man " crucified with Him. All that we are out of Christ is our old man. All that we are as flesh born of the flesh was judged, condemned and executed in our Substitute.

So the believer can say, " My old man was crucified "; " I have been crucified " (Gal. 2. 20); " I died " (Col. 3. 3): nevertheless, thank God, I am risen. " I live, yet not I, but Christ liveth in me."

VI. Application.

Let the unregenerate know that they have no substitute to stand between them and a holy God. Out of Christ they are exposed to wrath.

Let all who hope in Christ see to it that there has been a true identification by faith with Him.

Let the Saints rejoice that they are dead and risen with their Divine Head.

Substitution " In Christ "

Instead of Condemnation—Salvation (Rom. 8. 1; Acts 4. 12).
Instead of Eternal Death—Eternal Life (1 John 5. 11).
Instead of Bondage—Liberty (John 8. 36; Gal. 5. 1).
Instead of Old Sinful Nature—New Creation (2 Cor. 5. 17).
Instead of Sin—Righteousness (2 Cor. 5. 21).

LESSON 49

Christ Our Surety

I. Text. " By so much was Jesus made a Surety of a Better Testament " (Heb. 7. 22).

II. Main Lesson. A surety is defined as " a person who undertakes some specific responsibility on behalf of another who remains primarily liable; one who makes himself liable for the default or miscarriage of another, or for the performance of some act on his part " (Oxford Dictionary).

The Lord Jesus is our Surety in the double sense that He makes Himself responsible both to God and to us.

1. HE PLEDGES HIMSELF TO GOD to bring the sinner whose case He has undertaken into the New Covenant blessings.

2. HE PLEDGES HIMSELF TO US to bring us into those Covenant blessings.

Having made Himself responsible to God on our behalf, He had to discharge our debt and liability, and this He did on the Cross (Gal. 3. 13-15).

He was the Surety of the Covenant in a threefold sense:

(1) *In that He Ratified it by His Blood*, thus making it irrevocable. So His Blood was, He said, the Blood of the New Covenant.

(2) *He did all Needed* to procure its benefits for sinners.

(3) *He Gives Effect to the Covenant.* He is therefore Surety, Mediator, and Minister of the New Covenant (Heb. 7. 22 and 8. 6).

III. Scriptures to Study :

Examples of Suretyship.

Since the word " Surety " appears only once in the New Testament (Heb. 7. 22), we will give examples or illustrations from the Scriptures.

1. Genesis 43. 9. JUDAH UNDERTOOK WITH HIS FATHER JACOB TO BE SURETY FOR THE SAFE RETURN OF BENJAMIN.

" I will be surety for him: of my hand shalt thou require him: if I bring him not unto thee, and set him before thee, then let me bear the blame for ever."

He Tells Joseph (44. 32): " Thy servant became surety for the lad unto my father."

2. PAUL PLEDGES HIMSELF TO PHILEMON for any money owing to him by Onesimus. Philemon 18-19: " If he hath wronged thee, or oweth thee ought, put that on mine account; I Paul have written it with mine own hand, I will repay it."

3. JEREMIAH, FORETELLING OF ISRAEL'S FUTURE BLESS-ING (Jer. 30. 21), asks: " Who is this that engageth his heart to approach unto Me ? saith the Lord "; or, as the R.V. renders it, " Who is he that hath had boldness to approach unto Me ?" and in the margin, " *hath been surety* for his heart." An anticipation of Christ Who engaged His heart (became surety) for Israel.

4. JOB APPEALS TO GOD for defence against his accusers (Job 17. 3, R.V.). " Give now a pledge, be surety for me with Thyself; who is there that will strike hands with me ?"

5. DAVID CRIES TO GOD. Psalm 119. 122: " Be surety for Thy servant for good."

6. THE FOLLY OF SURETYSHIP. Proverbs 17. 18: " A man void of understanding striketh hands, and becometh surety in the presence of his friend."

7. THE DANGER OF IT. Proverbs 11. 15: " He that is surety for a stranger shall smart for it: and he that hateth suretyship is sure."

IV. Other Lessons on Suretyship.

1. THE DERIVATION OF THE WORD is from the Hebrew to mingle or mix, or to coalesce. It is used of those who married strange wives—the mingled seed in Ezra 9. 2; the surety and the one for whom he pledges himself being regarded as one (*cf.* Heb. 2. 11) in respect of the liability.

There is a suggestion of substitution here.

2. BECAUSE OF OUR DEFICIENCY we needed a surety. " In the first covenant made with Adam there was no surety, but God and men were the immediate covenanters " (Dr. Owen). But Adam failed. Man could not stand alone. He was therefore in great need of One to undertake for him, Who is able to meet the liability and secure the blessing.

3. OUR SURETY WAS A VOLUNTARY ONE. No obligation compelled Him to take up our case and stand pledge for us (*cf.* John 10. 18). It was love and compassion that led Him to take on Himself such heavy responsibility and to discharge so great a debt for our liberation.

4. A SURETY SMARTS FOR IT. " He that is surety for a stranger shall smart for it " (Prov. 11. 15). Therefore it is wise for a business man to avoid it. Only a man void of understanding strikes hands and pledges himself for another, especially if the liability is such that he cannot support.

A guarantor may be sure that he will be called upon to pay sooner or later. Therefore " He that hateth suretyship is sure."

But the Lord, knowing all the smart and sorrow it entailed, accepted it for our sakes.

> " When Blood from a Victim must flow
> Our Shepherd by pity was led
> To stand between us and the foe,
> And willingly die in our stead."

5. GOD NEEDED NO SURETY, for His word and promise cannot fail. All His promises are Yea and Amen in Christ. Christ did not guarantee God's Word to us; it needed no such confirmation or pledge for its fulfilment. He stood towards God as Surety for us, and towards us as assuring the promises to us. Not that God was failing in faithfulness, but that we were undeserving and incapable and needed such a Surety. As though He said, " You can never receive those promises because of sin and failure, but I will gain them for you and guarantee them to you."

6. A SURETY MUST BE ABLE TO PAY. This the Lord Jesus could do, for He had no sin of His own to atone for,

and could therefore take up our load of guilt and discharge it by the sacrifice of Himself.

7. A SURETY MUST BE A PERSON OF GOOD CREDIT. "Man had failed, and become bankrupt, all credit was gone, and therefore God could not treat nor trade with him any more, without a Mediator and such a Surety as Christ. 'Because they continued not in My covenant, and I regarded them not, saith the Lord.'" (Benjamin Keach, Heb. 8. 9.)

8. A CURIOUS APPLICATION. An old writer asks: "Hath Christ taken you (as a door) off the old hinges? Have you seen your want and beggary, and from hence chosen Christ for your Surety? It is only the broken man that seeks to his friend for security."

9. THE LORD FULFILS HIS SURETYSHIP TOWARD US by writing His Law upon our hearts, so that we respond to God in the obedience of faith and love. We become changed ones, a new creation. "I will put My fear in their hearts."

V. Application.

Do you feel your need of a Surety?

Have you found heart rest in the assurance that He has pledged Himself for you?

Have you His Law written on your heart? Do you love holiness, and find your happiness in Christ?

OUTLINE

As Our Surety

Christ pledged Himself to

- Satisfy the demand of justice.
- Undertake our liability.
- Redeem the lost.
- Enter into covenant with God for us.
- Turn again our captivity.
- Yield the perfected Kingdom to God (1 Cor. 15. 28).

Behold the Lamb of God

I. Text. "The next day John [the Baptist] seeth Jesus coming unto him, and saith, Behold the Lamb of God, which taketh away the sin of the world " (John 1. 29).

II. Main Lesson. Throughout the Bible the Lord Jesus is set before us as the Lamb of God.

In the *types* of the Law.

In the *prophecies* of the Prophets.

In the *Gospels* that recount His Death.

In the *Epistles* that teach the Doctrine.

In the *Revelation* as the Lamb upon the Throne.

The Lamb was always the sacrificial animal, as will be seen by its place in the Levitical Law (see IV. below).

Christ was God's Lamb in that, having been provided by God (Gen. 22. 8), He bore away the sin of the world.

The Lamb was, further, an emblem of Christ in its patient submission to death—He was led as a Lamb to the slaughter—and in its gentleness, reminding us of the meekness and gentleness of Christ.

III. Scriptures to Study :

Isaiah 53. 4-7. *The Lamb of God in Prophecy.* "Surely He hath borne our griefs, and carried our sorrows: yet we did esteem Him stricken, smitten of God, and afflicted. But He was wounded for our transgressions, He was bruised for our iniquities: the chastisement of our peace was upon Him; and with His stripes we are healed."

v. 6. *Our Guilt and His Load.* " All we like sheep have gone astray; we have turned every one to his own way; and the Lord hath laid on Him the iniquity of us all."

v. 7. *His Patience under Suffering.* " He was oppressed, and yet He humbled Himself [R.V.] and He opened not His mouth: He is brought as a Lamb to the slaughter, and as a sheep before her shearers is dumb, so He openeth not His mouth."

v. 8. *The Injustice Done to Him* (R.V.). "By oppression and judgment He was taken away; and as for His generation, who among them considered that He was cut off out of the land of the living: for the transgression of My people was He smitten" (R.V.M., "to whom the stroke was due").

1 Peter 1. 18, 19. *Redeemed with the Precious Blood of Christ.* "Forasmuch as ye know that ye were not redeemed with corruptible things, as silver and gold, from your vain conversation received by tradition from your fathers; but with the precious Blood of Christ, as of a Lamb without blemish and without spot."

v. 20. *This was Foreordained of God* (*cf.* Acts 2. 23). "Who verily was foreordained [of God] before the foundation of the world, but was manifest in these last times for you, who by Him do believe in God."

2. 21-23. *He Suffered also as an Example.* "Christ also suffered for us, leaving us an example, that ye should follow His steps: Who did no sin, neither was guile found in His mouth: Who, when He was reviled, reviled not again; when He suffered, He threatened not; but committed Himself to Him that judgeth righteously."

v. 24. *His Substitutionary Work.* "Who His own self bare our sins in His own body on the tree, that we, being dead to sins, should live unto righteousness: by whose stripes ye were healed."

IV. The Lamb in the Levitical Offerings.

1. In the PASSOVER (Exod. 12. 3). It was a Lamb whose blood was sprinkled upon the lintel and side posts of the door and saved the firstborn from the destroyer.

2. Every FIRSTBORN CHILD was redeemed with a lamb, as also the firstling of an ass (Exod. 13. 13).

3. Every MORNING AND EVENING a lamb was offered on the brazen altar in the Temple (Num. 28. 4).

4. Every SABBATH two lambs were offered (Num. 28. 9).

5. At the BEGINNING OF EACH MONTH seven lambs were offered (Num. 28. 11) with other offerings.

6. AT THE FEAST OF UNLEAVENED BREAD seven lambs were offered each day for seven days with other sacrifices (Num. 28. 17).

At the Feast of Firstfruits, seven lambs (Num. 28. 27).

At the Feast of Blowing of Trumpets, seven lambs (Num. 29. 2).

At the Feast of the Day of Atonement, seven lambs (Num. 29. 7).

At the Feast of Tabernacles, fourteen lambs each day, for seven days. On the eighth day seven lambs (Num. 29. 13 and 36).

7. THE LAMB might be for a Burnt Offering (Lev. 1. 10); for a Peace Offering (Lev. 3. 7); for a Sin Offering (Lev. 4. 32 and 35); for a Trespass Offering (Lev. 5. 6).

8. FOR THE PURIFICATION of women after childbirth, a lamb (Lev. 12. 6).

9. FOR THE LEPER, three lambs (Lev. 14. 10)—two he lambs and one ewe lamb.

10. At the OFFERING OF THE WAVE SHEAF (Lev. 23. 12), a lamb for a burnt offering.

11. FOR THE NAZARITE, when his days of separation were ended, two lambs, one he lamb for a burnt offering and one ewe lamb for a sin offering, and a ram for a peace offering (Num. 6. 14).

12. WHEN THE PRINCES OFFERED, each brought with other offerings one lamb for a burnt offering and five lambs for a peace offering (Num. 7. 15-17).

V. Other Lessons on Christ, the Lamb of God.

1. THE FIRST TIME THE WORD LAMB OCCURS in the Bible is in Genesis 22. 7, where Isaac asks his father as they go together to the sacrifice of Isaac, " *Where is the Lamb for a burnt offering* ?"

To which Abraham replies, " *My Son, God will provide Himself the* [R.V.] *Lamb for a burnt offering.*"

This is a remarkable case of first mention.

2. ABEL is, however, the first recorded as having offered " of the firstlings of his flock " (Gen. 4. 4), which, of course, implies a lamb.

He, we read in Hebrews 11. 4, did so " by faith," and "obtained witness that he was righteous "; and by that same lamb he, being dead, yet speaks of the precious Blood by which the sinner is justified.

3. THE PASSOVER LAMB* must be *without spot or blemish*, for Christ was without outward or inward failure or sin—holy, harmless and undefiled.

It must be *killed*, for it is not the blood, but the *shedding* of blood that ensures remission. The Son of Man *must* be lifted up; the corn of wheat *must* fall into the ground and die.

The blood *must be sprinkled*—that is to say, faith must apply the truth of Christ's death to its own case, must truly avail itself of the finished work.

" *Christ our Passover* " is sacrificed for us (1 Cor. 5. 7).

4. SAMUEL OFFERS A LAMB (1 Sam. 7. 9). The Philistines were gathered to battle, against Israel unarmed and defenceless. The people bid Samuel cry to God for them. Samuel does so, but offered a sucking lamb as a burnt offering, to teach the people that their sins must be purged before deliverance could be given. Then the Lord thundered upon the Philistines, and they were smitten before Israel.

5. JEREMIAH ADDS HIS TESTIMONY. Following Isaiah's wonderful prophecy (53), he says: " But I was like a lamb or an ox that is brought to the slaughter; and I knew not that they had devised devices against me, saying, Let us destroy the tree with the fruit thereof, and let us cut him off from the land of the living, that his name may be no more remembered " (Jer. 11. 19).

These words remind us of the words of the wicked husbandmen in the Parable of our Lord, " This is the heir: come, let us kill Him."

6. THE MEEKNESS AND GENTLENESS OF CHRIST. A lamb is the very symbol of innocency; it is inconceivable that it could harm or injure anyone.

It submits patiently and silently to death and suffering. So the Lord by His meekness under reproach, cruelty,

* A Lesson on the Passover is given in *Seventy Best Bible Stories*, No. 12, pp. 56-58.

and hatred leaves us an Example that we should follow. Reviled, He did not revile; suffering, He threatened not.

7. THE LAMB IN THE BOOK OF REVELATION. In this last book in the Bible the word Lamb occurs twenty-seven times. But it is a slightly different word. It is the diminutive of affection that is used (*arnion*). So that the poet is following the language of Scripture when He sings:

> " Dear dying Lamb, Thy precious Blood
> Shall never lose its power."

When John looked into Heaven he saw a Lamb as it had been slain upon the Throne—the Lion of the Tribe of Judah (5. 6). All the principalities and powers in Heaven and earth sang, " Worthy is the Lamb that was slain."

He saw the Bride of the Lamb coming down out of Heaven; He tells of the marriage of the Lamb; and He warns the rebellious nations of the Great Day of the wrath of the Lamb (6. 16).

VI. Application.

To the Sinner. " Behold the Lamb of God." Look and Live.

To the Believer. Follow the Lamb, looking on Him as He walked.

To the Preacher. Call to sinners, " Behold the Lamb of God," and warn them of the Great Day of His wrath.

The Lamb is the Lord

He is
{
Lord.
Advocate.
Mediator.
Brother.
}

By Death He has

Loosed us from our sins and made us
Accepted in the Beloved.
Made us nigh by the Blood.
Bought us with a Price.

We are thus Loosed, Accepted, Made nigh, Bought.

LESSON 51

Jesus the Mediator of the New Covenant

I. Text. " We have come to Jesus the Mediator of the New Covenant " (Heb. 12. 24).

II. Main Lesson. *A Mediator* is One who acts between God and man. "There is One Mediator (*mesites*) between God and man, the Man Christ Jesus " (1 Tim. 2. 5), and of course only One—for who dare usurp that office or substitute another in His place ?

We have seen Christ as Redeemer, Substitute, Advocate and Intercessor, Surety and High Priest; in all of these offices He occupies the place and carries on the work of Mediator.

It is specially as *Mediator of the New Covenant* we are to consider Him now.

What is a Covenant? A basis of relationship between God and man, a working agreement or contract.

The Covenant of Works was made with man, wherein he was promised life upon condition of perfect and personal obedience. This failed when Man sinned.

The Covenant of Grace " was made with Christ as the second Adam, and in Him with all the elect as His seed " (Longer Catechism, 31).

As Mediator He " interposed between God and man for the doing of all those things whereby a covenant might be established between them and made effectual " (Dr. J. Owen). So by His Mediation every believer is brought within the terms of the New Covenant and enjoys all its blessings.

III. Scripture to Study : Hebrews 8. 6-13

v. 6. *Christ has Obtained a more Excellent Ministry than that of the Law.* " But now hath He obtained a more excellent Ministry."

289

v. 6. *He is therefore Mediator of a Better Covenant.* "By how much also He is the Mediator of a Better Covenant, which was established upon better promises."

v. 7. *The First Covenant Faulty.* "For if that first covenant had been faultless, then should no place have been sought for the second."

v. 8. *God Promises a New Covenant.* "For finding fault with them [the children of Israel], He saith, Behold . . . I will make a New Covenant with the house of Israel and with the house of Judah."

v. 9. *It will be Unlike the Old Covenant.* "Not according to the Covenant that I made with their fathers . . . because they continued not in My Covenant, and I regarded them not, saith the Lord."

v. 10. *The New Covenant stated.* This is the Covenant (10-12):

I will put **My** laws into their mind, and write them in their hearts : and I will be to them a God, and they shall be to Me a people :

And they shall not teach every man his brother, saying, Know the Lord : for all shall know Me, from the least to the greatest.

For I will be merciful to their unrighteousness, and their sins and their iniquities will I remember no more.

---

v. 13. *The Old Covenant Passes off the Scene.* "In that He saith, A new Covenant, He hath made the first old. Now that which decayeth and waxeth old is ready to vanish away."

IV. Other Lessons from the Mediator.

1. CHRIST AND THE NEW COVENANT. "He is in the New Covenant the Mediator, the Surety, the Priest, the Sacrifice, all in His own Person " (Dr. J. Owen).

2. THERE MUST BE TWO PARTIES, for a " Mediator is not of one " (Gal. 3. 20). So that the believer must

consent in and to the Covenant—that is, must welcome
Christ as his Mediator and trust in Him as such. For the
Covenant is between God and Christ for all who are found
in Christ.

3. THE WORK OF THE MEDIATOR of the New Covenant
was twofold:

(1) He must *put away the enmity* or cause of offence
that kept man and God at a distance.

(2) He must *procure or purchase* the blessings offered in
the New Covenant.

Both these our Mediator did by His own Blood, so that
at the Last Supper He could say, "This Cup is the New
Covenant in My Blood, which is shed for many for the
remission of sins."

4. THE POSITION OF THE BELIEVER. He is brought in
Christ into Covenant relation with God—reconciled by
Blood, he becomes an inheritor of all the promises in the
Covenant. He enters by faith into the Promised Land—
that is, the sphere of the Promises.

They are all Yea and Amen—promised and assured—
in Christ Jesus.

5. THE BLESSINGS OF THE NEW COVENANT. It will be
seen that there are Seven Promises in it, as follows:

(1) *A Renewed Mind.* "I will put my laws into their
mind," so that they will understand them and see the
beauty of them.

(2) *A Changed or New Heart.* "And write them in
their hearts," so that they will love them, no longer find
them irksome or distasteful, but say of them, as David
did, " O how I love Thy law! it is my meditation all the
day "; or, as a Greater than David said, " I delight to do
Thy will: Thy law is within My heart."

(3) *A New Relationship.* "I will be their God "—not
only as He is the God of all as Creator, but in a new and
special sense, as the I AM to His saints. All that He is
as God He will be to them.

(4) *A New Privilege.* "They shall be My people." A
peculiar people (that is, for His own possession), zealous

of good works (Titus 2. 14), Called, Chosen, Elect, to be His witnesses in a dark world.

(5) *A New Knowledge of God.* "All shall know Me, from the least to the greatest." So John wrote to the little children, "Ye have known the Father"; and to the fathers, "Ye have known Him that is from the beginning" (1 John 2. 13).

(6) *A New Standing.* "I will be merciful to their unrighteousness." Having no righteousness of our own, He bestows upon us in grace a righteousness of God— a perfect robe in which we can stand before Him.

(7) *A New Joy of Remission.* "Their sins and their iniquities will I remember no more."

> "O happy day, O happy day,
> When Jesus washed my sins away."

6. Established upon Better Promises means that the New Covenant confirmed and assured to us in Christ far better promises than ever had been made to man before. For Eternal Life and a New Creation are ours in Christ, and these man did not know under any other promise.

V. Application.

Meditate upon the New Covenant.

Rejoice in Him who mediated it.

Yield in the obedience of faith to Him, that He may work all in us.

The Seven Promises of the Covenant with Abraham in Genesis 12. 2-3

1. I will make of thee a great nation.
2. I will bless thee.
3. And make thy name great.
4. Thou shalt be a blessing.
5. I will bless them that bless thee.
6. And curse him that curseth thee.
7. In thee shall all families of the earth be blessed.

SECTION VI

Our Lord Jesus Christ:
His Present Ministry

The Need of Jesus Felt.

Jesus, Lord, I need *Thy Presence*
As I journey on my way;
For without Thee I am lonely,
And my feet are apt to stray;
But if Thou wilt walk with me,
Life will calm and holy be.

Jesus, Lord, I need *Thy Wisdom*,
For perplexing problems press,
And without Thee I am foolish,
Nor can bear the strain and stress.
But if Thou wilt counsel me,
I shall true and upright be.

Jesus, Lord, I need *Thy Power*,
For temptations come and go,
And without Thee I am helpless
With no strength to meet the foe;
But if Thou wilt strengthen me,
Life will all-triumphant be.

Jesus, Lord, I need *Thy Guidance*—
Fire by night, and cloud by day,
For without Thee I am Guideless,
Neither do I know the way;
But if Thou dost lead me on,
I shall never walk alone.

Jesus, Lord, *Thy Love* so tender
Is my greatest need of all,
For without Thee pride and anger
From unguarded lips will fall;
But if Thou Thy love impart,
I shall have a gracious heart.

G. G.

Our Advocate with the Father

I. Text. "If any man sin, we have an Advocate with the Father, Jesus Christ the Righteous" (1 John 2. 1).

II. Main Truth. An Advocate is one who is called or summoned to aid another in his cause or defence. He is one who pleads, intercedes, or speaks for another.

Such is the Lord Jesus to His saints. He makes intercession for them before the Father.

Specially is this so when they have sinned. If any man (Christian) sin, we have an Advocate with the Father.

His plea is that the sin should not be laid to our charge because He Himself has died for the sins of His people, and they are therefore not to be imputed to them.

III. Scriptures to Study :

1 John 2. 1-2. *Christ our Advocate.* "My little children, these things write I unto you, that ye sin not. And if any man sin, we have an Advocate with the Father, Jesus Christ the Righteous: And He is the Propitiation for our sins: and not for ours only, but also for the sins of the whole world."

Hebrews 7. 21-28. *Christ our Priest and Intercessor.* "The Lord sware and will not repent, Thou art a Priest for ever after the order of Melchisedec."

v. 22. *And Surety of a Better Testament.* "By so much was Jesus made a surety of a better testament."

v. 23. *The Earthly Priests Died.* "And they truly were many priests, because they were not suffered to continue by reason of death."

v. 24. *Christ Continueth Ever.* "But this man, because He continueth ever, hath an unchangeable priesthood."

v. 25. *He ever Lives to Intercede.* "Wherefore He is able to save them to the uttermost that come unto God by Him, seeing He ever liveth to make intercession for them."

v. 26. *Such a Priest became us.* "For such an High Priest became us, Who is holy, harmless, undefiled, separate from sinners, and made higher than the Heavens."

IV. Illustrations of Advocacy.

1. ABRAHAM (Gen. 23. 32) pleads for Sodom that it may be spared if ten righteous souls be found in it. (A Lesson on this is found in *Seventy Less Known Stories*, No. 5, pp. 38-42).

2. ABRAHAM'S SERVANT (Gen. 24. 34-60) acts as advocate for his Master's son (Isaac) in the wooing of Rebecca.

3. JUDAH (Gen. 44. 18-34) acts as advocate on behalf of Benjamin, in whose sack Joseph's cup had been found.

4. MOSES is a frequent advocate.
He entreats Pharaoh for the children of Israel (Exod. 5. 1-9).
He entreats for Pharaoh that plague after plague be removed (Exod. 8. 8, etc.).
He entreats for the children of Israel after their sin in making the Golden Calf (Exod. 32. 11-13).

5. SAMUEL (1 Sam. 7. 5) prays for Israel after they had sinned in asking a king (see also 12. 23).
He prays for them when the Philistines threatened to destroy them (7. 9).
He prays for Saul, whom God had rejected for disobedience (1 Sam. 15. 11; 16. 1).

6. SOLOMON (1 Kings 8. 22-54) at the Dedication of the Temple.

7. ELIJAH AND ELISHA (1 Kings 17. 20 and 2 Kings 4. 33-35), each for the life of the child raised from the dead.

8. HEZEKIAH (2 Chron. 30. 18) for those unclean, that they might eat the Passover.
For the deliverance of Jerusalem from the hand of Sennacherib (2 Chron. 32. 20, with Isaiah).

9. NEHEMIAH (1. 4-11) for the City of Jerusalem, that it might be rebuilt.

10. ESTHER (7. 1-4) for the lives of her people, betrayed to destruction by the wicked Haman (see also Ezek. 9. 8, Dan. 9. 3-19).

11. STEPHEN (Acts 7. 60) for his murderers as he was dying.

12. THE LORD HIMSELF on the night in which He was betrayed (John 17), and for those who put Him to death (Luke 23. 34).

V. Other Lessons from Christ our Advocate.

1. COMMON MISTAKES AS TO ADVOCACY.

(a) *An Advocate does not Make or Invent a Case* for an offender; it would not be honest or honourable. He *presents* his client's case.

If he has a bad one, he advises him to abandon it or make terms (Matt. 5. 25 and Luke 6. 32).

If he has a good one, he presents it and pleads it with confidence.

(b) *An Advocate does not Plead with a judge to be Kind or Gracious.* Pleaders in our courts are not trying to touch the judge's hearts, *nor do they ask the judge to be just.* The judge's character is not their concern.

So our God does not have to be persuaded to be gracious or merciful or a just judge: He is all of these.

(c) *A Judge is not Moved by Sentiment* or pathos. He pronounces judgment on righteous lines.

Let us not think that Christ is more loving or merciful than God (that would be blasphemy); the advocacy is based on great facts.

2. WHAT DOES OUR ADVOCATE PLEAD BEFORE GOD ?

Of course, not any excuse for our sinning. The sin must be confessed and self-judged and put away. There is no plea in mitigation of it. Sin is the abominable thing which God hates. He can never overlook or excuse it.

But the Lord pleads :

(a) *The Merit of His Finished Work;* the efficacy of His precious Blood; the value of His One Great Sacrifice for sins once for all. For the sake of Christ the sinner is accepted and forgiven.

> " Whence to me this waste of Love ?
> Ask my Advocate above.
> See the cause in Jesus' face
> Now before the Throne of Grace.

> " There for me the Saviour stands,
> Shows His wounds and spreads His hands.
> God is Love; I know, I feel,
> Jesus lives and loves me still."

(b) *The Promise of the Father.*   To this all the prophets give witness, that Remission is assured to every believer. For the Father Himself loveth us and delights in mercy. No sin is laid to the charge of God's elect (Rom. 8. 33, Psa. 32. 2, Rom. 4. 6).

(c) *The Covenant and Oath.*   In the New Covenant it is written, " Their sins and their iniquities will I remember no more " (Heb. 8. 12; 10. 16-17).   Whenever the child of God draws near to the Father on the ground of the blood, he is met with grace, and no more remembrance is made of his sins.

This has been confirmed by an oath; not only has God promised but sworn (Heb. 6. 17), so that the believer has this double assurance of the grace of forgiveness.

> " His oath, His Covenant, His Blood,
> Support me in the o'erwhelming flood."

(d) *The Election of Grace.*   That the one for whom He pleads is one of the called and elect.   That he has truly repented and believed in the Lord Jesus, and has been born again of the Holy Spirit, and is indwelt of the same Spirit.

For all such absolute satisfaction has been made for sin by their Sinless Substitute.   They are therefore " dead to sin " and " dead to the law."   Its curse has been met.   It has no longer dominion over them.   There is no condemnation for those in Christ (Rom. 8. 1).

Thus the believer can say:

> " God will not payment twice demand:
> Once at my bleeding Surety's hand,
> And then again at mine."

So that the believer, while often conscious of sin and failure, does not despair. He sings with holy joy:

> " Before the Throne of God above
> I have a strong, a perfect plea:
> A great High Priest Whose Name is Love,
> Who ever lives and pleads for me."

3. Our Responsibility. There are always two sides to every truth.

While our Advocate above secures that we shall not perish, and assures us that sin shall not be so laid to our charge as to condemn us, yet we need to confess and judge and put sin away.

For while the Judge will not condemn, the Father will not show us His favour if we have grieved the Holy Spirit. Fellowship is broken. Communion needs to be restored and parental forgiveness received, and this is promised as follows:

" If we confess our sins, He (the Father) is faithful and just to forgive us our sins, and to cleanse us from all unrighteousness " (1 John 1. 9).

4. Justification and Parental Forgiveness. A judge cannot forgive; he must be satisfied if he is to acquit the offender. This has been done for every believer; the Judge of all the Earth, having been satisfied in the Cross of Christ, *justifies* freely all who believe in Jesus (Rom. 3. 24).

But a Father can Forgive. The child who offends does not appear before a judge who must condemn, but before a father who forgives on true repentance and confession.

Justification is therefore once for all.

Forgiveness as often as the need is felt.

VI. Application.

Let us make our calling and election sure, for if we are not true believers our sins are still upon us.

Let us rejoice in our redemption and justification if we are truly found in Christ.

Let us not sin, but if overtaken let us confess it and know that we have an Advocate with the Father and, for His sake, forgiveness.

Jesus, Our Great Priest*

I. Text. "We have such an High Priest, who is set on the right hand of the throne of the Majesty in the Heavens" (Heb. 8. 1).

II. Main Lesson. The Lord Jesus is our Great Priest. His office as such is:

1. To OFFER GIFTS AND SACRIFICES FOR SINS (Heb. 5. 1 and 8. 3). This He did once for all when He offered up Himself (7. 27).

2. To MAKE INTERCESSION FOR HIS PEOPLE (7. 25), and this He is enabled to do effectually because He ever liveth and is no longer subject to death.

3. To SAVE TO THE UTTERMOST all that come to God by Him (7. 25)—that is, to the very end, so that none of those given Him of God is lost (John 6. 39 and 17. 12).

4. To HAVE COMPASSION ON THE IGNORANT, AND THEM THAT ARE OUT OF THE WAY (5. 2). This He can do because He has Himself suffered.

5. To MINISTER THE BLESSINGS OF THE NEW COVENANT (8. 6). "A minister of holy things" (R.V.). Having as Surety obtained them and as Mediator discharged all the liability, He now ministers them to His people.

6. To TEACH THE LAW OF GOD (Mal. 2. 7). "The priest's lips should keep knowledge, and they should seek the law at His mouth." The Lord still says, "Learn of Me." None teacheth like Him.

7. To PRESENT THEIR PRAYERS TO GOD with His own for them (Rev. 8. 3 and 5. 8); for our prayers are full of foolishness often. We know not what we should pray for as we ought (Rom. 8. 26; Jas. 3. 2-3).

---

* A Lesson on Melchizedek, the King Priest, is found in *Seventy Less Known Stories*, No. 2, pp. 21-26. The comparison is omitted, therefore, in this study.

8. To Represent them before God in all Things
(Heb. 5. 1). "He is ordained for men in things pertaining
to God." In all our dealings with God He undertakes
for us, maintaining our position and supplying all our need.

III. Scriptures to Study:

Hebrews 2. 17. He became like unto His brethren, that
He might be a Merciful and Faithful High Priest.

Hebrews 3. 1-2. We must consider Him the Apostle and
High Priest of our confession, Who was faithful to Him
that appointed Him.

Hebrews 4. 14-16. Seeing He has passed into the
Heavens, let us hold fast, since He is touched with the
feeling of our infirmities. Let us come boldly to the Mercy
Seat.

Hebrews 5. 1–8. 1. These chapters treat of the Great
Type of Priesthood, Melchizedec (see footnote on p. 300),
and shows in what aspects he foreshadows the Blessed
Son of God. Chiefly in that He is in striking contrast to
the Aaronic priesthood because He " ever liveth " and
hath an unchangeable priesthood, and is therefore able to
save to the uttermost all that come to God by Him.

IV. Other Lessons from the Study.

1. Aaron and Christ. Aaron is a type of Christ
chiefly by *Contrast*, whereas Melchizedec was a type by
Likeness.

The contrast between Aaron and Christ is as follows:

(a) *Aaron was of the Tribe of Levi*, but the Lord Jesus
was of the Royal Tribe of Judah. Therefore He could
not be a priest on earth (Heb. 7. 12-14).

(b) *Aaron's was an Earthly Priesthood* with a *Worldly
Sanctuary* (a Tabernacle on the earth), but Christ is in
Heaven and is seated on the right hand of the Majesty
on High.

(c) *Aaron was of a Dying Race*, not able to continue by
reason of death (Heb. 7. 23), but Christ ever liveth in the
power of an endless life.

(d) *Aaron was Appointed without an Oath.* This indicates
that his office was temporary only. Christ was appointed

with an oath: "I have sworn, and will not repent, Thou art a Priest for ever."

(e) *Aaron was a Man with Infirmities* (Heb. 7. 28), but the Son of God was " consecrated for ever "—holy, harmless, undefiled, and separate from sinners (7. 26).

(f) *Aaron Offered Continually Sacrifices* that could never take away sins, but Christ offered One Sacrifice for ever, sanctifying and perfecting for ever (Heb. 10. 14).

(g) *Aaron was a Sinner* and had to offer for himself, but Christ needed not to do this, being without sin (Heb. 7. 27).

(h) *Aaron's Offering was Never Done*: he never sat down; but Christ, having offered the One all-sufficient sacrifice, sat down, His work completed.

(i) *Aaron was a Man :* Christ was the Son of God, both God and man, the Lord from Heaven.

(j) *Aaron was a Priest only :* The Lord Jesus was King and Priest, uniting in His own Person the threefold office of Prophet, Priest, and King.

2. THE PRIESTLY ROBES that Aaron wore were symbolical of the character and office of Christ as our Great Priest. They should be studied in Exodus 28. 1-43. They are called " Holy Garments for glory and for beauty."

They consisted of " a breastplate, and an ephod, and a robe, and a broidered coat, a mitre, and a girdle " (v. 4).

Upon the stones in the breastplate were engraven the names of the twelve tribes, so that the Priest bore them on his heart; and again on the two onyx stones on his shoulders, so that he bore them on the place of strength. In the breastplate was the Urim and Thummim by which he enquired of the Lord.

On the mitre was a crown of gold, bearing the inscription, " Holiness to the Lord."

On the fringe of his robe were golden bells and pomegranates, symbols of testimony and fruitfulness.

All of which are rich in spiritual meaning, which space forbids us to enter upon.

3. NO EARTHLY CASTE OF PRIESTS NOW. A Christian minister is never as such called a priest (*hiereus*) in the

New Testament, but all believers have been constituted " a kingdom of priests " unto God (Rev. 1. 6).

An Holy Priesthood (1 Pet. 2. 5) " to offer up spiritual sacrifices acceptable to God by Jesus Christ."

A Royal Priesthood (v. 9) to show " forth the praises of Him Who hath called you out of darkness into His marvellous light."

The result is:

(*a*) *To Pretend to be a Priest* in some sense that other believers are not is presumption.

No priest is needed between Christ and His people. All have direct approach to Him.

(*b*) *To Attempt to Offer Sacrifices for Sin* as a priest is fearful blasphemy, since by one offering Jesus perfected for ever them that are sanctified (Heb. 10. 14).

4. DR. WATTS's BEAUTIFUL HYMN expresses these things in graceful verse:

> Jesus ! in Thee our eyes behold
> A thousand glories more
> Than the rich gems and polished gold
> The sons of Aaron wore.
>
> They first their own sin-offering brought
> To purge themselves from sin;
> Thy life was pure, without a spot,
> And all Thy nature clean.
>
> Fresh blood, as constant as the day,
> Was on their altars spilt;
> But Thy One Offering took away
> For ever all our guilt.
>
> Their priesthood ran through several hands,
> For mortal was their race;
> Thy never-changing office stands
> Eternal as Thy days.
>
> Once in the circuit of a year,
> With blood, but not his own,
> Aaron within the Veil appears,
> Before the Golden Throne.

> But Christ, by His own precious Blood,
>   Ascends above the skies.
> And in the presence of our God
>   Shows His own sacrifice.

V. Application.

Let the believer dwell much upon the glories and excellences of Christ as his Great Priest.

Let him beware of all the pretensions of the various castes of priests in Christendom.

Let us make daily use of Christ in all our needs.

Let us as a holy and royal priesthood offer our spiritual sacrifices of thanksgiving and seek ever to show forth His praises.

OUTLINE

We have a Priest

Who is
- Perfect (without personal sin).
- Royal (King as well as Priest).
- Intercessor (at God's right hand).
- Entered (into Heaven by His own blood).
- Saving (to the uttermost).
- Touched (with the feeling of our infirmities).

No mere man can be all these to us.

Once for all ($\dot{\epsilon}\phi\acute{a}\pi a\xi$)

" Offered up Himself " (Heb. 7. 27).
" Entered into the Holiest " (Heb. 9. 12).
" Sanctified us by offering of His Body " (Heb. 10. 12).
" The faith delivered to the Saints " (Jude 3).

Christ as Lord

I. Text. " Let all the House of Israel know assuredly that God hath made that same Jesus, Whom ye have crucified, both LORD and Christ " (Acts 2. 36).

II. Main Lesson. The Blessed Saviour Jesus is "the Lord from Heaven " (1 Cor. 15. 47). He is LORD of ALL (Acts 10. 36).

(a) *In His Essential Deity.* He is Jehovah-Jesus.

The Hebrew word Jehovah is translated in the LXX " KURIOS," which is always rendered "Lord," so that " Lord Jesus " is equivalent to " Jehovah-Jesus." Christ Himself emphasized this in quoting Psalm 110. 1, "The Lord said unto My Lord " (*cf.* Heb. 1. 8).

(b) *As the Heir of All Things.* By Him and to Him are all things. When He came into the world He came unto His own [things] (John 1. 11).

(c) *In the Ultimate Purpose of God* (1 Tim. 6. 15). " Which in His times He shall show, Who is the Blessed and Only Potentate, the King of kings, and Lord of lords " (see also Rev. 19. 16).

(d) *As the One Who Died and Rose again to be our Saviour.* God hath exalted Him at His own right hand to be a Prince and Saviour (Acts 5. 31).

Those who confess Him as Lord are saved (Rom. 10. 9).

(e) *As the Head of His Church*, over which He rules as " Master of the House," Whom His saints confess as Lord and Head over all things to the Church.

III. Scriptures to Study :

Matthew 7. 21-23. *It is not Enough to Say " Lord, Lord," if there is no Obedience.* " Not every one that saith unto Me, Lord, Lord, shall enter into the Kingdom of Heaven; but he that doeth the Will of My Father which is in Heaven."

vv. 22-23. *To those who Sin the Lord will Refuse any*

Knowledge of Them. " Many will say to Me in that day, Lord, Lord, have we not prophesied in Thy Name ? and in Thy Name cast out devils ? and in Thy Name done many wonderful works ? And then will I profess unto them, I never knew you; depart from Me ye that work iniquity."

Luke 19. 12-27. *The Parable of the Pounds.* The Citizens Refuse to Recognize the Lordship.*

v. 14. " But His citizens hated Him, and sent a message after Him, saying, We will not have this Man to reign over us."

v. 27. *They are Slain before Him.* " But those Mine enemies, which would not that I should reign over them, bring hither, and slay them before Me."

John 13. 13. *Jesus rightly Called Lord.* " Ye call Me Master and Lord: and ye say well; for so I am. If I then, your Lord and Master, have washed your feet, ye also ought to wash one another's feet."

Romans 10. 9 (R.V.). *Christ must be Confessed as Lord with the Mouth.* " If thou shalt confess with thy mouth Jesus as Lord, and believe in thine heart that God hath raised Him from the dead, thou shalt be saved."

1 Peter 3. 15 (R.V.). *Christ must be Sanctified as Lord in the Heart.* " But sanctify Christ as Lord in your hearts: and be ready always to give an answer to everyone that asketh you a reason for the hope that is in you with meekness and fear."

IV. Other Lessons from the Study.

1. Christ is Lord of All.

The Prophets announced it. Isaiah 7. 14: " A Virgin shall conceive, and bear a Son, and shall call His Name Immanuel " (God with us). (See also Isa. 9. 6; Mal. 3. 1.)

The Forerunner proclaimed it. " Prepare ye the way of the Lord " (Matt. 3. 3).

The Lord Himself asserted it (see above, John 13. 13).

His Parables illustrated it. Matthew 25. 19: " The Lord of those servants cometh."

The Resurrection manifested it (Rom. 1. 3-4). " Jesus

---

* For a Lesson on this Parable, see *Seventy Less Known Bible Stories* No. 54, pp. 251-254.

Christ our Lord . . . declared to be the Son of God with power . . . by the resurrection from the dead."

The Apostles preached it:

At Pentecost (Acts 2. 36). "That same Jesus . . . both Lord and Christ."

In the House of Cornelius (Acts 10. 36). "He is Lord of all."

The Book of the Revelation consummates it (Rev. 19. 16). "He hath on His vesture and on His thigh a name written, *KING of KINGS and LORD of LORDS.*"

2. Christ must be Confessed as Lord for Salvation. Romans 10. 9 (R.V.): "If thou shalt confess with thy mouth Jesus as Lord . . . thou shalt be saved."

It is not enough to believe about Christ; the real issue in the matter of Salvation is that Christ must be yielded the place of LORD, and be received and confessed as such.

The Suggestion that He can be Received as Saviour without being Lord is False. He does not save rebels. There must be submission (that is, true repentance towards God) before there can be salvation. (My little tract *Prince and Saviour*, 1d., makes this very clear.)

Psalm 2 makes this plain. God has set His King on His holy hill of Zion (6) and declared Him to be "My Son" (7), and all nations (10) are called upon to "*Serve the Lord* with fear. . . . *Kiss the Son* [with the kiss of submission and allegiance], lest He be angry, and ye perish" (11-12).

3. An Old Writer's Testimony. Walter Marshall, in his *Gospel Mystery of Sanctification* (A.D. 1620), says:

"Why doth a man seek a pardon if he intend to go in rebellion and stand out in defiancy of his Prince ? They seek a pardon in a mocking way, and intend not to return unto obedience. . . .

"To take part of His Salvation and leave out the rest ! But Christ is not divided. . . .

"They would be saved by Christ, and yet be out of Christ in a fleshly state: whereas God doth free from condemnation only those who are in Christ."

4. CHRIST MUST BE SANCTIFIED AS LORD IN THE HEART FOR HOLINESS (1 Pet. 3. 15 (R.V.) as above).

Lord of Conscience, that it may be a safe guide in all morals.

Lord of Mind, so that no evil thoughts are allowed, but all brought to the obedience of Christ (2 Cor. 10. 5).

Lord of Will, that no purpose or plan may be made in independence of Him.

Lord of Spirit, so that the temper is under His control.

Lord of Heart, so that the affections do not stray to unworthy objects.

(My tract *Jesus Lord in the Heart* (1d.) enlarges on this.)

5. CHRIST MUST BE PREACHED AS LORD. 2 Corinthians 4. 5 (R.V.): "For we preach not ourselves, but Christ Jesus as Lord, and ourselves as your servants for Jesus' sake."

All men must be called to submission to Him, for He will one day sit as Judge Who is now Lord and Saviour.

There is much preaching that calls on men only to believe—"Only-believism" it has been not unfairly called. Men are told to "trust Jesus to take them to Heaven when they die," who are nevertheless living in the practice of sin and in rebellion against His laws.

They neither yield to His authority; acknowledge His Lordship; nor walk in His obedience; yet are encouraged to hope for salvation.

Salvation is by receiving Christ (John 1. 12)—not in one capacity only, but both as Saviour and Lord.

6. CHRIST MUST BE GIVEN THE PLACE OF LORD IN THE ASSEMBLY. There is "One Lord, One Faith, One Baptism" (Eph. 4. 5). Those who gather in His Name do so under His Lordship. He is "the Master of the House," the Lord of His Servants.

Others who seek to lord it over His inheritance are usurping His authority (1 Pet. 5. 3).

7. CHRIST SHOULD BE LOOKED FOR AS THE LORD FROM HEAVEN. "For the Lord Himself shall descend from

Heaven," and His saints "be caught up together . . . in the clouds, to meet the Lord in the air" (1 Thess. 4. 16-17).

Such is the hope of the Church.

V. Application.

To Sinners. Have we Confessed Christ as Lord ? Beware of saying, "Lord, Lord," and never knowing Him.

To Saints. Have we Sanctified Christ as Lord in our hearts ?

To Preachers. Are we faithfully Preaching Christ as Lord ?

OUTLINE

Lord and Saviour

As Saviour to LOOSE (us from our sins).
As Lord to LEAD.
As Saviour to OPEN (the Door).
As Lord to be OBEYED.
As Saviour to REDEEM.
As Lord to RULE.
As Saviour to DELIVER.
As Lord to DIRECT.

We have a LORD who saves
And a SAVIOUR who lords.

How can He SAVE if He does not
{ Live in us ?
Order our way ?
Regulate our actions ?
Dictate His will ?

Jesus, the Saviour

I. Text. "Thou shalt call His Name JESUS: for He shall save His people from their sins" (Matt. 1. 21).

II. Main Lesson. A Redeemer is a Saviour; so also the Lord Jesus is both Redeemer and Saviour; but the title Saviour has reference more specially to His work in delivering His people from their sins.

Our study, therefore, is, How does He accomplish this? Our Salvation is Fourfold:

1. From the *Guilt* of Sin—by His Blood.
2. From the *Bondage* or Reign of Sin—by His Risen Power.
3. From the *Love* of Sin—by Regeneration.
4. From the *Presence* of Sin—at His Coming.

Each of these is an advance on the last. It is little use forgiving a man if he remains under the power of sin; or forgiving and liberating him if he still loves and desires his sin; or doing all this and leaving him with no hope of ever being free from the presence of sin—that is, the law of sin and death in his yet unredeemed body.

III. Scriptures to Study:

Matthew 1. 21. *The Name Jesus Given before Birth.* "She shall bring forth a Son, and thou shalt call His Name JESUS: for He shall save His people from their sins."

Luke 2. 8. *The Message to the Shepherds.* "There were in the same country shepherds abiding in the field, keeping watch over their flock by night."

v. 9. *The Glory of the Lord Shines on Them.* "And, lo, the Angel of the Lord came upon them, and the glory of the Lord shone round about them: and they were sore afraid."

vv. 10-11. *The Angel Announces a Saviour.* "And the Angel said unto them, Fear not: for, behold, I bring you good tidings of great joy, which shall be to all people.

For unto you is born this day in the City of David a Saviour, which is Christ the Lord."

v. 12. *He Gives Them a Sign.* " And this shall be a sign unto you; Ye shall find the babe wrapped in swaddling clothes, lying in a manger."

v. 13. *A Heavenly Host Join in Praise to God.* " And suddenly there was with the angel a multitude of the heavenly host praising God, and saying."

v. 14. *Their Message.* " Glory to God in the highest, and on earth peace, goodwill toward men."

IV. Some Titles of our Salvation.

1. A Great (1 Sam. 19. 5) or So Great Salvation, because it is not a temporal, but an

2. Eternal Salvation (Isa. 45. 17 and Heb. 5. 9), even the

3. Salvation of the Soul (Heb. 10. 39; 1 Pet. 1. 9). It is a

4. Common Salvation—that is, proclaimed to all men.

5. *Christ is spoken of* as The Horn of My Salvation (2 Sam. 22. 3), which means

6. The Strength of Salvation (Isa. 33. 6).

7. *It is figured* as the Shield (2 Sam. 22. 36; Psa. 18. 25); the Rock (2 Sam. 22. 47; Psa. 90. 1); the Tower (2 Sam. 22. 51) of my Salvation—each helping us to understand how Christ is our Saviour by becoming to us all that these symbolize.

8. *We read too of the* Joy (Psa. 51. 12); the Truth (Psa. 69. 13); the Helmet (Isa. 59. 17; Eph. 6. 17); the Knowledge (Luke 1. 77); the Garments (Isa. 61. 10); the Cup (Psa. 116. 13); the Wells (Isa. 12. 3); and the Lamp (Isa. 62. 1) of Salvation—teaching the character and value of the Salvation we have in Christ.

9. *It is communicated to us by the* Gospel (Eph. 1. 13); the Word (Acts 13. 26); the Way (Acts 16. 17); and the Hope (1 Thess. 5. 8) of Salvation, to those who shall be *Heirs* of Salvation.

V. From What are we Saved ?

1. From the WRATH TO COME (Rom. 5. 9 and 1 Thess. 1. 16).

2. From our SINS (Matt. 1. 21).

3. From this PRESENT EVIL WORLD (Gal. 1. 4).

4. From our ENEMIES (Luke 1. 71).

5. From SO GREAT A DEATH (2 Cor. 1. 10).

6. From the POWER OF DARKNESS (Col. 1. 13).

7. From the LAW (Rom. 7. 6), its curse and burden.

8. From EVIL MEN (2 Thess. 3. 2).

9. From the BONDAGE OF CORRUPTION (Rom. 8. 21).

10. From the FEAR OF DEATH (Heb. 2. 15) and ALL OUR FEARS (Psa. 34. 4).

VI. Other Lessons from the Study.

1. THE MEANING OF THE WORD SALVATION. It means Deliverance, Liberty, and Freedom from all that dishonours God and all that oppresses and disgraces us.

To be saved means to be set free, to be brought into glorious liberty, so that we, being delivered from our enemies, can serve God in righteousness and holiness all the days of our life.

It goes beyond this life and promises us Eternal Salvation, perfect liberty for ever, even from the presence of Sin.

2. A TWOFOLD USE OF THE WORD. The word Salvation is used sometimes in a wide general sense, as when we read " Salvation is of the Lord," or " Mine eyes have seen Thy Salvation "; but at others it is used in the more restricted sense given above—that of Deliverance. As, for example, in Romans 5. 9, where it is said to follow on Justification: " Being now justified by His Blood, we shall be saved from wrath "; and again in verse 10: " Being reconciled to God by the death of His Son, we shall be saved by His life."

Here it will be noticed that Salvation is said to be " by His life."

Salvation—that is, Deliverance and Liberty—follows on Justification and Reconciliation. It is found in the Risen Living Saviour.

3. How does Christ Save His People from their Sins?—that is, from actually going on sinning.

First note it is *His People* whom He saves. Until we are reconciled by the death and justified by His Blood we cannot expect Him to set us free or rescue us from the power and dominion of our sins.

This liberty is for those who are His people.

We often hear the words " Jesus saves," but we do not hear it explained how.

In the Main Lesson (II.) we saw it was a fourfold salvation from the Guilt, Reign, Love, and Presence of Sin.

From the Dominion and Love of Sin we are saved by being brought into a new creation, and by the indwelling Spirit given *a nature that hates sin* (1 John 3. 9), and by the power of the risen Christ are given the victory *as we walk by faith* and in the Spirit.

4. A Conditioned Salvation. It will be seen, then, that our liberty depends upon our walk and our work. (This cannot be said of our Justification, which is " to him that worketh not ": Rom. 4. 5.)

We must *Walk by the Spirit* if we would not fulfil the lusts of the flesh (Gal. 5. 16), and we must *Work out our own Salvation* with fear and trembling, as God works in us, to will and to do of His good pleasure (Phil. 2. 12) if we would be free.

A careless walker or a lazy child of God will not enjoy either power or liberty; he will still be the servant of sin and subject to evil tempers.

Salvation from sinning is the privilege of the spiritual man only.

5. Preaching Salvation. It is important to remember the above distinction when preaching the Gospel of God. We must call to men, " Be ye reconciled to God " (2 Cor. 5. 20) before we tell them Jesus will save them from their sins.

Salvation follows on Reconciliation; let us not reverse the order.

When with David I can say, " I am Thine," then I can add, " Save me."

The Lord delivers His saints.

6. THE SAVING OF THE SOUL. This expression (Heb. 10. 39; James 5. 20) must be understood aright. It means the deliverance of the life, the man himself (for a man *is* [not has] a soul), from all that mars it—from besetting sins, pride, evil tempers, selfishness, and a thousand other sorrows that sin has introduced.

This is not accomplished at justification, but is *a lifelong business*. I need to see that my soul (myself) is delivered from all these things. Only then can I honestly say that my soul is saved, though I may say I am reconciled to God, have eternal life, and shall never perish. It is a good thing to have the soul really and fully saved.

7. NOW IS OUR SALVATION NEARER than when we believed (Rom. 13. 11). This, of course, refers to the Grace that is to be brought to us at the Coming of Christ. For then we shall receive the Adoption—that is, the Redemption of the Body (Rom. 8. 13). There will then be no more law of sin and death in our members, and we shall be for ever with the Lord in a glorified body, fashioned like unto His glorious body.

VII. Application.

Let the Sinner see that he is reconciled to God through the death of His Son, for till then there is no Salvation for him.

Let the Saint walk by the Spirit and work out his own salvation with fear and trembling, or he will never know Liberty.

Let the Servant of God entreat men to be reconciled to God, promising them a full Salvation.

Let us all look forward with joy to our Salvation, drawing every day nearer.

Jehovah-Tsidkenu—the Lord Our Righteousness

I. Text. " This is the Name whereby He shall be called, THE LORD OUR RIGHTEOUSNESS " (Jer. 23. 6).

II. Main Lesson. The sinner led to see his true state before God confesses " All our righteousnesses are as filthy rags " (Isa. 64. 6). He further acknowledges that he can never attain to righteousness in God's sight by his own efforts, nor by endeavouring to keep the holy commandments.

> " Not the labour of my hands
> Can fulfil Thy law's demands.

For by the law is the knowledge of sin.

But in Christ he finds righteousness. " In the Lord have I righteousness " (Isa. 45. 24). He learns that " a Righteousness from God hath been manifested (Rom. 3. 21, R.V.) . . . even the Righteousness of God which is by faith in Jesus Christ."

So that Christ is made unto him Righteousness (1 Cor. 1. 30), or, in other words, " Christ is his Righteousness." He can therefore rejoice that his Righteousness is in Heaven, and that he is Justified, accounted Righteous, when he believes in Jesus.

III. Scripture to Study : Romans 3. 19-26.

v. 19. *All the World Guilty before God.* " Now we know that what things soever the Law saith, it saith to them who are under the Law: that every mouth may be stopped, and all the world may become guilty before God " (R.V., " be brought under the judgment of God ").

v. 20. *The Law can Never Justify.* " Therefore by the deeds of the law there shall no flesh be justified in His sight: for by the Law is the knowledge of sin."

v. 21. *A Righteousness from God Manifested.* " But

315

now the righteousness of God without the Law is manifested, being witnessed by the Law and the Prophets."

v. 22. *It is by Faith in Jesus Christ.* " Even the Righteousness of God which is by faith of (R.V. " in ") Jesus Christ unto all and upon all them that believe."

vv. 22-23. *All alike are Sinners.* " For there is no difference: for all have sinned, and come (fall, R.V.) short of the glory of God."

v. 24. *Justification is Gratuitous and Free.* " Being justified freely by His grace through the redemption that is in Christ Jesus."

v. 25. *Christ having been Set Forth by God as a Mercy Seat.* " Whom God hath set forth to be a Propitiation through faith in His Blood."

v. 25. *So declaring that He was Righteous in Passing Over the Sins of the Past.* " To declare His righteousness for the remission (because of the passing over, R.V.) of sins that are past, through the forbearance of God."

v. 26. *And that He might righteously Justify Sinners now.* " To declare, I say, at this time (present season, R.V.) His Righteousness: that He might be Just, and the Justifier of him which believeth in Jesus."

IV. Some Figures of Righteousness.

Righteousness has a double meaning:

1. *A Right Relationship to God.* To be right with God, to have a perfect standing before Him, as one who is justified—*Our Position.*

2. *Righteous Conduct and Life* resulting from our relationship to God—*Our Practice.*

(1) *A Robe or Clothing* is a common simile used in the Bible for the Righteousness we have from God. " *The Gift of Righteousness* " (Rom. 5. 17).

Isaiah uses it (61. 10): " He hath clothed me with the garments of salvation, He hath covered me with the Robe of Righteousness."

The thought is of Righteousness imputed to us as a robe put upon us.

Job used it (29. 14): " I put on righteousness, and it clothed me: my judgment was as a Robe and a Diadem."

In the Psalms we read it (132. 9): " Let thy priests be clothed with righteousness."

Our Lord used the figure in the Parables.

The Prodigal had the Best Robe put on him.

The Man who came into the Marriage not having on a Wedding Garment was càst out.

In Revelation (19. 8) we read of the Bride arrayed in fine linen—" the fine linen is the Righteousness of saints."

(2) Armour is another figure used for Righteousness.

In Ephesians 6. 14 we read of the " Breastplate of Righteousness "; and in Isaiah 59. 17, " He put on righteousness as a Breastplate "; and in 11. 5 of " righteousness as the girdle of his loins."

In 2 Corinthians 6. 7 of " the armour of righteousness on the right hand and on the left."

Righteousness is a protection against all the assaults of the enemy.

(3) The Great Mountains. " Thy Righteousness is like the great mountains " (Psa. 36. 6), suggesting the firm foundation and stability of the eternal principles of righteousness upon which God's Throne is established (Psa. 97. 2; 111. 3).

(4) A Mighty Stream and Waves of the Sea (Isa. 48. 18). " O that thou hadst hearkened unto My commandments ! Then had thy peace been as a river, and thy righteousness as the waves of the sea."

Amos 5. 24. " Let judgment run down as waters, and righteousness as a mighty stream."

The strong and even flow of the life is like that of a deep and silent river.

(5) Various Similes. " The *paths* of righteousness " (Psa. 23. 3); " Righteousness as the *Light* " (Psa. 37. 6); " the *Gates* of Righteousness " (Psa. 118. 19); the *City* of Righteousness " (Isa. 1. 26); " *Trees* of Righteousness " (Isa. 61. 3); " the *Sun* of Righteousness " (Mal. 4. 2); " the *Law* of Righteousness " (Rom. 9. 31); " the *Fruits* of Righteousness " (2 Cor. 9. 10); " a *Crown* of Righteousness " (2 Tim. 4. 8); a " *Sceptre* of Righteousness " (Heb. 1. 8).

Suggesting Righteousness in all the different aspects and walks of life.

V. Other Lessons on Righteousness.

1. RIGHTEOUSNESS IN CHRIST. The Believer abandons all hope of righteousness in himself, seeing himself to be guilty without excuse and under condemnation. He can do nothing to remove his guilt, any more than a murderer can do anything to get rid of the sentence of death pronounced upon him.

He therefore flees to Christ, in Whom he finds a righteousness, the free gift of God to all who put their faith in Christ.

2. DR. JOHNSON'S REPLY. Dr. Johnson was the guest of Lady Macleod at Dunvegan Castle. She asked him, "Is not man naturally good?" His reply was: "No, madam; no more than a wolf."

Since the fall this is true. All sinned in Adam and fall short of the glory of God in all their ways.

3. IMPUTATION is the word used of the gift to us of God's righteousness. The Bible speaks of three *Imputations*:

(a) *The Imputation of Adam's* sin and its consequences to all his seed. "By one man sin entered into the world, and death by sin; and so death passed upon all men, for that all have sinned" (Rom. 5. 12).

(b) *The Imputation of our Sins to Christ.* As on the Day of Atonement the High Priest put the sins of the people upon the head of the scapegoat (Lev. 16. 21), so God hath laid upon Christ the iniquity of us all (Isa. 53. 6), so that He was "made sin" and "made a curse" for us, by having our sin and our curse imputed to Him and laid to His account.

(c) *The Imputation of Righteousness to us.* As He became sin, so we when reconciled become "the righteousness of God in Him" (2 Cor. 5. 21).

So we read, "Abraham believed God, and it was imputed to him for righteousness," and so it is to all who believe (Rom. 4. 3 and 22-25).

"Abraham was justified as a believer, and not as one who sought righteousness by works."

4. RIGHTEOUS PRACTICE RESULTING FROM RIGHTEOUS-NESS IMPUTED. The two aspects of righteousness are never separated. "He that doeth righteousness is righteous." That is to say, the justified believer reveals that he is righteous by righteousness in walk and life (1 John 2. 29).

5. The people of God have ever loved to sing of these things:

> "Jesus, Thy Blood and Righteousness
> My beauty are, My glorious dress;
> 'Mid flaming worlds, in these arrayed,
> I shall with joy lift up my head."

And again:

> "When I stand before the Throne,
> Dressed in beauty not mine own.
> Then, Lord, shall I fully know,
> Not till then, how much I owe."

And again:

> "At that Day we pray, Lord Jesus,
> To be found of Thee in peace,
> Wearing not our filthy raiment,
> But Thy Robe of Righteousness."

VI. Application.

To the Sinner. How dost thou think to appear before God in filthy rags?

To the Believer. Rejoice in thy beautiful garments, and keep them always unspotted.

To the Preacher. Call men to wash their robes and make them white in the Blood of the Lamb.

Our Righteousness

We must be RIGHTEOUS
- in CHRIST (by imputation).
- in CONSCIENCE (by sincerity).
- in CONDUCT (by obedience).
- in CALLING (by honesty).
- in CHARACTER (by spiritual growth).

Jesus, made Unto Us Sanctification

I. Text. " Of Him (God) are ye in Christ Jesus, Who was made unto us Wisdom and Righteousness and Sanctification and Redemption " (1 Cor. 1. 30, R.V.).

II. Main Lesson. Sanctification or Holiness has a double meaning just as Righteousness has.

Righteousness is a right state or relationship before God resulting in right conduct, so *Sanctification* means to be separated to God and set apart for Him, resulting in a life of truth, purity, and love, or a likeness to Christ.

Christ is made unto us Sanctification in the sense that by His Blood He not only redeemed us so that we are *justified* but purchased us so that we belong to God. We are constituted *a holy or separated people* whose future aim is to be holy even as our God is holy.

III. Scriptures to Study : Hebrews 10. 10-15.

v. 10. *We are Sanctified in the Will of God by Christ's Offering.* " By the which will we are Sanctified through the offering of the Body of Jesus Christ once for all."

vv. 11-13. *His One Sacrifice Availed to Take Sins Away.* " And every priest standeth daily ministering and offering oftentimes the same sacrifices, which can never take away sins: but this Man, after He had offered One Sacrifice for sins for ever, sat down on the right hand of God; from henceforth expecting till His enemies be made His footstool."

vv. 14-15. *We are Perfected for Ever, by the One Offering.* " For by One offering He hath perfected for ever them that are Sanctified. Whereof the Holy Ghost is a witness to us."

Hebrews 13. 12-14:

v. 12. *Jesus Sanctified us by His Blood.* " Wherefore Jesus, that He might sanctify the people with His own Blood, suffered without the gate."

vv. 13-14. *Let us Separate to Him.* " Let us go forth

therefore unto Him without the camp, bearing His reproach.
For here we have no continuing city."

1 Thessalonians 5. 23-24:

v. 23. *A Prayer for Sanctification.* "The very God of
Peace sanctify you wholly; and I pray God your whole
spirit and soul and body be preserved blameless unto the
coming of our Lord Jesus Christ."

v. 24. *God is Faithful.* "Faithful is He that calleth
you, Who also will do it."

IV. **Illustrations of Sanctification.** To sanctify a person
or thing means to declare that it belongs to God and is
set apart for His sole use. It is holy.

1. THE FIRSTBORN (Exod. 13. 2). "Sanctify unto Me all
the firstborn." Those who had been saved by the blood
sprinkled on the door posts at the Passover.

2. AARON AND HIS SONS (Exod. 29. 44). This family
was separated and set apart for the Priest's office.
Only one of the family of Aaron could be appointed
High Priest.

3. THE TABERNACLE, ITS FURNITURE AND OFFERINGS
were sanctified or hallowed by the sprinkling of blood
and the holy anointing oil upon them (Exod. 29. 44,
30. 25-33).

4. THE SABBATH was a hallowed or sanctified day
(Deut. 5. 12; Jer. 17. 22). It was set apart for man's rest
and for God's glory.

5. THE JUBILEE YEAR—that is, the fiftieth year—was
to be hallowed or sanctified (Lev. 25. 10). Slaves were
to go free; debts released; and mortgaged lands to return
to the owners.

6. THE NAME OF GOD (Matt. 6. 9; Exod. 20. 7). There
was to be no light or profane use of the Sacred Name. To
swear in that name was to dishonour it.

7. A FAST OR A SPECIAL ASSEMBLY (Joel 2. 15) could
be sanctified, set apart for the purpose of national repentance.

V. Other Lessons on Sanctification.

1. ANOTHER RENDERING OF OUR TEXT (1 Cor. 1. 30). "But you—and it is all God's doing—are in Christ Jesus: He has become to us a wisdom which is from God, consisting of righteousness and sanctification and deliverance; in order that it may be as Scripture says, He who boasts, let his boast be in the Lord" (Weymouth).

Some would read it, "righteousness and sanctification which constitute our double deliverance (or redemption)," righteousness from the curse of the Law and sanctification from the defilement of our nature.

So that we are justified and cleansed and separated to God.

2. THE BLESSING OF SANCTIFICATION. Many regard Sanctification as a second blessing following on Justification.

John Wesley, General Booth, Dr. Torrey, and many another preached this. Wesley described the blessing in his experience thus. Writing to Elizabeth Longmore, March 6th, 1760, he said, "I felt my soul was all love. I was so stayed on God as I never felt before, and knew that I loved Him with all my heart . . . and the witness that God had saved me from all my sins grew clearer every hour . . . I have never since found my heart wander from God."

3. EVERY BELIEVER HAS BEEN SANCTIFIED. It is clear from the Scriptures we studied (see III. above) that every true child of God has been "sanctified by the offering of the Body of Christ once for all" (Heb. 10. 10) and "perfected for ever" (Heb. 10. 14) as to our acceptance, standing and approach to God. The Blood gives us a perfect ground on which to stand before God. We enter the holiest by the Blood of Jesus. In this sense Sanctification is not a second blessing.

4. EVERY BELIEVER SHOULD SANCTIFY HIMSELF (1 Pet. 3. 15; 1 Thess. 4. 4). He is called unto holiness, and bidden cleanse himself from all filthiness of the flesh and spirit, "perfecting holiness in the fear of the Lord" (2 Cor. 7. 1).

This is not once for all except in resolve and purpose, but is by faith and patience, by patient continuance in well-doing.

There is *daily need of cleansing* from the defilement of the walk, from contact with the world around us. The believer must keep himself pure, washing himself in the pure water of the Word which is given for our daily sanctification (John 17, 17; Eph. 5. 26; Psa. 119. 9; 1 Pet. 1. 22).

5. CHRIST SANCTIFIED AS LORD IN THE HEART. In 1 Peter 3. 15 (R.V.) we are exhorted to sanctify Christ as Lord in our hearts. This means to give Him the place of Lord over all our powers—the Conscience, the Mind, the Will, the Temper and the Affections.

If these are under the control of the Lord we shall be sanctified in the inner life, the heart.

VI. Application.

Let the Sinner remember that without holiness no man shall see the Lord.

Let him know he can never put away his own guilt or change his own heart. His only hope is to flee to Christ.

Let the Saint follow after holiness; let him perfect holiness in the fear of the Lord, exercising himself unto godliness, and working out his own salvation with fear and trembling.

OUTLINE

SANCTIFIED
- By God the Father (Jude 1).
- In the Name of the Lord Jesus and in the Spirit of our God (1 Cor. 6. 11).
- In Christ Jesus (1 Cor. 1. 2).
- By the Holy Ghost (Rom. 15. 16).
- By the Blood of the Covenant (Heb. 10. 29).
- Through the Truth (John 17. 19).
- By Faith (Acts 20. 32 and 26. 18).

Christ the Wisdom of God

I. Text. " We preach Christ crucified, unto the Jews a stumblingblock, and unto the Greeks foolishness; but unto them which are called . . . Christ the Power of God, and the Wisdom of God " (1 Cor. 1. 24).

II. Main Lesson. Man by his unaided wisdom and searching can never find out God (Job 11. 7).

As a fallen sinner his foolish heart has become darkened (Rom. 1. 21). There is none that understandeth (Rom. 3. 11) or seeketh after God.

Man, until reconciled to God in Christ, is out of his mind, in the dark and blind. His wisdom is foolishness (1 Cor. 1. 20) with God. He will never see clearly nor understand until Christ, Who is the Light of life, saves him, and brings him into His marvellous light (1 Pet. 2. 9).

Then Christ is his Wisdom, for in Him he has both the Truth and the Light and Grace to use these aright, and this is true wisdom.

III. Scriptures to Study : Proverbs 8. 22-36.

v. 22. *Christ Foreshadowed as Wisdom Personified.* " Jehovah possessed Me in the beginning of His way, before His works of old."

vv. 23-29. *He was from all Eternity—before Creation.* " I was set up from everlasting, from the beginning, or ever the earth was. When there were no depths, I was brought forth; when there were no fountains abounding with water. Before the mountains were settled, before the hills was I brought forth. . . . When He appointed the foundations of the earth."

v. 30. *He was Daily God's Delight.* " Then I was by Him, as One brought up with Him; and I was daily His delight, rejoicing always before Him."

v. 31. *His Joy in Creation and in Man.* " Rejoicing in the habitable part of His earth; and my delights were with the sons of men."

vv. 32-33. *His Appeal to the Children of Men.* "Now therefore hearken unto Me, O ye children: for blessed are they that keep My ways. Hear instruction, and be wise, and refuse it not."

vv. 34-36. *The Blessing of Hearing Wisdom.* "Blessed is the man that heareth Me . . . For whoso findeth Me findeth life, and shall obtain favour of the Lord. But he that sinneth against Me wrongeth his own soul: all they that hate Me love death."

Man's Wisdom Foolishness with God (1 Cor. 1. 18-24).

vv. 18-20. "For the preaching of the Cross is to them that perish foolishness; but unto us which are saved it is the power of God. For it is written, I will destroy the wisdom of the wise. . . . God hath made foolish the wisdom of this world."

vv. 21-24. *Christ Crucified the Wisdom of God.* "After . . . the world by wisdom knew not God, it pleased God by the foolishness of preaching [or the foolish thing preached, (R.V.M.)] to save them that believe. For the Jews require a sign, and the Greeks seek after wisdom: but we preach Christ crucified, unto the Jews a stumblingblock, and unto the Greeks foolishness; but unto them which are called, both Jews and Greeks, Christ the Power of God, and the Wisdom of God."

IV. Other Lessons on Wisdom.

1. THE WISDOM AND THE WORD. In the Old Testament Christ is spoken of as Wisdom, for wisdom is hidden and not revealed until it is spoken.

Now that God has spoken to us by His Son (Heb. 1. 1-2), Christ is called the Word (John 1. 1).

So that the Hidden Wisdom became the Manifested Word.

2. WISDOM PERSONIFIED. In the passage we studied (Prov. 8. 22-36) Christ is foreshadowed as the Wisdom of God—dwelling with Him from Eternity, present with Him at Creation, delighting in the Children of Men.

No passage could more strikingly set forth the Essential Deity of Christ and His Oneness with the Father than this profound passage.

3. THE WISDOM THAT IS FROM ABOVE. James, our Lord's brother, wrote in his Epistle a description of the Wisdom that is from above (3. 17). It has been suggested that he is there describing the noble and beautiful character of his Divine Brother as he saw it manifested in the carpenter's shop and lowly cottage home in Nazareth.

It is very simple in its holiness and purity.

The Wisdom that is from above is:

First Pure : for no sin or uncleanness stained His holy life.

Then Peaceable—not peace at any price, but first pure, no doubt rebuking sin and refusing all unrighteousness; but subject to this, always making and keeping peace.

Gentle or kind, going about doing good and not pleasing Himself.

Easy to be Entreated, Full of Mercy and Good Fruits, and always

Without Partiality, never taking sides, but being equally loving to all, and *without Hypocrisy,* sincerity and truth marking all He said and did.

4. THE WISDOM OF GOD IN CHRIST CRUCIFIED. The world despises and rejects Salvation coming to us through a Crucified Saviour. It is a stumblingblock to the Jew and foolishness to the Greek, yet is God's highest wisdom. In choosing how He would save fallen man, He elected in His Perfect Wisdom to do so by the Cross because it revealed:

(1) HIS GREAT LOVE. Could anything else have showed that Love more than the Gift of His One Son, His Wellbeloved, for us men ?

(2) HIS PERFECT RIGHTEOUSNESS. Sin must be dealt with in a way consistent with His character as Judge of all the Earth. It was so dealt with on the Cross.

(3) HIS MIGHTY POWER. Who could put sin away by " making Christ to be sin for us," but One Who was Omnipotent ?

Who else could lay on Him the iniquity of us all ?

(4) His Abounding Grace to the Sinner. A free and full Salvation preached through the Blood of the Cross to " whosoever believeth on Him."

(5) An Exposure of the Sinfulness of Sin. It is at the Cross we see the guiltiness of our iniquity:

> " Oh, how vile my lost estate,
> Since my Ransom was so great !"

(6) A Perfect Example of obedience unto death; of suffering wrongfully, of meekness and love.

How better could these have been shown ?

(7) A Full and Perfect and Eternal Salvation based upon that Finished Work, the One Sacrifice.

These and a hundred other wonders displayed in the Cross reveal to us the Wisdom of God in Christ Crucified.

5. Christ Made to us Wisdom. In practice as we walk in the obedience of faith under His guidance we prove Christ to be our Wisdom. He is our wonderful Counsellor, He resolves all our doubts; answers all our hard questions, and teaches us to walk in the paths of wisdom.

6. The Folly of this World's Wisdom. By leaving God out of their reckoning and rejecting Christ, wise men are beating the air. They are like blind men discoursing on colour; or deaf men seeking to teach music; or untravelled men describing lands they have never visited.

Until men receive Christ (God's only Revelation of Himself) they will be like children working a sum the first figure of which is false; or like the astrologers of old who sought to discover the order of the Heavens while they made the Earth the centre of the Solar system instead of the Sun.

Christ must have His right place if man is to be truly wise.

7. Wisdom is the Principal Thing (Prov. 4. 7). Therefore seek Christ, or the Principal thing in life is missing. " The Fear of the Lord is the beginning of Wisdom " (Prov. 9. 10).

" Happy is the man that findeth Wisdom " (Prov. 3. 13).

V. Application.

To Wise Men. Beware of fleshly wisdom (2 Cor. 1. 12). Be not wise in your own conceits.

To the Thoughtful. " If any lack wisdom, let him ask of God, Who giveth . . . liberally."

To the Seeker. Look at the Cross and see in it the wisdom of God in Salvation.

OUTLINES

Wise and Otherwise

WISE in Heart (Prov. 10. 8).
WISE in Christ (1 Cor. 4. 10).
WISE unto Salvation (2 Tim. 3. 15).
WISE unto that which is Good (Rom. 16. 19).
WISE as Serpents (Matt. 10. 16).

Otherwise

WISE in thine own eyes (Prov. 3. 7).
WISE in his own conceits (Prov. 26. 5, 12; 28. 11; Rom. 11. 25).
WISE after the flesh (1 Cor. 1. 26).
WISE in this world (1 Cor. 3. 18).
WISE to do evil (Jer. 4. 22).

Wisdom is the Principal Thing

Wise unto Salvation (2 Tim. 3. 15).
Instructed in the Way of the Lord (Acts 18. 25).
Strong in the Grace that is in Christ Jesus (2 Tim. 2. 1).
Delighting in Thy Law (Psa. 119. 70).
Obedient to the Faith (Acts 6. 7).
Mortifying the deeds of the body (Rom. 8. 13).

SECTION VII.

Our Lord Jesus Christ:
His Varied Characters

The Glory of His Grace

(Tune, " Lux Eoi," G.B. 542.)

Glorious God, our Heavenly Father,
 We would worship at Thy feet;
In the Name of Jesus gather,
 Standing in His love complete.
Hushed our hearts in adoration,
 Filled our lips with happy praise,
In the holy contemplation
 Of the Glory of Thy Grace.

Grace that found us lost ones straying
 In the paths of shame and pride;
Grace Thy perfect love displaying,
 In the Saviour crucified;
Grace that brought us to repentance;
 Grace that gave like precious faith;
Grace that has revoked the sentence
 That assigned us unto death.

Grace that wrought a new creation,
 Seated us in Christ above,
With the holy, heavenly nation,
 In the realm of light and love;
Grace that brought us the adoption,
 Sons and daughters of our God!
Grace that gave us acceptation
 In the Christ the Well-beloved.

Holy God Who art a Spirit,
 By the Spirit we draw near,
Through the Saviour's blood and merit,
 Worship Thee with godly fear.
Unto Him Who loved and loosed us,
 Made us kings and priests to Thee,
We ascribe all praise and honour
 Unto all Eternity.

G. G.

Jesus, the Captain of Our Salvation

I. Text. " It became Him, for Whom are all things, and by Whom are all things, in bringing many sons unto glory, to make the Captain of their Salvation perfect through sufferings " (Heb. 2. 10).

II. Main Lesson. The word Captain is *Archēgos*. It comes four times in the New Testament, and is translated by three different words—*Prince* (Acts 3. 15, 5. 31), " The Prince of Life "; *Author* (Heb. 12. 2); and, as in our text, *Captain*.

Two other words are translated " Captain " in the New Testament, but neither of them is applied to Christ (Acts 4. 1, 21. 31). So we consider Christ as the Captain of Salvation; the Prince of Life; and the Author of Faith to His people.

In Isaiah 55 we read that God hath given Him for *a Leader and Commander* of the people.

He is our Joshua Who leads us on to victory, bringing us into the Promised Land—that is, into the enjoyment of all the Promises of God.

III. Scriptures to Study :

Joshua 5. 13. *Joshua outside Jericho Sees a Man with a Sword Drawn in his Hand.* " And it came to pass, when Joshua was by Jericho, that he lifted up his eyes and looked, and, behold, there stood a man over against him with his sword drawn in his hand."

v. 13. *Joshua Challenges Him.* " And Joshua went unto Him, and said unto Him, Art Thou for us, or for our adversaries ?"

v. 14. *The Lord Answers that He is Captain of the Lord's Host.* " And He said, Nay; but as Captain of the Host of the Lord am I now come."

v. 14. *Joshua Worships Him.* " And Joshua fell to the earth, and did worship, and said unto Him, What saith my Lord unto His servant ? "

v. 15. *The Lord Bids Him Remove his Shoes.* " And the Captain of the Lord's host said unto Joshua, Loose thy shoe from off thy foot; for the place whereon thou standest is holy. And Joshua did so."

Joshua 6. 2. *The Lord Promises him Victory.* " And the Lord said unto Joshua, See, I have given into thine hand Jericho, and the king thereof, and the mighty men of valour."

Hebrews 2. 10-18:

v. 10. *Our Captain Perfected through Suffering.* " It became Him . . . in bringing many sons unto glory, to make the Captain of their Salvation perfect through sufferings."

v. 11. *He is Identified with His People.* " For both He that sanctifieth and they who are sanctified are all of one; for which cause He is not ashamed to call them brethren."

v. 14. *He took Flesh and Blood that through Death He might Defeat the Devil.* " Forasmuch then as the children are partakers of flesh and blood, He also Himself likewise took part of the same; that through death He might destroy him that had the power of death, that is, the Devil."

v. 15. *He Delivers them from Fear of Death.* " And deliver them, who through fear of death were all their lifetime subject to bondage."

v. 17. *He became a Merciful and Faithful High Priest.* " Wherefore in all things it behoved Him to be made like unto His brethren, that He might be a merciful and faithful High Priest in things pertaining to God, to make reconciliation for the sins of the people."

v. 18. *He is able to Help.* " For in that He Himself hath suffered being tempted, He is able to succour them that are tempted."

IV. Some Notable Captains in the Old Testament.

1. Abraham, who defeated the five kings and delivered Lot, whom Melchizedec met on his return with bread and wine (Gen. 14. 14-24).

2. MOSES AND JOSHUA, the Leaders of the children of Israel out of Egypt across the Wilderness and into the Promised Land. For a Great Battle, see Exodus 17. 8-16.

3. DEBORAH AND BARAK; GIDEON; JEPHTHAH; and SAMSON in the days of the Judges.

4. SAUL AND JONATHAN, of whom we read that " they were swifter than eagles; they were stronger than lions " (2 Sam. 1. 23), but, alas ! whom sin defeated.

5. DAVID, who slew Goliath and led his people into victory wherever he went.

6. DAVID'S MIGHTY MEN, whose names and deeds are recorded in 2 Samuel 23. 8-39 and 1 Chronicles 11. 10-47.

7. ASA; JEHOSHAPHAT; AMAZIAH; UZZIAH; HEZEKIAH and others of the Kings of Judah, who were great warriors and whom God used to deliver His people.

V. Other Lessons on Christ our Captain.

1. A CAPTAIN IS TO LEAD. He goes before His army. So Christ is Captain, Prince or Author of our Salvation, our Life and the Object of our Faith.

In all these things He is our Leader and shows us the way. He became our Salvation in His death, our Life in His Resurrection, and Author of our Faith in His Example; for He walked the path of Faith on earth so that we might follow His steps.

2. A CAPTAIN GIVES VICTORY. So our Lord Jesus conquered all our foes and gives us the victory over them. *Victory is GIVEN, not GAINED.*

Therefore we read that Christ overcame all our enemies for us. " Fear not," He says, " I have overcome *the world.*" " He destroyed the Devil in His death, and made an end of sin, so that it can no longer reign over us."

We are therefore said to have overcome them all.

" *Ye have Overcome the Wicked One* " (1 John 2. 14 and 5. 18).

" This is the victory that *hath overcome* the *world,* even our faith " (1 John 5. 4-5, R.V.).

They that are Christ's *have crucified* the *flesh* (Gal.

5. 24). So that our Captain has given us victory over all, the World, the Flesh and the Devil.

Let us stand fast in that Liberty wherewith He has set us free.

3. A CAPTAIN MUST BE OBEYED. No Captain can lead an army to victory if it revolts against His commands.

The very first essential to victory is prompt and loyal obedience to the Leader.

Here so many fail. They want victory over sin, but they do not obey their Captain.

His orders, given *through the Word*, through the *convictions of the Spirit*, and through *conscience*, are disregarded, and so there is defeat.

4. A CAPTAIN PROMOTES THOSE WHO PLEASE HIM. So Paul warns us not to be entangled with the affairs of this life, that we may please Him Who hath chosen us to be His soldiers (2 Tim. 2. 4).

Service is appointed according to faithfulness. Some are Vessels unto honour—to some a great door and effectual is opened.

It is true that whoso is faithful in that which is least is faithful also in much. It is these the Lord appoints to more honourable service.

It will be so hereafter in the Kingdom; we shall be rewarded with higher service according to our faithfulness in service down here.

5. OUR CAPTAIN CALLS US TO ENDURE HARDNESS, as good soldiers of Jesus Christ (2 Tim. 2. 3).

Those who suffer with Him now will reign with Him hereafter.

Those who are afraid, let them return home; those who prefer self-indulgence, let them resign their commission; they are a danger in the army.

6. A CAPTAIN DESTROYS THE ENEMY WHO REFUSES TO SUBMIT. So we have the last graphic figure of Christ in Revelation 19. 11-21, leading His armies to execute judgment upon rebels against His authority and rule. He appears on a white horse, a sharp sword going out of

His mouth to rule the nations with a rod of iron. He is called Faithful and True, and on His vesture and thigh a name is written, King of kings and Lord of lords.

VI. Application.

Do we confess Christ as our Captain ?

Are we among those whom He has called to be His soldiers ?

Are we loyal, obedient and ready to endure hardness ?

Let us stand in the Victory He gives.

Let us look for the reward He promises.

OUTLINES

Our Captain calls us to Seven Things

1. Confess His Name (Matt. 10. 36).
2. Come after Him (Cross bearing) (Matt. 16. 24).
3. Consecration (1 Chron. 29. 5).
4. Constancy (1 Chron. 28. 7).
5. Courage (Josh. 1. 7).
6. Combat (2 Tim. 2. 3).
7. Conquest (Rom. 8. 37).

Titles of our Captain

Captain of the Lord's Host (Josh. 5. 15).

Author of Salvation (Heb. 5. 9).

Prince and Saviour (Acts 5. 31).

True and Faithful (Rev. 19. 11).

Alpha and Omega (Rev. 1. 8).

Intercessor (Heb. 7. 25).

Nail in a Sure place (Isa. 22. 23)

Jesus—the Rock of Ages

I. Texts. " They did all drink the same spiritual drink: for they drank of that Spiritual Rock that followed them: and that Rock was Christ " (1 Cor. 10. 4).

" The Lord is My Rock and My Fortress " (Psa. 18. 2).

II. Main Lesson. The Land of Palestine is a very rocky and in parts mountainous one. It is no wonder that the prophets found in their rocks and hills emblems of their God, their Refuge and Saviour.

The use of the expression " My Rock " is very frequent, and is specially applied to Christ.

The strength of the hills specially appealed to them, so that we read, " Trust ye in the Lord for ever: for in the Lord JEHOVAH is Everlasting Strength "; or, as the margin renders it, " *The Rock of Ages* " (Isa. 26. 4) (R.V., " An everlasting Rock ").

Our lesson, then, is of some of the Rock-like Qualities that are found in Christ.

III. Scripture to Study :

Deuteronomy 32. The Song of Moses—references therein to the Rock.

vv. 3-4. *The Lord is the Rock, Perfect in all His Ways.* "I will publish the Name of the Lord: ascribe ye greatness unto our God. He is the Rock, His work is perfect: for all His ways are judgment: a God of truth and without iniquity, just and right is He."

vv. 9-15. *Israel's Folly in Lightly Esteeming their Rock.* " The Lord's portion is His people. . . . He found him in a desert land, and in the waste howling wilderness; He led him about, He instructed him, He kept him as the apple of His eye. As an eagle stirreth up her nest, fluttereth over her young, spreadeth abroad her wings, taketh them, beareth them on her wings: So the Lord alone did lead him. . . . But Jeshurun waxed fat, and kicked . . .

then he forsook God which made him, and lightly esteemed the Rock of his salvation."

v. 18. " Of the Rock that begat thee thou art unmindful, and hast forgotten God that formed thee."

v. 29. *The Rock of the Enemy not like our Rock.* " O that they were wise, that they understood this, that they would consider their latter end !"

v. 30. " How should one chase a thousand, and two put ten thousand to flight, except their Rock had sold them, and the Lord had shut them up ?"

v. 31. " For their rock is not as our Rock, even our enemies themselves being judges. . . ."

v. 37. " Where are their gods, their rock in whom they trusted ?"

Psalm 62. 1-8 (the " Only " Psalm):

God only our Rock, Salvation and Defence

v. 1. " Truly [only] my soul waiteth upon God: from Him cometh my Salvation."

v. 2. " He only is my Rock and my Salvation; He is my defence; I shall not be greatly moved."

v. 5. My soul, wait thou only upon God; for my expectation is from Him."

v. 6. " He only is my Rock and my Salvation: He is my defence; I shall not be moved."

v. 7. " In God is my Salvation and my Glory: the Rock of my strength, and my Refuge, is in God."

v. 8. " Trust in Him at all times; ye people, pour out your heart before Him: God is a Refuge for us."

IV. Titles and Blessings of Our Rock.

1. The Titles.

Rock of my Salvation (Psa. 62. 2). This can be illustrated from Psalm 40. 2, " He brought me up also out of an horrible pit . . . and set my feet upon a Rock."

Rock of my Strength (Psa. 62. 7), in the sense of a Refuge —a strong hiding-place into which the believer can run and hide.

" Be Thou my Strong Rock, for an house of defence to save me " (Psa. 31. 2).

Rock of my Refuge (Psa. 94. 22), a similar term. " A Strong Tower from the enemy " (Psa. 61. 3).

The Rock that is Higher than I (Psa. 61. 2), suggesting a soul sinking in deep waters finding a Rock on to which he can climb and find Salvation.

2. THE BLESSINGS FROM THE ROCK.

Moses was put *in a Cleft of the Rock* (Exod. 33. 22), while the glory of God passed by.

David found *Refuge and Salvation* in the Rock (as above).

The Kenites (Num. 24. 21) built their *nest in the Rock*, and Balaam said of them, " Strong is thy dwelling-place."

From the Rock come:

Water (Exod. 17. 6, Psa. 78. 20), when smitten by Moses —a type of the Holy Spirit given after Jesus had been smitten under the curse of a broken law.

Oil (Deut. 32. 13), a figure of refreshment—" oil to make his face to shine," the comfort of the Holy Ghost.

Honey (Deut. 32. 13 and Psa. 81. 16), sweet and sustaining food, as both Jonathan (1 Sam. 14. 29) and Samson (Judg. 14. 8) found, and even our Lord after His resurrection (Luke 24. 42).

Fire (Judg. 6. 21). When the Angel of the Lord visited Gideon.

Shadow from the Heat (Isa. 32. 2). "A man (the man Christ Jesus) shall be as an Hiding-Place . . . as the Shadow of a Great Rock in a weary land."

A Foundation. For our Individual Faith (Matt. 7. 24); for those who hear and do the Word of God are like a man who built his house upon a Rock.

For the Church (the body of Christ), founded upon Christ, against which the Gates of Hell cannot prevail (Matt. 16. 18; 1 Cor. 3. 11).

V. Other Lessons from the Rock.

1. THE CHIEF THOUGHT IS STABILITY. Something that nothing can shake or move.

So if our faith is in Christ, He will never let us be confounded. We have a Kingdom that cannot be moved.

Our foundations are unshakable.   Nothing can destroy our hope.

2. THEN WE HAVE STRENGTH.   In the Lord Jehovah is Everlasting Strength, or the Rock of Ages.

" The Strength of the Hills is His also."

The Lord is a Strong Rock to all who trust in Him. They find courage and endurance for every need. They can say, " The Lord is my Strength and my Song."

3. THERE IS SAFETY.   Like the feeble conies that make their homes in the rock, so that neither eagle, vulture, fox nor other enemy can reach them, so the believer is hidden in Christ his Rock.

4. THERE IS STANDING.   As described in Psalm 40. 2, " He brought me up out of an horrible pit, out of the miry clay, and set my feet upon a Rock."

> " On Christ, the Solid Rock, I stand;
>   All other ground is sinking sand."

5. THERE IS SHELTER.   Such as Mr. Toplady found in the great crack in the Rock in Burrington Combe from the passing storm, an event that led him to write the favourite hymn:

> " Rock of Ages, cleft for me,
>   Let me hide myself in Thee."

How many a troubled and storm-beaten child of God has found peace and quiet and true rest in Christ his Rock !

6. THERE IS SUPPLY.   We have seen above how many things come from the Rock: Water for the thirsty soul; Oil to make the face to shine; Honey to sweeten our lives; and many other good things.

Indeed, in Christ are full supplies of all things necessary for life and godliness.   We have only to draw upon them.

7. THERE IS SATISFACTION.   Comfort under the Shadow of a Mighty Rock in a dry and thirsty land.

"The water that I shall give him," Jesus said, " shall be in him a well of water springing up into everlasting life," of which if a man drink he shall never thirst again.

It is water from the Smitten Rock, the Gift of the Holy Ghost from Him Who died and lives again.

8. THERE IS SINGING (Isa. 42. 11). "Let the inhabitants of the Rock sing, let them shout from the tops of the mountains."

Those who know Christ as their Rock can well sing for all the fulness of blessings found in Him. "My people," says He, "shall sing for joy of heart."

VI. Application.

Is your house being built on the Rock?

Have your feet been set upon that Rock?

Have you found in Christ all those things that are spoken of above of the Rock?

Seven Rocks in Scripture

ETAM, where Samson dwelt (Judg. 15. 8).

MERIBAH, the Smitten Rock (Exod. 17. 7 and Num. 20. 1-11).

ADULLAM, in which David hid (1 Chron. 11. 15).

BOZEZ and SENEH, where Jonathan and his armour-bearer climbed up (1 Sam. 14. 4).

OREB, where the Prince of Midian was slain (Judg. 7. 25).

RIMMON, where the Benjamites were beaten (Judg. 20. 47).

Where the TOMB was, in which Jesus lay (Matt. 27. 26).

Some Sure Foundations

For our FAITH (2 Tim. 2. 19).

For our CHARACTER (Luke 6. 48; 1 Tim. 6. 19).

For our WORK (1 Cor. 3. 10).

For our SALVATION (Isa. 28. 16; 1 Pet. 2. 6).

For the CHURCH (Matt. 16. 18).

For the HEAVENLY CITY (Rev. 21. 14).

Jesus Christ, the same Yesterday, and Today, and For Ever

I. Text. "Jesus Christ is the same yesterday and today, yea and for ever" (Heb. 13. 8, R.V.).

"Thou art the same, and Thy years shall not fail" (Heb. 1. 12).

II. Main Lesson. The unchangeable character of our Lord Jesus Christ. He is ever the same. As He was in the days of His flesh, so is He now exalted upon the Throne. As He was from Eternity, as He was when we first knew Him, so He ever remains.

Time does not alter His heart towards His people, nor His compassion for lost sinners.

He never grows weary; His patience is never exhausted; His hands never grow heavy in intercession for His people (as did those of Moses, Exod. 17. 12).

Though we have changeable moods and dispositions and tempers, He is not subject to these infirmities, but is invariable in perfect wisdom, love and power.

III. Scriptures to Study : Hebrews 1. 8-12.

v. 8. *The Son is God for Ever and Ever.* "Unto the Son He saith, Thy Throne, O God, is for ever and ever."

vv. 8-9. *His Sceptre is a Sceptre of Righteousness.* "A sceptre of righteousness is the sceptre of Thy Kingdom. Thou hast loved righteousness, and hated iniquity; therefore God, even Thy God, hath anointed Thee with the oil of gladness above Thy fellows."

v. 10. *The Son is the Creator of all Things.* "Thou, Lord, in the beginning hast laid the foundation of the earth; and the Heavens are the works of Thine hands."

vv. 11-12. *Creation will Perish ; the Son Remains Unchanged.* "They shall perish; but Thou remainest; and they all shall wax old as doth a garment; and as a vesture shalt Thou fold them up, and they shall be changed: but Thou art the same, and Thy years shall not fail."

Hebrews 13. 5-8:

vv. 5-6. *The Lord has Promised never to Leave us.*
"He hath said, I will never leave thee, nor forsake thee.
So that we may boldly say, The Lord is my Helper, and
I will not fear what man shall do unto me."

v. 7. *The Guides to be Remembered and their Faith Followed.*
"Remember them which have the rule over you, who have
spoken unto you the Word of God: whose faith follow,
considering the end of their conversation" ("the issue of
their life," R.V.).

v. 8. *Their View of Life Stated.* "Jesus Christ the same
yesterday, and today, and for ever."

IV. Other Lessons on the Unchangeable Lord.

1. "I AM JEHOVAH, I CHANGE NOT, therefore ye
sons of Jacob are not consumed" (Mal. 3. 6).

We are again and again told that God is not a man that
He should lie or repent.

"The Strength of Israel will not lie nor repent: for He
is not a man, that He should repent" (1 Sam. 15. 29).

This does not mean that God does not alter His methods
and ways of dealing with men, and this is sometimes
spoken of as God repenting (1 Sam. 15. 11); but as to His
character, the truth and grace of all His ways, He is unchangeable. He will never alter as to His attitude towards
sin, His grace toward the sinner who repents, or His
faithfulness in all His dealings with His people.

There is no variableness nor shadow of turning with
Him (Jas. 1. 17).

And this is true of Christ, Who is Himself God.

2. THE SAME YESTERDAY. Some speak of the "good
old days," as if they were better than today. This is a
mistake. "*Say not thou, What is the cause that the former
days were better than these? for thou enquirest not wisely
concerning this*" (Eccles. 7. 10).

To talk in this way is to suggest that God is not the
same as He was yesterday; but it is not true. As He was
in Abraham's day, in Moses' day, in David's day, in Elijah's
day, and in the days when He walked on earth in humiliation, so He is today: the same.

What wonders He wrought " yesterday." And He will still work wonders of grace for those who, like the saints of yesterday, put their trust in Him.

3. THE SAME TODAY. Is His Love less today? Surely not. Is His Power less? Truly not. Is His arm shortened that it cannot save or His ear heavy that it cannot hear? Verily not.

Men are today proving that God is still the Living God, that the God of Elijah yet hears and responds to the cry of His people.

Let any put it to the test. Have faith in God. Venture on His grace and power, and they will prove that He is the same today as yesterday.

> " Change and decay in all around I see:
> O Thou Who changest not, abide with me."

4. THE SAME TOMORROW. What rest of heart is found in believing this! " *Take no thought for the morrow,*" Jesus said (Matt. 6. 34); for when tomorrow comes there will still be a Faithful God, and an unchangeable Christ, as there was yesterday and is today.

The Lord will not die or change in the night; as surely as the sun will rise tomorrow, so will He be present with us.

When tempted to worry about the morrow, say to your soul, " Jesus is the same tomorrow," and you will find " tomorrow will take thought for the things of itself."

Indeed, there may be no tomorrow for us in this scene of sin and death. It may find us with the Lord.

> " I change, He changeth not;
> The Christ can never die.
> His Love, not mine, the resting-place;
> His Truth, not mine, the tie."

5. THERE IS NO CHANGE IN THE GOD OF THE OLD TESTAMENT AND THE NEW TESTAMENT. The suggestion that the God of the Old Testament is different from the Gracious Christ of the New is a heresy that must be rejected with scorn.

The God in Genesis 1, Who made the world so fair, Who

saw it all very good and blessed it, is the same all through the Bible, full of grace and truth—it was these same characteristics that were seen in Christ (John 1. 14). Judgment is as terrible in our Lord's life as anything in the Old Testament (*e.g.*, Luke 19. 27; Matt. 10. 28, 25. 46). Grace is as beautiful in the Old Testament as anything in the New (*e.g.*, Jer. 31. 3; Hos. 3. 19, 11. 8; Deut. 32. 10-12).

6. AN UNCHANGEABLE PRIESTHOOD. The Lord Jesus is specially commended to us because of this. He continueth ever, He never dies.

Yesterday (February 14th, 1939) the Pope was buried, and for the present there is no Pope. Christendom's pseudo-priest is dust and ashes, a man in whose nostrils his breath was and is not, and there is none to do his office. Thank God the True Great Priest of all Believers hath an unchangeable priesthood. He ever liveth, will never again see death, and so is able to save to the uttermost all that come unto God by Him. We need no other.

7. THE CONTINUING EFFICACY OF HIS FINISHED WORK. "The blood cleanseth;" it never ceases to be effective for the believer. The ground of our faith is the same for ever: it is the One Sacrifice for sins. It avails for all and for all time. There is and can be no change here.

> "Jesus, I know, has died and lives:
> On this firm Rock I build."

8. HIS FIDELITY TO HIS PROMISES WILL NEVER CHANGE. The promises are all Yea and Amen in Him.

No promise He ever made can alter; they are recorded in the unchangeable Word, and His faithfulness will never fail. Though we are unfaithful, He remaineth faithful; He cannot deny Himself.

9. UNCHANGEABLE IN A CHANGING WORLD. Fashions change; the creeds and doctrines of men alter with the times; modern theologians vary as the wind and tide; science, ever uncertain, gets out of date and becomes folly. There is no stable rock upon which we can stand except upon *Christ as revealed by the Spirit through the Scriptures.*

He changeth not. "For ever, O Lord, Thy Word is settled in Heaven." "The Word of the Lord endureth for ever."

10. Though all be lost, Christ Remains. Riches take to themselves wings and fly away; health gives way and leaves us weak and often afflicted; friends die or lose their affection; slander robs of the good name. All seems lost ! But Thou, Lord Christ, remainest; Thou art the same yesterday, and today, and for ever.

11. The Exhortation Based on the Fact is found in the next verse (Heb. 13. 9): " Be not carried about with divers and strange doctrines."

V. Application.

Avail yourself of this unchangeable Saviour.

Beware not to rest in the uncertain things of life and be not blown about by winds of doctrine.

Seek to be stedfast, unmoveable, always abounding in the work of the Lord.

Seven Faithful Ones

God is Faithful (1 Cor. 1. 9).
Christ is Faithful (Rev. 19. 11).
Abraham was Faithful (Gal. 3. 9).
Moses was Faithful (Num. 12. 7).
Daniel was Faithful (Dan. 6. 4).
Paul was Faithful (1 Tim. 1. 12).
Timothy was Faithful (1 Cor. 4. 17).
" Be thou faithful."

The Sun of Righteousness—the Bright and Morning Star

I. Texts. " Unto you that fear My Name shall the Sun of Righteousness arise with healing in His wings " (Mal. 4. 2).

" I am the Root and the Offspring of David, and the Bright and Morning Star " (Rev. 22. 16).

II. Main Lesson. While the Heathen and the Apostates of the natural seed of Abraham turned to various forms of Sun worship, the worship of Baal, the faithful refused to give the glory that belonged to the Creator to the creature, however wonderful and brilliant; yet they were glad to look upon the Sun and Morning Star as beautiful types or figures of Christ.

Christ was their Sun of Righteousness, and to them He was the Bright and Morning Star.

As the Sun is the centre of the Solar System, illuminating all with its glorious light, so is Christ the Centre of His Church, around which she revolves and has her being, from which she derives all her light and health.

So also is He the Bright and Morning Star, the Herald of a New Day that is to dawn.

The Holy Spirit has adopted this language. The Sun was made to rule the day (Gen. 1. 16), so Christ the Sun of Righteousness shall arise with healing for this sin-stricken world in His wings, and reign for ever and ever.

III. Scriptures to Study : Genesis 1. 1-5, 16-18.

vv. 1-2. *The Creation.* " In the beginning God created the Heaven and the Earth. And the earth was without form and void; and darkness was upon the face of the deep. And the Spirit of God moved upon the face of the waters."

v. 3. *God's first Recorded Utterance.* " And God said, Let there be light: and there was light."

vv. 4-5. *Day and Night Instituted.* " And God saw the light, that it was good: and God divided the light from the darkness. And God called the light Day, and the darkness He called Night. And the evening and the morning were the first day."

v. 16. *The Sun and Moon Appointed.* " And God made two great lights: the greater light to rule the day, and the lesser light to rule the night: He made the stars also."

vv. 17-19. *They are set in the Firmament to Rule.* " And God set them in the firmament of the Heaven to give light upon the earth, and to rule over the day and over the night, and to divide the light from the darkness: and God saw that it was good. And the evening and the morning were the fourth day."

Numbers 24. 15-19. *Balaam's Fourth Parable.*

vv. 15-16. *Balaam's Open Vision.* " And he took up this parable, and said, Balaam the son of Beor hath said, and the man whose eyes are open hath said: He hath said, which heard the words of God, and knew the knowledge of the Most High, which saw the vision of the Almighty, falling into a trance, but having his eyes open."

v. 17. *He Foretells of a Star and Sceptre to Rise out of Israel.* " I shall see Him, but not now: I shall behold Him, but not nigh: there shall come a Star out of Jacob, and a Sceptre shall rise out of Israel, and shall smite the corners of Moab. . . . Out of Jacob shall come He that shall have dominion, and shall destroy him that remaineth of the city."

IV. Christ Likened to the Sun and Star.

1. In the Transfiguration (Matt. 17. 2) we read, " His face did shine as the Sun."

In Revelation 1, where the Lord is seen walking among the candlesticks, we learn (1. 16), " His countenance was as the Sun shineth in his strength."

In Revelation 21. 23. The Holy Jerusalem " had no need of the sun, neither of the moon to shine in it: for the glory of God did lighten it, and the Lamb is the Light thereof."

2. In an old book entitled " A KEY TO OPEN SCRIPTURE METAPHORS," by Benjamin Keach (1856), I find in the index " Sun of Righteousness, Christ is in thirty-four particulars, p. 418." From these I extract and abbreviate the following:

(1) *There is but One Sun.* So there is one Mediator.

(2) *The Sun is a Fountain of Light,* as Jesus is the Light of the world.

(3) *The Sun is Matchless for Beauty.* So is Christ altogether lovely.

(4) *The Sun Loves to Communicate its Light.* So of His fulness have we all received.

(5) *The Sun Obeys God's Order in Setting and Rising.* So Christ died, and rose again at the commandment of the Father.

(6) *The Sun Shines upon the Just and Unjust.* So the Lord sends the Gospel of Grace to good and bad alike.

(7) *The Sun Rules the Day.* So Jesus Christ is the Great Potentate, Lord of lords.

(8) *The Sun is a Great Light*—" 166 times bigger than the earth " (but see page 27). So Christ is infinite in power, wisdom, and grace.

(9) *The Sun Lightens the Moon* so that it rules the night. So Christ shines upon the Church so that it is the light of the world.

(10) *The Sun is Constant in its Motions.* So the Lord is faithful to His promises.

(11) *The Sun Never Wearies.* So our Lord fainteth not, nor is weary.

(12) *The Sun Drives away Mists and Fogs.* So the Lord dispels the darkness of unbelief and doubt.

(13) *The Sun Produces the Seasons,* day and night, summer and winter. So Christ meets our recurring needs.

(14) *The Sun Softens Wax and Hardens Clay.* So Christ blesses the repentant and hardens the obdurate sinner.

(15) *The Sun is sometimes Hidden by Clouds.* So Christ veils Himself at times for our discipline.

(16) *The Sun is Terrible for Scorching Heat,* so is He to the wicked, whom He will consume.

(17) *The Sun may be Eclipsed.* So we may fail of the light of our Lord's face if aught come between.

(18) *The Sun Drowns the Glory of Lesser Lights.* So Christ causes the things of earth to grow strangely dim.

(19) *The Sun Ripens Fruit.* So does Christ the Fruit of the Spirit.

(20) *It is a Pleasant Thing for the Eyes to Behold the Sun* (Eccles. 11. 9). So it is to faith to see Jesus.

3. In the same great tome, " CHRIST IS THE MORNING STAR IN EIGHTEEN PARTICULARS, p. 476." Of these we select and reduce the following:

(1) *It is the Harbinger of the Rising Sun.* So the night is far spent, the day (of our Lord's return) is at hand. Christ seen by faith now is the promise of His being seen face to face then.

(2) *The Morning Star is the same as the Evening Star.* The planet Venus is each in turn according to its position at certain times. So Christ is Alpha and Omega, the First and Last, the One Who sank in death and rose in resurrection.

(3) *It has an Honourable Name—the Son of the Morning.* So Christ is the Dayspring from on high Who hath visited us. He has the Name above every name.

(4) *It is Beyond All other Stars for Beauty.* So is Christ excelling in beauty to His saints.

Further points are : " It is a terror to evil men, who haste away at its appearing "; " it is useful to guide mariners "; " it doth chiefly govern pleasant and delightful plants "; " it causes gentle storms in winter and moderate heat in summer "; " it is the cause of beauty "; " it doth most service in winter because the nights are longer "; and so on—for all of which qualities we cannot vouch ! But our Lord is more than all these to us.

4. THE STAR IN THE SCRIPTURES.

Balaam's Prophecy (Num. 24. 17), as set out above.

The Star of Bethlehem (Matt. 2. 2) that led the Wise Men of the East to the infant Christ.

The Dayspring from on High (Luke 1. 78), of which Zacharias sang at the birth of John the Baptist.

The Bright and Morning Star (Rev. 22. 16)—a Name taken by Christ to Himself.

V. Other Lessons of Christ as the Sun and Star.

1. CHRIST, THE EFFULGENCE OF THE GLORY OF GOD (Heb. 1. 3, R.V.). Just as the sunshine is the brightness and blessing of the Sun and in essence the same, so Christ is to the believer the Shining of God's Face lifted up upon him. "The Lord God is a Sun." He has shined forth in His Co-equal Son.

2. THE BEAUTY OF THE SUN is beyond expression. Its light, warmth, heat, and quickening power all speak of Christ. To keep in His Love; to walk in the Light of His Countenance; to enjoy His power resting upon us; to feel the warmth of His sympathy, is like keeping in the sunshine of a morning without clouds.

Thinking of Christ as our Sun, we can truly say: " It is a pleasant thing for the eyes to behold the Sun."

3. THE MORNING STAR. As the morning star heralds the dawn, so Christ is to His people now the Bright and Morning Star, foretelling the sunrise of a new and better day. In Hosea 6. 3 we are exhorted, " *Let us follow on to know the Lord : His going forth* [or, as some would render it, ' His coming again '] *is as sure as the morning* [as certain as the sunrise]: *and He shall come unto us as the rain, as the latter rain* [' He shall appear the second time ' (Heb. 9. 28)] *that watereth the earth* " (R.V.).

VI. Application.

Let us enjoy the Sunshine of the Presence of the Lord.
Let us seek to reflect it to others.
Let us rejoice in the Morning Star that heralds the dawn.

The Stars

Sang for joy at Creation (Job 38. 7).
Bowed to Joseph in his dream (Gen. 37. 9).
Fought for Israel against Sisera (Judg. 5. 20).
Fell upon the earth at the opening of the sixth seal (Rev. 6. 13).

Alpha and Omega

I. Texts. " I am Alpha and Omega, the Beginning and the Ending, saith the Lord, which is, and which was, and which is to come, the Almighty " (Rev. 1. 8).

" I am Alpha and Omega, the First and the Last " (Rev. 1. 11).

II. Main Lesson. Alpha (A) and Omega (Ω) are the First and Last letters of the Greek alphabet, the Beginning and Ending of it.

Just as the alphabet includes the whole of the language, so Christ is All in all to His people, the Beginning and Ending of everything to them.

The Oxford Dictionary contains an enormous number of words belonging to the English language, amounting to some hundred thousand and more. Every one of them is made up from the twenty-six letters of our alphabet. As the A to Z include all, so does Christ embrace the whole of the believer's life and hope.

He begins with Christ, he ends with Christ: to him Christ is the First and the Last.

III. Scriptures to Study : Revelation 1. 8 and 11, 21. 6, 22. 13. The four occasions when the words occur, showing their context.

Revelation 1. 8-11. *Christ Reveals Himself to John on the Isle of Patmos.* " I am Alpha and Omega, the Beginning and the Ending, saith the Lord, which is, and which was, and which is to come, the Almighty.

" I, John, . . . was in the isle that is called Patmos, for the Word of God, and for the testimony of Jesus Christ. I was in the Spirit on the Lord's day, and heard behind me a great voice, as of a trumpet, saying, I am Alpha and Omega, the first and the last: and, What thou seest, write in a book, and send it unto the Seven Churches which are in Asia."

Revelation 21. 5-7. *All Things New.* " He that sat

upon the Throne said, Behold, I make all things new.
And He said unto me, Write: for these words are True and
Faithful.

"And He said unto me, It is done. I am Alpha and
Omega, the beginning and the end. I will give unto him
that is athirst of the fountain of the water of life freely.
He that overcometh shall inherit all things; and I will be
his God, and he shall be My son."

Revelation 22. 12-14. *He is Coming Quickly.* "Behold, I come quickly; and My reward is with Me, to give
every man according as his work shall be.

"I am Alpha and Omega, the beginning and the end,
the first and the last. Blessed are they that do His
commandments (have washed their robes, R.V.), that
they may have right to the tree of life, and may enter
in through the gates into the City."

Colossians 2. 9-10. *Complete in Christ.* "In Him
dwelleth all the fulness of the Godhead bodily. And ye
are complete in Him, which is the Head of all principality
and power."

Colossians 3. 11. *Christ is All and in All.* "There is
neither Greek nor Jew, circumcision nor uncircumcision,
Barbarian, Scythian, bond nor free: but Christ is all, and
in all."

IV. Other Lessons from the Alpha and Omega.

1. CHRIST, THE FIRST AND LAST, the Eternal God. "In
the Beginning was the Word," and "Thy years fail not:
Thou remainest." He inhabits Eternity. The terms "the
First and the Last" are intended to express Eternity.
Such is our Lord and Saviour—"Having neither beginning
of days nor end of life" (Heb. 7. 3). "From everlasting
to everlasting," God over all, blessed for evermore.

2. CHRIST, THE BEGINNING AND END OF CREATION.
The Beginning, in that all things were made by Him, and
without Him was not anything made that was made
(John 1. 3; Col. 1. 16; Heb. 1. 2 and 10).

The End, because in the fulness of time God will gather
together in one all things in Christ both in Heaven and
earth; even in Him—He being the Heir of all things.

3. CHRIST, THE ALPHA AND OMEGA OF SALVATION. *The Alpha*, in that He came forth from the Father to seek and to save that which was lost. Having purged our sins, He took His seat at the right hand of power.

> " Done is the work that saves,
> Once and for ever done."

The Omega, in that He will perfect that which He has begun, never ceasing His gracious work until He presents us faultless before the presence of God with exceeding joy.

4. CHRIST THE FIRST AND LAST OF THE BELIEVER'S HOPE. When the sinner *first* trusted in Him it was the beginning of days to him. He entered upon a new life by new birth.

That day old things passed away, all things became new, and all things were of God.

The believer's hope is at the *last* to see and be for ever with the Lord.

So Christ is the First and Last of all his hopes.

5. CHRIST THE ALL IN ALL to those who trust Him.

His Power is their All, for without Him they can do nothing.

His Love is All to them: He is all their desire.

His Supply is their all-sufficiency. They are complete or filled full in Him. This has been the song of the Saints all down the ages:

> " Thou, O Christ, art all I want,
> More than all in Thee I find " (WESLEY).

> " Dear Name, the Rock on which I build,
> My shield and hiding-place,
> My never-failing Treasury filled
> With boundless stores of grace " (NEWTON).

This is what the Apostle meant when he said, " For to me to live is Christ."

6. CHRIST THE FIRST AND LAST IN THE INVISIBLE WORLD. When John fell at the Lord's feet as dead, He laid His right hand on him, saying:

"Fear not; *I am the First and the Last*: I am He that liveth, and was dead; and, behold, I am alive for evermore, Amen; and *have the keys of Hell and of Death*."

He ordained and established that invisible world, the region of the dead and the place of retribution, and it is He alone Who has the keys to open or to shut.

Let the sinner fear Him Who is able to cast both body and soul therein.

7. THE COMFORT THIS BRINGS. That Christ is All in All to the believer. He realizes his safety in Him, and rejoices in having One Who will never change, never pass away; Who has undertaken His eternal salvation, and Who, having begun the good work in him (the Beginning), will never give up till He finishes it (the End), and brings him home to glory.

Let us, then, run our race with patience, looking unto Jesus, the Author and Finisher of Faith.

V. Application.

Let us rejoice in Him Who sees the end from the beginning,
Who perfects every work He begins,
Who is the Sum of all our hopes—" All and in All."

The Lord Jesus was the

FIRST {
BEGOTTEN of the Father (Heb. 1. 6).
BORN from the Dead (Col. 1. 18).
BORN of every creature (Col. 1. 15).
To LOVE us (1 John 4. 19).
To PREACH the Gospel (Heb. 2. 3).
FRUITS of them that slept (1 Cor. 15. 20 and 23).
And the LAST (Rev. 1. 11; 22. 13).

The Last Adam

I. Texts. " The first man Adam was made a Living Soul; the last Adam was made a quickening Spirit" [R.V., " became a Life-Giving Spirit "] (1 Cor. 15. 45). " Adam . . . who is the Figure of Him that was to come " (Rom. 5. 14).

II. Main Lesson. Adam the First is said to be a Figure of Adam the Last—that is, the Lord Jesus Christ.

Each is the Federal Head of a Race—Adam of the first Creation, Christ of the New Creation.

The first result of Adam's sin was that death came into the world and passed upon all men.

This was met by the Death and Resurrection of Christ; just as all die in Adam, so all are raised in Christ. All mankind rise from the dead, good and bad alike.

THE QUESTION OF THE SECOND DEATH depends upon a man's continuing under the Headship of Adam or by faith becoming a member of Christ. So Death and Life are presented to all, and the sinner entreated to " Choose Life " (Deut. 30. 19; Jer. 21. 8).

The sinner's doom depends on his receiving or rejecting Christ, the Head of the New Creation, and Life in Him (John 5. 40).

" *They which receive* " (Rom. 5. 17) the gift of righteousness, and are found in Christ, reign in life by Him.

They that are Christ's will rise at His Coming. He is the Firstfruits: they are the Harvest.

The Grace in Christ far outweighs the Ruin in Adam. Where sin abounded, Grace did much more abound.

The Glory of the New Creation far transcends the glory of the first.

III. Scripture to Study : Romans 5. 12-19.

v. 12. *Sin Entered the World by One Man.* " As by one man sin entered into the world, and death by sin; and so death passed upon all men, for that all have sinned."

v. 13. *Sin not Imputed where no Law.* " (For until the Law sin was in the world: but sin is not imputed when there is no law."

v. 14. *Nevertheless, Death Reigned through Adam.* " Nevertheless, death reigned from Adam to Moses, even over them that had not sinned after the similitude of Adam's transgression."

v. 14. *Adam is the Figure of Christ.* " Who is the Figure of Him that was to come."

v. 15. *The Offence not like the Free Gift.* " But not as the offence, so also is the free gift."

v. 15. *Because the Grace far Outweighs the Sin.* " For if through the offence of one many be dead, much more the Grace of God, and the Gift by Grace, which is by One Man, Jesus Christ, hath abounded unto many."

v. 16. *And because One Sin brought Condemnation, whereas the Free Gift Covered many Offences.* " And not as it was by one that sinned, so is the gift: for the judgment was by one to condemnation, but the free gift is of many offences unto justification."

v. 17. *And because by Adam Death Reigned, whereas by Christ we Reign in Life.* " For if by one man's offence death reigned by one; much more they which receive abundance of grace and of the gift of righteousness shall reign in life by One, Jesus Christ.)"

v. 18. *So Judgment Came by Adam and Justification by Christ.* " Therefore as by the offence of one judgment came upon all men to condemnation; even so by the Righteousness of One the free gift came upon all men unto justification of life."

v. 19. *By Adam many were made Sinners ; by Christ many are made Righteous.* " For as by one man's disobedience many were made sinners, so by the obedience of One shall many be made righteous."

1 Corinthians 15. 21-23, 45-49:

v. 22. *As in Adam all Die, so in Christ all are Raised.* " For as in Adam all die, even so in Christ shall all be made alive."

v. 23. *Each in his Own Order.* " But every man in his own order: Christ the Firstfruits; afterward they that are Christ's at His Coming."

v. 45. *The First Adam a Living Soul; the Last Adam a Life-giving Spirit.* "The first man Adam was made a living soul; the last Adam became a life-giving Spirit" (R.V.).

v. 47. *The First Man of the Earth; the Second Man the Lord from Heaven.* "The first man is of the earth, earthy: the second man is the Lord from Heaven."

v. 49. *We shall Bear the Image of the Heavenly.* "And as we have borne the image of the earthy, we shall also bear the image of the Heavenly."

IV. **References to Adam in the New Testament.** Nine times the name occurs:

1. As THE ANCESTOR OF CHRIST (Luke 3. 38), where the Lord's genealogy ends, "which was the son of Adam, which was the son of God."

2. TWICE IN ROMANS 5. (as III. above), showing that all sinned and death reigned in him.

3. THREE TIMES IN 1 CORINTHIANS 15. (as III. above), showing that resurrection came through Christ, the Last Adam, as death through the first.

4. As THE FIRST FORMED (1 Tim. 2. 13), confirming the Old Testament narrative as a fact.

5. As WILFULLY SINNING (1 Tim. 2. 14). "Adam was not deceived, but the woman being deceived was in the transgression."

6. ENOCH was the seventh from Adam (Jude 14).

V. **Other Lessons from Adam.**

1. REPRESENTATIVE MEN. We are familiar in ordinary life with acting and incurring liability or securing benefit in a representative.

When war was declared in 1914 we were all at war; when peace was signed by our statesmen we all enjoyed peace again.

Those who acted acted in a representative capacity. A father acts as the head of the household; a member of parliament as for a district.

The Puritans spoke of such as " *Common Men* "—that is, acting as common to all they stood for.

Not all are Common Men or Federal Heads, but both Adam and Christ are so regarded.

2. THE TWO ADAMS. The First Adam sinned us all, and in him we all died.

The Last Adam graced us all, and in Him we all may live.

The First Adam's *One Sin* " brought death into this world and all our woe."

The Last Adam's *One Act of Righteousness* (Rom. 5. 18, R.V.) brought us the free gift unto justification of life.

The First Adam in the *Garden of Eden* cried, " My will, not Thine, be done "; the Last Adam in the *Garden of Gethsemane* cried, " Not My will, but Thine, be done."

3. NONE DIE THE SECOND DEATH FOR ADAM'S TRANS-GRESSION. All Adam's race pass into the realm of death for his sin, for in him all sinned; but all are called out of death by the resurrection which came through Christ. The second death was no part of the penalty pronounced on Adam's sin.

The second death is for Christ rejecters; all in resurrection stand upon the ground of personal responsibility.

Where there has been no responsibility there will be grace found.

(See my *The Heathen in Relation to the Gospel* (2d.), from the publishers.)

4. " IN ADAM " AND " IN CHRIST." As " in Adam " we are constituted sinners and come under judgment, so " in Christ " is salvation found.

Note that Salvation and Life are *in* Christ, not a gift apart from Him. We cannot have them if we have not Christ.

" Neither is there Salvation *in* any Other."

" *In* Whom we have redemption through His Blood."

" God hath given to us Eternal Life, and this life is *in* His Son. He that hath the Son hath the life."

To be " found *in* Christ " was the Apostle's ambition, for in Him he found a righteousness that was perfect.

We are " accepted *in* the Beloved."

5. More " in Christ " than Lost " in Adam." The Superabundance of Grace, as it has been called, is wonderful. Where sin abounded, Grace did much more abound.

We find in the New Creation far more than was lost in the old.

> " In Christ the sons of Adam boast
> More than their first forefather lost."

6. The Threefold Superiority of Grace as set out in Romans 5. 15-17. The three contrasts are:

v. 16. *Sin and Grace.* How infinitely superior is grace to sin—sin working death, but grace working righteousness.

v. 16. *One and Many.* One sin wrought all the havoc in the world, but the free gift of grace covers a multitude of sins.

v. 17. *Death and Life.* How much more glorious is the reign of life than that of death !

7. The First Creation and the New Creation. The first is but the Porch to the new. Man was not made for the first, but for the New Creation; he is here under discipline and preparation for the better country. The first creation is *temporal*, the new creation is eternal. The first creation is *a parable* of the new creation, the visible teaching us of the invisible.

The *Head of the New Creation* is Christ, the Lord from Heaven; to be found in Him is to become a New Creation (2 Cor. 5. 17).

The *Old Creation* travails in pain and groans, having been subjected to vanity in hope (Rom. 8. 19-20). It will be " delivered from the bondage of corruption into the glorious liberty of the children of God."

VI. Application.

Let us see that we are " found in Christ."

Let us rejoice in Christ, the Head of the New Creation.

The Lord's Walk on Earth was a Rebuke to Every form of Pride

PRIDE OF BIRTH.

" She brought forth her firstborn Son and wrapped Him in swaddling clothes, and laid Him in a manger " (Luke 2. 7).

PRIDE OF ANCESTRY.

" Is not this the carpenter's Son ?" (Matt. 13. 55).

PRIDE OF PLACE.

" Can any good thing come out of Nazareth ?" (John 1. 46).

PRIDE OF APPEARANCE.

" When we shall see Him there is no beauty that we should desire Him " (Isa. 53. 2).

PRIDE OF PRAISE.

" He is despised and rejected of men " (Isa. 53. 3).

" They laughed Him to scorn " (Matt. 9. 24).

PRIDE OF WEALTH.

" The Son of Man hath not where to lay His head " (Luke 9. 58).

PRIDE OF SELF-ESTEEM.

" I am meek and lowly in heart " (Matt. 11. 29).

PRIDE OF SUPERIORITY.

" I am among you as He that serveth " (Luke 22. 27).

PRIDE OF LEARNING.

" How knoweth this Man letters, having never learned ?" (John 7. 15).

PRIDE OF STRENGTH.

" He was crucified through weakness " (2 Cor. 13. 4).

PRIDE OF REPUTATION.

" He made Himself of no reputation " (Phil. 2. 7).

PRIDE OF POWER.

" The Son of man can do nothing of Himself " (John 5. 19).

PRIDE OF SPEECH.

" I have not spoken of Myself, but the Father which sent Me, He gave Me a commandment, what I should say, and what I should speak " (John 12. 49).

PRIDE IN DEATH.

" My God, My God, why hast Thou forsaken Me ?" (Matt. 27. 46).

SECTION VIII.

Our Lord Jesus Christ:
His Future Glory

The Coming of the Lord

As we see the day approaching
  And Thy coming drawing near,
We rejoice in Thee with trembling,
  While we serve Thee, Lord, with fear.
Soon that Day, foretold, expected,
  And for which we've hoped so long,
Will in rapture burst upon us
  With a Resurrection Song.

At that day we trust, Lord Jesus,
  To be found of Thee in peace,
Wearing not our filthy raiment,
  But Thy Robe of Righteousness,
Clothed in Garments of Salvation
  And adorned with grace divine,
Working out with fear and trembling
  Full Salvation, ours, yet Thine.

We would so abide in Thee, Lord,
  That when Thou shalt soon appear,
We with boldness may salute Thee,
  Knowing naught of slavish fear;
For with this bright Hope upon Thee
  We our lives would purify,
Not to be ashamed before Thee,
  When we meet Thee in the sky.

Some of us may sleep in Jesus
  Ere that Holy Day shall be:
Whether sleeping, whether waking,
  We shall rise and live with Thee.
So amid the present darkness,
  We will comfort each his heart;
We shall all be changed, be like Thee,
  And be with Thee where Thou art.

G. G.

Christ, Who is Our Hope

I. Texts. "Our Lord Jesus Christ, which is our Hope" (1 Tim. 1. 1).

"Christ in you, the Hope of Glory" (Col. 1. 27).

II. Main Lesson. Hope is Faith for the Future (Rom. 8. 24-25). The Christian Hope is no uncertain thing. It is both "sure and stedfast" (Heb. 6. 19), and since it is placed in Christ, the true Object of our Hope, it cannot be disappointed.

As the Believer looks back to *the Finished Work of Christ* as the ground of his Hope of Salvation, as he looks up to the *Great High Priest on the Throne* as the Hope of Continuance, so he looks forward to the *Coming of Christ* as the Hope of Future Blessedness.

The Full Assurance of Hope keeps the soul happy, in the anticipation of soon seeing, being with, and being like the Lord Jesus.

III. Scripture to Study : Hebrews 6. 11-20.

v. 11. *Exhortation to the Full Assurance of Hope.* "We desire that every one of you do show the same diligence to the Full Assurance of Hope unto the end."

v. 12. *Faith and Patience Needed to Inherit Promises.* "That ye be not slothful, but followers of them who through faith and patience inherit the promises."

vv. 13-14. *God Confirmed His Promise to Abraham by an Oath.* "For when God made promise to Abraham, because He could swear by no greater, He sware by Himself, saying, Surely blessing I will bless thee, and multiplying I will multiply thee."

v. 15. *Abraham Patiently Endured.* "And so, after he had patiently endured, he obtained the promise."

vv. 16-18. *Two Immutable Things on which Hope is Based.* "For men verily swear by the greater: and an oath for confirmation is to them an end of all strife.

Wherein God, willing more abundantly to show unto the heirs of promise the immutability of His counsel, confirmed it by an oath: that by two immutable things, in which it was impossible for God to lie, we might have a strong consolation, who have fled for refuge to lay hold upon the hope set before us."

v. 19. *Our Hope like the Anchor of the Soul.* "Which Hope we have as an Anchor of the Soul, both sure and stedfast, and which entereth into that within the veil."

v. 20. *The Forerunner has Entered in for us.* "Whither the Forerunner is for us entered, even Jesus, made an High Priest for ever after the Order of Melchizedec."

IV. Our Hope Defined.

1. THE HOPE OF SALVATION (1 Thess. 5. 8). The full assurance that we shall never perish, but in the day of judgment and wrath we shall be eternally saved.

2. THE HOPE OF ETERNAL LIFE (Tit. 1. 2 and 3. 7). God has promised that those who believe in Jesus shall have eternal life (John 3. 16). It is His Great Gift (Rom. 6. 23); we therefore confidently expect it.

3. THE HOPE OF THE GOSPEL (Col. 1. 23)—that is, the Salvation promised to us in the Good News from Heaven.

4. THE HOPE OF RIGHTEOUSNESS BY FAITH (Gal. 5. 5) —that is, our expectation that by faith in Jesus we are justified and shall stand before God without charge or condemnation.

5. THE GOOD HOPE THROUGH GRACE (2 Thess. 2. 16). The assurance that rests not on merit but grace, not of worth but the free gift of God.

6. THE HOPE OF HIS CALLING (Eph. 1. 18) and "OF YOUR CALLING" (Eph. 4. 4)—that is, the glorious position and prospect to which He has called and we have been called.

7. THE HOPE OF THE PROMISE (Acts 26. 6)—that is, of Resurrection, of which Paul testified before King Agrippa.

8. THE HOPE OF GLORY (Col. 1. 27; Rom. 5. 2). Glory here manifested in and through us by Christ in us, and the Glory to be revealed when He comes again.

9. THAT BLESSED HOPE (Tit. 2. 13). This refers to the coming again of Christ to take us to be with Himself, as described in 1 Thess. 4. 14-18.

10. A LIVELY HOPE (1 Pet. 1. 3). That is a vital thing in our lives, the hope for the grace that is to be brought to us at the coming of our Lord Jesus.

V. Other Lessons on Hope.

1. THE GROUND OF HOPE. Hope, like Faith, must have something on which to rest.

This ground is *the Promise of God*. All that God has promised we may safely hope for.

Our Promised Land is the inheritance of the Promises of God. These we enter into by faith and patience.

2. OUR HOPE CONFIRMED BY OATH. In order that our Hope may be doubly assured to us, God has confirmed His promises to us by an oath. Acting as man acts, so as to encourage us (Heb. 6. 16), He could only swear by Himself, for there is nothing greater.

So the *Heirs of Promise* (believers) have two immutable (unchangeable) things on which to base their hopes—His Promise and His Oath.

3. OUR HOPE LIKE AN ANCHOR. The anchor that holds the ship in a storm is unseen; it is hidden in the depths of the sea. So Christ our Hope is unseen, having passed within the Veil (Heb. 6. 19). Our Hope is like the cable that holds on to the unseen anchor. We trust in Christ, Who has entered into Heaven for us.

> " We have an anchor that keeps the soul
> Stedfast and sure while the billows roll,
> Fastened to the Rock that cannot move,
> Grounded firm and deep in the Saviour's love."

4. CHRIST IN YOU, THE HOPE OF GLORY (Col. 1. 27). This is said to be a secret, " the mystery which hath been hid from ages . . . but now is manifested," that Christ would actually indwell His saints, and that this would be their Hope of Glory.

Hope of Glory has a double meaning—a present hope of becoming like Christ now, being changed from glory to glory into the same image (2 Cor. 3. 18), and the hope of future glory with Him, when He comes to reign. Christ in us effects both of these.

5. WE ARE SAVED BY HOPE (Rom. 8. 24). This really means we are saved *in anticipation of good things*, with a definite purpose set before us. God has saved us with a great hope in view, which He will bring about in His own time. So we hope for our Hope, and are saved both by the hoping and in view of the hope set before us.

Our Hope draws daily nearer, so let us go on hoping, with the full assurance of Hope—that is, a well-founded hope.

6. REJOICING IN HOPE (Rom. 12. 12 and 5. 4). The clearer our Hope, the greater will be our Joy. The better we understand the Hope set before us in the Gospel, the more we shall desire it and delight in anticipation of it.

The more we love the Lord, the more intense will be our anticipation of seeing and being with Him, and, better still, being like Him.

7. VAIN HOPE. John Bunyan made Mr. Ignorance in *Pilgrim's Progress* get one called Vain Hope to row him across the river of death. In other words, he died in a vain hope and perished. Such is the fate of those *who make gold their hope* (Job 31. 24), like the Rich Fool in the Parable (Luke 12. 16) or Dives (Luke 16. 19).

Such, also, is *the Hypocrite's Hope* (Job 8. 13). It is like a spider's web, a flimsy hope that will perish. The hypocrite is like one who hatches cockatrice's eggs (Isa. 59. 5); a viper breaks out to sting him.

VI. Application.

See that your Hope is well founded—that you have the Promise of God for the Hope that is in you—lest you die like Ignorance with a Vain Hope.

Let us rejoice in Hope of the Glory of God.

Let us see that Christ truly dwells in our hearts by faith, and is thus in us the Hope of Glory.

Behold, the Bridegroom

I. Text. " Behold, the Bridegroom cometh; go ye out to meet Him " (Matt. 25. 6).

II. Main Lesson. The Lord Jesus is the Bridegroom of the Church.

He is her Lover, for we read, " He loved the Church, and gave Himself for it . . . that He might present it to Himself a glorious Church " (Eph. 5. 27).

He will come again and take His bride to Himself. The Church is seen under the figure of a City, the Heavenly Jerusalem, descending out of Heaven, " prepared as a Bride adorned for her husband " (Rev. 19. 7, 21. 2 and 9-11).

The Marriage Supper of the Lamb will follow (Rev. 19. 9 and 17). In the Kingdom the Bride will sit with Him upon His Throne (Rev. 3. 21).

III. Scripture to Study : Ephesians 5. 22-32.

vv. 22-24. *Wives are to be Subject to their Husbands as the Church is to Christ.* " Wives, submit yourselves unto your own husbands, as unto the Lord. For the husband is the head of the wife, even as Christ is the Head of the Church: and He is the Saviour of the Body.

" Therefore as the Church is subject unto Christ, so let the wives be to their own husbands in everything."

v. 25. *Husbands should Love as Christ Loved the Church.* " Husbands, love your wives, even as Christ also loved the Church."

vv. 25-26. *The Lord's Love and Care for His Church.* " And gave Himself for it; that He might sanctify and cleanse it with the washing of water by the Word."

v. 27. *He Will Present it to Himself a Glorious Church.* " That He might present it to Himself a glorious Church, not having spot or wrinkle, or any such thing; but that it should be holy and without blemish."

vv. 28-29. *So Men ought to Love their Wives as Themselves.* " So ought men to love their wives as their own bodies. He that loveth his wife loveth himself. For no man ever yet hated his own flesh; but nourisheth and cherisheth it, even as the Lord the Church."

v. 30. *We are Members of Christ's Body.* " For we are members of His body, of His flesh, and of His bones."

v. 31. *Therefore a Man should Cleave to his Wife.* " For this cause shall a man leave his father and mother, and shall be joined unto his wife, and they two shall be one flesh."

v. 32. *This is a Mysterious Figure of Christ and His Church.* " This is a great mystery: but I speak concerning Christ and the Church."

IV. Some Brides of Scripture.

Eve, the first bride, of the first Adam, is a type of the Church in that she was his body, as is the Church the bride and the body of the last Adam.

Adam was in a deep sleep when God took Eve from his side; so Christ begat His bride, the Church, by His death.

Sarah, the wife of Abraham, was a type of the Church in that she was a figure of the Heavenly Jerusalem (Gal. 4. 26). " The Jerusalem which is above is free, which is the mother of us all." The heirs of faith are children of Abraham by the free woman.

Rebekah, the bride of Isaac, gives us a beautiful type of God seeking a bride for His Son, sending the Spirit across the desert to win her (Gen. 24). Isaac met her on the way, and took her to be his wife and loved her.

Rachel, the beloved wife of Jacob, despised of Leah because she was barren, but of whom the language might be used, " Rejoice, thou barren that bearest not . . . for the desolate hath many more children than she which hath an husband " (Gal. 4. 27 and Isa. 54. 1).

Asenath, the bride of Joseph in Egypt—a figure of the Gentile stranger, who is one body with the elect bride (Eph. 2. 15-22); as also is Zipporah, the bride of Moses (Ex. 2. 21).

V. Other Lessons of the Bridegroom.

1. THE CHURCH THE BRIDE. The Scriptures that teach us that the Church is the Bride of Christ are the following:

Ephesians 5. 22-32, set out above (III.), in which we are told that the marriage relationship is a figure of Christ and the Church.

2 *Corinthians* 11. 2, where the Apostle says, "I have espoused you to One Husband, that I may present you as a chaste virgin to Christ."

Romans 7. 4, where we read, "Ye also are become dead to the Law by the Body of Christ; that ye should be married to another, even to Him Who is raised from the dead, that we should bring forth fruit unto God."

John 3. 29, where John the Baptist speaks of himself as the Friend of the Bridegroom, who rejoiced to hear His voice, adding, "He that hath the Bride is the Bridegroom."

2. THE TESTIMONY OF CHRIST HIMSELF.

Matthew 9. 15, *Mark* 2. 19 *and Luke* 5. 34. "Can the children of the bridechamber mourn, so long as the Bridegroom is with them? But the days will come when the Bridegroom shall be taken from them, and then shall they fast."

Matthew 22. 2-10. The Parable of "a Certain King which made a marriage for His son."

Matthew 25. 1-13. The Parable of the Ten Virgins who went forth to meet the Bridegroom. "At midnight there was a cry made, Behold, the Bridegroom cometh, go ye out to meet Him. . . . They that were ready went in with Him to the marriage."

3. THE BRIDE IN THE BOOK OF REVELATION.

Revelation 21. 2. *Under the Figure of a City.* "I John saw the Holy City, New Jerusalem, coming down from God out of Heaven, prepared as a Bride adorned for her husband."

v. 9. *An Angel bids him come and see the Bride.* "There came one of the seven angels . . . and talked with me, saying, Come hither, I will show thee the Bride, the Lamb's wife. And he carried me away in the Spirit

. . . and showed me that great city, the Holy Jerusalem, descending out of Heaven from God, having the glory of God."

(For a lesson on the Heavenly City, see *Seventy Less Known Bible Stories*, No. 70, pp. 311-316.)

Revelation 22. 17. *The Voice of the Bride* is heard in the last appeal of the Bible: " And the Spirit and the Bride say, Come."

4. THE MARRIAGE OF THE LAMB. Revelation 19. 7-8. " Let us be glad and rejoice, . . . for the marriage of the Lamb is come, and His wife hath made herself ready. And to her was granted that she should be arrayed in fine linen, clean and white: for the fine linen is the Righteousness of saints."

v. 9. " Blessed are they which are called unto the marriage supper of the Lamb."

Under this figure the consummation of the mutual Love of Christ and His Church is figured.

5. A MISTAKEN INTERPRETATION. Some have sought to make Israel the Bride of the Lamb, but this is certainly unsound, for Israel is always spoken of as a married woman, alas ! unfaithful to her Lord, Who entreats her to return unto Him in such language as this: " Turn, O backsliding children, saith the Lord; for I am married unto you " (Jer. 3. 14). " For thy Maker is thine Husband; the Lord of Hosts is His Name. . . . The Lord hath called thee as a woman forsaken . . . and a wife of youth " (Isa. 54. 5-6). " How shall I give thee up, Ephraim ? how shall I deliver thee, Israel ?" (Hosea 11. 8). Such language is not suitable of the chaste Virgin to be presented to Christ.

6. LOVE SHOWS ITSELF IN THREE WAYS:

Desire, as the Psalmist sang, " There is none on earth that I desire beside Thee " (73. 25).

Delight in its object: " Delight thyself also in the Lord " Psa. 37. 4); and

Devotion (Psa. 119. 38): " Thy servant, who is devoted to Thy fear."

It is thus the Lord loves the Church. His desire is toward them and His delight is in them, and He devoted Himself to them, even laying down His life to purchase His bride. It is so the Church should respond to His Love.

7. THE SATISFYING NATURE OF THE LOVE OF CHRIST. The Song of Solomon has this for its theme.

" Thy Love is better than wine " (1. 2); " He brought me into His banqueting house, and His banner over me was Love " (2. 4); " How much better is Thy love than wine " (4. 10); " Love is strong as death " (8. 6); " Many waters cannot quench love " (8. 7).

> " The love of Jesus, what it is,
>   None but His loved ones know."

VI. Application.

Let us thank God for the assurances of Love to us as revealed in Christ.

Let us keep our garments white against the day when the Bridegroom shall come.

Let us respond to the Love of Christ with true devotion.

The Qualities of True Love

THE
- STRENGTH of Love (Cant. 8. 6).
- COMFORT of Love (Phil. 2. 1).
- LABOUR of Love (1 Thess. 1. 3).
- CONSTRAINT of Love (2 Cor. 5. 14).
- BREASTPLATE of Love (1 Thess. 5. 8).
- SINCERITY of Love (2 Cor. 8. 8).
- PROOF of Love (2 Cor. 8. 24).

" PERFECT Love casteth out Fear " (1 John 4. 18).

Seven Visions of Christ

I. Text. "God speaketh once, yea twice, yet man perceiveth it not. In a dream, in a vision of the night " (Job 33. 14-15).

II. Main Lesson. God has down the ages revealed Himself to man in Visions.

The Seven of these Visions that we are to study are all of Christ, and help us to understand something more of His Glory. Each of them has a distinctive lesson to teach us. They form a valuable part of the revelation of Christ that we have in the Scriptures.

III. The Seven Visions.

1. ISAIAH'S VISION (Isa. 6. 1-9). In the year that king Uzziah died, he saw the Lord Jesus (see John 12. 41) sitting upon a high throne. Seraphim worshipped Him, crying, "Holy, holy, holy, is the Lord of Hosts: the whole earth is full of His glory."

The sight causes Isaiah to cry: " Woe is me," and to confess his uncleanness. A Seraph touches his lips with a live coal from the altar. His sin is purged, and he hears a voice saying: "Whom shall I send ?" He answers: " Here am I; send me," and receives his commission to go and preach to a rebellious people.

2. EZEKIEL'S VISION (Ezek. 1. 4-28). He sees a Throne with a rainbow round it, and the likeness as the appearance of a man above upon it: " This was the appearance of the likeness of the glory of the Lord."

The Throne is supported by four Living Creatures (5), having faces of a man, a lion, an ox, and an eagle; these were accompanied by wheels, " so high that they were dreadful," full of eyes, which went and returned as a flash of lightning. All was " like a fire infolding itself " (4).

Ezekiel hears a voice that sends him to the rebellious

nation to warn them of judgment, and yet to give promise of future blessedness.

3. DANIEL'S VISION (Dan. 7. 9-14). He also sees the Ancient of Days upon a Throne, "like the fiery flame, and his wheels as burning fire." A fiery stream of judgment issued from the Throne.

Then he beheld One like the Son of Man come with the clouds of Heaven, and came to the Ancient of Days, and they brought Him near unto Him. And there was given to Him a world-wide kingdom and everlasting dominion which should never be destroyed.

4. THE DISCIPLES' VISION ON THE HOLY MOUNT (Matt. 17. 1-9; 2 Pet. 1. 16-18). Peter, James and John see the Lord transfigured: His face did shine as the sun, and His raiment was white as the light. Moses and Elijah talk with Him of the death (exodus) He was to accomplish at Jerusalem. A Voice from Heaven addresses Him: "This is My Beloved Son, in Whom I am well pleased."

5. JOHN'S VISION ON THE ISLE OF PATMOS (Rev. 1. 12-20). John hears a great voice, as of a trumpet, and, looking round, sees One like the Son of Man walking in the midst of Seven Golden Candlesticks. He has seven stars in His right hand. He is arrayed in Priestly robes, and out of His mouth went a sharp two-edged sword. He sends messages to the Seven Churches of Asia.

6. THE LAMB IN THE MIDST OF THE THRONE (Rev. 5. 6-14). A Throne is set in Heaven, with One sitting thereon, and a rainbow round about. Four and twenty thrones with elders in white and crowns of gold. A sea of glass and four Living Creatures round the Throne.

No one is found worthy to open the book in the right hand of Him upon the Throne, until the Lion of the tribe of Judah, the Root of David, seen in the midst of the Throne as a Lamb Slain, having seven horns and seven eyes.

All fall before Him and sing a new song, "Worthy is the Lamb that was slain."

7. THE RIDER ON A WHITE HORSE (Rev. 19. 11-16). The last Symbolic Vision of Christ in the Bible. Behold, a

white horse. He that sat thereon was called Faithful and True. He went forth to judge and make war, His eyes as a flame, a name no man knew, many diadems, and His garment dipped in blood—His Name, the Word of God.

An army on horses, in white linen, followed Him—out of His mouth a sharp sword. He will tread the wine-press of the wrath of Almighty God.

On His vesture and thigh a name written, KING of KINGS and LORD of LORDS.

These Visions are not the only ones to be found in the Scriptures. The study may be continued profitably.

IV. Other Lessons from the Vision.

1. THE VALUE OF A VISION. Spiritual realities cannot well be expressed in material form. They lose their dignity, beauty, and sense of power by being made into images or pictures. That is why idols are so strenuously forbidden: they degrade the thought of God.

But a Vision is something beyond the limitations of idols; it transcends the material and expresses glorious conceptions in a way that impresses the mind as nothing on earth could do. Material things, as crowns, robes, etc., assume a symbolic form far beyond actuality, and so fill the mind with spiritual ideas and truths. In the Seven Visions chosen Christ is seen in a glorious dignity that nothing merely earthly could give Him. We feel we know Him better and esteem Him more highly as the result.

2. A DISTINCTIVE LESSON FROM EACH VISION. One thing is common to them all—the Glory of Christ, in most of them seated upon a glorious Throne; and this gives us the clue to each. The Lord Jesus is seen in different capacity in each of them.

(a) *In Isaiah's Vision* we see Christ as *LORD of HOSTS*, worshipped by Angels, who cry: " Holy, holy, holy "— Whose glory fills not only the Temple but the whole earth. His Deity is hereby established. From this Glorious Lord Isaiah receives his commission to the rebellious nation.

(b) *In Ezekiel's Vision* Christ is seen as *RULER and UPHOLDER* of all things—mighty angels as a flame of fire doing His will; wheels within wheels working out His providence.

Ezekiel, strengthened by the vision, is sent to the distressed nation to tell them of the glory departed returning in power.

(c) *In Daniel's Vision* we see the Lord Jesus as *KING*, receiving an Eternal Kingdom that shall never pass away.

(d) *In the Transfiguration* the Lord Jesus is seen in the *GLORY that should follow on SUFFERING*.

He spoke with Moses and Elias of the Exodus He was to accomplish, while He revealed to the disciples the majesty of His presence.

(e) *In John's Vision on Patmos* the Lord, walking among the Lampstands, is seen as *HEAD of the CHURCH and HIGH PRIEST* of His people, ministering to their needs and counselling and warning them.

(f) *In the Vision of the Lamb upon the Throne*, Christ is seen as the *OBJECT of WORSHIP* of all the principalities and powers in Heaven and earth, specially of those redeemed from all nations by His Blood.

(g) In the last vision, of *the man on the White Horse* with the armies following, the Lord is seen as the *JUDGE and EXECUTOR of the WRATH of GOD*, reducing the nations to obedience and destroying the enemies of God.

3. EXALTED THOUGHTS OF CHRIST. It is important that we should have noble and elevating thoughts and conceptions of our Lord Jesus Christ.

To have mean and low ideas of Him is practically to be ignorant of Him.

To talk of *the Historic Christ* in a way that would reduce the thought of Him to that of a long-since-dead character in history is to do Him grave dishonour.

To formulate ideas of our own, or to receive other men's thoughts of Christ, is to depart from reality.

There is only One Christ of God; it is He Whom the Scriptures set before us under the Inspiration of the Spirit.

It is possible to have " Another Jesus," a mere fancy of the mind. Let us beware of this.

4. THE HEAVENLY VISION comes to all true believers sooner or later, when Christ becomes to them more than a man, more than One they have heard about. They know Him by a revelation to their own souls individually.

In *Pilgrim's Progress* Christian bade Hopeful ask Ignorance:

"*Ask him if ever he had Christ revealed to him from Heaven.*" It is a question we might well put each of us to his own heart.

5. *The Danger of Visions.* Yet there is a danger of relying on dreams and visions. Many foolish and hurtful things have resulted from doing so. Cranks have multiplied as a consequence and absurd sects been started, depending on some supposed revelation or vision—as the Swedenborgians, the Mormons and the Irvingites. Visions are not to found doctrine upon, but when truly of God they strengthen faith and rejoice the heart. They will (if of God) be such as do not do outrage to the revelation already given in the Scripture.

V. Application.

Ponder the Glories of Christ as discovered in these Visions.

Seek for a personal revelation of Christ to the soul— a heart experience rather than a head knowledge.

Faith's Vision

The Patriarchs saw the Promises afar off (Heb. 11. 13).
Moses endured as seeing Him Who is invisible (Heb. 11. 27).
We see Jesus Crowned (Heb. 2. 9).
The believer sees the Son (John 6. 40).
Faith sees the Glory of God (John 11. 40).
We see now through a glass darkly, but then face to face (1 Cor. 13. 12).

The Hope of Israel

I. Texts. " He shall be great, and shall be called the Son of the Highest: and the Lord God shall give unto Him the Throne of His father David " (Luke 1. 32).

" Rabbi, Thou art the Son of God; Thou art the King of Israel " (John 1. 49).

II. Main Lesson. God has not cast away His people (Israel) whom He foreknew. For the gifts and calling of God are without repentance (Rom. 11. 2 and 29).

They are to be restored to favour again.

Their " blindness " will continue only until the fulness of the Gentiles be come in (Rom. 11. 25), and then all Israel shall be saved, and the Deliverer (Christ) shall come and turn away ungodliness from Jacob.

The veil will be removed from their heart when they turn to the Lord (2 Cor. 3. 15-16).

Till then Jerusalem will be trodden down of the Gentiles (Luke 21. 24), as it is today.

But Israel will be gathered again into their own land, and the two kingdoms (Judah and Israel) become one under the rule of Christ. Once more they will be the centre of God's government in the world, and Jerusalem become a Praise in the earth.

So that Christ is the Hope of Israel.

III. Scripture to Study : Romans 11. 1-29.

vv. 1-2. *God has not Cast away His People Israel.* " I say then, Hath God cast away His people ? God forbid. . . . God hath not cast away His people which He foreknew."

vv. 2-4. *Elijah's Plea against them and God's Answer.* " Wot ye not what the Scripture saith of Elias ? how he maketh intercession to God against Israel. . . . But what saith the answer of God unto him ? I have reserved to Myself seven thousand men who have not bowed the knee to Baal."

vv. 5-6. *So there is still an Election of Grace.* "Even so then at this present time also there is a remnant according to the election of grace . . . and because of grace, it is not of works."

vv. 7-10. *The Election has Obtained what Israel Failed of.* "What then ? Israel hath not obtained that which he seeketh for; but the election hath obtained it, and the rest were blinded." (Psa. 69. 22 and Isa. 6. 9 and 29. 10 quoted in confirmation.)

vv. 11-14. *Have they Stumbled to Fall ? No, but through their Fall Salvation has come to the Gentiles.* "Have they stumbled to fall ? God forbid: but rather through their fall Salvation is come to the Gentiles, to provoke them to jealousy. If their fall be the riches of the Gentiles; how much more their fulness ?"

v. 15. *The Receiving of them will be Life from the Dead.* "If the casting away of them be the reconciling of the world, what shall the receiving of them be, but life from the dead ?"

vv. 17-24. *The Parable of the Olive Tree.* Israel, like natural branches, was broken off; Gentiles, like wild olives, were grafted into the Olive Tree. Beware, for God can graft them in again, and thou standest by faith.

v. 25. *The Mystery of Israel's Blindness.* "For I would not, brethren, that ye should be ignorant of this mystery . . . that blindness in part is happened to Israel, until the fulness of the Gentiles be come in."

vv. 26-27. *Then all Israel to be Saved.* "And so all Israel shall be saved; as it is written, There shall come out of Sion the Deliverer, and shall turn away ungodliness from Jacob," according to the Covenant.

v. 28. *So they are Enemies, yet Beloved.* "As concerning the Gospel, they are enemies for your sakes: but as touching the election, they are beloved for the fathers' sakes."

v. 29. *God never Fails of His Purpose.* "For the gifts and calling of God are without repentance."

IV. **The Future of Israel as Foretold by the Prophets.** The Dispersion of Israel and the Destruction of the Temple and City of Jerusalem took place in A.D. 70, as foretold by Christ (Matt. 24. 2).

1. It will last until " the Times of the Gentiles be Fulfilled " (Luke 21. 24), or, as the Apostle says, " until the fulness of the Gentiles be come in " (Rom. 11. 25).

Jerusalem to this day remains trodden down of the Gentiles.

2. There will be a Restoration of Israel. The Lord taught this. A time was to come for them when they would say of Him, " Blessed is He that cometh in the Name of the Lord " (Matt. 23. 38-39).

The Psalm from which this is quoted (Psa. 118. 21-26) tells us that the Stone they rejected would become the headstone of the corner; it would be a day in which Israel would rejoice.

Micah (4. 6-8) says that Israel that was cast off would be made a strong nation, over which in Zion the Lord would reign for ever: " The Kingdom shall come to the daughter of Jerusalem."

Isaiah (11. 11, 12) tells of the dispersed being gathered from the four corners of the earth.

(See also Isa. 54. 7, 62. 4 and 12; Jer. 23. 5-8; Joel 3. 16-21; Amos 9. 11-15.)

3. They will Return to their Land in Unbelief. It is not until they are gathered into their own land that they are cleansed (Ezek. 36. 24-28) and given a new heart.

(See also Ezek. 20. 34-42, 34. 11-31; Isa. 27. 12-13.)

4. The Two Nations (Judah and Israel) will become one again, like the two sticks in the prophet's hand (Ezek. 37. 16-22), with One King over them; but before this—

5. There will come a Time of Unparalleled Tribulation for them, called the time of Jacob's Trouble, or the Great Tribulation, which began at the Dispersion and will finally be headed up under Anti-Christ, who will seek to exterminate them.

All nations will be gathered together against them at the Great Battle of Armageddon.

(See Jer. 30. 4-11; Ezek. 21. 1-17, 38. 14-23; Dan. 12. 1; Zech. 12. 2-3, 14. 1-2; Matt. 24. 15-23; Rev. 20. 7-9.)

6. IN THE MIDST OF THEIR DISTRESS THE LORD WILL
APPEAR FOR THEIR DELIVERANCE. His feet will stand on
the Mount of Olives (Zech. 14. 4), and He will go forth
and fight against the nations and deliver them with a
great Deliverance.

7. THE NATION WILL REPENT AND ACKNOWLEDGE THEIR
MESSIAH. Lo, this is our God; we have waited for Him;
we have waited for Him, and He will save us (Isa. 25. 9-12,
27. 1-9; Zech. 14. 3-8).

8. THE LORD WILL BECOME KING IN THEIR MIDST AND
THE MILLENNIAL REIGN BEGIN. He will sit upon the Throne
of David, and the elect people will become the centre of
His government, and Jerusalem be made a praise in
the earth (Ezek. 37. 24-38, 48. 35; Jer. 33. 7-9; Zech.
14. 9).

V. Other Lessons from Israel.

1. ISRAEL'S FALL AND CASTING OFF. Already after the
First Captivity their glory had largely departed.

Five things were Missing from the Second Temple that
were the chief glory of the nation in the first:

(1) *The Ark* of the Covenant with the Tables of Stone.

(2) *The Holy Fire* that fell from Heaven in Solomon's
Temple.

(3) *The Urim and Thummim*, whereby they asked
Counsel of God.

(4) *The Spirit of Prophecy*.

(5) *The Shekinah Glory*, the Visible Presence of Jehovah.

2. SINCE THE DISPERSION IN A.D. 70. We read in Hosea
3. 4-5 that they were to remain for many days *without a king*
(or, *the* king of God's appointment); for Herod, an
Idumæan, they never regarded as their true king.

Without a Prince, a true leader or Saviour.

Without a Sacrifice, for only at Jerusalem might sacrifices
be offered (Deut. 12. 11-14), and it was to continue trodden
down of the Gentiles.

Without an Image—that is, an image to false gods; for
even from this sin, to which they were so prone, they would
be restrained.

Without an Ephod, in which was the Urim and Thummim. No longer would they ask counsel thus from the Lord. And—

Without a Teraphim, a false oracle as contrasted with the true. A Teraphim was a speaking oracle of the heathen. This remains true, for the Dispersion still continues.

3. AFTERWARDS. "Afterwards shall the children of Israel return and seek the Lord their God, and David their King, and shall fear the Lord and His goodness in the latter days " (Hosea 3. 5).

This sums up the future Hope of Israel, of which we read so many details elsewhere in the prophets (see IV. above).

4. CHRIST, THE HOPE OF ISRAEL. "Let Israel hope in the Lord: for with the Lord there is mercy . . . and He shall redeem Israel from all his iniquities " (Psa. 120. 7-8).

" Let Israel hope in the Lord from henceforth and for ever " (Psa. 131. 3).

The Angel Gabriel (Luke 1. 31-32) said to Mary, " Thou shalt call His name Jesus . . . the Lord God shall give unto Him the Throne of His father David."

Mary Sang (Luke 1. 54-55), " He hath holpen His servant Israel, in remembrance of His mercy; as He spake to our fathers."

Zacharias Prophesied (Luke 1. 68-69), " Blessed be the Lord God of Israel; for He hath visited and redeemed His people, and hath raised up an Horn of Salvation for us in the house of His servant David."

5. THE LORD TOLD OF JERUSALEM BEING TRODDEN DOWN of the Gentiles and of a great Tribulation, but of the Son of Man coming to deliver: " Lift up your heads; your redemption draweth nigh " (Luke 21. 27-28).

Then they would see Him again, and say, " Blessed be He that cometh in the Name of the Lord " (Matt. 23. 38, 39).

The Apostle Paul (Acts 28. 20) said, " For the Hope of Israel I am bound with this chain."

He said that Christ had come to confirm the promises made to the fathers (Rom. 15. 8); that God had not cast

away His people (Rom. 11. 1-2), but that one day it would
turn to the Lord (2 Cor. 3. 16) and the Veil be lifted and
a Deliverer come to Jacob, and all Israel be saved (Rom.
11. 26).

6. ISRAEL GRAFTED INTO THE OLIVE TREE AGAIN (Rom.
11. 17-24). The Olive Tree represents the Testimony of God
on earth. Israel was originally this tree, but was broken
off because of unbelief, and the Election of Grace from among
the Gentiles grafted in as a wild olive; but Israel would be
grafted in again, and once more become fruitful and the
Witness of God on the Earth.

VI. Application.

Pray for the Peace of Jerusalem.
Let us beware, for by faith we stand.
Let us rejoice with Israel in their Hope.

Names of Jerusalem

The City of the Great King (Psa. 48. 1; Matt. 5. 5).
The City of God (Psa. 46. 4; 48. 1).
The City of Solemnities (Isa. 33. 20).
The City of Righteousness (Isa. 1. 26).
The City of Truth (Zech. 8. 3).
The Faithful (Isa. 1. 21), Holy (Neh. 11. 1), Beautiful
    (Psa. 48. 2), Great (Jer. 22. 8) City.
The Joy of the whole earth (Psa. 48. 2).
The Perfection of Beauty (Lam. 2. 15).

In His Millennial Glory

I. Text. " I saw the souls of them that were beheaded for the witness of Jesus . . . and they lived and reigned with Christ a thousand years " (Rev. 20. 4).

II. Main Lesson. A time is coming when the Lord will reign upon the earth, and righteousness and peace be established.

This period is called the Millennium, or the Thousand Years.

The only direct reference to a thousand years' reign is in Revelation 20, which we study below; but many of the prophets foretell such a period of earthly prosperity and blessing for Israel, in which all the nations shall share. As to whether it will be only *an actual thousand years* or a longer, undefined period, we must not be too dogmatic. Since all the numbers in the Book of Revelation are symbolical, this too may be.

Whether Christ will reign in His actual bodily presence on the Throne of David or by His representative we cannot be certain, though many Scriptures seem to suggest that He is the " David " referred to (Ezek. 37. 24).

The Millennium comes to an end by the release of Satan from his prison (Rev. 20. 7) and a final outbreak of rebellion under Gog and Magog. So that we must not confound the Millennium with the Everlasting Kingdom of our Lord Jesus Christ.

III. Scriptures to Study : Revelation 20. 4-10.

v. 4. *After Satan was Bound for a Thousand Years, those who had been Martyred Reign with Christ.* " I saw thrones, and they sat upon them, and judgment was given unto them: and I saw the souls of them that were beheaded for the witness of Jesus, and for the Word of God, and which had not worshipped the beast, neither his image, neither had received his mark upon their foreheads, or in their hands; and they lived and reigned with Christ a thousand years."

v. 5. *The Rest of the Dead Remain in their Graves.* "But the rest of the dead lived not again until the thousand years were finished. This is the first resurrection."

v. 6. *They are Priests of God and of Christ.* "Blessed and holy is he that hath part in the first resurrection: on such the second death hath no power, but they shall be priests of God and of Christ, and shall reign with Him a thousand years."

v. 7. *Satan Loosed Again.* "And when the thousand years are expired, Satan shall be loosed out of his prison."

v. 8. *He Heads a Rebellion.* "And shall go out to deceive the nations which are in the four quarters of the earth, Gog and Magog, to gather them together to battle: the number of whom is as the sand of the sea."

9. *They Besiege Jerusalem and are Consumed.* "And they went up on the breadth of the earth, and compassed the camp of the saints about, and the beloved city: and fire came down from God out of Heaven, and devoured them."

Isaiah 65. 17-25:

v. 17. *New Heavens and a New Earth Created.* "Behold, I create new heavens and a new earth: and the former shall not be remembered."

v. 18. *Jerusalem a Rejoicing.* "Behold, I create Jerusalem a rejoicing, and her people a joy."

v. 19. *No more Weeping in it.* "I will rejoice in Jerusalem, and joy in my people: and the voice of weeping shall be no more heard in her."

v. 20. *Long Life will Distinguish that Time.* "There shall be no more thence an infant of days, nor an old man that hath not filled his days: for the child shall die an hundred years old; but the sinner being an hundred years old shall be accursed."

vv. 21-22. *Houses Will be Built and Vineyards Planted.* "They shall build houses, and inhabit them; and plant vineyards, and eat the fruit of them. . . . Mine elect shall long enjoy the work of their hands."

v. 23. *They will not Labour in Vain.* "They shall not

labour in vain . . . for they are the seed of the blessed
of the Lord."

v. 24. *Their Prayers will be Answered.* "Before they call, I
will answer; and while they are yet speaking, I will hear."

v. 25. *Nature will be no Longer Red in Tooth and Claw.*
" The wolf and the lamb shall feed together, and the
lion shall eat straw like the bullock: and dust shall be the
serpent's meat. They shall not hurt nor destroy in all
My holy mountain."

IV. Seven Aspects of the Millennium.

1. God's King on the Throne.

Psalm 2. 6. " Yet have I set My King upon My Holy
Hill of Zion," to rule with a rod of iron over the uttermost
parts of the earth. The Lord Jesus is called the Holy One
of Israel, our King (Psa. 89. 18). He is to reign in righteousness (Isa. 32. 1); He is Jehovah-Tsidkenu (Jer. 23. 5-6);
and "David My Servant," the One Shepherd (Ezek. 37. 24);
"Jehovah," "One Lord, and His Name One " (Zech. 14. 9).

2. Its Nature. It includes all who take part in the
first Resurrection. It is Universal, Peaceful, Righteous
and Everlasting, in that it will merge into the Future
Eternal Kingdom.

Daniel 7. 13-14: It is over all peoples, nations, and
languages (v. 27); " the people of the saints " participate
in the rule.

Righteousness and Equity and Faithfulness (Isa. 11. 1-9)
will mark it, and death to the wicked, and Peace, Quiet,
and Assurance as the result of righteousness (Isa. 32. 17-18).

3. Converted Israel will enjoy their land again (Isa.
4. 2-6). Brought into the New Covenant (Jer. 31. 31-40),
they continue as a nation before God, never to be plucked
up or thrown down for ever (Ezek. 36. 25-38), their land to
become as the garden of Eden.

The two Kingdoms will be one nation in their land again
(Ezek. 37. 22).

4. Jerusalem the Metropolis. Ezekiel 48. 35. The
Name of the City from that day shall be Jehovah-Shammah,
The Lord is there.

All nations will flock to it (Isa. 66. 20).

It will be a Praise in the earth (Isa. 62. 7), a rejoicing, and her people a joy (Isa. 65. 18).

Jerusalem will be called the Throne of the Lord (Jer. 3. 17).

5. THE NATIONS BLESSED. They will say, Come ye, and let us go up to the mountain of the Lord; for the Word of the Lord will go out from Jerusalem. They will beat their swords into plowshares, and learn war no more (Isa. 2. 4).

Jacob will take root, and Israel bud and blossom, and fill the face of the world with fruit (Isa. 27. 6). They will be for a light to the Gentiles, and carry Salvation unto the end of the earth (Isa. 49. 5-6. See also Isa. 52. 1-10 and Jer. 3. 17).

6. A TIME OF JOY. A feast of fat things unto all people (Isa. 25. 6); of songs and everlasting joy (35. 10, 51. 11); sorrow and mourning flee away. No more hunger or thirst (Isa. 49. 7-23), and so prosperous that the place shall be too narrow for them.

They will be like a watered garden (Jer. 31. 12).

7. CHANGES IN THE NATURAL WORLD. Wild beasts will become tame (Isa. 11. 6-9, 65. 25).

No lions or ravenous beasts (Isa. 35. 9).

Thorns and briars give place to firs and myrtles (Isa. 55. 13).

All nature will clap their hands and sing (Isa. 55. 12).

Rich harvests: the plowman will overtake the reapers (Ezek. 36. 29-30; Amos 9. 13).

Life will be lengthened (Isa. 65. 20).

V. Other Lessons from the Millennium.

1. PERFECT GOVERNMENT. The world has never seen perfect government. All kinds have been tried again and again—Kings, Despots, Dictators, Republics, Democracies and Communist—but all have failed. Man has never been blessed with a rule of perfect righteousness and peace.

In the Millennium this will be his happy lot.

Christ will reign, wars will cease, life will be safe, and the lands fruitful and prosperous; the people multiply and dwell in harmony.

2. MAN'S LAST TRIAL. He has been tried without Law (from Adam till Moses); under Law since Sinai; under Judges; under Kings; under Grace since Jesus died. He has proved himself a failure, a rebel, and a sinner.

Now under perfect government, without any political or social grievance, he will be given his last chance.

He will show himself unchanged, and at the instigation of Satan rise up in final rebellion, only to be destroyed.

3. A GODLY REMNANT. All down the ages God has had an Election of Grace—Noah in the lawless days; Abraham under the promise; the Godly Remnant in Israel under Law; the Church under Grace.

They will reign with Him in the Millennium.

4. PREPARE NOW FOR SERVICE THEN. Our faithfulness here will fit us for service then. The Lord evidently taught this in many places (see Matt. 24. 45-47, 25. 21-23; Luke 12. 42-44).

We are told that if we suffer with Him we shall reign with Him (2 Tim. 2. 12).

VI. **Application.**
Let us pray, " Thy Kingdom come."
Let us prepare now for service then.

The Believer's Hope in Christ

Caught up to meet Him (1 Thess. 4. 17).
Be for ever with Him (1 Thess. 4. 17).
Be glorified together (Rom. 8. 17).
Reign with Him (2 Tim. 2. 12).
See His face (Rev. 22. 4).
Serve Him (Rev. 22. 3).
Be like Him (1 John 3. 2).

The Judge of Quick and Dead

I. Texts. "He commanded us to preach unto the people, and to testify that it is He which was ordained of God to be the Judge of Quick and Dead" (Acts 10. 42).

"He hath appointed a day, in the which He will judge the world in righteousness by that Man Whom He hath ordained" (Acts 17. 31).

II. Main Lesson. God has committed all judgment unto the Son (John 5. 22), and given Him authority to execute judgment, because He is the Son of Man (27, R.V.)

He will judge His people at the Bema or Judgment Seat of Christ.

He will judge the wicked at the Great White Throne.

Judgment will be according to works; according to truth (Rom. 2. 2); and by the secrets of men (Rom. 2. 16).

III. Scriptures to Study.

1. As to the Judgment Seat of Christ.

2 Corinthians 5. 10. "We must all appear before the Judgment Seat of Christ; that every one may receive the things done in his body, according to that he hath done, whether it be good or bad."

Romans 14. 10-13. "Why dost thou judge thy brother? or why dost thou set at nought thy brother? for we shall all stand before the judgment seat of Christ. For it is written, As I live, saith the Lord, every knee shall bow to Me, and every tongue shall confess to God. So then every one of us shall give account of himself to God. Let us not therefore judge one another any more."

1 Corinthians 3. 11-13. "For other foundation can no man lay than that is laid, which is Jesus Christ.

"Now if any man build upon this foundation gold, silver, precious stones, wood, hay, stubble; every man's work shall be made manifest: for the day shall declare it, because it shall be revealed by fire."

2. As to the Great White Throne (Rev. 20. 11-15).

v. 11. "I saw a Great White Throne, and Him that sat on it. . . . I saw the dead, small and great, stand before God; the books were opened: and another book was opened, which is the Book of Life."

v. 12. *All Judged according to their Works.* "And the dead were judged out of those things which were written in the books, according to their works."

v. 13. *The Sea and Death and Hades Give up their Dead.* "And the sea gave up the dead which were in it; and death and hell . . . and they were judged every man according to their works."

v. 14. *The Lake of Fire the Second Death.* "Death and Hell were cast into the Lake of Fire. This is the second death. And whosoever was not found written in the Book of Life was cast into the Lake of Fire."

IV. Other Lessons on Judgment.

1. The Judge. The Lord Jesus has been ordained of God the Judge of Quick and Dead (Acts 10. 42).

The reason is because He is Son of Man.

Having lived on earth and become a man, He is the better fitted to judge men.

He will discover the secrets of all hearts and the true attitude of each toward Himself.

It will be the wrath of the Lamb that the Christ rejecter will have to fear.

2. The Day Appointed. Paul told the Athenians that God had fixed the day of judgment (Acts 17. 31).

It is variously called "the Day of Wrath and revelation of the righteous judgment of God" (Rom. 2. 5); "the Day of Judgment and Perdition (R.V., Destruction) of ungodly men" (2 Pet. 3. 7); "the Judgment of the Great Day" (Jude 6); "the Great Day of His Wrath" (Rev. 6. 17).

3. The Principles of Judgment.

According to Truth (Rom. 2. 2). There will be no miscarriage of justice there.

No Escape and No Excuse (Rom. 2. 1-3). To condemn sin in others will not excuse it in ourselves.

According to his Deeds. Judgment must of necessity be on the ground of works.

Without Respect of Persons (Rom. 2. 11). No favouritism. The great lady who said she hoped God would "respect the quality" will be mistaken.

By the Law for those who sinned under Law, and *by the Conscience* for those who had no law (Rom. 2. 12-15).

By the Secrets of Men. Not by their profession or outward conduct, but by the thoughts and intents of the heart.

By the Word of God (John 5. 45, 12. 48). The fearful words to the Rich Man in Hell tell us this: "They have Moses and the prophets, let them hear them."

According to the Gospel (Rom. 2. 16)—the rejection of Christ being the great matter.

4. THE TWO JUDGMENTS. The first is of those believers who share in the first resurrection.

They will not "come into judgment" in the sense of being "condemned with the world" (John 5. 24; 1 Cor. 11. 32; and Rom. 8. 1). For them there is no condemnation, being "in Christ Jesus."

But they will stand before the judgment seat of Christ, at which only the redeemed appear, and at which they will each give an account of himself and be manifested, receiving praise or rebuke, reward or loss, according as his conduct since conversion merits. After the Millennium the Final Judgment of the dead before the Great White Throne will take place, as described in Rev. 20. 11-15 (see III. above).

5. MATTERS DEALT WITH AT THE BEMA.

(a) *Personal Conduct,* the deeds done in the body (2 Cor. 5. 10).

It will be a time of manifestation. We shall be made manifest before the judgment seat—nothing hidden, no disguise, the real truth will be known; we shall be seen by all as we actually are.

(b) *Our Treatment of our Brethren* (Rom. 14. 10). Quarrels will be dealt with, as also evil speaking or unkind treatment. Any fraud will be avenged (1 Thess. 4. 6) and any advantage taken of a brother dealt with.

Harmony among brethren must be secured, that they
may live together in peace and love through eternity.

(c) *Works will be Reviewed and Tested* (1 Cor. 3. 11).
The whole will go through fire, that the rubbish may be
burnt up. All good and honest work will receive its due
reward, even to a cup of cold water given in the name of a
disciple (Matt. 10. 42).

6. THE SCENE AT THE GREAT WHITE THRONE.

(a) *The Throne is Great and White*, speaking of power
and purity—in themselves appalling to the guilty.

(b) *The Face of the Judge*—such that earth and Heaven
fled from it. For holiness is awful to the unclean and
impure.

(c) *The " Dead, Small and Great."* Those dead towards
God: dead in trespasses and sins. Earthly distinctions,
" small and great," matter not there. All stand before
God.

(d) *Books were Opened*, reminding us that our sins are
recorded in the Books of God's Remembrance.

(e) *Another Book—the Lamb's Book of Life*, wherein are
recorded the names of the regenerate: those who have
received the gift of Eternal Life.

(f) *All were Judged according to their Works.* Equal
justice and perfect righteousness will be there.

(g) *The Second Death*—not, as the first death, for Adam's
transgression, but for having rejected Christ ; having
turned from the Light (John 3. 19-21); for refusing the
free offer of Eternal Life; for having chosen sin, disobedience,
and death.

7. THE LAKE OF FIRE. Five times this expression is
used in the last chapters of Revelation and nowhere else
in the Bible, although fire is frequently used in the Scriptures
in association with judgment.

John the Baptist used the expression " unquenchable
fire " (Matt. 3. 12); our Lord the expressions " Hell-fire "
(Matt. 5. 22); " a furnace of fire: there shall be wailing and
gnashing of teeth "; " Everlasting fire " (Matt. 18. 8-9);
" the fire that never shall be quenched (Mark 9. 43, 48),
where their worm dieth not, and the fire is not quenched."

He, moreover, told the story of the rich man in Hades "tormented in this flame" (Luke 16. 24).

Evidently the Lord desired to make the fate of the wicked terrifying. They will never be able to say they were not warned. But only a Friend warns, and none need perish.

V. Application.

Let the Sinner fear lest he go to "this place of torment."

Let the Saint rejoice in the grace that has saved him from so great a death.

Let the Servant of God be careful to warn sinners with all love.

The Day of Judgment Described

The Day of Judgment and Perdition (2 Pet. 3. 7).

The Judgment of the Great Day (Jude 6).

Eternal Judgment (Heb. 6. 2).

Judgment without mercy (Jas. 2. 13).

The Resurrection of Damnation (John 5. 29).

Everlasting shame and contempt (Dan. 12. 2).

The Day of Wrath and revelation of the righteous judgment of God (Rom. 2. 5).

The Great White Throne (Rev. 20. 11).

The Second Death (Rev. 20. 14).

The Lake of Fire (Rev. 20. 15).

Everlasting Destruction from the presence of the Lord (2 Thess. 1. 9).

Index

393